D0261917

LANCASHIRE COUNTY LIBRARY

3011813248189 0

Britain Goes to War

Britain Goes to War

How the First World War Began to Reshape the Nation

Edited by

Peter Liddle

Pen & Sword
MILITARY

First published in Great Britain by
PEN AND SWORD MILITARY
an imprint of
Pen and Sword Books Ltd
47 Church Street
Barnsley
South Yorkshire S70 2AS

Copyright © Peter Liddle and Contributors, 2015

ISBN 978 1 47382 820 9

The right of Peter Liddle and Contributors to be identified
as the authors of this work has been asserted by them
in accordance with the Copyright, Designs and Patents Act 1988.

A CIP record for this book is available from the British Library.

All rights reserved. No part of this book may be reproduced or transmitted
in any form or by any means, electronic or mechanical including
photocopying, recording or by any information storage and retrieval
system, without permission from the Publisher in writing.

Printed and bound in England by
CPI Group (UK) Ltd, Croydon, CR0 4YY

Typeset in Times by CHIC GRAPHICS

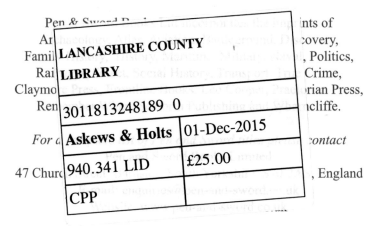

Pen & Sword Books ~~~~~~~~~~~~~~~~~~~~~~~~ ints of
Ar~~~~~~ covery,
Famil LANCASHIRE COUNTY ~~~~~~~~~~~~~~ , Politics,
Rai LIBRARY ~~~~~~~~~~~~~~~~~~~~~~~~~~~~ Crime,
Claymo~~~~~~~~~~~~~~~~~~~~~~~~~~~~~~~~~~ rian Press,
Ren 3011813248189 0 ~~~~~~~~~~~~~~~~~~~~ cliffe.

For a	**Askews & Holts**	01-Dec-2015	contact
47 Churc	940.341 LID	£25.00	, England
	CPP		

Contents

List of Plates

Acknowledgements

There would have been no conference had it not been for the Board of Weetwood Hall Hotel and Conference Centre, Leeds, deciding that in addition to hosting conferences externally organised, Weetwood would mark the occasion of the centenary of the outbreak of the First World War by mounting its own gathering. Hence my first thanks must go to that body and in particular to the former Pro Chancellor of Leeds University, Colonel Alan Roberts, for suggesting to the Board that I might be useful in the academic direction of the conference. My second note of appreciation is towards the team with which I worked for two years in the planning process. My colleagues were Martin Hicks, the Managing Director of Weetwood, Peter Chubb, the Development Director and, as Military Consultant, Alan Roberts. We all had ideas, shared enthusiasm, worked hard and knit well as a team.

My thanks are due to Weetwood's staff, seen and unseen. The praise recorded by delegates in this direction was well deserved. Peter Chubb's administration from the start and throughout was first class: Speakers and delegates were made to feel at home by friendly, courteous and efficient staff, and the facilities and cuisine fully lived up to the Hall's high reputation.

I had little difficulty in persuading chosen Speakers to come to Weetwood but I would like to mention one in particular, the friend of all First World War historians I imagine, John Bourne. John was generous in giving me so much of his time in discussing the programme and suggesting Speakers. Their brief was to share knowledge accessibly with our target audience – the general public with an interest in the Great War – and it was consistently followed. I thank them all for the research undertaken, the presentations, and the fulfillment of another element in the briefing – and I am sure by instinct too – their engagement with the delegates. An outstanding feature of the five days.

By great good fortune we assembled delegates who contributed in large measure to the successful proceedings. Congenial fellowship, agreeable discussion, insightful questions, shrewd suggestions and relaxed friendly coffee or lunchtime gossip on everything under the sun from career stage comparison and home location – we had guests from Australia, the States, France, the Netherlands and from Edinburgh to Romsey in the United Kingdom – to the merits of the beers and wine on hospitality offer, ensured for many of us, altogether the most delightful atmosphere imaginable.

Further elements which made the conference memorable and a factor of remembered enjoyment in the preparation of this book in addition to those special tastings of Timothy Taylor's beers and the wine of the English Wine Company, were a quite fabulous evening of original Yorkshire-based wartime film presented by the Yorkshire Film Archive, an evening of shared wartime songs, the 'presence' of a 1918 dispatch rider with his period motor bike and a Royal Navy farrier with his forge, a marvellous display of miniature railway modelling of Western Front reality, the Corps of Drums of the Yorkshire Volunteers, a Piper and a Bugler for the Last Post and then Reveille. I have recently read the expression 'a manly tear' and it is appropriate for one's reaction to this military display of musicianship – tears of pride and sadness, so fitting in our commemoration. All the men and women engaged in providing these supporting activities added something quite distinctive to our enjoyment and I would like to record that here.

We were blessed in having as our Patron, Jerolama, the Lady Haig, who engaged fully in the academic, social and commemorative proceedings. During the conference she was able to inspect some of Field Marshal Sir Douglas Haig's books which she had recently presented to the Liddle Collection in the University's Brotherton Library.

Turning specifically to the book, I thank my colleagues for their chapters which have taught me so much and I believe have introduced so accessibly, expert knowledge and helpful interpretation of a wide range of topics, some of fundamental importance and all of interest to anyone with a 'feel' for the Great War. Relatedly, working with Stephen Chumbley, the book's sharp-eyed, very well-informed copy editor has again been invaluable to me.

The illustrations in the book are from many sources, private, institutional and public. Where permission to publish was necessary, it was readily provided and, as Editor, gratefully I acknowledge this generous support for our collective endeavour.

Penultimately I would like to acknowledge the interest shown from the start by Rupert Harding of Pen and Sword Books. It is my hope that his confidence in the vision of a book following upon the conference will be justified.

My final thanks in the preparation of this book is to my wife Louise, not just for the formatting and finding where I had put this or that on the computer, and most particularly for locating, with Matthew Richardson's advice, additional photographic images, but for the joy of our companionship in this and in everything – how fortunate I am.

Peter Liddle
Mickley, North Yorkshire, November, 2014

Introduction

A hundred years after the outbreak of the First World War, how should British people with an interest in their heritage reflect upon this anniversary? As we look back at August 1914, by definition we are separated from our forebears because we know what was going to happen and by definition they did not. We know the war is going to last for more than four years; we know it is going to be terribly costly in lives and in disablement; it is going to prove ruinous to the economy of the nation; it will set the bell tolling on our Imperial position; and we may emerge as one of the victors but we have to do it all over again and at still greater cost a generation later. It really does, or can, seem very puzzling and in our lack of comprehension it has always been tempting to search for blameworthy figures to hold to account for the striking deficit in the ledger of sacrificial effort and reward, or the real consequences behind the show of victory.

Our sadness at the cost of the war stands beyond dispute but the recourse to war in 1914, the nature and cost of the war that followed, the way it was prosecuted, the problems faced by the 'directors' of the war as they wrestled with its challenges, what it meant for the servicemen on the fighting fronts and the civilians in industry, factory, farm and household, these are certainly topics deserving of study designed towards achieving a clearer understanding of the war with which the 1914 generation was faced. They faced it, of course, not as we do today as a matter of academic debate, but as a matter of daily anxiety, interminably prolonged and without knowing what further tribulations tomorrow might bring.

It was along the lines of trying always to keep within sight the 1914 perspective – the then commonly-held values and outlook – that the Weetwood Conference programme was constructed. It was considered essential that we looked first at why and how Britain became involved in a world war when, neither in government nor in public awareness, was there any such anticipation, with problems enough at home demanding attention. In any sense was the nation prepared for such a war? How did it respond to a crisis which was not short-lived but was to seem indefinitely extended?

There were pre-war perceptions of the Royal Navy being not merely the bulwark defence of the country but its means swiftly to defeat the foe. How was this expectation played out? Just how proficient and how adequate was the Regular Army and with what speed and efficiency was an expansion of the Army recruited? As well as a close look at the Regular Army in action in Belgium and France during the first months of the war, we chose to look in particular at a battalion of regulars from the Green Howards and at the raising of the New Armies.

Our initial focus was upon the prime 1914 issues for Britain and the most significant happenings in that year, sometimes viewed through a close lens, but by design the programme, also took us into less familiar byways; British and German civilian internment, the fundamentally important matter of the technology and efficiency of infantry weapons used by the Western Front antagonists, and of their guns and howitzers too.

We wanted to examine the way animals were employed and treated; how to explore the Great War history likely to be found within our own families, and to learn of the sportsmen who responded to the call to arms. There were further topics, this time perhaps more to be expected, the early stages of air warfare, the expansion of the nursing services and the experience of the professionally trained and then the wartime volunteer nurses in the new circumstance of a cataclysmic world war.

There were excursions during the week, integral to the conference theme, two of them the subject of chapters in this book; the 1914–18 documentary riches of the Liddle Collection in the Library of the University of Leeds, and the evocative Great War evidence in Lawnswood Cemetery, Leeds.

It may be noted that, on one occasion, two chapter authors do not agree with each other on a major issue, and then, more frequently, there are divergent views on some significant point of detail. I do not see it as my role as Editor to attempt adjudication in these areas of dispute. There is in all cases further suggested reading material for the reader puzzled by these instances, and not sure whom to endorse.

There may be further 1914–18 conferences at Weetwood following upon this centenary conference and it is the editor's hope that this book will be the first of several which offer valuable insights into the First World War as it undergoes re-examination. The subject is surely of inexhaustible interest. Town after town has been re-discovering, or unearthing, not only the tragic personal histories of its citizens – and often their brave deeds too – but showing regional pride in publicising such information. New generations are learning of their community's collective achievements during the war years, something which might have been quite outside their knowledge as a result of social or industrial changes during the intervening years. The city of Sunderland makes no ships today; in 1914–18 the nation was hugely dependent on the Wear's ship-building yards. There is scant vestige in Crayford or Bexley Heath or Erith of the building of Vickers aircraft there in the Great War, similarly in Kingston, Surrey, of Sopwiths, and in Cricklewood of the making of Handley Page machines. Tanks are no longer made in Lincoln, their birthplace. Romsey may have riding and pony clubs today, as does every community, but during the war it had a massive 'warhorse' remount establishment, something now generating quite inspiring commemorative activity, as is the case in Hartlepool relating to the site of the coastal gun battery which responded to the German shelling on 16 December 1914.

Every city, town or village has something of the Great War, or more than something, on which to reflect. There are more than enough tragic events, the shelling of Hartlepool, Whitby and Scarborough – Lowestoft and Yarmouth too – the dreadful toll of the Gretna rail crash, the explosions at munition works in

Silvertown and Leeds, the locations of Zeppelin and aircraft bombing, but there are associations with more positive reasons for commemoration, most notably, the communities which can celebrate 'their' Victoria Cross award citizens.

For example, of the twenty-five awards of the Victoria Cross to Yorkshiremen, eight were born in Leeds. Then, staying with Yorkshire's broad acres, the tailoring firm of Burton and Burton in Leeds made uniforms for more than a quarter of the entire British armed forces and one may reasonably presume that the mills of Pudsey, Stanningley, Bradford, Dewsbury, Halifax, Elland, Huddersfield and other West Riding towns manufactured the cloth and dyed it for that percentage and perhaps more. Steam engines made in Hunslet puffed their way along the narrow-gauge light railways behind the Western Front along track much of which was made in Gildersome and the admirably enterprising Halifax Great War Society has successfully 're-discovered' and promoted awareness of a whole range of sites in the town having First World War significance.

Every region of the country has reason to identify with a related war necessity, from leather and servicemen's bootmaking, to flax and aeroplane fuselage and wing fabric, from coal production to corn harvest, from netting herrings to fabricating steel, and to the location of almost forgotten weapon research establishments like that at Orfordness. Arguably the most exceptional survivor of the war is now receiving the conservational and promotional care it deserves at Stow Maries in Essex, the miraculously little-changed First World War airfield. Professional and amateur 'sleuths' are revealing places, people, institutions, buildings, associated with a war effort hitherto unmatched in the history of the United Kingdom and mapping the vestigial remains of such enterprise.

The Press, Radio and Television have of course been active in promoting awareness of the centenary year. It may be said that not all the dramatic reconstructions pleased the purist but the pragmatist might retort that there is no such thing as bad publicity and through the Media more people have been drawn into the anniversary being commemorated. That must be a good thing. Awareness of our past may well have led to interest in it, fuelling a potential fascination, an appetite for more information, the beginning of understanding and so of respect for the endurance, resilience, ingenuity, enterprise, the very spirit of our forebears. If this book were to encourage some part of that process. then all who have contributed to it will feel well-rewarded.

PART ONE

Chapter 1

The Origins of the First World War Revisited[1]

* * *

Gary Sheffield

The 1919 Treaty of Versailles, which formally ended the war with Germany, stated that it was the aggression of Germany and its allies which has brought about the war. In the disillusioned aftermath of a terribly bloody and destructive war, such views were challenged. David Lloyd George, a key member of the government that took Britain to war in August 1914 and Prime Minister from 1916 to 1922, argued in the 1930s that 'Nobody wanted war' but 'nations backed their machines over the precipice'.[2] Lloyd George reflected the Zeitgeist eloquently expressed in 1929 by the American historian, Sydney B. Fay: 'No one country and no one man was solely, or probably even mainly, to blame'.[3]

From the 1960s until just before the centenary of the July Crisis however, the scholarly consensus was that, *pace* Lloyd George and Fay, the aggression of Germany and Austria-Hungary was indeed the primary reason for the outbreak of war. That consensus has been challenged by the work of Margaret MacMillan and, especially, Christopher Clark, whose 2012 book, *The Sleepwalkers*, came to essentially the same conclusion as Lloyd George and Fay.[4] These books have attracted much support in the media. Once again the spirit of the age seems to dislike the allocation of blame for the outbreak of the First World War. However, such views remain in a minority among scholarly historians. An impressive array of evidence points the finger at Berlin and Vienna for turning a somewhat tense international situation, exacerbated by a series of crises in the Balkans, into a world war.[5] The politico-military elite in Berlin and Vienna took a series of decisions that at best were appallingly risky gambles taken in the full knowledge that they were likely to bring about general war. At worst, they were deliberately aggressive moves to achieve hegemony. In either case, they were not the decisions of sleepwalkers. Geoffrey Wawro, in his book *A Mad Catastrophe* – the very title states the author's view of Austro-Hungarian policy in 1914 – argues that:

> We must reconsider the origins of the First World War and carve out a new
> place for the Austrians. Austria-Hungary wasn't the essentially decent but
> charmingly slipshod power that muddled through and into war . . .
> Austria's Great War was built on the reckless gamble that the monarchy's
> internal problems could be fixed by war. They couldn't.[6]

A bestselling book by a respected British journalist and historian, Sir Max
Hastings, also firmly rejected the 'sleepwalkers' line.[7] Thus, at the centenary of
the outbreak of the Great War, the reasons why the states of Europe came to blows
are the subject of 'history wars', with scholars on both sides of the debate
passionately arguing their case.[8]

The debate about the origins of the war is not just an arcane matter of interest
only to historians. It addresses the meaning of a conflict that killed millions. If the
war were accidental, did that mean it was also preventable, and by extension those
millions had died for nothing? This chapter argues that, far from being caused by
statesmen stumbling or sleepwalking into war, the Great War of 1914 to 1918 was
the product of conscious decisions taken by individuals, and that it is simply untrue
that the blame should be spread fairly evenly among the eventual belligerents.
Rather, the guilty parties were to be found among the decision-making elite of
Imperial Germany and Austria-Hungary.

The creation of the German Empire in 1871, following the defeat of France by
a Prussian-led German coalition, did not, as might have been expected, cause
general conflict. Instead, under the guidance of the 'Iron Chancellor', Otto von
Bismarck, a new international equilibrium was created. The accession of Kaiser
Wilhelm II to the throne in 1888 destabilised this situation. Obsessed with envy
of his British mother's homeland, and in all likelihood mentally unbalanced,
Wilhelm dismissed Bismarck and attempted to rule as well as reign. Wilhelm's
maladroit interventions on the international scene worsened a situation created by
the new direction in German foreign policy commenced in the 1890s, a drive to
gain colonies and expand German power and economic influence. Germany
alienated Russia and France, who made common cause. Britain moved from
regarding Germany as a friendly power to seeing it as a potential enemy, largely
because of an ill-conceived attempt to build up a fleet to rival the Royal Navy.
Alarmed at this threat to their security, the British picked up the gauntlet. By 1912
Germany had clearly lost the naval arms race and had seen Britain move into the
Franco-Russian camp. However, there was no formal alliance committing Britain
to go to war in support of either Russia or France. The ententes between London
and Paris and London and St Petersburg were not aimed at Germany and owed
much to the desire of colonial rivals to come to terms. Moreover, Sir Edward Grey,
the Liberal Foreign Secretary, in fact favoured a consensual approach to resolving
international disputes, along the lines of the nineteenth-century Concert of Europe.
After the 1912 Balkan War, he had helped broker a peace settlement during a
conference in London where he had by no means always favoured his entente

partners: he sided with Austria over some key issues.[9] The fact that Britain was to enter the war in August 1914 and thus turn the entente into a genuine power bloc owed much to badly-judged German strategy.

In recent years, the role of Austria-Hungary in bringing about the First World War has come to the forefront. Germany had beaten Austria in a short war in 1866 but the two powers had reached a *rapprochement*, with a treaty, inspired by distrust of Russia, being signed in 1879. Austria-Hungary, as the state was formally renamed in 1867, was a multinational, multilingual empire ruled by the House of Hapsburg. Nationalism posed a threat to the Hapsburg Empire's internal cohesion and even its very existence. Shut out of its traditional spheres of influence in Italy in 1859, and Germany seven years later, Austria-Hungary increasingly looked to the Balkans. However, the Austro-Hungarians faced a rival force in the form of Balkan nationalism, which was backed by Russia, which saw itself as the protector of the South Slav people. International tensions were heightened when in 1908 Vienna formally annexed the Ottoman provinces of Bosnia-Herzegovina, territories that had been ruled by Austria-Hungary for thirty years. The annexation was seen by the Austro-Hungarian leadership as a way of forestalling the growth of the small independent state of Serbia, which aspired to rule over all Serbs, including the large number domiciled in Bosnia-Herzegovina. In the face of German support for Austria-Hungary, neither Russia nor the small independent state of Serbia were willing to push the issue to the point of war (the former was weakened by its recent defeat at the hands of Japan, and its Entente partners had proved unwilling to back Russia's stance).

The 1908 Bosnia crisis was extremely destabilising. It brought to an end Russian and Austria-Hungarian collaboration in keeping things calm in the Balkans and enhanced Russian suspicion of Austrian intentions in the area. Also destabilising was Italy's seizure of Libya from the Ottoman Empire (Turkey) in 1911, which placed the world on alert that the Ottoman Empire, the 'sick man of Europe', might be on the point of collapse. This possibility came a step closer in 1912, when a coalition of Balkan states attacked Turkey and rapidly captured much of its European territory. The victorious powers then fell out in a second war in 1913, from which Serbia emerged with its territory, population and power greatly enhanced. Understandably, the Austrians were alarmed at this development.

The decision-makers in Vienna seized upon the assassination on 28 June 1914 in Sarajevo, the capital of Bosnia-Herzegovina, of Archduke Franz Ferdinand, the heir to the dual monarchy, as an opportunity to settle accounts with Serbia once and for all. The assassin was a young Bosnian Serb, Gavrilo Princip, and the murder was seen by Vienna as a direct challenge by Serbia. Actually, Princip was an extremely low-level member of a powerful secret society, the 'Black Hand'.[10] Central authority in Serbia was weak. Dragutin Dimitrijević (known as 'Apis'), the head of Serbian military intelligence, was also the leader of the Black Hand, and he supplied the eventual assassins with weapons. But even the Black Hand could not control the activities of its members, and it may have been a 'freelance' killing by local activists.[11]

The fact that the Serbian Prime Minister, Pašić, could not stop Apis from sending death squads into Hapsburg territory perhaps, as Clark and Lang argue, puts Serbia in the category of a rogue state, although failing state might be a more accurate description. However, the connection between official Serbia and the assassins was opaque: clear evidence to link Princip and the Serbian government was distinctly lacking, and there was no clamour by the public in the Hapsburg Empire for war with Serbia.[12] The fact that Austria-Hungary did little for three weeks and then delivered a draconian ultimatum to Serbia, most of which Belgrade promptly accepted, diminished the international sense that Serbia was a rogue state. As it was, had there been an international conference, Britain would have been very likely to have supported Austria-Hungary, as in previous Balkans crises.[13] Serbia would almost certainly have been punished, although not destroyed. The Sarajevo crisis did not override security concerns of other powers about the situation in the Balkans to the extent of their being willing to give Austria-Hungary a free hand. Yet Austria-Hungary ignored the interests of other states. If any country behaved as a rogue state in the summer of 1914, it was Austria-Hungary. It wanted a local war with Serbia, even though there was no guarantee that this would not drag in Russia, and escalate into a general war.

Austria-Hungary looked to their senior partner for support. Without Germany's backing it is extremely unlikely the Austro-Hungarian Empire would have gone ahead with the attack on Serbia. Emperor Franz Josef wrote to the Kaiser on 4 July 1914 that Austria-Hungary wanted to 'eliminate Serbia as a power factor in the Balkans'.[14] On the following day, Count Hoyos, from the Austrian Foreign Ministry, and the Austro-Hungarian ambassador, Count von Szögyény-Marich, had high-level discussions in Berlin. Their request for support met a sympathetic hearing from the Kaiser, and Arthur Zimmerman from the German Foreign Office. Later Wilhelm convened a meeting with General Erich von Falkenhayn, Theobald von Bethmann-Hollweg, the Chancellor, and Baron Moriz von Lyncker, the head of the Kaiser's Military Cabinet. The meeting 'considered the question of Russian intervention and accepted the risk of general war'.[15]

That evening Szögyény-Marich sent a telegram to Vienna:

> The Kaiser authorised me to inform our gracious majesty that we might in this case, as in all others, rely upon Germany's full support . . . [but] this action must not be delayed. Russia's attitude will no doubt be hostile, but for this he had for years prepared, and should a war between Austria-Hungary and Russia be unavoidable, we might be convinced that Germany, our old faithful ally, would stand by our side. Russia at the present time was in no way prepared for war, and would think twice before it appealed to arms.[16]

Thus on 5 July 1914, Wilhelm II issued what has become known to history as the 'blank cheque' of unconditional support to Austria-Hungary, a decision rubber-stamped by Zimmerman and Bethmann-Hollweg the following day.

Germany and Austria-Hungary were united in seeking a decisive confrontation with Serbia, no matter what the risk. Count Forgách of the Austrian Foreign Ministry privately wrote on 8 July that Berchtold was:

> determined . . . to use the horrible deed of Sarajevo for a military-clearing up of our impossible relationship with Serbia . . . With Berlin we are in complete agreement. Kaiser & Reich Chancellor etc more decided than ever before; they take on board complete cover against Russia, even at the risk of a world war which is not ruled out, they consider the moment as favourable & advise to strike as soon [as possible] . . .[17]

At first, the crisis was slow-burning, in part because Tisza, the Hungarian Prime Minister, had to be persuaded to support military action against Serbia. With some reservations, he agreed on 14 July. Alarmed at the developing situation, on 18 July S. D. Sazonov, the Russian Foreign Minister, told Austria-Hungary that Russia would not tolerate the undermining of Serbian independence. This clear warning to Vienna was reinforced by French President Raymond Poincaré's message to the Austrian ambassador in St Petersburg on 21 July, pointedly reminding him of the friendship between Russia and Serbia, and that France was allied to Russia.[18] This unmistakably-drawn red line was ignored by the Austro-Hungarians, who, on 23 July, delivered an ultimatum to the Serbian government, the terms of which were so severe that Sazonov's reaction on hearing them on the 24th was 'It's a European war'. Nevertheless, to the surprise of the statesmen of Europe, on 25 July, Pašić accepted all but one relatively minor clause of the ultimatum. In spite of inflicting national humiliation upon Serbia, and achieving what any disinterested observer would regard as more than adequate revenge for the assassination, on 28 July Austria-Hungary declared war. Belgrade was shelled on the following day. The British Foreign Secretary, Sir Edward Grey, deeply alarmed at the turn of events, called in the German ambassador on 29 July to urge mediation and to warn that Britain might get involved in a general war on the side of France and Russia.

Russia responded by mobilising on 30 July. In turn, Germany issued an ultimatum to Russia on the next day, and followed that by declaring war on Russia on 1 August, and on France on the 3rd. Germany demanded that neutral Belgium allow German troops to cross its territory. When the request was refused, the German army invaded Belgium on 4 August. This was the trigger for Britain's declaration of war. With the exception of the Ottoman Empire, which joined the Central Powers in late October, and Italy, which initially remained neutral, 5 August 1914 found all of Europe's Great Powers at war.

The Austrian elite had a sense that the credibility, perhaps the very existence, of the Empire was at stake. The wars of 1912–13 had gravely weakened its position in the Balkans, which was the only sphere of influence that it had left. To strike against the newly powerful and confident Serbia gave Austria-Hungary a chance to stop the rot. Recent research has shown that Vienna had no concrete war aims, and powerful individuals such as Conrad von Hotzendorf, the Austrian Chief of Staff, were pessimistic about the chances of success. But Austria-Hungary's decision-making elite wore blinkers, focusing on the reckoning with Serbia at all costs. For Austria-Hungary, and Germany, 'war had become an aim and an end in itself'.[19]

The motives of the German leaders in 1914 are deeply controversial. The work of the German historian Fritz Fischer has been seminal. He argued that the war was caused, in the uncompromising German title of his first book, by 'Germany's grab for world power'.[20] The Balkan crisis was escalated in spite of Berlin clearly understanding it was likely to lead to Russian involvement and hence a general European war. Fischer highlighted the so-called 'War Council' of 8 December 1912, at which, he argued, the decision was taken that war would be launched about eighteen months later, in part for domestic reasons: 'The war provided an opportunity to assert and strengthen the old social and political order and to assimilate the Social Democrats as well.'[21] Fischer set out clear continuities between the foreign policies of the Kaiser's Germany and those of the Third Reich. His ideas no longer command support in their entirety. Fischer's interpretation of the meeting of 8 December 1912 has been rejected by many historians, although it cannot be dismissed out of hand. John Röhl has recently argued that 'the military-political discussions on that Sunday morning fit seamlessly into a decision-making process whose origins went far back, and which finally led to Armageddon in the summer of 1914'.[22] Certainly, they are at the very least indicative of the willingness of the German political and military High Command to contemplate war. The central role Fischer ascribed to domestic concerns in Germany's path to war has largely been debunked, but Fischer's arguments about the aggression of German foreign policy before the war, the preparedness of the German leadership to court war in pursuit of diplomatic objectives, and their decision to initiate war remain fundamentally sound. German leaders, trusting in their military strength, were set apart from their opposite numbers in the other Great Powers (apart from the Austrians) by their willingness to threaten to unleash a European conflict to obtain foreign policy goals.[23]

By manipulating the crisis, Germany hoped to divide the three Entente powers.[24] In previous Balkan crises, Britain and France had been reluctant to support Russia, and there appeared to be an opportunity for Germany to break up the Entente without war. Bethmann-Hollweg believed that Britain could be kept out of the war. German behaviour from 5 to 30 July can be characterised as a policy of 'calculated risk' or 'brinkmanship'. The blank cheque gave the go-ahead to the Austro-Hungarians to launch a limited and local Third Balkan War, but Germany was probably in this period only prepared to risk a general conflict, rather than to actively create one. In the end, the leadership in Berlin decided to take that fatal extra step, against an extraordinary background of chaotic decision-making. By issuing an ultimatum to Russia on 31 July, Germany initiated a general European war.[25]

The leadership in Berlin in July 1914 had a 'strike-now-better-than-later' mentality. Niall Ferguson, among others, has argued that Germany began a preventive war out of fear of Russia.[26] In October 1913 Russia had begun its 'Great Military Programme', increasing troop numbers and expanding strategic railways.[27] The German Secretary for Foreign Affairs in July 1914 privately stated that 'Russia will be prepared to fight in a few years. Then she will crush us by the number of her soldiers; then she will have built her Baltic fleet and her strategic railroads'.[28] However, there is simply no credible evidence that Russia was planning a war of aggression.[29] The case that the Russians deliberately manipulated the July Crisis to begin a war that would allow the seizure of Constantinople and the Straits is weakened by the absence of any evidence in the documentary records.[30]

The context of the Great Military Programme was the rebuilding of the reputation and strength of the Czarist state after the twin catastrophes of defeat at the hands of Japan and the failed 1905 revolution. The possession of large and effective armed forces can increase the international standing of a state, and add weight to a state's diplomacy. A weakened Russia had been humiliated during the 1908 Bosnian Crisis. Russian leadership was determined that that should not happen again.

There was a whole world of difference between Russia's decisions in July 1914, which were backed by France, and those of the Central Powers. Russia responded defensively to the crisis provoked by the Austrian ultimatum to Serbia on 23 July 1914. The Russian reaction was governed by the determination not to let its vital national interests in the Balkans be attacked. Sazonov, the Foreign Minister, saw the threat in stark terms, warning a ministerial meeting on the following day that Russia's very status as a great power was at risk if Austria-Hungary was allowed to get away with this flagrant attempt to reduce Serbia to vassal status. The influential Agriculture Minister, A. V. Krivoshein, recognised the risks involved, but believed that only 'by making a firm stand' was there a chance of deterring Germany.[31] French support – and as it happened President Poincaré and his Prime Minister, René Viviani, were in St Petersburg from 20 to 23 July on a prearranged visit – was forthcoming, as it was not in 1908, and it was important in stiffening Russian resolve. Poincaré was a keen supporter of the agreement with Russia. Shortly after becoming President, he informed the then Russian Foreign Minister that he would 'not fail to use [his influence] to ensure . . . the sanctity of the policy founded on the close alliance with Russia'.[32] During the July Crisis, Poincaré viewed supporting Russia as vital to keeping that country out of the arms of Germany, and avoiding the nightmare of an immensely strong power bloc, a revival of the nineteenth-century League of Three Emperors, which would leave France isolated and marginalised. Thus Austria-Hungary's bid to halt its decline as a great power by attacking upstart Serbia was resisted by both Russia and France, which feared for their future as great powers if they were to do nothing.[33]

Russian preliminary moves towards mobilisation on 26 July were not intended to trigger a war: rather, in line with Krivoshein's advice, they were warning shots intended to underline the seriousness of the Austrian move against Serbia, and to help persuade Vienna and Berlin, even at this late stage, to draw back. It was also a necessary step in preparing Russia for war should the worst happen. Initially the plan was to mobilise only in certain areas, to underline that this was a response to Austria, so pre-mobilisation moves were not extended across Russia. It was hoped that Germany would read this limited move as evidence that the Czar's government was seeking to avoid provocative measures. In the event, St Petersburg ordered on 30 July a full mobilisation in response to the Austrian attack on Serbia. As one official explained: 'a partial mobilization could be carried out only at the price of dislocating the entire machinery of general mobilization' – should the war spread beyond the Balkans, the Russians 'would be powerless to defend ourselves on the frontiers of Poland and East Prussia'.[34] Russian mobilisation proved a gift to the German government as it allowed it to portray the war as a defensive one. This was important in rallying otherwise wavering sections of German society behind the government.

There was nothing inevitable about the British entry into the war. In late July and at the beginning of August 1914 the Liberal government of H. H. Asquith was deeply divided over the issues of war and peace, and this reflected the state of opinion in the country as a whole. Various church groups and the Labour movement had no love for the Czar's regime, and there was a widespread belief that a quarrel in the Balkans was no concern of Britain's. While some Cabinet ministers, such as the Foreign Secretary, Sir Edward Grey, and Lord Haldane, the Lord Chancellor, believed that Britain should uphold the balance of power by supporting France, there were others who took a contrary view. Even Asquith himself initially thought that Britain should stay out of the war. One of the most influential members of the Cabinet was David Lloyd George, the Chancellor of the Exchequer and the radical Welsh conscience of the still-powerful Nonconformist lobby. If Lloyd George pushed his opposition to British participation in the war to the point of resignation, the government would probably have collapsed. And yet, on 4 August, Asquith's government, with Lloyd George remaining a prominent member, brought a largely united nation into the war.

What changed the situation was the German invasion of Belgium.[35] Both Britain and Germany (the latter through the predecessor state of Prussia) had guaranteed the independence and neutrality of Belgium by a treaty of 1839. That a major power should simply rip up an international agreement was regarded as a moral outrage, causing genuine anger. Before 1914, German war planners had been aware of the likely consequences of violating Belgian neutrality, but had chosen to ignore them. It is well within the realms of possibility that had Germany attacked France without marching through Belgium, Britain would have stayed out of the war, or at least there would have been a political crisis resulting in the delaying of British support for France. This could have had catastrophic consequences for the French. German strategic myopia thus gratuitously added an enemy to the forces ranged against them and threw away an opportunity to gain a major advantage in the initial campaign in the West.

Grey has been harshly criticised for not making it clear, early in the July Crisis, that Britain would stand by France and Russia. If he had done so, or so the argument goes, Germany could have been deterred from starting the war.[36] This is unfair on two levels. First, the realities of British party politics meant that Grey was unable to give this assurance. A statement of this kind would have lacked credibility and would almost certainly have been attacked from within the Liberal Party and may even have led to resignations from the Cabinet. Second, it is bizarre to assign war guilt to a man who strenuously worked for peace, proposing mediation on six occasions during the July Crisis. Grey's principal mistake was failing to see, until very late in the day, that the Concert of Europe, which had worked well during the Balkan crises of 1912–13, would not work this time because, far from restraining Austria-Hungary, Germany was actively encouraging its ally to go to war.

Niall Ferguson has put forward the argument that the British were wrong to fight in 1914. Had they stayed out, Germany would have won and a 'Kaiser's European Union' would have emerged. This Panglossian view has not achieved wide acceptance among historians. In reality, quite apart from the moral dimension of failing to resist blatant aggression and breaches of international law (in 2013 a prominent academic theologian argued persuasively that according to the Christian principles of just war, Britain was right to fight in 1914[37]), the consequences of a German victory would have been cataclysmic for Britain. The British had every reason to be concerned about the German invasion of Belgium. Maintaining maritime security by keeping the coast of the Low Countries out of the hands of a hostile power had been a staple of British foreign policy for centuries. German occupation of Belgium posed a similar threat to the occupation of the same territory by another naval rival, Revolutionary and Napoleonic France, a century before, and provoked the same response. Similarly, opposition to attempts to achieve hegemony by Continental powers had led Britain to join many coalitions to restore the balance of power. Had Britain turned its back on France and Russia in 1914, Germany probably would have won the war. Britain would have been isolated, friendless, facing a continent controlled by an autocratic and aggressive foe in which democracy had been largely snuffed out. Britain could well have been faced with a war against Germany some time after 1914 which the British would have had to fight without allies. For Britain, the war that broke out in August 1914 was a very traditional conflict. The Germany of Wilhelm II joined the Spain of Philip II and the France of Louis XIV and then Napoleon on the roll-call of aggressors that Britain had opposed over the years.[38] Well might King George V say to the US Ambassador, 'My God, Mr Page, what else could we do?'[39]

So far, this chapter has considered diplomacy and high politics, but of course they did not take place in a vacuum. Some writers consider that the war was precipitated by four modern horsemen of the apocalypse, that is militarism, alliances, imperialism and nationalism. These all played a role in creating the conditions in which war broke out, but none of them individually or in combination can be said to have 'caused' the First World War. There is, for instance, no evidence that arms races necessarily lead directly to conflict. Certainly, the Anglo-German naval building competition before the First World War destabilised relations between the two states, but it was the German army's invasion of Belgium that was the *casus belli* for Britain. The context of military build-ups helped create an atmosphere of uncertainty and distrust between the Powers, which fed into the wider mood of militarism; not just readiness to use armed force in support of state policy, but the excessive admiration of military culture, deference to armed forces, belief in the benefits of war, and Social Darwinist thinking.[40]

The so-called 'war by timetable' debate argues that rigid military plans tied the hands of politicians during the crucial days of July and August 1914. There was a general fear that being slower to mobilise than any enemy would be at a disadvantage from the start. When the weathercock Kaiser on 1 August suddenly demanded that the German armies be sent against Russia alone, sparing France, General Helmuth von Moltke, the Chief of the General Staff, had to say 'no'. There was no alternative to the Schlieffen Plan by which the bulk of the German army would be deployed in the west, and it was logistically impossible to unpick it at that stage.[41] In that armies were dependent on carefully-choreographed mobilisation plans, which rested on the use of railways which were inherently inflexible, the 'war by timetable' idea contains some truth. However, the notion that civilian leaders were hustled into war by aggressive generals does not bear scrutiny. Both the German and Austro-Hungarian Army Chiefs of Staff had been urging war for some years, but only in the summer of 1914 were their strident demands finally aligned with the decision of the politicians to go to war. While these men were far more influential than their counterparts in France, Russia and Britain, their views were not determinant in tipping the deliberations of those who in fact would make Vienna and Berlin in favour of war.

The network of alliances has been blamed for causing a wider war by a sort of 'domino effect', and more generally, the international system has also been put in the dock for failing to maintain the peace. The existence of rival power blocs did not make a major war inevitable. Instead, such groupings can actually bring stability to a situation, not least through deterrence and the disciplines imposed by being a member of an alliance or coalition. However, in the instance of 1914, a good case can be made that the problem was not that alliances were too strong, but that they were too weak. Italy, to the anger of its Triple Alliance partners, remained neutral in 1914, and compounded this betrayal by joining the other side in 1915. Germany believed that the Triple Entente rested on foundations sufficiently insecure so that the bloc could be broken apart over the July Crisis with or without war. Britain was not formally allied to either Russia or France, and the Franco-Russian alliance was perceived in Berlin as being shaky. Indeed, 'a fundamental problem which contributed to the outbreak of war was the *lack* of a fully effective balance of power in Europe – not its existence'.[42]

While imperfect, the international system had accommodated Germany under Bismarck's rule: it was decisions of his successors to pursue more confrontational paths that led to its failure. Paul W. Schroeder has blamed the spirit of 'New Imperialism' that set in after about 1870, which often rewarded aggression, especially, but not solely, in extra-European empire-building.[43] Following this logic, Austria-Hungary and Germany in 1914 were simply behaving as Britain had behaved towards the Boer republics in 1899, the United States towards Spain a year earlier, or Serbia towards the Ottoman Empire and its Balkan neighbours in 1912–13. While imperialist mentalities probably contributed to the corrosion of the Concert of Europe, this argument is not entirely satisfactory. Contemporaries, influenced by attitudes that today would be seen as racist, saw a clear difference between behaviour of this sort beyond Europe, or a small power's activities in the borderlands of the Balkans, and a Great Power threatening the interest of its peers by aggressive activity in Europe proper. The fact that in crises in 1905–06, 1908–09, and 1911–12, German leaders pursued a policy of brinkmanship by threatening war, was destabilising.

The German perception of being 'encircled' by the Triple Entente was exaggerated – it was not the case that Britain would automatically support Russia and France in time of crisis – and was, in any case, a self-fulfilling prophesy. France and Russia had come together in 1892–4 out of fear of Germany. Subsequent German bellicosity had done nothing to relieve their anxieties, and had served to add Britain to the Entente as a 'country member'. Moreover, the choice of Germany and Austria-Hungary to reject Grey's numerous attempts to resurrect the Concert of Europe, and thus settle Vienna's dispute with Belgrade by international cooperation, points to the importance of decisions taken by individual statesmen and governments in the 'failure' of the international system, which can be made to work only if the principals wish it to do so. The Bulgarian crisis of 1878, which had been dealt with through an international conference, offered a clear precedent for coping with the crisis initiated by the Sarajevo assassination. While the strains placed upon the international system by the irreconcilable pressures of Serb nationalism and Austro-Hungarian interests in the Balkans should not be underestimated, it is quite possible that a settlement could have been brokered by the Great Powers in July 1914 – if Berlin and Vienna had wished for one: but they did not.

It was once fashionable to blame the outbreak of the war on imperialism, the drive to acquire colonies, raw materials and markets overseas. Following V. I. Lenin, Marxists saw German *Weltpolitik* in economic terms, with capitalists urging on foreign policy, which in turn led to a clash with other capitalist states, whose capitalists too provided a 'hidden hand' behind the foreign policies of the Great Powers. To quote Frank McDonough, 'In this view, millions of people were being sacrificed to ensure the future domination of one group of monopoly capitalists over another'.[44] Superficially, events such as the capture of German colonies in

Africa and the Pacific by troops of the British and French empires, the carving of a vast German empire out of the ruins of Imperial Russia, and the dismemberment of the Ottoman Empire in the post-war peace process, supported this theory. However, such 'imperialism' was the by-product of a war begun for different reasons. The various empires picked up additional territories from defeated enemies almost out of force of habit, as for example the British had done in the Seven Years War a century-and-a-half earlier. That was what empires did.

The 'imperialism' thesis is counterbalanced by the 'improbable war' argument recently propounded by the British-based German historian, Holger Afflerbach. He argues that the outbreak of war took many people across Europe by surprise, including key military and political decision-makers, who took dangerous risks because of a belief 'that peace was secure'.[45] Certainly, there were many reasons why a major war might seem improbable. The economies of Europe were increasingly interdependent. In an influential book of 1910, Norman Angell argued that the notion that states could gain by war was a 'great illusion'. Rather, it was 'impossible' for a state to 'enrich itself by subjugating . . . another'.[46] In addition, other factors such as international law bound states together. The paradox in thinking in Europe before 1914 has been well-expressed by Michael Neiberg: there was a bizarre mixture of pessimistic certainty in the inevitability of war on the one hand, and an equally optimistic certainty on the other hand that war had become an impossibility in the modern world.[47]

The idea that rampant nationalism drove Europe into war in 1914 is wrong. It was a classic cabinet war, and the reactions of the common people to its outbreak ranged from outright enthusiasm to outright opposition. The mostly young, affluent men who gathered in city centres to cheer for war were emphatically not representative of the masses, who reacted to the news of war with fear, apprehension and fatalism. War was seen as something to be endured, and certainly not to be greeted with joy. The growth of nationalistic feeling and hatred for enemies was a product of the war as the casualty lists grew ever longer, people suffered privations and the true ghastliness of modern industrialised warfare became all too evident.[48] Abstract forces such as 'nationalism', 'imperialism' and 'militarism', the system of alliances and issues such as Anglo-German naval rivalry, did not cause the war, although they may all have contributed towards making it more likely.

The outbreak of war in August 1914 was wholly avoidable. There were certainly tensions, but as David Stevenson has written: 'The European peace [in 1914] might have been a house of cards, but someone still had to topple it.' The First World War came about because key individuals in Austria-Hungary and Germany took conscious decisions to achieve diplomatic objectives even at the cost of conflict with Russia and France. The response of Russia, France and eventually Britain to the events in the Balkans, and their consequences, were essentially reactive and defensive. The response of the Great Powers in limiting the damage from previous Balkan crises strongly suggests that had the Austrians and Germans wished it, the crisis of summer 1914 could have been resolved by the cooperation of the international community which would have isolated and punished Serbia but left its independence and security intact. On this occasion however, Austria-Hungary and Germany wanted war.

Notes

1. An earlier version of this chapter appeared in my *Short History of the First World War* (London: Oneworld, 2014). I am grateful to Fiona Slater and Oneworld for permission to reproduce some material that first appeared in this book.
2. David Lloyd George, *War Memoirs*, abridged edition, Vol. II (London: Odhams, c. 1938), pp. 33–4.
3. Quoted in Annika Mombauer, *The Origins of the First World War: Controversies and Consensus* (Harlow: Pearson, 2002), p. 85.
4. Margaret MacMillan, *The War that Ended Peace* (London: Profile, 2013); Christopher Clark, *The Sleepwalkers: How Europe Went to War in 1914* (London: Allen Lane, 2012).
5. Annika Mombauer, *The Origins of the First World War: Diplomatic and Military Documents* (Manchester: Manchester University Press, 2013), pp. 24–5.
6. Geoffrey Wawro, *A Mad Catastrophe: The Outbreak of World War I and the Collapse of the Hapsburg Empire* (New York: Basic Books, 2014), p. 383.
7. Max Hastings, *Catastrophe: Europe Goes to War, 1914* (London: Collins, 2013). For another book by a respected historian aimed at the popular market that rejects the 'sleepwalkers' hypothesis, see Saul David, *100 Days to Victory* (London: Hodder and Stoughton, 2013).
8. For example, Richard J. Evans, 'Michael Gove's History Wars', *Guardian*, Review section, 13 July 2013, and Gary Sheffield, 'It was a Great War. One that saved Europe', *The Times*, 3 February 2014.
9. Vernon Bogadnor, 'The Shadows Lengthen', *History Today*, Vol. 64, No. 8 (August 2014), pp. 21–2.
10. For Princip see Tim Butcher, *The Trigger: Hunting the Assassin who Brought the World to War* (London: Chatto and Windus, 2014).
11. Richard C. Hall, 'Serbia', in Richard F. Hamilton and Herger H. Herwig, *The Origins of World War I* (Cambridge: Cambridge University Press, 2003), pp. 106–08.
12. Clark, *Sleepwalkers*, pp. 56–8; Sean Lang, *Why the First World War Broke Out* (London: Searching Finance, 2014) p. 63; D. C. B. Lieven, *Russia and the Origins of the First World War* (London: Macmillan, 1983), pp. 139–40; Michael Neiberg, *Dance of the Furies: Europe and the Outbreak of World War I* (Cambridge, MA: Belknapp Press, 2011), p. 18.
13. Bogadnor, 'The Shadows Lengthen', pp. 21, 23.
14. Gordon Martel, *The Origins of the First World War* (London: Longman, 1996), p. 79.
15. Richard F. Hamilton and Herger H. Herwig, *Decisions for War, 1914-1917* (Cambridge: Cambridge University Press, 2004), p. 62.
16. Quoted in Martel, *Origins*, p. 100.
17. Quoted in Annika Mombauer, 'The First World War: Inevitable, Avoidable, Improbable or Desirable? Recent Interpretations on War Guilt and the War's Origins', *German History* Vol. 25 No. 1 (2007), p. 84.
18. Luigi Albertini, *The Origins of the War of 1914*, Vol. II (New York: Enigma Books, 2005 [1952]), p. 193.
19. Mombauer, 'The First World War', p. 94.
20. The English title was the less inflammatory *Germany's Aims in the First World War* (New York: Norton, 1967).
21. Fritz Fischer, *World Power or Decline: The Controversy over Germany's Aims in the First World War* (New York: Norton, 1974), p. 84.
22. John Röhl, *Wilhelm II: Into the Abyss of War and Exile 1900-41* (Cambridge: Cambridge University Press, 2014), p. 911.

23. Mark Hewitson, *Germany and the Causes of the First World War* (Oxford: Berg, 2004), pp. 3–4, 228–9. Hewitson sees the German leadership as acting from a sense of confidence rather than 'weakness and despair' (p. 228).
24. My ideas in this paragraph have been particularly informed by Hewitson, *Germany*, Holger H. Herwig, 'Germany', in Hamilton and Herwig, *Origins*, and Hew Strachan, *The First World War* Vol. I, *To Arms* (Oxford: Oxford University Press, 2001), pp. 86–91.
25. Herwig, 'Germany', pp. 178–85.
26. Herwig, 'Germany', p. 187; Niall Ferguson, *The Pity of War* (London: Allen Lane, 1998), pp. 98–101.
27. For details, see David Alan Rich, 'Russia', in Hamilton and Herwig, *Origins*, pp. 212–14.
28. Quoted in Martel, *Origins*, p. 101.
29. For the view that Russian aggression was a major factor for launching the war, see Sean McMeekin, *The Russian Origins of the First World War* (Cambridge, MA: Belknapp Press, 2011). For a convincing counterview that stresses Russia's deterrent stance, see Ronald B. Bobroff, 'War accepted but unsought: Russia's growing militancy and the July Crisis, 1914', in Jack S. Levy and John A. Vasquez, *The Outbreak of the First World War: Structure, Politics and Decision-Making* (Cambridge: Cambridge University Press, 2014).
30. Bobroff, 'War accepted', p. 239.
31. Lieven, *Russia*, pp. 142–4.
32. Quoted in Albertini, *Origins*, Vol. I, p. 413.
33. John F. V. Keiger, *France and the Origins of the First World War* (New York: St Martin's Press, 1983), pp. 165–8; Eugenia C. Kiesling, 'France', in Hamilton and Herwig, *Origins*, p. 234.
34. Martel, *Origins*, pp. 80–1, 106.
35. For Britain's entry into the War, see Keith Wilson, 'Britain', in Keith Wilson (ed.), *Decisions for War* (New York: St Martin's Press, 1995).
36. These arguments are summarised in Mombauer, *Origins*, pp. 191–6; Mombauer is moderately sympathetic to Grey.
37. Nigel Bigger, 'Was Britain Right to Go to War in 1914'? *Standpoint*, September 2013, http://standpointmag.co.uk/node/5143
38. Gary Sheffield, *Forgotten Victory: The First World War – Myths and Realities* (London: Hodder Headline, 2001), pp. 33–40.
39. Quoted in Bogadnor, 'Shadows Lengthen', p. 25.
40. David Stevenson, *Armaments and the Coming of War in Europe 1904-1914* (Oxford: Oxford University Press, 1996), p. 40; in general, James Joll and Gordon Martel, *The Origins of the First World War* (Harlow: Pearson, 2007).
41. Herwig, 'Germany', in Hamilton and Herwig, *Origins*, p. 168.
42. Frank McDonough, *The Origins of the First and Second World Wars* (Cambridge: Cambridge University Press, 1997), p. 33.
43. Paul W. Schroeder, 'Stealing Horses to Great Applause: Austria-Hungary's Decision in 1914 in Systemic Perspective' in Holger Afflerbach and David Stevenson (eds), *An Improbable War? The Outbreak of World War I and European Political Culture Before 1914* (New York: Berghahn, 2007), pp. 28–32.
44. McDonough, *Origins*, p. 36.
45. Holger Afflerbach, 'The Topos of Improbable War in Europe Before 1914', in Afflerbach and Stevenson, *Improbable War?*, pp. 161–82.
46. Norman Angell, *The Great Illusion*, quoted in J. D. B. Miller, 'Norman Angell and Rationality in International Relations', in David Long and Peter Wilson, *Thinkers of the Twenty Years Crisis: Inter-War Idealism Reassessed* (Oxford: Clarendon Press, 1995), pp. 104–05.
47. Neiburg, *Dance of the Furies*, p. 79.
48. Neiberg, *Dance of the Furies*, pp. 123, 235–6. See also Jeffrey Verhey, *The Spirit of 1914: Militarism, Myth and Mobilization in Germany* (Cambridge: Cambridge University Press, 2000); Catriona Pennell, *A Kingdom United: Popular Responses to the Outbreak of the First World War in Britain and Ireland* (Oxford: Oxford University Press, 2012).

Suggested Further Reading

Afflerbach, Holger, and David Stevenson (eds), *An Improbable War? The Outbreak of World War I and European Political Culture Before 1914* (New York: Berghahn, 2007).

Clark, Christopher, *The Sleepwalkers: How Europe Went to War in 1914* (London: Allen Lane, 2012).

Fischer, Fritz *Germany's Aims in the First World War* (New York: Norton, 1967).

Hamilton, Richard F., and Holger H. Herwig, *Decisions for War, 1914-1917* (Cambridge: Cambridge University Press, 2004).

Levy, Jack S., and John A. Vasquez, *The Outbreak of the First World War: Structure, Politics and Decision-Making* (Cambridge: Cambridge University Press, 2014).

Mombauer, Annika, *The Origins of the First World War: Controversies and Consensus* (Harlow: Pearson, 2002).

Mombauer, Annika, *The Origins of the First World War: Diplomatic and Military Documents* (Manchester: Manchester University Press, 2013).

Neiberg, Michael, *Dance of the Furies: Europe and the Outbreak of World War I* (Cambridge, MA: Belknapp Press, 2011).

Wawro, Geoffrey, *A Mad Catastrophe: The Outbreak of World War I and the Collapse of the Hapsburg Empire* (New York: Basic Books, 2014).

Chapter 2

British Readiness for War

* * *

John Bourne

How ready for war was Britain in 1914? This question needs to be 'unpacked' before an answer can be attempted. It depends what is meant by 'Britain', what is meant by 'ready' and – ultimately – what is meant by 'war'.

The British Government

War is an act of state. The British declaration of war in August 1914 was made by Royal Prerogative.[1] There was no parliamentary debate or division.[2] There was no referendum. Much less was there any attempt to 'run' the decision for war past 'focus groups' to see how it would 'play' with the working classes, whose views were thought to be important but whose response was uncertain. The decision for war was made by a small number of senior politicians, chief among them the Prime Minister, Herbert Asquith, the Foreign Secretary, Sir Edward Grey, the Chancellor of the Exchequer, David Lloyd George, and the First Lord of the Admiralty, Winston Churchill. They were members of one of the most politically and socially progressive administrations in British history up to that time. They had challenged and broken the political power of the House of Lords, bastion of the landed aristocracy, and laid the foundations of a welfare state, paid for out of increased taxation of the 'idle rich'. For the government's enemies in Parliament and the press, during one of the most divisive periods in modern British political history, Asquith and his colleagues were almost as bad as socialists. It is therefore difficult to portray the Liberal government as one of 'warmongers' looking for any opportunity to start a conflict.

It was, however, undoubtedly a government of Imperialists, even among its most radical members. 'Imperialists' is used here in the neutral sense of 'people who believed the Empire was important'. This included virtually everyone in the parliamentary political spectrum. From our perspective the Empire appears to be something of a poisoned chalice,[3] but there were few – if any – British statesmen who could conceive a future of political progress, social stability and economic prosperity at *home* that was not an *Imperial* future. Ensuring the long-term safety and security of the British Empire was therefore a priority of British policy. The government was certainly 'ready' to go to war in defence of this aim, as it demonstrated in August 1914. This does not mean that the government welcomed war or was expecting it.

In the early years of the twentieth century, successive British governments pursued a policy of *détente*. This was designed to limit the possibilities of military conflict with the Empire's potential enemies, which did not really include Germany. Although the two world wars against Germany fundamentally changed British perceptions of that country, there was nothing inevitable – or even probable – about an Anglo-German war before 1914. There were British statesmen, notably Joseph Chamberlain and David Lloyd George, who believed Germany was one of Britain's 'natural allies', not one of her 'natural enemies'. The failure to conclude an Anglo-German alliance rose from mutual incompatibility rather than mutual antagonism.[4] The Second Boer War had brought home to the British just how vulnerable the Empire was in a rapidly changing world. Chamberlain's proposed solution to this problem, based on tariff reform and a radical reordering of imperial economic and military resources, succeeded only in dividing the Unionist Party and handing a crushing electoral victory to the Liberals in 1906. Instead, Britain would look to safeguard the Empire, not by increasing its own military power, but by diplomatic approaches to the nations that threatened it most: the United States, Japan, France and Russia.

The search for a diplomatic solution to the British imperial dilemma was begun in 1901. The Hay-Pauncefote Treaty with the United States saw Britain abandon its opposition to a canal across the Isthmus of Panama controlled by one country, a position that had been firmly held ever since the Clayton-Bulwer Treaty of 1850. The Hay-Pauncefote treaty marked, in effect, British recognition of American dominance of the Western hemisphere. British dependence on imports of food from North America alone made going to war with the United States unthinkable and no British government was prepared to think it. Whether this view of the world was reciprocated quite so warmly in the United States, especially in the US Navy, is another matter. Britain and the USA were very far from being allies but no one in Britain was prepared to make the USA an enemy.

The following year, 1902, saw Britain abandon a century of 'splendid isolation' by concluding a peacetime alliance with Japan. This was the most striking illustration of the British sense of imperial overstretch and global weakness. The alliance provided for British neutrality in a war between Russia and Japan and for British support for Japan in a war between Russia and Japan in which Russia was joined by another European power. The alliance seemed to contain any threat to the British Empire in Asia and the Far East by making an ally of Japan and by encouraging an enemy of Russia. The Japanese alliance had undoubted short-term benefits for the British, not least during the First World War, but it was essentially a cynical exercise in power diplomacy that made a Russo-Japanese war much more likely. When this came, in 1904, the outcome – a crushing Japanese victory – had an enormous impact on colonial peoples, being characterised by Geoffrey Barraclough as 'the French Revolution of Asia'. The consequences of this for the long-term future of the British Empire were as profound as they were malign.

Russia's only likely ally in a war against Japan was France. At the turn of the century British relations with France were much more fractious than they were with Germany and threatened to break out into open war, especially over the 'Fashoda Incident' in 1898. Once prospects of an Anglo-German alliance dimmed, however, improving relations with France, living under a powerful sense of threat from its eastern neighbour, became a more realistic possibility. Even so, the famous Anglo-French *entente* of 1904, negotiated by the Unionist Foreign Secretary, Lord Lansdowne, burst like a bombshell in the world of European diplomacy. (The *entente* also owed much to the intervention of King Edward VII, an intervention that earned him the title 'Edward the Peacemaker', an indication that France was thought of as a much more likely enemy than Germany.) The substance of the *entente* seems, from this distance, remarkably trivial, being principally concerned with adjusting spheres of interest in North Africa and the Middle East and resolving fishing rights on the Grand Banks and in the St Lawrence. It was not what was agreed, however, that was important, but the fact that anything was agreed at all. The *entente*'s real significance was essentially symbolic; the fact that it represented a diplomatic coming together of Britain and France. The British never saw the *entente* as an alliance or intended it to be anti-German, but this was not how the Germans saw it. German determination to break the Anglo-French *rapprochement*, during the first Moroccan Crisis of 1905 and, more especially, during the second Moroccan Crisis of 1911, had the effect – typical of pre-war German diplomacy – of strengthening it. British military preparations following the second Moroccan Crisis arguably took on a much more overtly anti-German aspect.

The Anglo-Russian Convention of 1907 is, perhaps, much more surprising than the *entente* with France. Russia was the greatest potential threat to the British Empire in India. Sir Edward Grey took the opportunity of Russia's defeat in the war against Japan to extract from her favourable understandings on matters of mutual imperial concern, especially on the frontiers of India, in Afghanistan and Persia. Reducing the potential for conflict with Russia in Asia had been a fundamental aim of British diplomacy since the 1890s. Grey achieved something of a coup. He was, however, severely criticised for this, not least by members of the parliamentary Liberal party who loathed Tsarist autocracy. For some later critics, as well, this seemed an '*entente* too far' and one that limited even further Britain's room for manoeuvre in July and August 1914.

The weeks that followed the assassination of the Archduke Franz Ferdinand on 28 June 1914 are usually referred to as 'the July Crisis'. In Britain, however, that might be more accurately characterised as the 'last week of July Crisis'. The Cabinet showed no anxiety about the European situation, of which there was no discussion between 28 June and 24 July, when news of the Austrian ultimatum to Serbia broke. The Cabinet was fully focused on preventing war, but the war it was fully focused on preventing was a civil war in Ireland. In the last week of peace Grey was the only statesman who seriously tried to prevent the outbreak of a European war, but later critics, including – hypocritically – Lloyd George, accused Grey of not taking a firm enough line with Germany. Grey did not do this because he had no mandate from the Cabinet. Had he sought one, he would almost certainly have been opposed by Lloyd George. The Cabinet, in all likelihood, would have split, and even the government have fallen. The government only became 'ready' for war at the very last minute, when there seemed no other realistic choice and after the Germans had obligingly violated Belgian neutrality.[5] Grey and Asquith would have argued for a declaration of war even if Germany had not violated Belgian neutrality, but it is doubtful whether the Cabinet, the Liberal party or the country would have followed them, at least not with the degree of political and national solidarity that was shown.

The decision that faced the British government in early August 1914 was not whether to start a war, but whether to join in a war that had already started. The Foreign Office official Eyre Crowe summed up the dilemma: 'Should this war come and England stand aside, one of two things must happen: Either Germany and Austria win, crush France and humiliate Russia . . . [Then] what will be the position of friendless England? Or France and Russia win. What would be their attitude towards England? What about India and the Mediterranean?'[6] Crowe was a committed anti-German and it is significant that he did not see the Germans as the only problem, but the French and Russians too. Grey agreed with him. After the fateful decision was taken, the Foreign Secretary summarised Britain's reasons for going to war. 'If we did not stand by France and stand up for Belgium against this aggression, we should be isolated, discredited and hated; and there would be nothing before us but a miserable and ignoble future.'[7] From a British perspective a 'perfect storm' had blown up. British opposition to a hegemonic and aggressive power dominating the Low Countries was a central and historic aspect of British foreign policy. This alone made it difficult for Britain to stand aside, but abandoning France and Russia would undermine the whole edifice of *détente* so carefully constructed over the previous thirteen years. It is bitterly ironic that British determination to lower the temperature of international relations and to make conflict less likely was what ultimately dragged her into the conflagration in 1914.

The British Armed Forces

The British government in August 1914 intended to fight the war with the military resources it already had at its disposal. Were these forces ready for war?

Britain was pre-eminently a naval power. Despite increased competition from the USA, Japan, France, Italy and Austria-Hungary, as well as Germany, Britain remained *the* naval power. The naval 'arms race' with Germany had been convincingly won by the British by 1912. The British knew this and so did the Germans. Admiral Lord Fisher, First Sea Lord from 1904 to 1910, had presided over a revolution in naval warfare, creating an efficient, modern, fast, all big-gun fleet that was expected to play a decisive role in any future war.[8] The Royal Navy was clearly of the view that such a war would almost certainly be against Germany, an event that some in the navy not only expected but also welcomed. The navy was 'ready'.

The Royal Navy was confident of success. It had not only the means but also a plan. Fisher characterised this as the 'policy of steady pressure'. In order for this pressure to tell, the Royal Navy had to maintain supremacy at sea. Naval supremacy would keep Britain inviolate, allow her to conduct world trade unmolested and to maintain the flow of imports, especially of food, which were vital to a country that produced only 120 days of food a year from domestic resources in 1914. This was Clausewitz's 'principle of protection'. Failure to uphold this principle could lose the war, but it was not enough in itself to win it. Victory would come from the ruthless offensive use of naval power. The main element was a blockade of Germany. German failure to break the blockade would, eventually, compel her to end the war through economic exhaustion and financial bankruptcy. This economic warfare was not simply a matter of physically obstructing German sea trade. The strategy would also utilise Britain's domination of international banking, communications and shipping to achieve a German economic implosion. Few naval strategists believed that Germany could afford not to contest the blockade. After all, Germany was a substantial naval power. At some point, the German High Seas Fleet would have to come out of port and attempt to relieve the stranglehold that the Royal Navy was applying. This would give the Royal Navy the opportunity it craved to destroy the German fleet in a battle of annihilation in the North Sea, a new Trafalgar. This would be the decisive moment of the war and Britain's principal contribution to Allied victory. Britain's allies would be encouraged, neutrals would be intimidated and economic warfare against Germany could be prosecuted even more ruthlessly. Although this plan was not to work out as seamlessly as hoped, weakened principally by the hostility of the neutral United States and the disappointment of the Battle of Jutland, the role of economic warfare in the eventual defeat of Germany is often over-looked because of the hold on the British imagination of 'trench warfare'.[9]

The war that the government believed it had entered – certainly Sir Edward Grey believed this – would be from the British perspective a naval war utilising British economic and financial power. This war would not be a short one. One of the most pervasive, but absurd, myths about the Great War is that 'everyone' expected it to be 'over by Christmas'. It is actually difficult to find 'anyone' who believed this. The war Britain proposed to fight would take time. This was clearly understood. The German economy would not collapse overnight. British strategic planning was based on the long haul, but this seemed to be achievable on the basis of 'business as usual'. The unhappy reality of the Great War from a British perspective was that Britain fought the war she had to, not the war she wanted to. The war she had to fight was a land war of attrition. This came as an enormous shock, for which no preparatiohs had been made and for which measures were introduced only reluctantly and slowly under the discipline of events. Neither the British government nor the British army was 'ready' for this kind of war.

'In every respect the Expeditionary Force of 1914 was incomparably the best trained, best organized, and best equipped British Army which ever went forth to war,' declared the British Official Historian, Sir James Edmonds.[10] This judgement has proved a captivating one. The British Expeditionary Force (BEF) of 1914 remains clothed in an aura of military sanctity. Despite the Kaiser's famous dismissal of Britain's 'contemptible little army', the reputation of the BEF as an elite force of combat-hardened veterans found much support in German opinion, especially after the First Battle of Ypres, during which young, inexperienced German volunteers were flung against Britain's Regulars with disastrous results, a 'massacre of the innocents'. In reality, the BEF's fighting capability left much to be desired.

The British Army of 1914 was undoubtedly a much improved institution from what it had been a decade earlier. The force for change was the chastening experience of the war in South Africa. Two important committees were set up: the Elgin Commission was charged with investigating the conduct of the Boer War; and the Esher Committee was charged with reform of the army. Remarkably, these committees worked quickly and effectively and reforms soon followed. A Committee of Imperial Defence was established in 1902, with a brief to co-ordinate British defence planning. An Army Council and a General Staff were established in 1904 and the post of Commander-in-Chief abolished. The War Office was radically re-organised. Any chance that the army would successfully oppose the recommended reforms was dished by the appointment of Richard Haldane as Secretary of State for War in 1905. Prominent among Haldane's advisers was General Sir Gerald Ellison, who had been Secretary to the Esher Committee. There was to be no turning back.

Haldane's reforms did not stop at the recommendations of the Elgin Commission and Esher Committee. He established the Officers' Training Corps and the BEF (1908). The mobilization of the BEF was constantly practised and improved under the watchful eye of the Director of Military Operations, Henry Wilson. Arrangements with the General Post Office, the railway companies and the shipping lines, were perfected. When the call came, the BEF's mobilization ran like a well-oiled machine. To that extent, at least, the BEF was 'ready'.

Haldane also successfully overcame the entrenched opposition of the Volunteer movement and created a new Territorial Force (TF) (1908) that was organised along Regular Army lines. The TF was intended to be a financially and politically acceptable means of solving Britain's perennial lack of efficient auxiliary forces. Haldane envisaged the TF as a future source of reinforcements for the Expeditionary Force, but in order to get the necessary legislation through Parliament, where it was assailed from left and right, he was compelled to limit the TF's role to home defence. Despite the best efforts of King George V, the TF never really caught the public imagination. Its members were derided as 'Saturday night soldiers'; they greeted the outbreak of war 36,000 men below establishment. Only five complete units had signed the 'Imperial service obligation' that allowed them to be used abroad. When the war came, the military burden would fall on Britain's small Regular army and its Reserves.

The army also showed a capacity for reform from within. The Staff College was transformed under the leadership of three powerful commandants, Henry Rawlinson (1903–6), Henry Wilson (1907–10) and William Robertson (1910–13). The Directorates of Operations and of Staff Duties at the War Office revised British military 'doctrine' and administrative procedures in the important *Field Service Regulations Part I: Operations* and *Field Service Regulations Part II: Administration* (1909), publications in which the future Commander-in-Chief of the BEF, Douglas Haig, played an important role. The army was also re-kitted and rearmed, adopting the Short Magazine Lee-Enfield rifle (1907), with its ten-round detachable magazine and drop-handle bolt that made for rapid firing, the 'sword-pattern' bayonet (1907), the 18pdr quick-firing field gun (1904) and the 4.5in howitzer (1908), staples of British field artillery throughout the war. British field service uniform was also transformed. The Burrowes Committee, chaired by Major Arnold Burrowes of the Royal Irish Fusiliers, designed innovative webbing, known as the 1908 Pattern Web Equipment. Practical and ergonomic, it proved highly adaptable to the conditions of trench warfare and served the British soldier well. The training of ordinary soldiers greatly improved, focusing on field craft, on small unit tactics, based on the principle of fire and manoeuvre, and on shooting skills (known in the British army as 'musketry'), in which the Commandant of the School of Musketry at Hythe, Major N. R. McMahon, was a key figure.[11]

There were also other changes that could be interpreted as those of a country readying itself for war. The foundations of the 'Security State' were laid in the years before 1914 with the establishment of the Secret Service Bureau (1909), later split into the Security Service (MI5)[12] and the Secret Intelligence Service (SIS or MI6),[13] the passing of the Official Secrets Act (1911) and the drafting of the War Book (1911). The War Book was the achievement of Major Adrian Grant-Duff, Assistant Secretary (Military) of the Committee of Imperial Defence. It was drawn up in the immediate aftermath of the second Moroccan Crisis ('Agadir') in April 1911. It is therefore difficult to see the War Book as anything other than preparation for a war against Germany. It laid down the administrative arrangements to be carried out by all departments of the central government in the event of war. When war came, the British civil service was undoubtedly 'ready'.

The second Moroccan Crisis also saw the British army draw up plans for closer co-operation with the French in the event of a war against Germany.[14] Henry Wilson was, once again, a leading player. At a famous, some would say infamous, meeting of the Committee of Imperial Defence on 23 August 1911, Wilson, a fluent and facile lecturer, worsted his namesake, Admiral Sir Arthur Wilson, the First Sea

Lord. The result, according to some, was the adoption of a 'Continental strategy' by Britain, in which the BEF would be immediately sent to France to fight on the left flank of the French armies, where Wilson believed it would be 'the decisive force, at the decisive place, at the decisive time'.[15] But when the war broke out, the British government behaved as though this decision had never been taken and Wilson was compelled to make his case again.

Britain's armed forces had undergone a period of rapid change and improvement between the end of the South African War and the outbreak of war with Germany. Without this it is difficult to see how Britain could have intervened so quickly in the land war, mobilising an expeditionary force and deploying it safely to France, where it confronted the main advance of the German army within nineteen days of the declaration of war. But there were grave limitations to British military readiness.

There were two principles underpinning British military reform. The first was financial parsimony; the second was the priority afforded to imperial policing. One of the most impressive things about the Haldane reforms is that they were achieved without increasing military spending. In reality, they were achieved *because* Haldane did not seek an increase in the Army Estimates. Parliament eventually showed itself willing to fund Fisher's 'Dreadnought revolution' in the Royal Navy, which was central to the protection of the country's independence and liberty.[16] There was, however, a deep-seated reluctance to spend money on the army, whose libertarian credentials were less clear than the navy's. This ancient fear was sharpened at a time when monies had to be found for social reform in a political environment, even among many Liberals, that was hostile to high taxation. The consequences of financial stringency were that the Regular Army remained small and unlikely to intimidate potential enemies. It also meant that it was sometimes denied important new weapons, notably the machine-gun, on a scale that advocates of 'firepower', like McMahon, wanted.[17]

The establishment of the BEF was deliberately intended to give the British government the ability to intervene quickly in a Continental war, but it was never the focus of British military policy. The BEF was fixed at six infantry divisions and a cavalry brigade (later raised to a cavalry division). This force structure owed nothing to a careful consideration of Britain's actual or potential political obligations or strategic intentions. It was simply the largest force available once the demands of imperial policing had been met. Since the early 1880s British infantry regiments had been organised on a two-battalion system, in which one battalion remained at home and one served abroad. The home battalions acted in part as training and re-supply units for the battalions serving abroad. As a consequence, home battalions were rarely up to their war establishment of 1,070 men, a number of whom at any one time would also have been soldiers still under training and those too young to be sent on active service. As the BEF was to be created from home-based battalions, the shortfall would have to be remedied by calling up the Reserves.[18] The proportion of Reserves in BEF infantry battalions has been put as high as 60 per cent. The proportion would have varied from unit to unit, but 60 per cent is a realistic figure. The 1st Battalion Cameronians was reinforced by 600 Reservists in August 1914;[19] the two Regular battalions of the Royal Welsh Fusiliers needed 342 men and 489 men to bring them up to war establishment.[20] Some Reservists would have been recently with the colours but others may have been out of the army for several years and unfamiliar with changes in weaponry, uniforms and tactics. As the punishing retreat from Mons soon demonstrated, many were far from 'match fit'. Few soldiers, Regular or Reservist, would have previously been in combat. The BEF's limitations and achievements in 1914 must be set in the context of its being essentially a Reserve force.

The problems experienced by the BEF at the battalion level were magnified higher up the chain of command. The army was lacking in experienced commanders and even more in experienced staffs.[21] Of the formations that made up the BEF, only the Aldershot Army Corps (which became I Corps upon mobilization) had any real peacetime existence; the other elements existed mainly on paper and had to be extemporised with scratch staffs. The consequences of this were all too apparent in the early fighting. The army was woefully short of heavy artillery, which was of little utility in imperial policing. The field artillery remained wedded to forward support of the infantry, which was to prove costly in the early battles and had to be virtually abandoned after the battle of Le Cateau on 26 August.[22] The field artillery was armed almost exclusively with shrapnel shell, a deadly weapon against troops in the open, but of limited effectiveness against the earthworks that characterised the onset of trench warfare. The United Kingdom had inadequate space for large-scale manoeuvres, which meant that the level of 'all-arms co-operation' achieved by the BEF was wholly inadequate, a serious weakness that could not be compensated by the rifle skills of individual infantrymen. The BEF was barely 'ready' for the war it was required to conduct in 1914 and hopelessly ill-prepared for the war of attrition with which it was faced in the years to come.

The British People

It is always tempting with great events like the First World War to seek their 'origins' in long-maturing causes and to portray Europe as being 'readied' for war by decades of nationalism, militarism, imperialism and propaganda. Evidence for the 'militarization' of British society hangs by the thin evidential threads of institutions such as the Boys' Brigade (1883), the Church Lads' Brigade (1891), Empire Day (first celebrated on 24 May 1902)[23] and, most of all perhaps, the Boy Scouts (1908). Recent scholarship has raised serious objections to the validity of this argument, not only in Britain but also more widely in Europe.[24] The picture of a Europe politically and culturally readied for war has been replaced by that of a Europe in which the great powers were not seeking war, certainly not a general European war, the outbreak of which came as a profound shock and into which the civilian populations entered in an atmosphere of grim resignation and determination, not a frenzy of mindless jingoism. Professor Michael Neiberg asked the rhetorical question of his audience at the University of Wolverhampton in June 2014: 'Did young men in the streets of Wolverhampton in August 1914 believe that their lives had been unfulfilled because they had not been given the opportunity to kill a German?' The answer is clearly 'no'. The British government did not act as it did in the opening days of August 1914 in response to a popular clamour for war. Among national newspapers only *The Times* took a consistent interventionist line. Among the provincial press, much perused by politicians as a source of 'public opinion', there was general concern and sober reflection on the potentially disastrous consequences of a European war, not 'universal unthinking enthusiasm'.[25] Opinion only became reluctantly converted to British intervention after the German invasion of Belgium.

British society on the eve of the Great War was overwhelmingly urban and industrial. Perhaps as much as 80 per cent of the population could reasonably be characterised as 'working class'. The question 'were the British people ready for war' is therefore really a question of whether the working class was 'ready' for war. There was a general recognition in government that what the working class believed, wanted or would accept would be important in ensuring a satisfactory outcome to the war, but there was less certainty what these beliefs, desires and limits were. Official nervousness may be detected in one of the first acts of the government after the outbreak of war, the passing of the Defence of the Realm Act (DORA) on 8 August. DORA was partly intended to protect the country from the 'enemy within' of foreign nationals, but granted wide-ranging powers that could be used to control domestic dissent and 'encourage morale'. Given the tumultuous history of working-class unrest in the previous decade, this legislation may be thought prudent.

The British working class has proved a disappointment to the British left. Then, as now, there was a large proportion of working-class Conservatives, Disraeli's 'angels in marble'. Even at the moment of its 1945 electoral triumph, the Labour Party was not able to equate 'working class' with 'Labour voter'. Marxists attribute this phenomenon to 'false consciousness', in which capitalist institutional, ideological and material processes prevent the 'proletariat' from recognising its true interests. For others, on the right as well as the left, it is a result of working-class 'deference'. It is difficult to find much support for either of these theories in the decade before the outbreak of war. The British working-class was quite extraordinarily strike-prone in defence of its industrial interests, so strike-prone indeed that some, especially during the 'Triple Alliance' of miners, railwaymen and dockers in 1912, thought the country was on the brink of revolution. The British urban working class was the product of 150 years of economic and social change. During that time it developed characteristic institutions, such as the Co-Operative Movement, the friendly societies, the trade union movement and the nascent Labour party, and characteristic cultural values based on the pub, the club, the team and the 'fancy', that owed little or nothing to upper and middle class patronage, while retaining confidence in the monarchy and in Parliament.[26] Many were therefore surprised when working-class support for the war proved to be so strong and enduring.

Working-class males were to have an opportunity to display their readiness for war much sooner than anyone anticipated. Britain's plan for winning the war, as we have seen, rested on waging a ruthless economic war against Germany, utilising Britain's major military asset, the Royal Navy, and its strategic domination of world finances and trade. Britain's military commitment would be limited to the despatch of the small expeditionary force to France and, possibly, the despatch of other, even smaller, expeditionary forces to other parts of the periphery of the Central Powers where it was hoped and believed they would have an impact out of all proportion to their size. No one anticipated raising a mass army, counted in millions, and launching it against the main forces of the main enemy on the main battlefield. No one, that is, other than Lord Kitchener. Asquith's decision to 'reinforce' his government with the presence of the Empire's greatest living soldier was one of the most extraordinary and important of the war. Kitchener's impact was immediate. He argued that Britain must raise a mass army and be prepared to keep it in the field for at least three years. The function of these 'New Armies' would be to execute the *coup de grâce* on the German army that had been rendered ripe for defeat by the French and Russian armies. This would allow Britain not only to win the war but also to determine the peace in the long-term interests of the British Empire, a peace that would be directed as much against Britain's allies as her enemies. Kitchener's intervention, and the Cabinet's unquestioning acquiescence in it, changed everything. The war for which the government might have thought it was 'ready' changed overnight. This 'new war' put an even greater premium on working-class support.

The response to Kitchener's call to arms was certainly impressive. By the end of 1914 1,186,357 men had volunteered for the Regular Army and the Territorial Force; a further 1,280,362 men volunteered in 1915.[27] These numbers certainly show willingness, but military readiness was months, perhaps years, away. The appeal of military service to young and not-so-young British working-class men is complex and nuanced. It was not simply a matter of white feathers and peer pressure, though the latter was undoubtedly important.[28] Peter Simkins long ago dismissed the idea of a mindless rush to the colours by gullible young men intent on a lark.[29] He showed, in particular, that the peak of recruitment in 1914 came not in August but in the middle of September, when news of the BEF's precipitous retreat from Mons became known in Britain. There was always a more considered element to recruitment than is traditionally allowed. There were similar recruitment spikes in 1915 in response to the events on the battlefield. (Voluntary recruitment in 1915 was even more impressive than in 1914 because by then the true nature of the war had become apparent.) As late as the spring of 1918 more than 200 Staffordshire miners *volunteered* for military service in order to help repel the German offensives, then appearing to threaten an Allied defeat.[30]

Working-class support for the war was never absolute. The government could not heedlessly draw on a bottomless well of working-class patriotism. There was no industrial truce on the home front. Labour relations remained fractious, especially in the coalfields, despite the willingness of large numbers of miners to join the army. A wave of strikes across the Midlands engineering sector, vital to the war effort, in the spring and summer of 1917 so alarmed the government that Lloyd George was compelled to institute a Commission of Inquiry, chaired by the veteran trade unionist (and Minister of Labour) George Barnes. Thereafter, Lloyd George pursued a carrot and stick approach, locking up left wing 'agitators' while addressing many working-class grievances. Working-class pressure was instrumental in bringing about rent controls (1915) and a national system of rationing (July 1918). But in the end, no matter how reluctantly government and people entered upon the war, and no matter how demanding and costly the war became, neither government nor people showed themselves willing to exchange peace at the price of defeat. Like Mr Brightling, they were ready to see it through to the end.

Notes

1. A. J. P. Taylor gives a characteristic account of this in *English History 1914-1945* (Oxford: Oxford University Press, 1965), pp. 2–3.
2. The closest Parliament came to giving formal approval to the declaration of war was when it voted a credit of £100 million on 6 August. This was agreed without a division and with barely a debate.
3. This is one of the themes of Bernard Porter's *The Lion's Share: A Short History of British Imperialism* (4th edn. Harlow: Longman, 2004).
4. See Zara Steiner, *Britain and the Origins of the First World War* (2nd edn. Basingstoke: Palgrave Macmillan, 2003).
5. See Keith M. Wilson, 'The British Cabinet's Decision for War, 2 August 1914', *British Journal of International Studies*, 1 (1975), pp. 148–59.
6. Quoted in Keith M. Wilson, *The Policy of the Entente: Essays on the Determinants of British Foreign Policy, 1904-14* (1985), pp. 79–80.
7. Quoted in Steiner, *Britain and the Origins of the First World War*, p. 245.
8. See Nicholas A. Lambert, *Sir John Fisher's Naval Revolution* (Columbia, South Carolina: University of South Carolina Press, 2002).
9. See Nicholas A. Lambert, *Planning Armageddon: British Economic Warfare and the First World War* (London: Harvard University Press, 2012).
10. Sir James Edmonds, *History of the Great War: Military Operations France and Belgium 1914* (London: Macmillan, 1923), p. 10.
11. For a fuller treatment, see Spencer Jones, *From Boer War to World War: Tactical Reform of the British Army, 1902-1914* (Norman, OK: University of Oklahoma Press, 2012).
12. See Christopher Andrew, *The Defence of the Realm: The Authorized History of MI5* (London: Penguin, 2009).
13. See Keith Jeffery, *The Secret History of MI6, 1909-1949* (New York: Penguin, 2010).
14. Informal talks between the British and French general staffs had been taking place since 1905.
15. In this belief, Wilson was deluded. He later recognised this himself, declaring that six divisions were 'fifty too few' to take to a Continental war: Field-Marshal Haig commanded fifty-nine British divisions in the Great Advance of 1918.
16. Even so, Fisher was appointed First Sea Lord because of his promise to *cut* naval expenditure.

17. It is not true, however, that the British army was under-equipped with machine-guns compared with the German army. The allocations were exactly the same. McMahon also advocated adopting an automatic rifle, with which neither the British nor the Germans went to war.

18. The situation with the Reserves was somewhat muddled, as Alison Hine has demonstrated: 'Prior to 1908 the length of time spent on the Reserve was changed frequently and confusingly. In May 1902 the ratio between colour and reserve service of seven and five years respectively had been changed to three and nine years, in order to attract more recruits. This did not prove successful and in November 1904, as a result of a growing manpower crisis, the ratio of service was reversed to nine and three years. Then, in September 1906, the ratio reverted to the original seven and five years respectively. There was a potentially serious effect arising out of the rapid changes in length of service commitments: both the 1905–6 and the 1907–8 enlistments would be due to transfer to the Reserve in 1914' (Unpublished paper).

19. John Terraine (ed.), *General Jack's Diary* (London: Eyre & Spottiswoode, 1964), pp. 22–5.

20. David Langley, 'British Line Infantry Reserves for the Great War – Part 2: A Case Study of the Royal Welsh Fusiliers', *Stand To! The Journal of the Western Front Association*, 101 (September 2014), pp. 27–31.

21. For the limitations of the staff, see J. M. Bourne, 'Major General Sir Archibald Murray', in Spencer Jones (ed.), *Stemming the Tide: Officers and Leadership in the British Expeditionary Force 1914* (Solihull: Helion, 2013), pp. 51–69.

22. For the importance of Le Cateau in the history of the Royal Artillery, see Shelford Bidwell, *Gunners at War: A Tactical Study of the Royal Artillery in the Twentieth Century* (London: Arms & Armour Press, 1970), pp. 13–30.

23. The celebration of Empire Day, on Queen Victoria's birthday, began in Canada in 1898. It was introduced to Britain in 1902 by the ardent Imperialist, Lord Meath. It was not recognised as an official event until 1916. As a working-class child growing up in the industrial Midlands in the 1950s, Empire Day made no impact on me whatsoever. In fact, I had never heard of it until it was pointed out to me by my late colleague, Bob Bushaway, in the 1980s.

24. For Britain, see Adrian Gregory, *The Last Great War: British Society and the First World War* (Cambridge: Cambridge University Press, 2008) and Catriona Pennell, *A Kingdom United: Popular Responses to the Outbreak of the First World War in Britain and Ireland* (Oxford: Oxford University Press, 2012); for France, J. J. Becker, *1914: comment les Français sont entres dans la guerre* (Paris: Presses de la Fondation Nationale des Sciences Politiques, 1977) and *L'année 14* (Paris: A. Collin, 2004); for Germany, Jeffrey Verhey, *The Spirit of 1914: Militarism, Myth and Mobilization in Germany* (Cambridge: Cambridge University Press, 2000). For a Europe-wide perspective, see Christopher Clark, *Sleepwalkers: How Europe Went to War in 1914* (London: Penguin, 2013), Margaret Macmillan, *The War that Ended Peace: How Europe Abandoned Peace for the First World War* (London: Profile Books, 2014) and Michael Neiberg, *Dance of the Furies: Europe and the Outbreak of World War I* (Cambridge, Mass. and London: Belknap Press of Harvard University Press, 2010).

25. See Nick Beeching, 'The Provincial Press & the Outbreak of War. A Unionist View in Worcestershire', *Midland History*, 39 (2) (Autumn 2014), pp. 163–84

26. See Ross McKibbin, 'Why was there no Marxism in Great Britain?', in *The Ideologies of Class: Social Relations in Britain 1880-1950* (Oxford: Clarendon Press, 1991), pp. 1–41.

27. *Statistics of the Military Effort of the British Empire 1914-1920* (London: War Office, 1922), p. 364.

28. See David Silbey, *The British Working Class and Enthusiasm for War, 1914-1916* (London: Frank Cass, 2005) for a considered and convincing account.

29. Peter Simkins, *Kitchener's Army: The Raising of the New Armies, 1914-1916* (Barnsley: Pen & Sword Military, 2007).

30. See John Bourne, 'Burslem and its Roll of Honour 1914-1918', *Midland History*, 39 (2) (Autumn 2014), pp. 202–18.

Suggested Further Reading

Bowman, Tim, and Mark Connelly, *The Edwardian Army: Recruiting, Training and Deploying the British Army, 1902-1914* (Oxford: Oxford University Press, 2012).

French, David, *British Economic and Strategic Planning 1905-1915* (London: George Allen & Unwin, 1982).

Gilbert, Adrian, *Challenge of Battle: The Real Story of the British Army in 1914* (Oxford: Osprey, 2014).

Hart, Peter, *Fire and Movement: The British Expeditionary Force and the Campaign of 1914* (Oxford: Oxford University Press, 2014).

Jones, Spencer, *From Boer War to World War: Tactical Reform of the British Army, 1902-1914* (Norman, OK: University of Oklahoma Press, 2012).

Jones, Spencer (ed.), *Stemming the Tide: Officers and Leadership in the British Expeditionary Force 1914* (Solihull: Helion, 2013).

Pennell, Catriona, *A Kingdom United: Popular Responses to the Outbreak of the First World War in Britain and Ireland* (Oxford: Oxford University Press, 2012).

Steiner, Zara, *Britain and the Origins of the First World War* (2nd edn. Basingstoke: Palgrave Macmillan, 2003).

Chapter 3

The Shock of War: How Britain Entered the First World War

* * *

Catriona Pennell

As we work towards an emotive commemoration of the outbreak of WW1 we are also busy setting the scene by creating a 'living stage' reminiscent of the peaceful idyll of a pre-war summer's day 1914.[1]

The image that the summer of 1914 was the culmination of the long Edwardian idyll persists in the public imagination – as evidenced above – as the centenary commemorations of the First World War unfold. It stands in opposition to the rupture and disharmony brought by the outbreak of the First World War. Alice Meynell's *Summer in England*, 1914, which first appeared in *The Times* on 10 October 1914, contrasts the idyll of that last innocent summer with the terrible fall into war (although the war, in her view, is necessary to preserve that very beauty):

Most happy year! And out of town
The hay was prosperous, and the wheat;
The silken harvest climbed the down;
Moon after moon was heavenly-sweet,
Stroking the bread within the sheaves,
Looking twixt apples and their leaves.[2]

In the late 1920s, Winston Churchill, First Lord of the Admiralty in 1914, reflected that 'the spring and summer of 1914 were marked in Europe by an exceptional tranquillity'.[3] By the 1960s, the motif of a peaceful pre-war summer had cemented itself firmly within the historiography. Paul Fussell wrote, in 1975:

Although some memories of the benign last summer before the war can be discounted as standard retrospection turned even rosier by egregious contrast with what followed, all agree that the prewar summer was the most idyllic for many years. It was warm and sunny, eminently pastoral. One lolled outside in a folding canvas chaise, or swam, or walked in the countryside. One read outdoors, went on picnics, had tea served from a white wicker table under the trees.[4]

It was also echoed in popular histories, such as Lyn Macdonald's *The Roses of No Man's Land* (originally published in 1980) which describes the summer of 1914 as 'golden' preceding the moment when the world 'was about to come to an end'.[5] This nostalgia is, perhaps, unsurprising; looking back on 1914, after the tragedy of two (not entirely unrelated) world conflicts, the disappointment of peace, and the prospect of nuclear annihilation, the 'last summer of peace' must have appeared as a golden age, if only in contrast to what followed it.[6]

The sudden transition from peaceful idyll to bloody conflict – as this image suggests – implies that Edwardians would have felt a profound sense of shock at the announcement of Britain's entry into war on 4 August 1914. This chapter seeks to explore this notion. How shocking was the news of war for the people of Britain? To what degree had the British public been expecting a major conflict? How valid is this image of peaceful pre-war idyll? If the news of war did come as a surprise, can we ascribe that to the idyll people were living in that summer before? Or are there other explanations for this sense of shock?

An Expectation of War?

To some degree, an expectation of war had been building in the imaginations of people in Britain. Between 1871 and 1914, Britain was invaded by an army of fictional enemies, usually in the guise of an enemy spy. They landed 'in their thousands on bookstalls and in bookshops. They used the short story to establish themselves in hundreds of newspapers and magazines, successfully infiltrated dozens of popular stage plays, and were even spotted in cinemas and on the pages of children's comics'.[7] Invasion stories thrilled and entertained audiences in the late Edwardian era. According to John Gooch, one word could send 'a frisson of terror coursing down the middle class spine – invasion'.[8]

Since the mid-nineteenth century there had been an increasing awareness of the vulnerability of Britain to attack from across the Channel. The enemies in fiction reflected, to some extent, British foreign relations. It was an article by Sir George Chesney in *Blackwood's Magazine* in May 1871 entitled 'The Battle of Dorking' that truly placed the possibility of a *German* invasion in the minds of contemporaries. It became a book and caused such dismay amongst an already nervous public that the then Prime Minister, William Gladstone, felt it necessary to make a speech against its alarmism – a remarkable occasion in both political and literary history.[9] The story foretold the destruction of the Channel Fleet by a secret device and the subsequent landing of 200,000 Prussians. The British forces were easily defeated, owing to antiquated equipment and obsolete tactics.

Over the next thirty years, this precedent was imitated by a myriad of writers, its popularity enhanced by the fact that invasion had now entered official discourse with debates ranging from the proposed construction of the Channel Tunnel in 1882–3 to the lack of dreadnoughts in the British navy.[10] Many of the earlier accounts still presented the French as the putative foreign oppressor, but from the turn of the century the needle of anxiety switched direction to Germany. In *The Riddle of the Sands*, published in 1903, Erskine Childers devised the ideal myth in which to convey the anxieties of a nation beginning to be alarmed about a menace from overseas. The espionage novel revealed in a stage-by-stage account the discovery of German plans to invade England.[11] The story seemed as if it ought to be true, and therefore caused a sensation when it came out, selling several hundred thousand copies.[12] *The Riddle of the Sands* was swiftly followed by William Le Queux's *The Invasion of 1910* published in serial form in the *Daily Mail* in 1905. The story described a German invasion of the British Isles where the *Uhlans* (German cavalry) wreaked havoc in every town from Hull and York to Southend-on-Sea.[13] The book was published in 1906, translated into twenty-seven different languages, and sold over one million copies.[14]

Some more sceptical observers view these stories, and in particular their links with key newspaper editors of the day, as no more than propaganda; an opportunity to play on the fears of ordinary people in order to forward political campaigns and increase circulation figures. Newspaper magnate Alfred Harmsworth's 1895 electoral campaign was based on 'The Siege of Portsmouth', a series published in his newly-acquired Portsmouth *Evening Mail* that sensationalized Britain's lack of naval preparedness, playing on Conservative supporters' concerns in an effort to combat the local Liberal paper.[15] Leading members of the National Service League, founded in 1901 to advocate for conscription, utilised fears of invasion to further their campaign. Harmsworth went on to commission Le Queux to write *The Invasion of 1910* precisely to keep readers of the *Daily Mail* informed on the need for a stronger navy and for universal military service. However, alarmist as these stories were, and manipulative in their desire to promote a political manifesto and boost sales, there can be no doubt that they expressed the fears of many Edwardians.

The growth of German imperialism, the disputes with France (in east and north Africa) and later with Germany (Morocco), and the decision to abandon the traditional policy of isolation, were all factors that helped to encourage an expectation of war in Britain. National anxieties about the British army's ability to defend the Empire or repel a foreign invasion came to a head during the South African War of 1899–1902. Although the better-equipped, better-trained and larger British army eventually exhausted its Boer enemy into submission, it took a long and costly three years.[16] It was probably this event, more than any other, which destroyed for ever the confidence the British population – of all classes and political persuasions – had in their empire.[17] It compounded a sense of national foreboding.

The *Daily Mail*, one of the most popular dailies of the time and usually the champion of Britain's imperial strength, warned in December 1900 that 'England is entering stormy seas and the time may be near when we shall have to fight for our life'.[18] Statistics, for example, that showed, in the same year, that 90 per cent of recruits were unfit to serve in the British Army, fuelled fears that Britain – indeed, the very state of the population – was in decline and sparked various 'national efficiency' reforms, such as the Education Act (1902), subsidised school meals (1906) and school medicals (1907).[19] A sense of a disaster narrowly averted, triggered a tremendous upsurge of interest in the military in Edwardian Britain, not only in terms of positive heroic portrayals in the adventure stories of G. A. Henty and H. Rider Haggard amongst others, but also in the negative 'fear fiction' described above. Christopher Andrews suggests that the spy novel was born in Edwardian Britain from 'a new sense of imperial frailty'.[20] Spy and invasion stories, I. F. Clarke observed, belong to the literature of patriotism and mainly concern the 'future greatness of the fatherland'.[21] Spy fiction, adds David Stafford, is a literature of 'national passions and phobias' and its genesis was 'inextricably linked with the crisis of confidence in British power and security that obsessed the Edwardian age'.[22]

Wars, such as the South African War, fuelled popular imaginations but, in reality, were remote to ordinary British people. Given the naval competition with Germany, many assumed the key point in a future war would be a new Trafalgar.[23] Those who did contemplate a large land battle tended to think of it in Napoleonic terms: one decisive battle, admittedly bloody, but brief – a new Waterloo. Whilst images of Britain's future war varied depending on the individual, and these images often conflicted with each other, it would be fair to suggest that most people in Britain, regardless of rank or position, were anxious. The South African War had removed the complacency bred during the long years of peace and led to a loss in national self-confidence.[24] The expectation of war was increasingly a part of Edwardian consciousness.[25] How would that play out in the July Crisis of 1914?

An Improbable War

On 28 June 1914, in Sarajevo, the capital of Bosnia, Gavrilo Princip, a Bosnian Serb student who had become involved with a Serbian terrorist group, the Black Hand, fired two shots in quick succession. Within minutes he had killed Archduke Franz Ferdinand, heir to the Habsburg throne, and his wife Sophie. Princip's aim – as a member of a nationalist movement favouring a union between Bosnia-Herzegovina and Serbia – was to end Austria-Hungary's rule over Bosnia-Herzegovina through any means possible. Exactly one month later, on 28 July, Austria-Hungary declared war on Serbia. What had begun as the Third Balkan War would, within a week, become the First World War.[26]

It is impossible to put ourselves into the shoes of people who lived 100 years before us and try to ascertain whether or not they expected war in 1914. Even with the plethora of source material from the era of the First World War, such as contemporary diaries, letters and journals, it is unlikely that we will really know what people thought and felt in the past.[27] As Holger Afflerbach outlines:

The education, interests, and expectations of the population were too diverse. People in the countryside saw things differently from men in the cities; married people differently from single ones; and young people differently from the elderly. Military specialists were also sharply divided in their expectations of the duration and the outcome of a Great War.[28]

Nevertheless, in spite of all these differences, historians agree that the European populations feared the prospect of a great war but did not believe it to be on the immediate horizon.[29] The majority of educated people saw the current political circumstances, at the turn of the century, as imperfect but acceptable and improving. They believed the system of 'the balance of power' (or 'equilibrium') acted as a sufficient military deterrence.[30]

The 'July Crisis' (as it came to be known) of 1914, was essentially a localised Balkan conflict – of which there had been a number in the years leading up to 1914 – that expanded rapidly into a conflict that touched all areas of the globe. At the beginning of the twentieth century, British public engagement with this area of southeastern Europe was limited, partly because focus tended to remain on the 'Eastern Question' (the Ottoman Empire and its future) rather than the areas of the Balkans ruled by the Dual Monarchy of Austria-Hungary.[31] Disinterest (and disenchantment) had been exacerbated by the break in Serbian-British diplomatic relations following the assassination of King Aleksandar Obrenović and his wife, Draga, in June 1903.[32] Sir Edward Grey, the Foreign Secretary, had mediated between Austria and Serbia following the Austrian annexation of Bosnia in 1908, another spark of tension in the region that had failed to ignite into war.[33] The Balkan Wars of 1912 and 1913 naturally commanded the attention and energies of the European Great Powers. Although they had not managed to prevent them, they had worked together diplomatically to contain them: at the Ambassadors' Conferences of London and St Petersburg and militarily at Constantinople in November 1912 and again at Scutari in April 1913. Their efforts were the result of the Concert of Europe functioning to maintain the balance of power in a way that it had done on the continent since 1648.[34]

By 1914, there was little fear of war. The Graeco-Turkish War of 1897, the ethnic fighting in Macedonia, the two Balkan Wars and the Italian war with Turkey in 1911 all suggested that war in this region was not unusual. Contained warfare had become commonplace, a normal aspect of foreign relations. Hence, in the first half of July 1914, no one expected that the crisis would escalate into a 'Great War'. Contemporaries did, of course, consider an Austrian-Serbian conflict to be possible: 'in fact it was precisely because they believed in the improbability of a Great War that all parties involved assumed that it would be avoided; they could risk a local war against Serbia to stabilize both Austria-Hungary and, as a result, their own Triple Alliance system'.[35] Although neither the Treaty of London (May 1913) nor the Treaty of Bucharest (August 1913) settled territorial claims in the Balkans following the wars of 1912 and 1913, powerful restraints – particularly in the form of European diplomatic relations – were acting against war in the lead-up to the assassination in June 1914.[36]

Notable 'stars' within the 'European constellation' that had, to a large extent, contained the Balkans crises in 1912 and 1913 were Great Britain and Germany. Despite being bitter rivals for years, they suddenly found themselves cooperating with a good deal of cordiality.[37] Although debates about the origins of the First World War continue to thrive, some scholars are moving away from assessments that place blame squarely with Germany or that focus entirely on a sense of declining Anglo-German relations.[38] In fact, it is now understood that if there were two European countries that had a sense of allegiance and cultural affiliation in the years immediately preceding the outbreak of war, it was Britain and Germany.[39]

Merchants had long travelled between the two countries and, by the eighteenth century, new British industrial methods were of great interest to German industrialists. Ten thousand British students graduated from German universities in 1848. German influence on British thinking in education, theology, law, philosophy, music, literature and linguistics was unmistakable. By 1914, there were 57,000 Germans in Britain and around 18,000 British residents in Germany.[40] The two countries were huge trading partners; British Liberals admired German efficiency; the British Left envied the massive organisation of its Social Democrats and trade unions; and British intellectuals admired German universities. Thomas Weber's work has highlighted the strength of Anglo-German affinities among educational elites in the two countries.[41] There is no question that Anglo-German antagonism arose in the first decade of the twentieth century. However, the years 1911–14 saw more attempts to improve Anglo-German relations than further exacerbations of the rivalry.[42]

Although Lord Haldane, the British war minister, failed in his mission to Berlin in February 1912 to resolve Anglo-German antagonism after the Agadir crisis, the very fact it was undertaken indicates that Britain and Germany hoped that at least a détente was possible. Following the Haldane Mission, the naval arms race virtually disappeared as a point of contention between Britain and Germany, although there was no formal agreement on naval armaments. As well as cooperating during the Balkan crises of 1912–13, as discussed, Britain and Germany also reached mutually beneficial agreements over the Portuguese colonies and the Baghdad railway in August 1913 and June 1914 respectively. A fitting culmination of this cooperation was expressed by a group of British intellectuals on 1 August 1914, the eve of the First World War, in an open letter to *The Times*:

> We regard Germany as a nation leading the way in Arts and Sciences and we have all learnt and are learning from German scholars. War upon her in the interests of Serbia and Russia will be a sin against civilization . . . at this juncture we consider ourselves justified in protesting against being drawn into the struggle with a nation so akin to our own, and with whom we have so much in common.[43]

This letter, along with others signed in the following days (prior to Germany's invasion of Belgium on 4 August), may have been an increasingly minority opinion as the nation mobilised for war. However, the letters do indicate 'the residual feelings of British-German cultural affinity and mutual regard that blur the picture of clear-cut political and military confrontation culminating in the Great War'.[44]

War at Home

In addition to war being remote and improbable, for many British people the foreign tensions emerging in June and July 1914 were of little consequence in comparison with the profound unrest that was unfolding at home. The Liberal government, led by H. H. Asquith, was too preoccupied with a kaleidoscope of issues – the Scottish independence movement, the labour movement, suffragette unrest and the situation in Ireland – to be seriously considering a European conflict stemming out of what was perceived to be a localised Balkan dispute.[45] Although these domestic concerns were often separate in their roots, they were united 'by a common hothouse blossom of violence'.[46]

Serious problems were emerging in industrial relations. Between 1910 and 1914, the number of strikes increased fivefold, costing the economy around ten million working days. Spread across the engineering, textile, mining and shipbuilding industries, the 'Great Labour Unrest' was led mainly by the major unions conscious of their ability to bring economic life to a standstill. The strikes appeared to be a result of an increasing working class militancy which had numerous causes: shrinking wages, employer's attempts to increase efficiency in the face of foreign competition, expanding union membership (trade union membership rose from 2.5 million to 4.1 million between 1910 and 1914), and a realisation of the power of industrial action in the context of an increasingly independent and complex economy.[47] While some historians have also highlighted the revolutionary influence of socialism and syndicalism, Keir Hardie was probably more accurate when he summarised in Parliament: the workers were crying out for a 'fuller share of life'.[48] The Liberal government was inconsistent in the way it handled labour unrest. Sometimes it preferred supporting employers; in other cases it negotiated directly with the unions (as Lloyd George did in the railway strikes of 1907 and 1911). In certain circumstances, ministers were despatched with olive branches to quell the strikers; in others it chose confrontation, as evidenced with the deployment of troops to quell rioting Welsh miners in Tonypandy in 1911.[49]

However, to upper-class Edwardian men, the women's suffrage campaign was as alarming as the labour movement. By 1909, most women agitated by the inequities of the electoral system were members of the National Union of Women's Suffrage Societies (NUWSS) – the constitutional movement led by Millicent Fawcett. However, it was the militant organisation, the Women's Social and Political Union (WSPU) – nicknamed 'the suffragettes' – founded by Emmeline and Christabel Pankhurst, that was attracting the more attention. To keep the cause in the public eye and to attract new members, the tactics of the WSPU had become increasingly shocking. At first they heckled politicians and tried to disrupt meetings, but by 1912 suffragettes had resorted to attacks on property, including smashing the windows of West End clubs, and acts of arson. Cabinet ministers were often hounded and attacked when they appeared in public. Suffragette tactics became increasingly violent as they were subjected to rough treatment at the hands of both the police and the public.[50] Just as with the challenge of labour unrest, the government struggled to respond coherently. The WSPU was handed a propaganda coup in the form of the brutal and cruel force-feeding of imprisoned suffragettes on hunger-strike.[51] The government tried to regain the initiative with the so-called 'cat and mouse act' of April 1913 which allowed offenders to be released on medical advice on the condition that they resume their sentence when their health was restored. However, by June 1913, Emily Davison had been killed throwing herself in front of the King's horse at the Derby. Six months later, Sylvia Pankhurst declaimed that 'We will make ourselves a terror to Westminster; we will make the cabinet ministers shake in their shoes until they are afraid for their very lives'.[52] Ultimately, the tactics of persuasion would succeed as sympathy for the cause moved towards the 'suffragist' NUWSS. The large and peaceful 'Pilgrimage' of July 1913, which culminated in the gathering of 70,000 suffragists in Hyde Park, convinced Asquith to meet representatives of the movement and, consequently, signal his support for a women's suffrage bill in the next parliament.[53]

As if the two challenges of labour and the women's suffrage movement were not enough, the Liberals faced an even bigger threat in the form of Home Rule for Ireland. This was the most serious domestic crisis in the lead up to the outbreak of war in August 1914. The Liberal government had introduced a Home Rule Bill into Parliament in 1912, the aim of which was to grant self-government to Ireland. Although the bill was defeated in the House of Lords, it placed the government in an awkward position in relation to Ulster Protestants. As unionists, they were opposed to any form of devolution, in particular the creation of an all-Ireland home rule parliament in Dublin, and demanded the retention of all four Irish provinces within the United Kingdom. Debates on whether Ulster should be excluded produced considerable disarray on the Liberal backbenches. National self-determination for a united Ireland conflicted with minority rights and might also require coercion if implemented, thus conflicting with Liberal philosophy in two significant respects. According to the Chief Secretary, Augustine Birrell, to leave Ulster permanently out of the settlement 'would have been an outrage upon Irish unity . . . but to bring her in without bloodshed seemed impossible'.[54]

Eventually, on 9 March 1914, the cabinet offered Ulster counties the right to vote themselves out of the jurisdiction of a Home Rule parliament for six years but discussions, ultimately fruitless, continued about the time limit and area to be excluded.[55] By May 1914, the third Home Rule Bill had been passed three times as required by the recently ratified Parliament Act of 1911. However, both the

Unionists and the Conservatives used this two-year hiatus to build-up resistance in Ireland. The dominant elite in Ulster – the Protestant minority led by Captain James Craig and Sir Edward Carson – feared a loss of power and status. They established the Ulster Volunteer Force (UVF) of some 90,000 men and embarked upon a series of illegal gun importations. The Ulster Unionists had the support of the leader of the opposition Conservative Party, Andrew Bonar Law, even if they were to resort to violence. As a response to the establishment of the UVF, the Irish Nationalists formed their own volunteer army – the Irish (National) Volunteers (INV). The emergence of these private armies raised the prospect that civil war would erupt if a Dublin parliament were set up. King George V warned on 21 July that 'the cry of civil war is on the lips of the most responsible and sober-minded of my people'.[56]

Five days later, it was as if the King's fears were to be realised. A detachment of the King's Own Scottish Borderers fired on a crowd of Dublin civilians on Bachelors Walk – suspected of being INV gun-runners – killing three and wounding thirty-eight others. A fourth died two months later. The incident sparked outrage in Ireland and was relayed to people in Britain under frightening headlines suggesting slaughter and chaos in Dublin. The funeral of three of the victims, on 29 July, became a day of national mourning. Tensions reached an unprecedented level.[57] The over-reaction of the British in Dublin, coupled with their failure to act in Ulster, created a situation in which there were two opposing groups, both freshly armed, both with grievances against the government, and both willing to fight for their cause.[58] In this context, it is perhaps unsurprising that the ramifications of a royal assassination, over 1,000 miles away, were not at the centre of the attention of the people of Britain in July 1914.

Conclusion

In January 2014, in an interview with *The Observer* to mark the beginning of the centenary calendar, the eminent historian Margaret MacMillan was asked how she would feel if she were a British citizen, commencing the new year 100 years ago. She replied: 'I'd be fairly optimistic. I think I'd wake up and think "Thank God calm has prevailed" and be confident that the various conferences with ambassadors would be sorting stuff out.'[59] Her thoughts echo those of contemporaries. In early 1914, Vera Brittain was revising for her Oxford Scholarship examination at her family home in Buxton, Derbyshire. She no longer had time to be concerned with 'those tentative treaties in the too-inflammable Balkans'.[60]

While the British population had certainly considered war – and believed they could imagine its frightening contents – it was not an immediate reality. The popularity of 'future wars' as a fictional topic suggests that people were playing out their worst fears within the safety of their leisure time, as a form of sensational escapism. This holds true to this day with the popularity of mystery-detective thrillers by authors such as Dan Brown and Robert Harris. The international landscape in 1914 looked calm, particularly in comparison with previous years. The disturbances in the Balkans in 1912 and 1913 appeared to have been resolved. Anglo-German relations were improving to the point that the two countries were cooperating over issues of colonial and diplomatic significance. Kaiser Wilhelm of Germany was being hailed by some as a glorious peacemaker, having ruled for twenty-five years without conflict.[61] For the British government, domestic matters were causing far more instability than the global situation as it faced violent challenges from the labour and suffrage movements as well as a potential civil war in Ireland.

While any suggestion that the Edwardian summer of 1914 was a peaceful, sunny idyll consisting of cream teas and picnics is clearly problematized by the internal strife and unrest of domestic affairs, it is not to deny that the outbreak of war on 4 August 1914 came as a profound shock to the people of the United Kingdom of Britain and Ireland. Throughout most of July, the European situation received little serious attention in the national and local press. Many British people viewed Austro-Serbian tensions as an internal affair of the Austro-Hungarian Empire. The issue of Austro-Serbian relations was a matter of little significance compared to the approaching collision between the Liberals and the Conservatives over Ireland.[62] This sense of surprise and shock was exacerbated by the fact that Anglo-German relations had improved to the extent that people genuinely believed that the July 1914 crisis could be resolved through Anglo-German cooperation.

While it is difficult of course to make generalisations about how the whole population responded, the language used by contemporaries reflected a clear sense of shock and surprise.[63] These sentiments are neatly captured by two witnesses from 1914, to whom I shall give the last word: Mrs E. Moore, from Harlow, recalled that 'news of the imminence of war with Germany came as a shock to me for I was entirely unprepared to receive such news'.[64] Margery Corbett-Ashby was watching her husband play tennis in Woodgate, West Sussex on 4 August: 'In spite of growing uneasiness at the Kaiser's sabre-rattling, the thought of war between civilised nations seemed inconceivable, so the invasion of Belgium came like a thunderbolt.'[65]

Notes

1. 'Emus at the Lost Gardens', The Lost Gardens of Heligan, 20 March 2014, http://heligan. com/news-events/news-article/emus-at-the-lost-gardens, accessed 6 October 2014.
2. Alice Meynell, 'Summer in England, 1914', *The Times*, 10 October 1914, p. 9. Nosheen Khan, *Women's Poetry of the First World War* (Lexington, KY: University Press of Kentucky, 1988), p. 50. See also http://war-poets.blogspot.co.uk/2009/11/alice-meynell-summer-in-england-1914.html, accessed 6 October 2014.
3. Cited in Thomas Otte, *July Crisis: The World's Descent into War, Summer 1914* (Cambridge: Cambridge University Press, 2014), p. 138.
4. Paul Fussell, *The Great War and Modern Memory* (Oxford: Oxford University Press, 1975), p. 24.
5. Lyn MacDonald, *The Roses of No Man's Land* (2nd ed. London: Penguin, 1993), p. 2.
6. Jonathan F. Vance, *Death So Noble: Memory, Meaning, and the First World War* (Vancouver: UBC Press, 2011), p. 138.

7. Nicholas Hiley, 'Decoding German Spies: British Spy Fiction, 1908-1918,' in Wesley K. Wark (ed.), *Spy Fiction, Spy Films and Real Intelligence* (London: Routledge, 1991), p. 55.
8. John Gooch, *The Prospect of War: Studies in British Defence Policy, 1847-1942* (London: Frank Cass, 1981), p. 36.
9. I. F. Clarke, 'The Battle of Dorking, 1871-1914,' *Victorian Studies* 8, no. 4 (1 June 1965), p. 309.
10. I. F. Clarke, *The Tale of the Future from the Beginning to the Present Day: A Check-list of those satires, ideal states, imaginary wars and invasions, political warnings and forecasts, interplanetary voyages and scientific romances – all located in an imaginary future period – that have been published in the United Kingdom between 1644 and 1960* (London: 1961), p. 24.
11. Erskine Childers, *The Riddle of the Sands* (London: 1903).
12. I. F. Clarke, 'The Shape of Wars to Come', *History Today* 15 (1965), p. 111.
13. William Le Queux, *The Invasion of 1910 with a full account of the Siege of London* (London: 1906).
14. Samuel R. Williamson, *The Politics of Grand Strategy: Britain and France Prepare for War, 1904-1914* (Cambridge, Massachusetts: 1969), p. 97.
15. J. Lee Thompson, *Politicians, the Press, and Propaganda: Lord Northcliffe and the Great War, 1914-1918* (Ohio: 2000), p. 8.
16. Bill Nasson, *The Boer War: The Struggle for South Africa* (Stroud: The History Press, 2011).
17. Krishan Kumar, *The Making of English National Identity* (Cambridge: Cambridge University Press, 2003), p. 198.
18. *Daily Mail*, 31 December 1900, cited in David Stafford, *The Silent Game: the Real World of Imaginary Spies* (University of Georgia Press, 2012), p. 7.
19. Pat Thane, 'Government and Society in England and Wales, 1750–1914', in F. M. L. Thompson (ed.), *The Cambridge Social History of Britain, 1750–1950: Volume 3: Social Agencies and Institutions*, (Cambridge: Cambridge University Press, 1990), pp. 51–2.
20. Christopher M. Andrew, *Secret Service: The Making of the British Intelligence Community* (London: Heinemann, 1985), p. 34.
21. I. F. Clarke, *Voices Prophesying War: Future Wars 1763-3749* (Oxford: Oxford University Press, 1992), p. 125.
22. Stafford, *The Silent Game*, p. 7.
23. Jan Rüger, *The Great Naval Game: Britain and Germany in the Age of Empire* (Cambridge and New York: Cambridge University Press, 2007).
24. Hew Strachan, 'The Boer War and Its Impact on the British Army, 1902-1914', in Peter B. Boyden, Alan James Guy and Marion Harding (eds), *'Ashes and Blood': The British Army in South Africa, 1795-1914* (London: National Army Museum, 1999), p. 97.
25. Samuel Hynes, *The Edwardian Turn of Mind* (Princeton: Princeton University Press, 1968), p. 53.
26. S. R. Williamson Jr., 'The Origins of the War', in Hew Strachan (ed.), *The Oxford Illustrated History of the First World War* (Oxford: Oxford University Press, 2000), p. 9.
27. Helen B. McCartney, 'The First World War Soldier and His Contemporary Image in Britain', *International Affairs* 90, no. 2 (March 2014), p. 306.
28. Holger Afflerbach, 'The Topos of Improbable War in Europe before 1914', in Holger Afflerbach and David Stevenson (eds), *An Improbable War? The Outbreak of World War I and European Political Culture Before 1914* (Oxford: Berghahn Books, 2012), p. 170.
29. Jean Jacques Becker, *1914: Comment Les Français Sont Entrés Dans La Guerre* (Paris: Presses de la Fondation Nationale des Sciences Politiques, 1977); Catriona Pennell, *A Kingdom United: Popular Responses to the Outbreak of the First World War in Britain and Ireland* (Oxford: Oxford University Press, 2012); Jeffrey Verhey, *The Spirit of 1914: Militarism, Myth and Mobilization in Germany* (Cambridge: Cambridge University Press, 2000).
30. Afflerbach, 'The Topos of Improbable War in Europe before 1914', p. 170.

31. Eugene Michail, *The British and the Balkans: Forming Images of Foreign Lands, 1900-1950* (A&C Black, 2011), pp. 16–17.
32. 'Historical Notes: Brutal murder in Serbia: 1903', *Independent*, 29 June 1999, http://www.independent.co.uk/arts-entertainment/historical-notes-brutal-murder-in-serbia-1903-1103132.html, accessed 3 October 2014.
33. Michail, *The British and the Balkans*, p. 17.
34. Richard C. Hall, *The Balkan Wars 1912-1913: Prelude to the First World War* (London: Routledge, 2000), p. 142.
35. Afflerbach, 'The Topos of Improbable War in Europe before 1914', p. 172.
36. William Mulligan, *The Origins of the First World War* (Cambridge: Cambridge University Press, 2010).
37. Bernadotte E. Schmitt, 'Review of *The Diplomacy of the Balkan Wars, 1912-1913* by Ernst Christian Helmreich', *Political Science Quarterly* 54, no. 3 (1 September 1939), p. 450.
38. Christopher M. Clark, *The Sleepwalkers: How Europe Went to War in 1914* (London: Allen Lane, 2012); Sean McMeekin, *July 1914: Countdown to War* (London: Icon Books, 2013); Otte, *July Crisis*.
39. Dominik Geppert and Robert Gerwarth, 'Introduction', in Dominik Geppert and Robert Gerwarth (eds), *Wilhelmine Germany and Edwardian Britain: Essays on Cultural Affinity* (Oxford: Oxford University Press, 2008), p. 3.
40. David Blackbourn, '"As Dependent on Each Other as Man and Wife": Cultural Contacts and Transfers', in Geppert and Gerwarth (eds), *Wilhelmine Germany and Edwardian Britain*, pp. 19–20, 22.
41. Thomas Weber, *Our Friend 'the Enemy': Elite Education in Britain and Germany before World War I* (Stanford, CA: Stanford University Press, 2008).
42. Sean M. Lynn-Jones, 'Détente and Deterrence: Anglo-German Relations, 1911-1914', *International Security* 11, no. 2 (1986), p. 124.
43. 'Scholars' protest against war with Germany', *The Times*, 1 August 1914, p. 6.
44. Geppert and Gerwarth, 'Introduction', p. 1.
45. David Powell, *The Edwardian Crisis: Britain, 1901-1914* (Basingstoke: Macmillan, 1996); Alan O'Day (ed), *The Edwardian Age: Conflict and Stability, 1900-1914* (London: Macmillan, 1979).
46. Arthur Marwick, *The Deluge: British Society and the First World War* (London: Bodley Head, 1965), p. 26.
47. Norman McCord, Bill Purdue, and A. William Purdue, *British History 1815-1914* (Oxford University Press, 2007), p. 502.
48. Hansard Parliamentary Debates, 8 May 1912, vol 38, cc487-534, http://hansard.millbanksystems.com/commons/1912/may/08/industrial-unrest#S5CV0038P0_19120508_HOC_410, accessed 14 October 2014.
49. Alan G. V. Simmonds, *Britain and World War One* (London: Routledge, 2012), p. 16.
50. Martin Pugh, *The March of the Women: A Revisionist Analysis of the Campaign for Women's Suffrage, 1866-1914* (Oxford: Oxford University Press, 2000).
51. James Vernon, *Hunger: A Modern History* (Harvard University Press, 2009), p. 67.
52. 'Worst yet to come if Sylvia has way', *The Toronto World*, 4 December 1913, p. 1, http://news.google.com/newspapers?nid=22&dat=19131204&id=jXFSAAAAIBAJ&sjid=MikDAAAAIBAJ&pg=2885,2542582, accessed 14 October 2014
53. Simmonds, *Britain and World War One*, pp. 17–18.
54. Patricia Jalland, 'A Liberal Chief Secretary and the Irish Question: Augustine Birrell, 1907-1914', *The Historical Journal* 19, no. 2 (June 1976), p. 448.
55. Ian Packer, *Liberal Government and Politics, 1905-15* (Basingstoke: Palgrave Macmillan, 2006), pp. 70–1.
56. J. F. V. Keiger, 'Britain's 'Union Sacrée' in 1914', in J.-J. Becker and S. Audoin-Rouzeau (eds), *Les Sociétiés Européenês et La Guerre de 1914-1918* (Nanterre: Université de Paris X, 1990), p. 40.

57. Pennell, *A Kingdom United*, p. 23.
58. Ben Novick, 'The Arming of Ireland: Gun-Running and the Great War, 1914-16', in Adrian Gregory and Senia Pašeta (eds), *Ireland and the Great War: 'A War to Unite Us All'?* (Manchester: Manchester University Press, 2002), p. 98.
59. Elizabeth Day, 'January 1914: suffragettes, blizzards, exploration – but no hint of war', *The Observer*, 4 January 2014, http://www.theguardian.com/world/2014/jan/04/january-1914-no-hint-war, accessed 14 October 2014. See also Margaret MacMillan, *The War That Ended Peace: How Europe Abandoned Peace for the First World War* (London: Profile Books, 2013).
60. Vera Brittain, *Testament of Youth: An Autobiographical Study of the Years 1900-1925* (2nd ed. London: Virago Press, 1978), p. 69.
61. Charles Emmerson, *1913: The World before the Great War* (London: Bodley Head, 2013).
62. D. C. Watt, 'British Reactions to the Assassination in Sarajevo', *European Studies Review* 1, no. 3 (1971), p. 234.
63. Pennell, *A Kingdom United*, pp. 35–8.
64. Essex Record Office: T/Z 25/659 (1966).
65. Liddle Collection, Leeds: DF 036: Dame Margery Corbett-Ashby, 4 August 1914.

Suggested Further Reading

Afflerbach, Holger. 'The Topos of Improbable War in Europe before 1914', in Holger Afflerbach and David Stevenson (eds), *An Improbable War? The Outbreak of World War I and European Political Culture Before 1914* (Oxford: Berghahn Books, 2012).
Clark, Christopher M., *The Sleepwalkers: How Europe Went to War in 1914* (London: Allen Lane, 2012).
Emmerson, Charles, *1913: The World before the Great War* (London: Bodley Head, 2013).
Geppert, Dominik, and Robert Gerwarth, 'Introduction', in Dominik Geppert and Robert Gerwarth (eds), *Wilhelmine Germany and Edwardian Britain: Essays on Cultural Affinity* (Oxford: Oxford University Press, 2008).
Gooch, John, *The Prospect of War: Studies in British Defence Policy, 1847-1942* (London: Frank Cass, 1981).
Hall, Richard C., *The Balkan Wars 1912-1913: Prelude to the First World War* (London: Routledge, 2000).
Lynn-Jones, Sean M., 'Détente and Deterrence: Anglo-German Relations, 1911-1914'. *International Security* 11, no. 2 (1986), pp. 121–50.
MacMillan, Margaret, *The War That Ended Peace: How Europe Abandoned Peace for the First World War* (London: Profile Books, 2013).
McMeekin, Sean, *July 1914: Countdown to War* (London: Icon Books, 2013).
Mulligan, William, *The Origins of the First World War* (Cambridge: Cambridge University Press, 2010).
Nasson, Bill, *The Boer War: The Struggle for South Africa* (Stroud: The History Press, 2011).
O'Day, Alan (ed), *The Edwardian Age: Conflict and Stability, 1900-1914* (London: Macmillan, 1979).
Otte, Thomas, *July Crisis: The World's Descent into War, Summer 1914* (Cambridge: Cambridge University Press, 2014).
Pennell, Catriona, *A Kingdom United: Popular Responses to the Outbreak of the First World War in Britain and Ireland* (Oxford: Oxford University Press, 2012).
Powell, David, *The Edwardian Crisis: Britain, 1901-1914* (Basingstoke: Macmillan, 1996).
Pugh, Martin, *The March of the Women: A Revisionist Analysis of the Campaign for Women's Suffrage, 1866-1914* (Oxford: Oxford University Press, 2000).

Chapter 4

The National Response to the Outbreak of War, 1914

* * *

Edward M. Spiers

Ideally an evaluation of the British national response to the outbreak of war on 4 August 1914 should be based upon a comprehensive body of evidence but the material left by official papers, correspondence, newspapers, contemporary diaries and reminiscences hardly meets that standard. Consequently, indulging in broad generalizations such as Arthur Marwick's claim that 'British society in 1914 was strongly jingoistic and showed marked enthusiasm at the outbreak of war'[1] seems unwise, while assertions that in a 'rush' to the colours, men, fearing that they might miss out 'on a glorious adventure', engaged in 'almost lemming-like enlistment',[2] may be too extreme.

While there is scant evidence from 1914 to support the perception of the war's futility, as described by post-war critics,[3] anti-war feelings were still expressed, albeit by a small and marginalized minority.[4] What needs examining, as W. J. Reader observed, is the 'suddenness of the onset of war fever and the way in which it smothered all other national preoccupations', effectively focusing attention upon 'the quarrel with Germany, so that great reserves of bellicosity were concentrated behind the nation's military effort'.[5] By reviewing the immediate transition from peace to war, this chapter will consider how the 'national response' began and evolved, taking account of regional variations and a case study that compares the response in Leeds, a major urban conurbation, with the response in the North Riding, a vast rural community with an industrial border.

Hostility towards Germany was not new. Even before the end of the South African War (1899–1902), Alfred Harmsworth (later Lord Northcliffe), the proprietor of the best-selling *Daily Mail* and later *The Times*, forecast a German war in Europe that Britain could not avoid.[6] He was far from alone in his forebodings, and passions erupted subsequently over the naval arms race with Germany and the famous Dreadnought building programme of the late Edwardian era.[7] Britain, though, was not preoccupied with Germany during the month preceding the outbreak of war. Despite the assassination of Archduke Franz Ferdinand and his wife in Sarajevo on 28 June 1914, the principal British concerns encompassed the protests of the suffragettes, a succession of major industrial disputes and the opposition of Ulster Unionists to the prospect of Irish home rule. Extra-parliamentary agitation exacerbated the political divisions, with the Conservative opposition condoning Ulster loyalism, as manifested in the raising of the Ulster Volunteer Force, and the so-called 'Curragh mutiny'.[8]

Nor had the cabinet exhibited any enthusiasm about intervening in the European crisis. While Sir Edward Grey, the Foreign Secretary, had tried to broker a peace conference, H. H. Asquith, the Prime Minister, believed that Britain could avoid involvement in the prospective conflict. As late as 29 July 1914, he informed his mistress, Venetia Stanley, that 'Of course we want to keep out of it, but the worst thing we could do would be to announce to the world at the present moment that in no *circumstances* would we intervene.'[9] While *The Times* led Conservative newspapers in demanding that Britain stand up to Germany and Austria-Hungary, leading Liberal newspapers, notably A. G. Gardiner's *Daily News* and C. P. Scott's *Manchester Guardian*, upheld the policy of neutrality until 4 August. Similarly on 1 August 1914, the *Yorkshire Post* expressed its hope that Britain could 'preserve the peace consistently with the continuance of national interests' since it had 'no quarrel with Germany'.[10]

Only when it became clear that Germany intended to invade France and violate the neutrality of Belgium, which Britain and other powers had guaranteed under the Treaty of London (1839), did the cabinet, its main political opponents and much of the country find an issue upon which to rally. There were resignations – John Burns and Viscount Morley from the cabinet,[11] and J. Ramsay MacDonald from the chairmanship of the Parliamentary Labour Party after it voted in support of the government's request for £100 million in war credits[12] – but the degree of political unity was highly impressive. Most of the newspapers followed the government's lead; as the *Yorkshire Post* declared, once Germany refused to respect the neutrality of Belgium, its readers ought to accept that war had been forced upon the country, and that everybody had 'to support the Government wholeheartedly'.[13]

Of critical importance was the collapse of anti-war opposition. Radical opponents of intervention had proved utterly ineffectual. Bereft of coherent and effective leadership, their collective resolve evaporated in cabinet where the crucial decision to enter the war was taken. Sir John Simon, the Attorney General, and Earl Beauchamp, Lord President of the Council, withdrew their threatened resignations as evidence of German bellicosity mounted, while the prominent Quaker, J. A. Pease, preferred to resign his chairmanship of the Peace Society and remain as President of the Board of Education. Of the two who resigned from the cabinet, neither Burns nor Morley possessed the energy or the following to sustain their opposition. Fellow radicals in parliament and the press had formed two pressure groups, the Neutrality League and the British Neutrality Committee, to oppose intervention, but both organizations dissolved themselves on 5 August after the declaration of war. The radical debacle was complete.[14]

In the final throes of the pre-war period, non-intervention, which was not necessarily a pacifist proposition, found expression in several Liberal newspapers, half a million pamphlets, church sermons and resolutions from Labour and Liberal constituency parties. It had champions among the Liberal intelligentsia – Gilbert Murray, Bertrand Russell, L. T. Hobhouse and J. A. Hobson among others – trades unions, socialists and the Peace Society.

On Sunday 2 August 1914, anti-war rallies had been held all across the country, including a famous rally in Trafalgar Square where speakers such as James Keir Hardie, Arthur Henderson, Mary Macarthur, Will Thorne and George Lansbury deplored any prospect of British intervention in the imminent war.[15] Working-class solidarity though, proved as ephemeral as any other form of opposition during the unfolding crisis. Just as Arthur Henderson, the secretary of the National Executive Committee of the Labour Party, changed his mind and reluctantly supported the war, so did the veteran socialist H. M. Hyndman, who upheld the right of self-defence against the 'German military aggressionists', whom he dubbed the 'disturber of Europe'.[16] Many trades unions supported the war, mollified by the resolve of the government to fight, at least initially, without any recourse to conscription. The churches rallied overwhelmingly in support of the war and turned their wrath on German militarism. If patriotic support from the Church of England were only to be expected, many Nonconformists followed suit, including the Baptist pro-Boer veteran the Reverend Dr. John Clifford, who described the war as 'a fight for the rights of the human soul to freedom, independence and self-control against an arrogant, autocratic, swaggering and cruel military caste'.[17] Even the Society of Friends, which formally described the war as 'un-Christian' on 7 August, found its membership split over the conflict, as many younger Quakers enlisted.[18]

The Peace Society itself lost any sense of purpose and vitality when it refused to condemn the declaration of war.[19] In these circumstances individual pacifists made their own choices. Herbert Read (1893–1968), though a pre-war member of Leeds University Officers' Training Corps, had fondly hoped that international working-class solidarity would stop the war. Having seen this illusion shattered, this future anarchist recalled that the onset of war 'meant a decision: a crystallization of vague projects: an immediate acceptance of the challenge of life. I did not hesitate'. He secured a temporary commission in the Green Howards.[20] Conversely, the Cambridge don Bertrand Russell (1872–1970) sustained his pacifist activities while many of his best friends turned their pacifism into moral outrage against the Germans. Russell remained true to his pre-war beliefs but was amazed, nonetheless, to see that the London crowds had changed, and that 'average men and women were delighted at the prospect of war'.[21]

The London crowds, assembling on a Bank Holiday (3 August 1914) to cheer the outbreak of war, have fuelled further debate. Michael MacDonagh, a contemporary journalist with *The Times*, described how rival crowds – pro- and anti-war – had gathered in Trafalgar Square, whereupon the more vociferous pro-war multitude moved onto Buckingham Palace, where it sang patriotic songs and prompted King George V to 'appear on the balcony three separate times during the evening'.[22] At the approach of the decisive hour of eleven o'clock, when the ultimatum to Germany was due to expire, the crowd in its thousands returned to Whitehall where another crowd had already packed Downing Street. As David Lloyd George recollected, this was one of several 'warlike crowds' that had 'thronged Whitehall and poured into Downing Street, whilst the Cabinet was deliberating on the alternative of peace or war'.[23]

Adrian Gregory remains sceptical about the significance of these pro-war crowds. He argues that domestic surveillance capacity of the British state, unlike those of its Continental counterparts, was extremely limited, and so the claims of 'mass enthusiasm' lack substantive evidence. In the absence of any numerical estimate from the Metropolitan Police, he reckons that a mean of the newspaper calculations, about 8,000 people, suggests that the crowds were relatively small, and much smaller than the anti-war demonstrations on 2 August. As the Bank Holiday crowd also lacked any supporting demonstrations across the metropolis, Gregory argues that the demonstrations bore scant resemblance to the 'Mafficking' mobs that erupted in jubilation during the South African War. He claims, too, that politicians exaggerated the significance of these crowds to spread the blame for the war, and that the description of 'warlike' crowds only corresponds with the stereotype after the declaration of war.[24]

Given the sudden shift from peace to war, there was a considerable shock at the turn of events. Pockets of bemusement, incredulity and even residual anti-war opposition persisted, as demonstrated by the speeches of the Scottish Socialist John Maclean, who declared that: 'Let the propertied class go out, old and young alike, and defend their blessed property. When they have been disposed of, we of the working class will have something to defend and we shall do it.'[25] Such opposition was now extremely marginalized and contested vigorously. When Keir Hardie, the chairman of the Independent Labour Party, returned to Aberdare on 13 August 1914 and delivered a critique of the war in the Market Hall, he encountered extensive heckling and barracking as men and women sang 'Rule Britannia' and 'God Save The King'. A local journalist reported that 'it was quite impossible to hear Mr. Hardie, the uproar being deafening', and that a mob jostled and followed him through the streets after the meeting.[26] Facing such hostility, Hardie only recovered his popularity in Merthyr and Aberdare by modifying his anti-war stance: he was soon exhorting people to support 'our gallant defenders both by sea and land'.[27] Even the Union of Democratic Control (UDC), a left-wing pressure group set up after the declaration of war, and subsidized largely by the Society of Friends and individual Quakers, dared not call for an end to the war. Rather, it brought together a coalition of Radical and Labour activists to agitate for parliamentary control over foreign policy and an end to secret diplomacy. It also advocated peace by negotiation, the setting-up of an International Council, and peace terms that neither humiliated the defeated nation nor provided a pretext for future wars.[28]

Accompanying the marginalization of anti-war sentiment was the spy mania and anti-German hysteria whipped up by the popular press. As early as 11 August 1914, MacDonagh reported rumours that London was 'said to be full of German spies', and that Germans of long residence in Britain had already been arrested as spies or 'information agents'.[29] The 35,000 Germans were the third largest immigrant group after the Irish and Jews, and actual or supposed Germans soon became the object of popular suspicion, especially after the reports of German atrocities in Belgium. German shops were wrecked and plundered across the country, despite the desperate attempts of the shopkeepers to re-label sauerkraut and liver sausage as 'Good English Viands' or to fly Union Jacks over their doors. Innocent German residents felt compelled to change their names, dachshunds were kicked or stoned in the street and pigeons shot on sight in case they were carrying messages. Some twenty-two spies, including one who escaped before he could be arrested, were apprehended in 1914, and another fourteen suspects arrested later. Eventually the government responded to public pressure and interned 30,000 aliens, mainly on the Isle of Man, after all aliens had been compelled to register under the Aliens Restrictions Act of August 1914.[30]

Anti-German feeling of course persisted throughout the war, exacerbated by air raids and the sinking of the *Lusitania* with 1,198 fatalities on 7 May 1915 (precipitating riots in Liverpool and across the country, with seven dying in the East End). Two prominent casualties of the hysteria were Prince Louis of Battenberg, who was compelled to resign as First Sea Lord in October 1914 and had to change the family name to Mountbatten, and Lord Haldane, the Lord Chancellor, who was hounded by the press over his alleged pro-German sympathies and jettisoned from the coalition government, which was formed in May 1915.[31] This degree of hysteria derived largely from the shock at the outbreak of war and a search for scapegoats; possibly from popular anxieties fuelled by a generation of reading about imaginary wars in which an unprepared England becomes the target of espionage and the threat of German invasion;[32] and partly from the nature of the ensuing war in which civilians were becoming victims of the German military machine.

Amidst this range of emotions, enlistment into the armed forces expressed the national response to war in its most tangible form. The remarkable achievement of raising nearly two and a half million soldiers through voluntary enlistment by the end of 1915 would not have been possible without the political consensus attained in August 1914 – a consensus that contrasted sharply with the political divisions exposed by the South African War. By waiting until Germany had declared its readiness to violate Belgium's neutrality before declaring war, by appointing the hugely reassuring presence of Earl Kitchener of Khartoum as secretary of state for war on 5 August, and by relying upon voluntary enlistment to raise Kitchener's New Armies, Asquith's government maximized the degree of support for the war.

Horatio Herbert Kitchener was the key appointment; as a soldier who had spent most of his service career overseas, he was neither involved in any of the pre-war military controversies in Ireland nor associated, as Lord Roberts had been, with the pre-war campaign for compulsory military service. A towering, awesome presence, he appeared above party politics,[33] and, in accepting his post on 5 August, buttressed the government at a time when national unity was of paramount importance. Kitchener had his faults as an administrator, and used too little of the pre-war recruiting machinery initially, notably the County Associations of the Territorial Force, but he perceived correctly that this was going to be a long and costly war. In his recruiting appeals, for the first 100,000 on 7 August, with parliamentary approval for an additional 500,000, and another 100,000 on 28 August, he galvanized the recruiting process.[34]

Although voluntary recruiting became the essential measure of the national response, Kitchener anticipated different responses from the Celtic regions. In Ireland the authorities had allowed two proto-military movements to evolve during 1913 and 1914: the Ulster Volunteer Force, sworn to resist the imposition of Home Rule on Ulster, had enrolled about 85,000 members by May 1914 (or about one Protestant Ulsterman in three), while the Irish Volunteers, raised to reinforce the demands for Home Rule, numbered about 150,000 by July 1914. By comparison with the apparent efficiency of the Ulstermen, as reflected in their numerous retired officers, drill sergeants, and importation of 25,000 rifles and over 2,000,000 rounds of ammunition, the 'Irish Volunteers seemed ill-trained, under-armed and incompetent'.[35] On the outbreak of war, their respective political patrons (Sir Edward Carson and John Redmond) both supported the national cause in the hope of reaping political benefits. They bargained to embody their forces as divisions of the new army but Kitchener was much more sympathetic to the Ulster requests (conceding Ulster in the name of the 36th Division and the Red Hand of Ulster on their badges) than Redmond's suggestion that forces raised from these units should serve as Territorials for home defence. Kitchener, an Anglo-Irishman by birth and a Conservative by inclination, remained suspicious of nationalist motives and was reluctant to arm Irish nationalists.[36]

Meanwhile, as news of heavy losses in the retreat from Mons gained national attention, Carson responded on 28 August 1914, offering 35,000 Ulstermen as willing to enlist and serve abroad. He won the approval of the Ulster Unionist Council on 3 September with a remarkable speech, in which he declared that 'England's difficulty is not Ulster's opportunity; England's difficulty is our difficulty'.[37] He was duly allowed to raise the division, with local battalion titles and the appointment of senior officers who were sympathetic to the Unionist cause. Nevertheless, he had to enrol additional men from Liverpool and Glasgow, as the division failed to recruit its full establishment of 18,000 in Ulster.[38] Redmond was mollified by the passage of the Home Rule Bill on 18 September, despite its suspended implementation for a year or until the end of the war, and the promise of a new amending bill to settle the problem of Ulster, but Kitchener and his senior staff at the War Office would not countenance the formation of an Irish nationalist division. Even Redmond's plea that the 16th (Irish) Division, which had been organized from newly-raised battalions, should be called an 'Irish Brigade', and wear a distinctive badge, met with unyielding resistance. Even so, the Irish Volunteers probably contributed some 7,500 reservists to the Regular Army and another 24,000 new recruits.[39]

Kitchener had more problems in Wales, where many people had rallied behind the war effort but more out of loyalty to the Liberal government than any deeply rooted military tradition. The entire political dynamic was broken when David Lloyd George, the Chancellor of the Exchequer and a former pro-Boer activist, spoke publicly for the first time on 19 September 1914. He not only dashed the UDC's hopes of a further split in the cabinet but also appealed specifically for further Welsh support for the war. Dubbing the conflict as 'against barbarism', and describing the Prussian Junker as 'the road-hog of Europe', Lloyd George dwelt upon the threat to the 'little five-foot-five nations' of Belgium and Serbia (and implicitly Wales). He envisaged the raising of a 'Welsh Army' by drawing upon the martial heritage of medieval Wales.[40]

However welcome in the principality,[41] this proposal aroused scepticism in Kitchener, who objected to any reassignment of recently-raised Welsh battalions. As he told Asquith, he had doubts whether any 'purely Welsh regiment is to be trusted: they are (he says) always wild & insubordinate & ought to be stiffened by a strong infusion of English or Scotch'.[42] Kitchener, though, was less obstructive than Lloyd George recalled in his memoirs,[43] approving the concept of a Welsh Army Corps as early as 23 September, which enabled prominent Welshmen to form a National Executive Committee in Cardiff (29 September) to launch the project. Lloyd George, though, resented the instruction that all existing Welsh units should be brought up to establishment before recruiting afresh for the army corps, and then an order banning the speaking of Welsh in Territorial billets. He duly raised the issue of the Army Corps in cabinet. A 'royal row' followed, as Kitchener fought to keep some 40,000 Welsh recruits in their new divisions or in support of the three Welsh regiments at the front. Lloyd George rallied most of the cabinet behind his Welsh Army Corps, leaving Kitchener isolated: 'K', wrote Asquith, 'is much the most to blame: he was clumsy & noisy . . .'[44] On 30 October 1914, Kitchener accepted that a Welsh Army Corps should be established but never allowed the previously formed Welsh units to be attached to it, and only one division, the 38th (Welsh) Division, emerged from the agitation.[45]

Kitchener found Scotland much less troublesome. He simply summoned distinguished Scots to raise additional battalions for its famous regiments. By offering Lord Lovat, who had raised the Lovat Scouts during the South African War, the command of the Highland Mounted Brigade, he gave 'great satisfaction throughout the Highlands'.[46] The appointments also resonated across the Scottish diaspora,[47] including officers such as Major H. D. N. MacLean, D.S.O., to command the 6th King's Own Scottish Borderers, Major J. C. Grahame, D.S.O., who served on the Indian frontier, to command the 10th Highland Light Infantry, Lord Sempill of Fintray, who had served in the Sudan and the South African War, to command the 8th Battalion, the Black Watch, and Colonel D. W. Cameron of Lochiel, chief of clan Cameron, to command 5th Battalion, Cameron Highlanders. Cameron proved particularly energetic and wrote to the *Glasgow Herald*,

> I want to raise a thousand Highlanders for my battalion, and I have no doubt I shall have little difficulty in so doing; but, having regard to the fact that Highlanders are now scattered all over the face of the earth, I must especially appeal to the officials and committee of the different Highland county and clan societies in Glasgow, Edinburgh, and elsewhere to assist me in my endeavours by becoming my recruiting agents.[48]

He promised that men from each district of the Highlands would be kept in their own section, platoon or company, and appealed directly to regional and clan loyalties by expecting 'Highlanders from all parts of the globe to flock once again to the untarnished standard of the Camerons'.[49]

Lochiel, like other landowners, seized this opportunity to recover some of the power and status that had been challenged in Scotland since the 1880s. He did so by recruiting not only in the Highlands, where myths about land redistribution in the wake of military service appear to have boosted recruiting (and caused post-war discontent when they proved illusory), but also in the industrial belt of Scotland and overseas. Lochiel spoke at meetings of Highland and clan societies in Glasgow, advertised for recruits on Glasgow tramcars, marched his regiment through the streets of Glasgow, and even paraded it at Ibrox stadium, where 100 recruits were raised. He attracted a company for his 5th Battalion from the Glasgow Stock Exchange and another from the students of Glasgow University for the 6th Battalion. He ultimately raised four service battalions for the Queen's Own Cameron Highlanders.[50]

Where recruits failed to appear voluntarily, some landowners employed coercion: Hugo Charteris, the 11th Earl of Wemyss, threatened to dismiss any of his estate workers between the ages of eighteen and thirty who failed to enlist, while Lord Rosebery drove round his estates collecting young employees for recruitment.[51] Despite their readiness to serve, lairds and the sons of lairds were not necessarily the best of officers; Sir Ian Hamilton, a veteran Gordon Highlander, and then in command of the Territorial Forces retained for home defence, described the Scottish Territorial officers, other than those of the Lovat Scouts, as 'very inferior to the professional men from the Midlands, solicitors, doctors, architects & such'.[52]

Apart from the landed gentry, the Scottish response really flourished in the large municipal and industrial areas. The municipal authorities, politicians of all parties, employers, lawyers and men of the cloth, were all to the fore in the recruiting process, and once the political agencies supplemented the official recruiting offices and the Territorial associations, recruiting in 1914 proved highly innovative. There was advertising on tramcars for the first time, illuminated tramcars, recruiting vans sent to tour the remote districts of rural Scotland, and tramcars used as mobile recruiting booths in Edinburgh.[53]

Although the Scots never fully embraced the 'Pals' phenomenon, which became such a badge of pride among the industrial towns of northern England, the Glaswegian civic authorities and Chamber of Commerce led the way in raising three 'Pals' battalions for the Highland Light Infantry. Two prominent Edinburgh citizens and former Volunteers, Sir Robert Cranston and Sir George McCrae, raised two units for the Royal Scots, including the 16th Battalion made famous by its enrolment of footballers from the Heart of Midlothian club.[54] In sum, Scotland responded to the onset of war by raising 320,589 recruits through voluntary enlistment – the highest proportion in the United Kingdom.[55]

However welcome the contributions from the regions, they could only supplement the predominant response from England. This English response had to sustain the expanding ambitions of Kitchener as he strove to meet the demands of an unprecedented war. Just as voluntary recruiting for the peacetime army had depended upon recruitment in England, especially in its large urban centres that supplied about three-quarters of the annual intake,[56] so the response from the big cities, and particularly Greater London which housed seven million of the forty-four million people in the UK, was critical.

In early August 1914, when confronted with vast queues and congestion at its main recruiting offices, London opened new recruiting premises at Camberwell, Islington, Battersea, Fulham and Marylebone. It pioneered the 'Pals' concept when, in response to a suggestion from Major-General Sir Henry Rawlinson, then the Director of Recruiting at the War Office, Major the Hon. R. White raised over 1,600 City workers to form the 10th ('Stockbrokers') Battalion, Royal Fusiliers. London also sent the first Territorial unit, the London Scottish, to the Western Front, where it lost over half of its officers and men at Messines Ridge on 31 October 1914. Admittedly London was not always ahead of the provinces, as its recruiting peak in the first two weeks of September 1914 was less pronounced than the peak recorded across the rest of the UK, and local elites had to mount parades of troops, and organized rallies in Trafalgar Square, under the 'Wake Up London' campaign. By 30 April 1915, nonetheless, London had raised 257,878 recruits or 36.3 per cent of its eligible males.[57]

By the same date, Birmingham, Liverpool, Manchester and the North-East had also provided over 30 per cent of their eligible males as recruits (with Warwickshire and Northumberland both exceeding 40 per cent),[58] but the English response was far from uniform. If patriotism and a myriad of personal reasons contributed to the surge of enlistments in August and September (when 761,824 recruits or 15 per cent of the entire wartime enlistment occurred), so too did the onset of adverse economic conditions, which swept through the major towns and cities. Caused by the collapse of export markets in Europe, a protracted slump in the cotton industry and the curtailment of home orders, unemployment and short-term working surged in August and early September. It boosted recruitment before the receipt of large-scale orders for textiles, munitions, leather goods and other wartime requirements arrived in mid-September.[59] The famous 'rush' to the colours only occurred over the period 31 August to 11 September, when 295,278 men were recruited. This followed a second 'call' by Kitchener (28 August) for more men and an extension of the age limit to 35 years; the publication by *The Times* of the so-called 'Amiens despatch' on the plight of the British Expeditionary Force during the retreat from Mons; and the engagement of civilians in the recruiting process as well as the raising of numerous 'Pals' battalions by local communities. The 'rush' ended just as dramatically when the War Office raised the height limits to 5 foot 6 inches on 10 September 1914. At this time criticism persisted about information on separation and disability payments; the spectacle of recruits in civilian clothes, bereft of weapons, barracks or proper sanitary and feeding provisions; the rejection of 10 per cent of recruits as unfit for active service; and the censoring of news. In effect, these factors had the unintended consequence of implying that all eligible men were not needed, and that the nation could return to business as usual.[60]

The recruiting response varied across counties, with Yorkshire raising 168,426 recruits, or 26.3 per cent of its eligible males by 30 April 1915, a performance that was slightly below par but not as poor as that of Leicestershire or Derbyshire.[61] Within Yorkshire too, there were discrepancies between the various urban centres, and between those living in urban areas and those living in the countryside or in smaller market towns and villages. Some of those discrepancies can be illustrated by comparing the recruiting response of Leeds, the second largest urban area in the county (445,568 people in the 1911 census), with that of the North Riding, a vast, predominantly rural and sparsely populated recruiting district of the Yorkshire Regiment (Green Howards), in which Middlesborough was the largest town (104,787 people in the 1911 census).

The Green Howards, with its depot in Richmond, had a strong regimental reputation and a tradition of recruiting from beyond its district boundaries. At the outset of the war, only one of its two Territorial battalions was significantly under strength,[62] a shortage quickly remedied by the North Riding Territorial Association which opened recruiting offices in Malton, Whitby, Cloughton, Sowerby, Saltburn, Redcar, Guisborough and Stokesley, the boroughs of Middlesborough and Scarborough, and in Richmond. The regiment raised five service battalions in August and September 1914, with Middlesborough alone attesting 10,181 recruits and Richmond another 1,633 (not all of whom joined the Green Howards).[63] Even so, the response varied across the Riding; it was particularly impressive in the environs of Middlesborough, including small towns like Yarm, where 'about 10 per cent of the population . . . offered their services',[64] but much less so in the Leyburn office, which covered the area from Masham to Hawes. By the end of the first week in September, Leyburn had enrolled only 150 men since the war began, mostly from the Masham district, including twenty-eight from the Masham waterworks, a form of 'Pals' enlistment.[65]

By the end of January 1915, 17.3 per cent of Yorkshire's agricultural employees had entered the naval or military forces, marginally above the national average of 15.6 per cent out of the workforce of 1,135,000 for England and Wales.[66] Yet the recruiting enthusiasm waned in some rural communities and appeared to bypass others altogether. Recruiting in Richmond fell from 1,194 in September to 315 in October, and remained below 1,000 a month for the rest of 1914.[67] The response across much of Wensleydale and Ryedale occasioned all manner of speculation in the press and at public rallies. At meetings in Hawes and Pickering, local recruiting officers found few recruits and even encountered jeers and heckling; the reports on a series of rallies in Hawes described the second as 'again almost a failure, only one or two volunteering', while after the third in October 1914, 'none gave in their names'.[68] Although there were villages like Thornton Dale, where volunteering enjoyed the support of family, friends and the community generally,[69] in other isolated communities men felt little fear of invasion or need to enlist. They regarded war as something that soldiers did or saw no reason to volunteer as conscription was bound to follow; in the meantime they received higher wages as farmers sought to overcome the labour shortage.[70]

Undoubtedly the sheer size of the North Riding diminished the impact of the various recruiting campaigns. The Parliamentary Recruiting Committee (PRC) mounted recruiting tours of North Yorkshire, with carefully selected speakers. At various rallies, exhortations to enlist came from local elites, MPs, recruiting officers, senior churchmen and celebrities like Gertrude Bell, the redoubtable traveller, writer, fluent Arabist and daughter of the Lord Lieutenant of the North Riding, Sir Hugh Bell. Some of these efforts proved productive as in December 1914, when a PRC team toured the Thirsk and Malton division, covering 780 miles of country roads and holding fifty-four meetings, to attract 200 recruits.[71] Yet the yield overall was simply insufficient. In the previous month, the Green Howards had to find 62 per cent of its 715 recruits from outside Yorkshire, namely from Durham, Sunderland, South Shields, Bishop Auckland, Houghton and West Hartlepool.[72] As early as January 1915, the North Riding County Association, which was responsible for raising Territorial recruits for the Green Howards, debated the case for compulsory service. It postponed a decision but subsequent recruiting, apart from a brief revival during the New Year, fell below a hundred a month in April and May. Two recruiting marches through parts of the North Riding raised only nine men in April 1915 and 114 men in May 1915, and, on 21 May 2015, the Association voted decisively in favour of compulsory service.[73]

Although the outbreak of war reportedly produced 'a ready response' in Leeds, the town had never had a strong military tradition, and it took until 16 August before the local Territorial battalions, the 6th and 7th West Yorkshires (Leeds Rifles), reached their full strength.[74] As unemployment and short-time working were widespread during the first month of the war, unprecedented numbers offered themselves for enlistment, and it took only four days to raise 1,275 men for a businessmen 'Pals' battalion that excluded artisans and manual workers. This social exclusivity, and the failure to raise two workers' battalions, exacerbated class divisions in Leeds, which were then compounded by the sight of a huge crowd at the railway station, cheering the Leeds Pals as they went off to training. As one reporter observed:

> Ninety per cent of the recruits in Leeds have gone away to war, or to training in preparation for war without a cheer and without a song . . . It was the cheering that killed recruiting in Leeds. There has been no public protest, no outspoken contempt, but just silence and a huge drop in the rate of recruiting.[75]

In fact recruiting in Leeds had never been very good. During the height of the recruiting boom, Birmingham raised more men in three days than Leeds did in six weeks.[76] Leeds never raised another 'Pals' battalion whereas Barnsley, one-ninth of its size, raised two, and Hull, half of its size, raised four. In raising only 6,736 recruits from the start of the war until the end of 1914, Leeds suffered by comparison with Sheffield, a city of similar size, which raised 12,310 recruits.[77] As Leeds 'laggards' earned ridicule across Yorkshire, embarrassed the local press and provoked the wrath of Dr Stanley M. Bickersteth, the Vicar of Leeds,[78] the Leeds Chamber of Commerce rallied in defence at the end of 1914. It argued that recruiting in Leeds 'compares favourably . . . with that elsewhere' if due account were taken of its industrial contribution (later known as 'starred industries'), meeting orders for khaki cloth, uniform clothing, boots, small arms, cartridges and other munitions, and if allowances were made for the raising of two Territorial reserve battalions (required before the Leeds Rifles could serve abroad) as well as for Kitchener's Army.[79]

Such special pleading may have impressed post-war writers,[80] but the local elites and recruiting staff, assisted by the PRC, intensified their campaigns, recruiting for specific bodies, like the Leeds Bantams (the 17th [Service] Battalion, West Yorkshire Regiment) and units of the Royal Artillery, Army Service Corps, Royal Engineers and Royal Army Medical Corps. They employed all manner of techniques, including meetings, parades, Harry Lauder's bagpipers, the illuminated tram and later the canvassing of employers and door-to-door canvassing. They moved systematically through particular suburbs, trying to exert as much moral pressure as possible on the eligible men. There were still disappointments – the second battalions of the Leeds Rifles were not raised until February 1915 – and employees of the textile trade were among the least willing to enlist, hence the continuing references to Leeds 'slackers', and Councillor R. Escritt's remark in late August 1915 that 'the young men of Leeds had not done what they ought to have done . . . to put on khaki, play the man, and win the fight'.[81] Nevertheless, the recruiting response improved steadily in Leeds during 1915, outperforming all the major recruiting centres of Yorkshire and supplying the largest number of recruits for the Green Howards in November 1915.[82]

Despite the remarkable achievements of the voluntary system in enlisting 2,466,719 recruits from the outset of the war to the end of 1915, this response was insufficient. The government had tried to measure the response through a voluntary Householders' return (November–December 1914), which provided hopelessly incomplete data; then a National Register through the Local Government Board (completed on 15 August 1915) that revealed 5,012,146 men of military age were not in the forces, and that of these, 2,179,231 were single men of whom only 690,138 were in 'starred' occupations; and finally the door-to-door canvas across the country (apart from Ireland) under the scheme led by Lord Derby. This final effort, undertaken from 16 October to 15 December 1915, asked men between the ages of 18 and 40 to enlist or to attest their willingness to serve when summoned. As the canvas revealed that 2,182,178 men had neither enlisted, nor tried to enlist, nor attested, and that of these men 1,029,231 were bachelors, 651,160 of whom were not in 'starred' occupations, the voluntary system was doomed. Parliament's passage of the Military Service Act in January 1916 (by 431 votes to 39 on second reading) confirmed that voluntary recruitment was incompatible with the demands of a total war.[83]

The relative ease with which Parliament moved from voluntary recruiting to conscription showed how deep was the support for the war effort. Just as the political opponents of war had been marginalized from the outset, and anti-German passions had erupted, so the country responded in the most tangible way through a massive wave of voluntary recruiting. This had reached a peak in the 'rush' to the colours during August and September 1914, when 761,824 men joined as new recruits before they could be accommodated, equipped and properly trained. Thereafter, voluntary recruiting ebbed and flowed, without ever replicating the numbers raised in the first two months. However impressive in scale, the voluntary response had its limitations: it consumed huge resources in numerous recruiting campaigns and exacerbated divisions when units were raised on the basis of social exclusivity or when statistics were released that exposed comparative divisions between regions, major towns, or between towns and country, or when the system took married men before bachelors. Above all, it failed to prepare for fighting a total war when the demands of recruiting had to be assessed against the requirements of agriculture and the war industries. As John Osborne observed, 'a modern state demanded a more rational, more organized, and more egalitarian approach'.[84]

Notes

1. A. Marwick, *The Deluge: British Society and The First World War* (New York: W. W. Norton & Co., 1965), p. 309.
2. T. Royle, *The Kitchener Enigma* (London: Michael Joseph, 1985), pp. 256–7.

3. Mark Connelly, *The Great War, Memory and Ritual: Commemoration in the City and East (London: 1916-1939* (London: The Boydell Press for the Royal Historical Society, 2002), p. 8; see also D. Todman, *The Great War, Myth and Memory* (Hambledon and London: 2005), Ch. 4.
4. C. Pearce, *Comrades in Conscience: The story of an English community's opposition to the Great War* (London: Francis Boutle Publishers, 2001).
5. W. J. Reader, *At Duty's Call: A Study in Obsolete Patriotism* (Manchester: Manchester University Press, 1988), pp. 104–5.
6. R. Pound and G. Harmsworth, *Northcliffe* (London: Cassell, 1959), p. 252.
7. W. S. Churchill, *The World Crisis, 1914-1918*, 5 vols. (London: Thornton Butterworth, 1923–31), vol. 1, pp. 36–7; see also P. M. Kennedy, *The Rise of Anglo-German Antagonism 1860-1914* (London: George Allen & Unwin, 1980).
8. H. Strachan, *The First World War: Volume 1 To Arms* (Oxford: Oxford University Press, 2001), p. 131; I. F. W. Beckett (ed.), *The Army and the Curragh Incident 1914* (London: The Bodley Head for the Army Records Society, 1986), pp. 25–6.
9. H. H. Asquith to V. Stanley, 29 July 1914, in M. and E. Brock (eds), *H. H. Asquith: Letters to Venetia Stanley* (Oxford: Oxford University Press, 1982), pp. 132–3; see also M. Gilbert, *First World War* (London: HarperCollins, 1994), p. 22.
10. *Yorkshire Post*, 1 August 1914, p. 8; see also A. Gregory, 'British "War Enthusiasm" in 1914 a Reassessment', in G. Braybon (ed.), *Evidence, History and the Great War: Historians and the Impact of 1914-18* (New York: Berghahn Books, 2003), pp. 62–85, at pp. 73–4 and C. Clark, *The Sleepwalkers: How Europe Went to War in 1914* (London: Allen Lane, 2012), p. 541.
11. E. David (ed.), *Inside Asquith's Cabinet. From the Diaries of Charles Hobhouse* (London: John Murray, 1977), pp. 179–80.
12. D. Marquand, *Ramsay MacDonald* (London: Jonathan Cape, 1977), p. 169.
13. *Yorkshire Post*, 5 August 1914, p. 6.
14. C. Hazelhurst, *Politicians at War July 1914 to May 1915: A prologue to the triumph of Lloyd George* (London: Jonathan Cape, 1971), pp. 60, 98, 116; M. Caedel, *Pacifism in Britain 1914-1945: The Defining of a Faith* (Oxford: Oxford University Press, 1980), p. 32; David (ed.), *Inside Asquith's Cabinet*, p. 180; M. Swartz, 'A Study in Futility: The British Radicals at the Outbreak of the First World War', in A. J. A. Morris (ed.), *Edwardian Radicalism 1900-1914: Some aspects of British Radicalism* (London: Routledge & Kegan Paul, 1974), pp. 246–61.
15. K. Robbins, *The Abolition of War: The 'Peace Movement' in Britain, 1914-1919* (Cardiff: University of Wales Press, 1976), pp. 27–9, 34, and A. Gregory, *The Last Great War: British Society and the First World War* (Cambridge: Cambridge University Press, 2008), pp. 22–3.
16. Quoted in W. Kendall, *The Revolutionary Movement in Britain 1900-21: The Origins of British Communism* (London: Weidenfeld & Nicolson, 1969), p. 86.
17. J. Clifford, *The War and the Churches* (London: J. Clarke, 1914), p. 8; see also Robbins, *Abolition of War*, pp. 31–2.
18. M. E. Hirst, *The Quakers in peace and war: an account of their peace principles and practice* (London: The Swarthmore Press, 1923), p. 493 and Robbins, *Abolition of War*, pp. 32–3.
19. Caedel, *Pacifism in Britain*, p. 32.
20. H. Read, *Annals of Innocence and Experience* (London: Faber and Faber, 1946), pp. 137–8; see also H. Cecil, 'Herbert Read and the Great War', in D. Goodway (ed.), *Herbert Read Assessed* (Liverpool: Liverpool University Press, 1998), pp. 30–45.
21. B. Russell, *The Autobiography of Bertrand Russell*, 3 vols. (London: George Allen and Unwin, 1967–9), vol. 2, pp. 16–17.
22. M. MacDonagh, *In London during the Great War: The Diary of a Journalist* (London: Eyre & Spottiswoode, 1935), pp. 8–9.
23. Ibid. p. 9; D. Lloyd George, *War Memoirs of David Lloyd George*, 6 vols. (London: Ivor Nicholson & Watson, 1933–6), vol. 1, p. 65.

24. Gregory, 'British "War Enthusiasm" in 1914', pp. 68–9, 71–2, 78–9 and *Last Great War*, pp. 9–11, 13–16, 25–30.
25. Kendall, *Revolutionary Movement*, pp. 88–9.
26. 'War against War', *Aberdare Leader*, 15 August 1914, p. 6.
27. 'Cumnock Ministers and the War', *Merthyr Pioneer*, 5 September 1914, p. 5; see also Gregory, *Last Great War*, p. 12.
28. Among their leading members were Charles P. Trevelyan, Ramsay MacDonald, Norman Angell, Arthur Ponsonby and the journalist E. D. Morel: M. Swartz, *The Union of Democratic Control in British Politics during the First World War* (Oxford: Clarendon Press, 1971), pp. 28, 35–6, 39, 42, 69, 93.
29. MacDonagh, *In London during the Great War*, p. 15.
30. Ibid. p. 15; I. F. W. Beckett, *Home Front 1914-1918: How Britain Survived the Great War* (Kew, Richmond: The National Archives, 2006), pp. 149–50; see also P. Panayi, *The Enemy in Our Midst: Germans in Britain During the First World War* (Oxford: Berg, 1991).
31. Beckett, *Home Front*, pp. 150 and 153; Asquith to Venetia Stanley, 28 October 1914 in M. and E. Brock (eds), *Letters to Venetia Stanley*, p. 290; P. Ziegler, *Mountbatten: the official biography* (London: Collins, 1985), pp. 35–6; E. M. Spiers, *Haldane: an Army Reformer* (Edinburgh: Edinburgh University Press, 1980), pp. 11–13.
32. I. F. Clarke, *Voices Prophesying War* (2nd ed. Oxford: Oxford University Press, 1992), pp. 115–16, 118–28.
33. MacDonagh, *In London during the Great War*, p. 19.
34. Apart from prejudice against part-time soldiers, Kitchener had good reasons to set aside the Territorial Force, which had been raised for purposes of home defence. He still needed the nucleus of a force to guard against invasion, and he was not sure how many Territorials would volunteer for overseas or 'imperial' service, P. Simkins, *Kitchener's Army: The Raising of the New Armies, 1914-16* (Manchester: Manchester University Press, 1988), pp. 38–44, 60.
35. D. Fitzpatrick, 'Militarism in Ireland, 1900-1922', in T. Bartlett and K. Jeffery (eds), *A Military History of Ireland* (Cambridge: Cambridge University Press, 1996), pp. 379–406, at p. 386.
36. Royle, *Kitchener Enigma*, pp. 274–5.
37. I. Colvin, *The Life of Lord Carson*, 3 vols. (London: Victor Gollancz, 1932–6), vol. 3, p. 33.
38. T. Bowman, *Irish Regiments in the Great War: Discipline and Morale* (Manchester: Manchester University Press, 2003), pp. 64 and 66; I. F. W. Beckett, *The Great War 1914-1918* (2nd ed. London: Pearson, 2007), p. 293.
39. Fitzpatrick, 'Militarism in Ireland', p. 386; Simkins, *Kitchener's Army*, pp. 114–15.
40. *The Great War: Speech delivered by the Rt. Hon. David Lloyd George, M.P. (Chancellor of the Exchequer) at the Queen's Hall, London on September 19th 1914* (Toronto: Hodder and Stoughton, 1914), pp, 6, 10, 14–15; Swartz, *Union of Democratic Control*, pp. 28–9; and on lingering reservations in Welsh-speaking areas, see Gregory, *Last Great War*, p. 12 and C. Parry, 'Gwynedd and the Great War, 1914-1918', *Welsh History Review*, vol. 14 (1988–9), pp. 78–117.
41. 'Lloyd George's Great Speech', *Carmarthan Journal and South Wales Weekly Advertiser*, 20 September 2014, p. 7.
42. Asquith to Venetia Stanley, 30 October 1914, in M. and E. Brock (eds), *Letters to Venetia Stanley*, p. 298.
43. Lloyd George's memoirs are particularly unreliable on this issue, describing his campaign as one waged on behalf of one division when it was on behalf of a Welsh army corps (of two divisions), and summarizing the outcome as a 'handsome surrender' by Kitchener when Kitchener actually preserved his default position of not including previously-enlisted Welshmen in the 38th Division: Lloyd George, *War Memoirs*, vol. 2, p. 754.
44. Asquith to Venetia Stanley, 28 October 1914, in M. and E. Brock (eds), *Letters to Venetia Stanley*, p. 291; David (ed.), *Inside Asquith's Cabinet*, pp. 203–4.
45. Simkins, *Kitchener's Army*, pp. 96–9.

46. 'Highland Mounted Brigade', *Inverness Courier*, 28 August 1914, p. 5.
47. 'Kitchener Trying Daring Experiment. Nothing Like It Since the Times of Cromwell', *Poverty Bay Herald*, 20 October 1914, p. 3. The spelling mistakes in the New Zealand account are corrected in the text.
48. 'Cameron Highlanders', *Glasgow Herald*, 26 August 1914, p. 6.
49. Ibid.
50. 'Students and Lochiel's Camerons' and 'Result of Camerons' March', *Glasgow Herald*, 8 September 1914, p. 7 and 10 November 1914, p. 9; E. A. Cameron and I. J. M. Robertson, 'Fighting and Bleeding for the Land: the Scottish Highlands and the Great War', in C. M. M. Macdonald and E.W. McFarland (eds), *Scotland and the Great War* (Phantassie, East Linton: Tuckwell Press, 1999), pp. 81–102, at pp. 83–5; Lieutenant Colonel A. Fairrie, *'Cuidich 'N Righ': A History of the Queen's Own Highlanders (Cameron and Seaforth)* (Inverness: Regimental H. Q., 1983), pp. 77–81.
51. D. Young, *Forgotten Scottish Voices from the Great War* (Stroud, Gloucestershire: Tempus, 2005), p. 22.
52. Asquith to Venetia Stanley, 30 September 1914, in M. and E. Brock (eds), *Letters to Venetia Stanley*, p. 257.
53. 'Instructions to Political Recruiting Committees' and 'Church's Attitude. A War of Freedom', *Glasgow Herald*, 8 September 1914, p. 7 and 9 September 1914, p. 5; Young, *Forgotten Scottish Voices*, p. 25; E. A. Cameron, *Impaled Upon a Thistle: Scotland Since 1880* (Edinburgh: Edinburgh University Press, 2008), p. 107.
54. J. Alexander, *McCrae's Battalion: The Story of the 16th Royal Scots* (Edinburgh: Mainstream Publishing, 2004); T. Chalmers, *An Epic of Glasgow: History of the 15th Battalion, The Highland Light Infantry (City of Glasgow Regiment)* (Glasgow: John McCallum, 1934); T. Chalmers (ed.), *A Saga of Scotland: History of the 16th Battalion. The Highland Light Infantry (City of Glasgow Regiment)* (Glasgow: John McCallum, 1930); and J. W. Arthur & I. S. Munro (eds), *The Seventeenth Highland Light Infantry (Glasgow Chamber of Commerce Battalion) Record of War Service 1914-1918* (Glasgow: D. J. Clark, 1920).
55. Parliamentary Papers (PP), 'General Annual Reports on the British Army (including the Territorial Force from the date of embodiment) for the period from 1st October 1913, to 30th September 1919', Cmd. 1193 (1921), XX, p. 9; see also E. M. Spiers, 'The Scottish Soldier at War', in H. Cecil and P. Liddle (eds), *Facing Armageddon: The First World War Experienced* (Barnsley: Leo Cooper, 1996), pp. 314–35, at p. 315.
56. E. M. Spiers, *The Late Victorian Army 1868-1902* (Manchester: Manchester University Press, 1992), pp. 130–1.
57. The National Archives (TNA), WO 159/3, 'The War (August 1914 To 31 May 1915) Note by the Secretary of State for War', appendix 2; 'London and the recruiting boom', in https://greatwarlondon.wordpress.com/2014/9/28/london-and-the-recruiting-boom/ (accessed 11 October 1914).
58. TNA, WO 159/3, 'The War', appendix 2.
59. PP, 'State of Employment. Report to the Board of Trade on the State of Employment in the United Kingdom in October, 1914', Cd 7703 (1914-1916), XXI, pp. 5-6, 19-20; J. M. Osborne, *The Voluntary Recruiting Movement in Britain, 1914-1916* (New York: Garland Publishing, 1982), p. 74.
60. TNA, WO 159/19, Secretary of State for War, private office, 'Recruitment', n.d.; Osborne, *Voluntary Recruiting*, pp. 23, 75, 78, 80.
61. TNA, WO 159/3, 'The War', appendix 2; on the poor response of Leicestershire, see Gregory, *Last Great War*, pp. 88–9.
62. This was the 5th Battalion, which had only eighteen of its twenty-eight officers and 598 of its 979 men in 1913, PP, 'The Annual Return of the Territorial Force for the Year 1913', Cd 7254 (1914), LII, p. 64.
63. Calculated from the data in TNA, NATS1/398, 'Approximate Number of Recruits Raised Daily'.
64. 'Yarm's splendid effort', *Darlington and Stockton Times*, 5 September 1914, p. 3.

65. 'Response in Masham-Hawes District', *Yorkshire Herald*, 12 September 1914, p. 3.
66. PP, 'State of Employment. Report to the Board of Trade on the State of Employment in the United Kingdom in February, 1915', Cd. 7850 (1914-1916), XXI, p. 11; see also 'Malton. 200 Recruits for Lord Kitchener's Army', *Yorkshire Herald*, 11 September 1914, p. 3 and 'Why We Are At War', *Yorkshire Herald*, 18 September 1914, p. 5.
67. TNA, NATS1/398.
68. 'Mr. D'Arcy Wyvill's Appeal to the Men of the Dales', *Craven Herald*, 28 August 1914, p. 2, 'Recruiting in Wensleydale', *Craven Herald*, 4 September 1914, p. 4; 'The New Army. Recruiting Meeting at Hawes', *Yorkshire Herald*, 29 October 1914, p. 6; 'Wensleydale and the War', *Darlington and Stockton Times*, 31 October 1914, p. 8; and 'Recruiting Meeting at Pickering', *Malton Messenger*, 14 November 1914, p. 4.
69. 'Thornton Dale', *Weekly Supplement to the Yorkshire Herald*, 9 January 1915, p. 17.
70. C. Kernahan, *The Experiences of a Recruiting Officer: True Pictures of Splendid Patriotism* (London: Hodder and Stoughton, 1915), p. 29; 'Duty of Farm Workers', *Yorkshire Herald*, 11 November 1914, p. 8; 'Call for Recruits. Attitude of Ryedale Farmers', *Yorkshire Herald*, 7 November 1914, p. 8.
71. 'Thirsk and Malton Division's Successful Recruiting Campaign', *North Riding News*, 24 December 1914, p. 5.
72. Green Howards' Regimental Museum (GHRM), 'Enlistment Record Book 1914-1916'.
73. Ibid.; 'North Riding Territorial Association', *Yorkshire Herald*, 29 January 1915, p. 6; 'Wensleydale Recruiting March', *Yorkshire Herald,* 10 April 1915, p. 8; 'Green Howards' Recruiting March', *The Green Howards' Gazette*, vol. 23, no. 268 (1915), pp. 74-6; 'Call for Recruits. Compulsory Service Favoured', *Yorkshire Herald*, 22 May 1915, p. 6.
74. PP, 'Annual Return of the Territorial Force', p. 64; W. H. Scott, *Leeds in the Great War 1914-1918: A Book of Remembrance* (Leeds: The Libraries and Arts Committee, 1923), pp. 16–17.
75. 'Why Recruiting Stopped', *Leeds District Weekly Citizen*, 2 October 1914, p. 1; see also 'Recruiting in Leeds', *Yorkshire Post*, 27 August 1914, p. 8 and L. Milner, *Leeds PALS: A History of the 15th (Service) Battalion (1st Leeds) The Prince of Wales's Own (West Yorkshire Regiment) 1914-1918* (London: Leo Cooper, 1991), pp. 20–42.
76. 'Leeds Recruiting Figures Compared', *Yorkshire Evening Post*, 12 September 1914, p. 4.
77. TNA, NATS1/398.
78. 'In the Big Cities. Leeds and its Recruits', *Sheffield Daily Telegraph*, 18 November 1914, p. 6; 'Yorkshire Must Wake Up', *Leeds Mercury*, 15 October 1914, p. 4; 'Leeds Vicar's Outburst', *Leeds & District Weekly Citizen*, 4 December 1914, p. 2.
79. Scott, *Leeds in the Great War*, pp. 20–2.
80. Ibid, P. M. Morris, 'Leeds and the Amateur Military Tradition, The Leeds Rifles and Their Antecedents, c. 1859-1918', (unpublished PhD dissertation, University of Leeds, 1983), p. 321.
81. 'Leeds Bantams Campaign', *Leeds Mercury*, 24 August 1915, p. 4; 'Leeds Slackers', *Leeds Mercury*, 12 May 1915, p. 2; PP, 'State of Employment . . . December 1914', p. 5; Morris, 'Leeds and the Amateur Military Tradition', pp. 321–3.
82. TNA, NATS1/398 and GHRM, 'Enlistment Record Book 1914-1916'.
83. *Parliamentary Debates*, Fifth Series, vol. 77 (12 January 1916), col. 1736; Simkins, *Kitchener's Army*, pp. 121–2, 142–57; Osborne, *Voluntary Recruiting*, p. 105.
84. Osborne, *Voluntary Recruiting*, p. 132.

Chapter 5

War Readiness in Britain: the Royal Navy, August 1914 – January 1915

* * *

Dominic Tweddle

Basking in the long afterglow of Trafalgar, worshipping at the ceaselessly polished shrine of Nelson, and conscious of its immense material might, the Royal Navy faced the First World War with confidence. In July 1914 the Royal Navy mobilised for its summer manoeuvres, including a great fleet review at Spithead on 18 July there was no demobilisation, the fleet remaining in being at almost full strength and as the international situation deteriorated this looked increasingly prescient. As the British ultimatum to Germany expired at 2300 hours on 4 August, the fleet moved smoothly and efficiently to its war stations. On 5 August, the destroyers HMS *Lance* and HMS *Landrail* in company with the cruiser, HMS *Amphion*, spotted the German steam ferry *Königin Luise* laying mines off the Dutch coast. Having ordered her to stop, the British ships opened fire and *Königin Luise* was sunk.[1] After the war, a 4in Mark IX gun was preserved from HMS *Lance* as the gun which fired the first British shot of the First World War.[2] That it was a Royal Navy gun seemed somehow appropriate. Elsewhere, however, there were shots that should have been fired and were not, a subject returned to below.

The Royal Navy which mobilised so confidently in July 1914 was a navy transformed over the previous decade both in terms of technology[3] and organisation. In large part it was a navy remodelled to a blueprint developed by Admiral Sir John Arbuthnot Fisher, First Sea Lord 1904–10. He saw, understood, encouraged and marshalled both technological advance and the radical organisational changes which were necessary to underpin its use.[4]

For surface ships Fisher was the progenitor of the all big-gun battleship, HMS *Dreadnought*. Fisher saw that even the biggest and most modern battleships of his existing fleet were inadequate. They were relatively slow, carried armament of mixed calibre and were designed for relatively close-range engagements. For

Fisher what mattered were speed, heavy armour and big guns of a single calibre capable of engaging at long range. *Dreadnought*, powered by steam turbines rather than reciprocating engines and fuelled by coal which had oil sprayed onto it to increase the burn rate, could make 21 knots. She had armour of a maximum thickness of 11 inches, and ten 12in guns. At a stroke she had rendered every single battleship existing in every fleet obsolete.[5] The Germans ruefully referred to pre-dreadnought battleships as '*funf minuten*' ships. They would last that long in an engagement with a Dreadnought. Fisher, too, championed the battlecruiser, a more lightly armoured version of *Dreadnought*, able to move at higher speed, 25.5 knots in the case of the first battlecruiser, HMS *Invincible*. Speed was bought by sacrificing armour; *Invincible*'s armour had a maximum thickness of 4–6 inches.[6] As the war unfolded both the virtues and the drawbacks of the battlecruiser concept were revealed. The development of *Dreadnought*, of course, fed the Anglo-German naval race, but by 1914 Britain had decisively won that battle; she could deploy twenty-two Dreadnought battleships against Germany's fourteen – the Austro-Hungarian Navy scarcely counted. As the war progressed, Britain's lead in battleship production increased. The Grand Fleet entered the war 60 per cent more powerful than the next two most powerful fleets combined.

The superiority of the big-gun Dreadnought battleship and battlecruiser lay not only in weight of projectile fired, but in range. The Battle of Tsushima in 1905 had been fought at a range of around 6,000 yards,[7] but the latest Dreadnoughts entering service could fight at a range of around 20,000 yards. To achieve this, new methods of rangefinding and fire control had to be developed which were sophisticated enough to control all the big guns on a single ship together, allowing for such factors as wind speed, type of shell and even the rotation of the earth during the time the shell was in the air. *Dreadnought* had a workable system involving a 9ft rangefinder, Dumaresq fire-control calculator, and Vickers clock. The next step was director firing, controlling all of the guns centrally. A workable director-firing system had been developed by Percy Scott which needed a mechanical computer. Much scholarly ink has been spilt on which of the mechanical computers on offer was the better one, that developed by Dreyer or that devised by Pollen; at this distance in time it is impossible to know. All that can be said is that the system the Royal Navy had did the job.[8]

Fisher had embraced these technological changes with enthusiasm, and indeed had driven many of them. He had also long understood the potential of torpedoes, a late nineteenth-century development turned into an effective weapon by the opening of the twentieth century. Anti-submarine methods played an important part in his thinking, as did the provision of new classes of vessel which carried torpedoes as their main weapon system. In understanding the potential of torpedoes, Fisher too had clearly seen the potential of submarines. The first operational Royal Navy submarine, *Holland I*, which entered service in 1901, was probably more terrifying to its crew than to the enemy,[9] but, by 1914, powerful and effective submarines had been developed and deployed by the Royal Navy, particularly the 'E' class which played such a significant role in the war.[10] The potential of air power was also well appreciated. The Royal Navy was well behind the Germans in the use of airships, but was well ahead in aircraft. The first aircraft took off from a surface ship in 1911, a Short S.27 from the deck of HMS *Africa*; an alternative method of launching aircraft, the seaplane lighter, had also been developed. A lighter carrying a single aircraft was towed at high speed into the wind until take-off was achieved. The Royal Navy had developed aircraft both for scouting and for strike, including aircraft which could carry torpedoes.[11]

To co-ordinate all of this remained problematic. The telegraph allowed the Admiralty to communicate with bases across the globe: after all, almost every undersea telegraph line in the world was controlled by Britain. Wireless too was well-developed and well-disseminated across the fleet. The problem was that it was slow. Tests in 1911 showed that it took 10 minutes to transmit a 100-word message (5 minutes if it were not coded) but that it took 25 minutes to code it and 25 minutes to decode it[12] – hence the reliance on signal flags or semaphore lamps to control ships in the heat of battle. Given poor weather conditions, gun smoke and the general chaos of battle, this was less than satisfactory. Telegraph and radio had another downside: they allowed the Admiralty to try and control in detail the actions of commanders at sea, sometimes with disastrous results, as we shall see.

As well as building modern ships to new designs and specifications, Fisher was ruthless in scrapping the obsolete. The many ships he considered 'too weak to fight and too slow to run away' were axed. Even so, far too many of them survived in service, to prove Fisher embarrassingly accurate in his analysis of their capabilities. The ships that did survive were re-deployed. The Home Fleet was re-titled the Channel Fleet and its strength increased to twelve battleships, the Mediterranean Fleet was reduced to eight battleships and the armoured cruiser squadrons formerly attached to each fleet were re-organised into three new squadrons to be deployed where needed.[13] This plan was backed-up by major changes in naval education and training designed to improve technical knowledge and understanding, and to increase social mobility within the service.[14] Whether the Royal Navy was to have had the right staff structure is something which obsessed naval officers and commentators at the time, and has 'entertained' historians ever since, but as war changed and technology changed, so adjustments were made to the structure of the Naval Staff, although many functions remained the same.[15] The Naval Staff, however, did have an early stroke of good fortune. The Russians retrieved a German naval code book from SMS *Magdeburg* and passed it to the British. Room 40 was created to decipher German codes and played a vital role in ensuring that the Royal Navy continued to command the seas.[16]

It would, however, be futile to pretend that all was well with the Royal Navy in 1914. The service had changed very quickly in a short space of time. There were weaknesses in the supply of shells and in the quality of armour-piercing shell,[17] only rectified when unexploded German shells were recovered and copied. British mines also performed poorly up until 1917 when new types were introduced.[18]

Naval bases, particularly in the northern North Sea, remained to be completed and adequately protected. Breakneck change had also left the Royal Navy short of trained men, and there was one other legacy of the Fisher era, the bitterness between the Fisher and Beresford factions in the Royal Navy which had eventually damaged the careers of both men. This factionalism ran deep and soured personal relationships.

Before the war the Royal Navy had made a gallant attempt to advance a strategy in which there would be no British army engaged on the Continent. Instead, the Navy would use its mobility and land forces wherever they could threaten the enemy. This was a re-run of the strategy of the Napoleonic Wars, where it had not been conspicuously successful. As a result, it had been rejected as had the idea of close blockade, another Napoleonic relic completely unsuited to the modern era.[19] Consequently, at the start of the war the Royal Navy had three core tasks: to convey the British Expeditionary Force to France and to ensure its resupply and reinforcement; to establish and maintain a blockade of Germany; and to ensure the safety of Britain's trade worldwide, allowing her to draw both on the resources of empire and on the resources of the other nations mobilised by global trade. Of course this would mean bringing German units to battle wherever they could be found. Fighting a second Trafalgar, something which haunted the naval psyche, was not on the agenda and was not necessarily desirable. As Churchill remarked, Jellicoe commanding the Grand Fleet at Scapa Flow, was 'the only man who could lose the war in an afternoon', a comment on the deterrent effect of the Grand Fleet in being.[20] Of course the Germans would have plans of their own, and they would have to be deal with; a German invasion seemed a remote possibility although plans were developed to counter such an eventuality.[21]

The movement of the BEF to France was undertaken simply and effectively. Between 9 and 23 August, four infantry divisions and one cavalry division, with all their supplies, were moved without loss.[22] Across the whole of the four and a half years or war, thousands of shipping movements delivered supplies, ammunition and reinforcements in a constant stream, returning troops on leave and the injured to the United Kingdom. Not a single man or woman was lost. This was surely the most superbly-executed and most effective logistics exercise in the history of warfare. Men of the Royal Navy were lost in protecting this vital lifeline, to mines, torpedoes, and hit-and-run raids, however. The most tragic and unnecessary of those losses was the sinking of the cruisers *Aboukir*, *Hogue* and *Cressy* on the same day, 22 September, 1914. They were patrolling in line abreast and about two miles apart off the area of the Dutch coast known as the Broad Fourteens. As one ship was torpedoed by *U9*, the next stopped to pick up survivors and was torpedoed in turn. They were antiquated ships; the loss of which was of minimal importance, but the loss of trained men was a blow. Out of a complement of 2,200, 1,459 men were lost, many of them cadets straight from Britannia Naval College; this was not the Royal Navy's finest moment.[23]

Without too much difficulty, the Royal Navy imposed an effective blockade of

Germany. The Germans had expected a close blockade to be established. Instead, the Navy opted for a distant blockade, sealing off the main entrances and exits to the North Sea with a combination of minefields and patrol lines. With such large distances to control, it was inevitable that German ships would slip through, especially by using Norwegian territorial waters. Neutrals were stopped and searched and if carrying contraband were sent into British ports where their cargoes would either be seized or purchased. Neutrals, in particular the United States, were much exercised by the blockade. Throughout the nineteenth century it had been US policy to try and limit the ability of the Royal Navy to intercept their trade, and Britain had seemed to concede this with the London Declaration of 1909. This banned distant blockade and precluded Britain from stopping ships bound for neutral ports even if they were carrying contraband. There were also types of cargo which were permitted even though they could aid the enemy. Britain had announced at the beginning of the war that she would adhere to the declaration, and the Navy thus trod a fine line in enforcing its blockade. The problem was further exacerbated by the reluctance of the courts to condemn cargoes as contraband, often in the teeth of the evidence, bowing to the pressure of financiers who had worldwide trading interests and objected to their trade being interrupted. It has to be said that many of them were British! Britain controlled 50 per cent of the world's shipping and was the world's predominant trading and investing power, despite the rapid growth of the United States. The result was that the blockade was more porous than had been anticipated, and it was not until much later in the war that it became more fully effective. A merry dance developed with the Royal Navy, Germany and neutral powers all trying to circumvent the London Declaration. As the US Ambassador commented, the London Declaration 'would probably have given victory to Germany if the allies had adopted it'. Even so, the winter of 1915 was known as the Turnip Winter in Germany, so the blockade was making a difference from the outset, though not as great a difference as planned. Essentially, however, this weakness was political not naval.[24]

In retrospect, the greatest challenge posed to the Royal Navy in the first six months of the war was in securing the safety of British trade globally and dealing with the German surface units that threatened it. At the outset of the war there were German surface ships in the Mediterranean (SMS *Goeben* and *Breslau*), in the Caribbean (SMS *Karlsruhe*), off Mexico's Pacific Coast (SMS *Leipzig*), in the Caroline Islands (SMS *Scharnhorst*, SMS *Gneisenau* and SMS *Nürnberg*), off Japan (SMS *Emden*) and in the Indian Ocean (SMS *Königsberg*). There were also numbers of armed liners and supply ships on which the surface units depended.

The first encounter between British and German forces was in the Mediterranean. By 2 August, just before the outbreak of war, the Royal Navy was shadowing the German battlecruiser *Goeben* and light cruiser *Breslau*, which were in company. The British battlecruisers could not keep up and lost contact with *Goeben* and *Breslau*, but the German ships were shadowed by the cruiser, HMS *Gloucester*, which kept Admiral Troubridge, stationed at the mouth of the Adriatic, informed of their position. Troubridge moved to intercept with his flotilla of four armoured cruisers and eight torpedo-armed destroyers, but he had been ordered not to engage superior German forces, and he decided that *Goeben*, with her 11in guns, was superior to his ships which only carried 9.2in guns. He concluded that he was outranged and out-gunned and did not offer battle. HMS *Gloucester* kept in touch with the Germans and even engaged *Breslau* before being ordered by Troubridge to break off the action.[25] Troubridge's decision has rightly been compared unfavourably with Commodore Harwood's decision to engage *Graf Spee* at the opening of the Second World War. Harwood had one 8in cruiser and two 6in cruisers to take on a 'pocket battleship' with 11in guns. By a combination of superior tactics and sheer effrontery, he forced *Graf Spee* to retreat into the River Plate where she was eventually scuttled. Troubridge, in contrast, was court-martialled, and although acquitted, never served again. *Goeben* and *Breslau* escaped to Turkey where they were commissioned into the Ottoman Navy as the *Yavuz Sultan Selim* and *Midilli* respectively. Arguably they tipped the scales in Turkey's decision to join the Central Powers in the First World War, although the seizure of two Turkish Dreadnoughts being built in Britain in August 1914 was a significant factor too.

Elsewhere, German surface ships took the offensive, tackling British shipping and paralysing trade, a reaction out of all proportion to the losses inflicted which, on the grand scale of things, were insignificant. Insurance rates soared and it took government intervention in the market to restore some kind of order. It was evident that the German units would have to be hunted down and destroyed. HMAS *Sydney* sank *Emden* at the Cocos Islands on 9 November 1914, but by that time she had sunk 70,825 tons of shipping, bombarded Madras and Penang, and sunk a French destroyer and a Russian cruiser.[26] *Königsberg*, having sunk a single merchant ship and driven HMS *Pegasus* ashore, took refuge in the Rufiji River in German East Africa. She was blockaded by HMS *Dartmouth*, but was too far upriver to be reached by conventional naval gunfire. Eventually two monitors, HMS *Severn* and HMS *Mersey*, were despatched. They had a shallow enough draft to sail up river. The first attack on 6 July 1915 proved abortive, signals were not received from the spotting aircraft and *Konigsberg*'s shooting was accurate, aided by spotters on the river bank:

> Four men were seen up a tree on an adjacent island, evidently spotting by telephone to '*KONIGSBERG*'. These hastily descended when a 4.7' shrapnel burst over them and I have no doubt beat a hasty retreat or died a sudden death when 3 6' High Explosive shells fell amongst them. This undoubtedly spoilt the '*KONIGSBERG*'s' accurate shooting.[27]

On 11 July, *Severn* and *Mersey* returned to the attack. Spotting from the aircraft was this time effective:

I received a signal from the aeroplane 'I'm hit, send boat for us' after which the observer made 'all hits are right forward on '*KONIGSBERG*'. This I should say was one of the most gallant episodes of the war. A piece of shell right pierced through the water-jacket of the engine, which of course immediately commenced to fail; these two fellows went on flying over '*KONIGSBERG*' getting lower and lower, and ultimately put '*SEVERN*' on to the target: vitally important. About 2 minutes after that the engine seized up altogether and stopped. They then glided down towards me and made a perfect landing not very far from us, making spotting signals and corrections all the way down.[28]

Eventually *Königsberg* was left a burning hulk:

We continued to fire at '*KONIGSBERG*' until about 2.45 by which time she was burning everywhere, one funnel had fallen out of her, and 8 separate explosions had taken place in her, so I should think there was precious little left of her; the poor wretches on board must have had a terrible time.[29]

The commander of the German Pacific squadron, Admiral Graf von Spee, meanwhile concluded that he should try and return to Germany. He commanded a formidable force consisting of the armoured cruisers *Scharnhorst* and *Gneisenau*, together with the light cruisers *Leipzig* and *Nürnberg* and a flotilla of supply ships. He headed for Chile, making landfall at Coronel. It was off Coronel on 1 November 1914, that he encountered a weak British squadron commanded by Sir Christopher Craddock. Craddock had one modern cruiser, HMS *Glasgow*, together the superannuated armoured cruisers *Good Hope* and *Monmouth* and the armed liner, *Otranto*. The pre-dreadnought battleship HMS *Canopus*, which was meant to provide 'a citadel around which all our cruisers in those waters could find absolute security,'[30] presumably from its 12in guns, was 240 miles away, plagued by mechanical breakdowns. In any event, *Canopus'* guns were out-ranged by those of *Scharnhorst* and *Gneisenau* and even when her engines functioned, she was much slower than them as well. Cursed by orders from the Admiralty out of which no sane man could extract much sense, and with the example of Troubridge before him, Craddock elected to fight. It was a brave decision – he was outnumbered and outgunned. He rejected the option to cut and run using his superior speed to escape; he felt he could not abandon the much slower *Otranto*. Craddock's flagship, *Good Hope*, and *Monmouth* were sunk with all hands, *Glasgow* and *Otranto* escaped.[31] There are accounts of the battle from HMS *Glasgow*. Chief Yeoman of Signals, Henry Pine, wrote to his wife:

God knows as well as anyone that from the start we stood no chance of beating them but there was no talk of running away until it was absolute suicide to remain and it took a great deal to make our Captain leave the *Monmouth* . . .

God grant that I never see a sight like *Good Hope* was when she caught fire and blew up. Three times the *Monmouth* caught fire and got it under control and she must have been in an awful state before she was finally sunk but the pair of them never thought of giving in.[32]

Petty Officer S. G. Hobbs recorded:

After an hour's fighting the *GOOD HOPE* was practically stopped and when, just before our beam, a tremendous explosion occurred on board her, the flames reaching 200 ft . . . She was lost to view a few moments after and no doubt sank with all hands. . . . The *MONMOUTH* when last seen was down by the bow and turned towards the enemy, 75 flashes were counted half an hour later the enemy probably finishing her off. No survivors were saved.[33]

This was an inevitable and crushing German victory. When British officers were later able to debrief officers from *Gneisenau*, they discovered:

In the action off Valparaiso, the '*GNEISENAU*' fired 200 8in shell, and '*SCHARNHORST*' 400. The six inch guns were not used. 100 rounds of 8in were afterwards transferred to '*SCHARNHORST*' from '*GNEISENAU*' and at the commencement of the last action, there were 1100 rounds of 8in and 1000 rounds of 6in on board each ship.[34]

Good Hope and *Monmouth* had been blown to pieces in short order and at long range.

HMS *Canopus* and *Glasgow* headed for the Falkland Islands. They expected von Spee to capitalise on his victory and rapidly round Cape Horn and fall on the undefended settlement; *Canopus* was grounded to act as a fixed defensive position. Meanwhile decisive action was taken by the Admiralty under the newly-returned Fisher. The battlecruiser *Princess Royal* was despatched to cover the West Indies in case von Spee used the Panama Canal. The battlecruisers *Invincible* and *Inflexible*, under Sir Doveton Sturdee, were ordered south to the Falklands, leaving on 11 November. As a bonus, this enabled Fisher to get rid of Sturdee, his Chief of Staff at the Admiralty, whom he disliked and distrusted.[35] After a somewhat leisurely journey, Sturdee reached the Falklands on 7 December. With him, he had the cruisers *Carnarvon*, *Glasgow*, *Kent*, *Bristol* and *Cornwall* and the armed liner *Macedonia*. Fortunately for the British, von Spee had also been delayed, and only arrived off the Falklands on 8 December.

To his surprise, it was reported to von Spee that there were tripod masts in Port Stanley Harbour. This could only mean one thing – modern battlecruisers or battleships were present. Von Spee discounted the report and pressed on with his planned attack. It soon became painfully obvious that the discounted report was accurate and von Spee's squadron turned and ran. HMS *Kent* reported the events from her position at the mouth of Port Stanley harbour:

> I saw two cruisers steaming towards us, one big one with four funnels [*Scharnhorst*] and a smaller one with three funnels [*Nürnberg*) behind. Far away on the horizon I could see the smoke of three more cruisers approaching . . . The first two approached to within seven miles, just within gun range of me, then they must have caught sight of the *Invincible* and *Inflexible*, for they turned round and steamed away.[36]

Surviving German officers reported events on the *Gneisenau*:

> The presence of Battlecruisers was an undreamt-of possibility. The *GNEISENAU* and *NURNBERG* formed the advance squadron, and the Captain of the former would not believe his 1st Lieutenant's report that he could see 'two modern cruisers with tripod masts' and it was not till *CANOPUS* had fired twice that the captain was convinced . . . One of their officers on being brought on board of us asked 'who is this ship?', and on being told said '*INFLEXIBLE* you should be in the Mediterranean'.[37]

On a perfect day, the British ships set off in pursuit; the battlecruisers would deal with *Scharnhorst* and *Gneisenau* and the cruisers with the other ships; *Bristol* and *Macedonia* were detailed to deal with von Spee's supply ships. This kind of chase was what battlecruisers were designed for, to bring heavy guns to bear at high speed and long range. *Scharnhorst* and *Gneisenau* stood no chance and were rapidly sunk, only 176 men survived, von Spee and his two sons were not among them. It was as one-sided a contest as that fought at Coronel. HMS *Cornwall* reported:

> We pass under the sterns of the 'big ones' fighting their action, and it is like a football match, the whole of our ship's company (except of course the engine room brigade) assembled on the forecastle, cheering wildly every time their 12' guns went booming off.[38]

There is a contemporary account of the end of the *Gneisenau* as told by a German officer:

> The ship stopped firing and my Captain say to me, 'Why don't you fire?' I say 'Captain I cannot, I cannot speak to the guns'. The Captain then sent Lieutenant K —— (the 2nd gunnery officer) to look. He report that he cannot go round the ship, but that he can see all the guns and they are disabled or have no men. The fore turret is alright, but has only one round, there is ammunition below but it cannot come up.[39]

The captain ordered the ship scuttled. Of a crew of 780 men and 80 reservists, only about 300 were left alive at this point. Many more perished in the sea.

Of the German light cruiser actions, we have an eyewitness account of the sinking of *Nürnberg*. The chase was long and somewhat touch-and-go:

> I sent a message down to the engine room to do everything possible to increase speed . . . Then I got the sailors on deck to smash up all the wood they could find and pass it down to the stokeholds to put on the furnace – boats, accommodation ladder, hen-coops, lockers, capstan bars . . . Presently the old ship got a move on.[40]

Once battle was joined, however, HMS *Kent* soon overwhelmed *Nürnberg*:

> Then I crossed her bow and let her have it from all the starboard guns. I ordered 'Cease firing' and then tried to make out if her colours were still flying . . . as I got closer there was no mistake about it – there was a large German ensign flying at her peak. I gave the order to open fire again, keeping my glasses on the ensign. For five minutes all guns were firing on her and shell bursting all over her. Then I saw the ensign being lowered, and immediately ordered 'Cease firing'. Poor devils, I felt sorry for them.[41]

There was then the task of rescuing the Germans:

> It is near dusk now, 7.30 and we have been two hours in action. Up comes everyone from below, from casemates and turrets, to stare and rejoice, but they are all immediately hustled away to do what can be done to save life. All our boats are riddled, and none of them can be repaired for an hour. We do what we can with our life-buoys and lumps of wood paid astern, but it's mighty little, it's a loppy sea, and dreadfully cold. All this part was beastly.[42]

Only *Dresden* escaped from the long stern chase. She caused much worry, but was finally found by HMS *Glasgow*, HMS *Kent* and the armed liner *Orama* in the Juan Fernandez Islands in Chilean territorial waters. The British ships nonetheless attacked, as P.O. Hobbs recorded:

> At 9.10 at a distance of 8600 yards the *GLASGOW* opened fire followed immediately by *KENT* and *ORAMA* . . . our second salvo hit doing enormous damage, setting her on fire . . . 9.12 we opened fire for the second time . . . our shooting was excellent after two minutes 9.14 she hoisted a large white flag.[43]

After striking her colours *Dresden* was scuttled, despite the promise of her captain to take no such action. The captain of *Glasgow* apologised profusely (and no doubt entirely sincerely) to Chile for violating her neutrality. At a stroke, the remaining German threat in the Pacific was removed, and the German Pacific Squadron was prevented from entering the Atlantic to harass British trade with South America and the US.

There was now no surface threat to British trade anywhere other than in the North Sea; the major threat to the Royal Navy and to British trade now came from mines, but more particularly from submarines and torpedoes. The loss of the superdreadnought *Audacious* from striking a mine on 27 October had demonstrated the potency of the under-water threat, if any demonstration were needed.[44]

In the North Sea, the German High Seas Fleet was not idle. Its High Command wanted a fleet action with the Grand Fleet, provided that it could balance the disparity in numbers by engaging only a part of the Grand Fleet. A way of achieving this was to attack east coast towns in Britain hoping to draw out units of the Grand Fleet, while the whole of the High Seas Fleet was held in reserve ready to engage. The first raids fell on Lowestoft and Great Yarmouth on 3 November; very little damage was done, but attacking undefended towns did violate the rules of war and caused outrage in Britain.[45] The Grand Fleet had not engaged simply because it could not move units south quickly enough to engage the raiders before they withdrew. On 16 December, Whitby, Scarborough and Hartlepool were attacked. This time the damage was more severe with numerous casualties. The ensuing British propaganda posters record that seventy-eight women and children were killed and 228 women and children were injured; allowing for the inference that adult male casualties were expendable or at least, acceptable.[46]

On this occasion, forewarned by Room 40, the Commander-in-Chief of the Grand Fleet, Admiral Sir John Jellicoe, had sent the battlecruisers south together with a battle squadron commanded by Vice-Admiral Sir George Warrender, while Commodore Reginald Tyrwhitt's light cruisers had come north from Harwich. The Admiralty, however, did not know that the High Seas Fleet was also out. When the screening forces of the two fleets came into contact, Admiral Friedrich von Ingenohl, commanding the High Seas Fleet, turned for home, leaving his bombarding squadron to fend for itself. When the light screens of the British and German fleets clashed again, bungled signalling from Vice-Admiral Sir David Beatty's flagship (something of a *leitmotif* of Beatty's career as a fleet commander), led to the action being broken off and the British ships in contact with the enemy being recalled.

Several months earlier the first major naval engagement of the war had taken place, the Battle of Heligoland Bight on 28 August 1914. In this somewhat confused action, Commodore Roger Keyes, in command of the submarines of the Harwich Force, had suggested that his submarines lie on the surface in the Heligoland Bight and thus draw out the Germans towards Tyrwhitt's light forces which would also be in the area. The two Commodores requested support from the Grand Fleet to be on hand and, after some discussion, three battlecruisers were despatched together with

Commodore William Goodenough's 1st Light Cruiser Squadron. Jellicoe then followed on with four squadrons of the Grand Fleet. Tyrwhitt only became aware late in the day that Goodenough's ships were taking part and Keyes thought the only large British ships his submarines had to watch out for were HMS *Arethusa* and HMS *Fearless*; any other big ships would be German.

As the German and British forces engaged, a confused melee ensued. The Germans fed reinforcements into the battle, but their big ships could not get out, due to the state of the tide.[47] The Germans lost the destroyer *V-187* and the cruiser SMS *Mainz*. The end of *Mainz* is vividly documented in the account of Lt-Cdr Andrew Davies of HMS *Birmingham*:

> Meanwhile it was awful to see the effects of our shell on her. Great clouds of smoke and a flash & the third funnel was blown over. Then a hit on the broadside . . . a colossal column of smoke shot up about amidships, quite twice as high as her masts. I think a boiler must have burst . . . All of this time there were 3 of us *Southampton*, ourselves and *Falmouth* firing at her . . . Poor devils they must all have been lunatics by that time . . . Then we close to about 4000 (yards) and I fired a salvo & one or more shells hit just under the bridge, probably on the Conning Tower. The effect was awful, the whole fore bridge went up in a tremendous cloud of black smoke and white flame, men and iron thrown sky high. It was terrible to look at . . . The carnage was horrible to look at, all around the guns were heaps of dismembered bodies . . .[48]

At this point the battle was swinging away from the British when Beatty intervened with five battlecruisers, at high speed and across a minefield. The Germans were now totally out-gunned; in total they lost three light cruisers and a destroyer with three more light cruisers damaged. They lost 1,242 casualties to the Royal Navy's seventy-five. Despite these figures, this was not an impressive show. There had been muddle over what forces to deploy, poor communication in letting commanders know what forces were being deployed and where, offset by good luck in that none of the British ships sank any units on their own side! What the public perceived, was a spectacular and dashing victory. It would take the Battles of the Dogger Bank and Jutland to demonstrate that dash was not enough.

The final engagement of the Royal Navy's first six months of the war, the Battle of Dogger Bank, took place on 24 January 1915.[49] The German Commander in Chief, von Ingenohl, had allowed Admiral Franz von Hipper to reconnoitre the Dogger Bank with his battlecruisers and SMS *Blücher*, a large armoured cruiser. Room 40 had intercepted the signals setting up this plan and a trap was laid. Beatty's battlecruisers and Goodenough's light cruisers were despatched south, Tyrwhitt's light cruisers and destroyers came out from Harwich to rendezvous with the 3rd Battle Squadron made up of eight pre-dreadnoughts. Three ships of the 3rd Cruiser Squadron were also at hand. The plan proceeded flawlessly and Beatty made contact with the Germans. His ships, in the order, *Lion, Tiger, Princess Royal, New Zealand* and *Indomitable*, chased the German ships which made off as fast as they were able, in the order, from the rear, *Blücher, Moltke, Seydlitz* and *Derflinger*.[50] Here the plan unravelled. Beatty was controlling his forces using signal flags; it was important that his ships should engage every German ship both to damage the Germans and prevent them engaging him without harassment. His signals were ambiguous and as the battle proceeded his forces contrived to direct their fire on *Blücher* in the rear of the German squadron, leaving the rest of the German forces relatively unengaged. As events unfolded the German ships concentrated their fire on Beatty's flagship, *Lion*, which was so severely damaged it could not continue in the battle. Beatty shifted his flag, but by the time he could take command again, the Germans had fled, *Blücher* was finished and *Lion* was so badly damaged she had to be escorted back to Rosyth. The brief report from Lt-Cdr MacKinnon, gunnery officer of the battlecruiser *Indomitable*, records events slipping out of control:

At about 11.10 *Lion* hauled out of line, & the *Tiger* & *Princess Royal* continued in action against the leading ships, but shortly after the *New Zealand* altered course across our bows joined in the firing at the *Bleucher* [*sic*] followed a few minutes afterwards by the *Princess Royal* . . .[51]

By then *Blücher* had already taken a terrible beating, as reported from HMS *Indomitable*:

At 10.30 the *Bleucher* [*sic*]was again badly on fire, & we had closed in on her appreciably; at 10.35 the Captain told me to try a shot & so I ordered 'A' turret to fire at extreme elevation but the shot fell a long way short. At 10.45 'A' turret fired again & from then on we were firing at the *Bleucher* [*sic*], having been ordered to finish her off.[52]

However, she continued to resist for another hour and a half:

At 11.50 we ceased firing & the Destroyers closed in to save life. At 12.00 a torpedo passed about 30 yards ahead of us, obviously a parting shot from the *Bleucher* [*sic*]. At about 12.5 the *Bleucher* [*sic*] heeled over badly to Starboard & blew up & sank.

During the last ten minutes or so of the action we could see a number of men collected on the Quarter Deck, & it was a fearsome thought that these poor devils had the cold sea waiting for them outside the ship, a raging fire amidships, & also our shots bursting all around them. One man was seen to rush out on the Forecastle & whilst storming up & down was shaking his fists at us – however a shot bursting on the Forecastle put an end to his troubles.[53]

This was a victory of a kind but showed up painfully Beatty's flaws in handling a fleet: too much dash, too little training and too little cold calculation.

As the first six months of the war came to a close, the Navy had every reason to be pleased with its performance to date. Coronel had been a debacle, and the loss of *Cressy*, *Aboukir* and *Hogue* nothing short of fatuous, but every war has its fair share of the ill-considered and the fatuous. Of the four major battles fought – Heligoland Bight, Dogger Bank, Coronel and the Falklands, three had gone in the Royal Navy's favour, and because of the victory at the Falklands, the defeat at Coronel had no long-term adverse consequences.

Strategically the Navy had closed down the World War: British trade and forces flowed freely across the world's oceans without hindrance. The North Sea was the only arena for warfare between British and German surface naval forces, although the threat of the U-Boat remained a worrying factor. The blockade of Germany properly applied would eventually throttle her. British forces and supplies meanwhile flowed remorselessly across the Channel. What could possibly threaten Britain's naval might? What was to stop her winning the war as long as her military forces in Belgium and France avoided defeat? In fact, so it turned out. Despite the alarms of Gallipoli, the nail-biting Battle of Jutland, the anxious months it took in 1917 to devise means to neutralise the U-Boat threat in the North Atlantic to the British material capacity to wage the war, the Royal Navy ground down the German economy. This was a different type of naval warfare. There was no single crushing victory, but this was total war with the same Nelsonian goal of total victory. And after all, Germany lost her entire fleet, what could be more total? The pattern was set in the first six months, and relentlessly delivered across another four years of war.

In the preparation of this chapter I would like to thank my colleague, Matthew Sheldon, for his assistance in locating archival sources at the National Museum of the Royal Navy. Additionally, Captain David Bailey RN, made a timely donation to the museum of documents bearing on the first six months of the war. The scholarship of my colleague, Dr Duncan Redford, and that of Dr Mike Farquharson-Roberts, has also helped me immeasurably through their outstanding accounts of this period of naval history, and I would like to acknowledge my debt to them too.

Notes

1. M. Farquharson-Roberts, *A History of the Royal Navy: World War 1* (London and New York: I B Tauris, 2014), p. 49.
2. The gun belongs to the Imperial War Museum and is displayed at the National Museum of the Royal Navy, Portsmouth, where it is on long loan.
3. The best account of the technological change which overtook the Navy in the late nineteenth and early twentieth centuries is D. K. Brown, *Warrior to Dreadnought, Warship Design and Development 1860-1906* (Barnsley: Pen and Sword Books, 1997), and D. K. Brown, *The*

Grand Fleet, Warship Design and Development 1906-1922 (Barnsley: Pen and Sword Books, 1997).

4. An account of Fisher's work is provided by Nicholas A. Lambert, *Sir John Fisher's Naval Revolution* (Columbia: 2001).

5. D. K. Brown, *Warrior to Dreadnought*, p. 24.

6. Ibid, pp. 191–3.

7. Ibid, p. 14, n. 1.

8. For a more detailed account see D. K. Brown, *Warrior to Dreadnought*, pp. 180–2 and D. K. Brown, *The Grand Fleet*, pp. 46–7.

9. *Holland 1* is on display at the Royal Navy Submarine Museum, Gosport, a part of the National Museum of the Royal Navy.

10. D. Redford and P. D. Grove, *The Royal Navy, A History Since 1900* (London and New York: I B Tauris, 2014), pp. 15–16; D. K. Brown, *The Grand Fleet*, Chapters 6 and 9.

11. Redford and Grove, *The Royal Navy, A History Since 1900*, pp. 17–18. The topic will be covered more fully in B. Jones, *A History of the Royal Navy: Air Power and British Naval Aviation* (London and New York) forthcoming. See also D. K. Brown, *The Grand Fleet*, pp. 74–7

12. Farquharson-Roberts, *A History of the Royal Navy: World War 1*, pp. 28–31; Redford and Grove, *The Royal Navy, A History Since 1900*, pp. 16–17. A radio room of the period is on display at the National Museum of the Royal Navy in Portsmouth

13. Redford and Grove, *The Royal Navy, A History Since 1900*, pp. 25–6.

14. Ibid, pp. 10–12.

15. The topic is covered *in extenso* in Viscount Jellicoe of Scapa, *The Crisis of the Naval War* (London: New York, Toronto and Melbourne: 1920), pp. 1–31. Farquharson-Roberts, *A History of the Royal Navy: World War 1*, pp. 27–8.

16. Farquharson-Roberts, *A History of the Royal Navy: World War 1*, p. 30; H. Cleland Hoy, *O.B., or How the War Was Won* (London: 1932).

17. Farquharson-Roberts, *A History of the Royal Navy: World War 1*, pp. 229–30. see also D. K. Brown, *The Grand Fleet*, pp. 31–3.

18. Jellicoe, *The Crisis of the Naval War*, p. 231.

19. Redford and Grove, *The Royal Navy, A History Since 1900*, p. 33. To be fair, the idea of close blockade was not one espoused by Fisher, his successor was perhaps less thoughtful.

20. R. K. Massie, *Castles of Steel, Britain, Germany, and the winning of the Great War at Sea* (London: Ballantine Books, 2004), p. 681.

21. See Dr D G Morgan Owen, PhD research thesis, Exeter University, 2013.

22. Redford and Grove, *The Royal Navy, A History Since 1900*, p. 40.

23. Ibid, pp. 47–8.

24. See Nicholas A. Lambert, *Planning Armageddon: British Economic Warfare and the First World War* (Cambridge, MA: 2012).

25, Farquharson-Roberts draws a parallel with the River Plate action, *A History of the Royal Navy: World War 1*, p. 47.

26. A good modern account of the Pacific naval war is Farquharson-Roberts, *A History of the Royal Navy: World War 1*, pp. 53–61, for the *Emden* pp. 53–4.

27. Bailey papers. *The Sinking of the Königsberg*. A typescript report by the commanding officer, HMS *Mersey*, with manuscript annotated plan. National Museum of the Royal Navy Portsmouth.

28. Ibid.

29. Ibid.

30. The words are Churchill's: Farquharson-Roberts, *A History of the Royal Navy: World War 1*, p. 57.

31. Ibid, pp. 54–8.

32. National Museum of the Royal Navy, Portsmouth, item 1998/61.

33. National Museum of the Royal Navy, Portsmouth, unnumbered item.

34. Bailey Papers. *Report on the Gunnery of SMS Gneisenau*. A typescript report based on interviews with officers surviving from SMS *Gneisenau*. National Museum of the Royal Navy, Portsmouth.
35. He had been responsible for the deployment of *Aboukir*, *Cressy* and *Hogue* which arguably led to their sinking
36. Bailey Papers. *Account of the Battle of the Falkland Islands*. A typescript report by an officer on HMS *Kent*. National Museum of the Royal Navy, Portsmouth.
37. Bailey Papers. *Report on the Gunnery of SMS Gneisenau*.
38. Bailey Papers. *Account of the Battle of the Falkland Islands*.
39. Ibid.
40. Letter from the Commanding Officer of HMS *Kent* to his wife. Original held in the National Museum of the Royal Navy, Portsmouth. A printed copy is also preserved which seem to have had wider circulation
41. Ibid.
42. Bailey Papers. *Account of the Battle of the Falkland Islands*.
43. Diary of P.O Hobbs, HMS *Glasgow*. Privately printed. Copy in the National Museum of the Royal Navy, Portsmouth.
44. Redford and Grove, *The Royal Navy, A History Since 1900*, p. 46, fig. 2.2.
45. Farquharson-Roberts, *A History of the Royal Navy: World War 1*, p. 62.
46. Ibid., pp. 63–4, fig. 3.9.
47. Ibid., pp. 49–52, fig 3.4.
48. National Museum of the Royal Navy, Portsmouth.
49. Farquharson-Roberts, *A History of the Royal Navy: World War 1* 64-69, figs. 3.10 and 11
50. Bailey Papers. *The Battle of the Dogger Bank*. Typescript report by Lt-Cdr MacKinnon, HMS *Indomitable*. National Museum of the Royal Navy, Portsmouth
51. Ibid.
52. Ibid.
53. Ibid.

Suggested Further Reading

Farquharson-Roberts, M., *A History of the Royal Navy in World War 1* (London and New York: I B Tauris, 2014).
Redford, D., and Grove, P. D., *The Royal Navy, a History since 1900* (London and New York: I B Tauris, 2014).

Chapter 6

True Grit: Officers of the British Expeditionary Force and the Great Retreat, 1914

* * *

Spencer Jones

In 1914, Great Britain committed her military to the continent of Europe for the first time in just under a century. The army that went to France was known as the British Expeditionary Force (BEF) and was, in the words of the Official Historian Sir James Edmonds, 'incomparably the best trained, best organized and best equipped British Army which ever went forth to war'.[1] Captain Richard Meinertzhagen noted in his diary at the outbreak of the conflict that the BEF was 'terribly small, but a mighty weapon, for every soldier can shoot and every man is determined to fight . . . the Germans will soon find that out'.[2] The army needed all of its skills in 1914 as it was thrust into some of the most ferocious fighting of the entire First World War.

In August and September, the BEF unwittingly found itself facing the main thrust of the German invasion of Belgium and France. Substantially outnumbered, with its flanks exposed and with the French army seemingly in disarray, the BEF was in grave danger of encirclement and destruction. Its only option was to withdraw. The Great Retreat that followed was a gruelling march of approximately 200 miles, undertaken in heatwave conditions, with German pursuit in close proximity. Ultimately, the manoeuvre was a success. In early September, French commander, Joseph Joffre, hurled his forces into a counter-attack at the Battle of the Marne and turned the tide of the war. The BEF played a small but important part in this massive Franco-German clash which flung the invaders back to the line of the River Aisne. However, the Germans could not be moved from this defensive position, repelling British attacks at the Battle of the Aisne (13–15 September).

A relative lull followed as the armies settled into trenches and eyed one another across no-man's land. However, in October, the BEF redeployed to Flanders in an effort to turn the German flank and advance to assist the beleaguered Belgians at Antwerp. But the Allied advance stalled as the Germans launched a major offensive that aimed to capture the city of Ypres and surge onwards to the Channel coast. For just over a month the two armies were locked in ferocious combat as the Allies sought to resist the sheer weight of German attacks. Although the line buckled on several occasions, it ultimately held fast. By the time the fighting came to a close in mid-November, the Germans had been decisively defeated. The attackers' losses were so severe that Germany abandoned all hope of achieving victory on the Western Front in 1915.[3] Yet, although victorious, the cost to the BEF had been great. By the end of November, the army had suffered around 89,000 casualties from a total pre-war strength of approximately 250,000 men.[4] Indeed, the Battle of Ypres was proportionately the costliest battle fought by the British Army in the entire First World War.[5]

Although outnumbered and outgunned throughout the campaign, the training, tactics and sheer tenacity of the BEF had played an important part in Allied victory. The fighting reputation of the BEF has remained high for a century, although recent revisionism has raised certain questions about its battlefield performance.[6] However, whilst frequently justified, the praise heaped upon the officers and men of the British Army can distort perceptions of the fighting. Victory was by no means pre-ordained and the risk of complete destruction was very real.

Indeed, contemporary officers were relatively cautious in their assessment of the campaign. For example, Sir James Edmonds's description of the Great Retreat is comparatively cool and detached. He believed the withdrawal was 'in every way honourable to the Army' and applauded the discipline and morale of the soldiers.[7] The account stood in contrast to the retrospective of the First Battle of Ypres contained in the second volume, which praised the army for its tenacity and role in the Allied victory. However, an undercurrent of criticism directed against General Headquarters (GHQ) runs throughout both of the 1914 volumes of the *Official History*.[8] There is the sense that operations were mismanaged at the highest levels, and that the BEF's eventual success owed more to its training and tenacity than its commanders.[9] The clearest expression of this idea came from Thomas Snow, who had commanded 4th Division in 1914. Soon after the war he sent an account of the Great Retreat to Edmonds, noting 'I feel convinced that in some fifty years' time students of Military History will have begun to realise that the Retreat of 1914 was not what it has always been made out to be, an episode to be proud of.'[10] A slightly different account in Snow's private papers offered a similar assessment: 'I feel sure that that the day will come when the student of Military History discovers that the retreat of 1914, was not, as is now imagined, a great military achievement, but was a badly bungled affair only prevented from being a disaster of the first magnitude by the grit displayed by the officers and men.'[11]

This chapter will look at the performance of British officers on the campaign in greater detail and examine the nature of the 'grit' praised by Snow. The pace of the campaign and the intensity of the fighting made it difficult for any senior officer, be they British, French or German, to exercise effective overall control of an engagement. With the intentions of higher command frequently rendered irrelevant by the rapid pace of events at the front, much of the fighting devolved into 'soldier's battles' where the decision-making of subordinates and junior officers was paramount. As will be seen, the BEF's unique combination of experience, training and ethos, contributed to a particularly effective class of junior officers who would play a vital role in the ferocious combat of 1914.

* * *

On the eve of the First World War, the British Army was noticeably different in outlook and role from the vast conscript armies of the Continent. It was a small, all-volunteer force that took particular pride in long-held regimental traditions. Furthermore, its duties were quite unlike those of the armies of France, Germany, Russia and Austro-Hungary, who eyed one another warily across their respective borders and planned their campaigns against one another in minute detail. Although the British Army certainly gave thought to a war in Europe, necessarily it had to remain conscious of its role in defence of imperial obligations. This was no simple task. The imperial frontiers were a constant source of danger and low-intensity conflict. Indeed, in the reign of Queen Victoria (1837–1901) the British Army had been involved in a staggering 230 colonial wars.[12] The vast majority of these struggles ended in decisive British victories, but as contemporary army reformer Leo Amery observed: 'These wars against savages were by no means the child's play that foreign critics have often asserted.'[13] The dangers of colonial warfare were brutally illustrated by the notorious British defeats at Isandlwana (1879), Maiwand (1880) and Majuba Hill (1881), whilst the Italian disaster at the Battle of Adowa (1896) served as a stark warning of the cost of arrogance and complacency on campaign.

The sheer frequency of British colonial campaigns meant that the army's officer class was by far the most combat-hardened of any of the major European armies.[14] This served a valuable function. As Colonel W. N. Nicholson wrote after the First World War:

It is not possible in peace to gauge with certainty the war time qualities of any officer. Those whom we expect will succeed as commanders are not always a success; while some seemingly indifferent peace time soldiers do magnificently. Even courage, the primary virtue in a soldier, cannot be assessed with certainty. Unimaginative courage that goes baldheaded may balk from ignorance; while the imaginative man may find danger a stimulant or a paralysis.[15]

By virtue of educating a large proportion of its officers in the hard school of colonial warfare, the British Army alleviated many of the problems described by

Nicholson. Failure on imperial campaigns was frequently fatal to the career of a young officer. For example, in the Boer War (1899–1902), officers adjudged to have blundered in battle were sent far from the action to the town of Stellenbosch in the Western Cape, a much feared punishment known as 'Stellenbosching'. Few recovered from this humiliation.

Yet, although the army was ruthless with failure, it also rewarded success. Performing well in a small action boosted an officer's career prospects and brought him to the notice of his peers. More practically, it taught the young officer much about the realities of combat and the attributes required of a leader in battle. The skills of quick decision-making, personal initiative and retaining composure under fire would prove to be as valuable in 1914 as they were in earlier colonial clashes.

In 1914, the officers of the BEF possessed a vast fund of combat experience. Out of 157 infantry battalions, 138 were commanded by officers who had been on active service.[16] At both divisional and corps level, each formation was commanded by an officer who had seen action, with many of them having excelled in earlier conflicts.[17] Douglas Haig, commanding I Corps, had been unlucky not to be nominated for a Victoria Cross in 1898.[18] Horace Smith-Dorrien, commanding II Corps, had an astoundingly varied combat record. He had been one of just five officers to survive the disaster at Isandlwana and had subsequently fought in Egypt, India, Sudan and South Africa.[19] The senior staff officers of the army, Chief of Staff Archibald Murray and Sub-Chief of Staff Henry Wilson, both carried scars that served as a reminder of the dangers of frontier warfare; Murray had been shot in the stomach in the Boer War and was still troubled by the wound, whilst Wilson had a prominent facial scar as a result of a machete blow suffered during hand-to-hand combat in Burma.[20] At the very head of the army, Commander-in-Chief Field Marshal Sir John French had secured his reputation with his daring handling of the Cavalry Division in the Boer War. Indeed, it is often overlooked that of the senior commanders of all nationalities on the Western Front in 1914, French had the most battlefield experience and had commanded the largest formation in action.

Beyond providing proof of individual courage and competence, service in colonial wars had the important effect of providing a shared pool of experience. A large proportion of the officers of the BEF had served in the Boer War, a conflict where the British Army was forced to engage a tenacious, well-armed enemy in uniquely difficult terrain. Although ultimately victorious, the hard lessons learned in this war resulted in widespread tactical and organisational reform.[21] The shared experience of this major conflict encouraged trust in fellow veteran officers and, by virtue of a common ethos, precluded the need for a complex written doctrine.[22] The training manuals that emerged after the Boer War were concise, simple and reflected the fact they were aimed at a combat-hardened officer class. *Combined Training* and its successor *Field Service Regulations* were understated works that emphasised the need to avoid stereotypical tactics. Instead they emphasised flexibility, a respect for enemy firepower and the importance of individual initiative. *Field Service Regulations* took the important step of codifying the authority of the 'man on the spot', giving junior officers permission to disregard orders from higher authority if they felt it did not reflect the situation on the ground.[23] Inevitably, there were some officers who struggled to meet the required standards.[24] Yet overall, the combination of combat experience, solidified through thorough training, provided the BEF with a strong backbone of leaders. The 'grit' praised by Thomas Snow emanated from this group of core officers.

But learning from colonial warfare had its limits. The nature of these conflicts, which often took place in areas of wilderness far from British bases, inevitably limited the size of the armies engaged. Even the largest pitched battles of the Boer War, such as Paardeberg (18–27 February 1900) and Tugela Heights (14–27 February 1900), involved no more than 20,000 British soldiers – numbers comparable in strength to a single infantry division of 1914. Colonial warfare therefore provided little guidance on the handling of large bodies of troops. Unfortunately, this problem was exacerbated by a serious weakness with British peacetime training that would, in turn, have a baleful effect in the opening weeks of the First World War. This was the relative absence of what may be termed 'command level' manoeuvres: exercises designed to provide senior commanders with experience of commanding reasonably large forces, usually of divisional size or above.[25]

Large-scale annual manoeuvres were a relative novelty in the British Army of the time, having only been reintroduced in 1898.[26] Although well-intentioned, the scope and the scale of the exercises were greatly constrained by lack of suitable ground upon which to train, lack of funds to ensure the manoeuvres were conducted with units at full strength, and simple lack of experience in organising and umpiring these types of events.[27] The work that was carried out had some benefit but the learning was uneven. Contemporary reports from the Inspector General of Forces sounded a note of caution. In 1910, the report noted that he could 'not discover that any appreciable progress is apparent in the higher leading of the troops', further stating: 'Commanders of the higher units in writing their appreciations [of manoeuvres] seldom seemed to be imbued with that instinctive knowledge and perception of strategic principles which can only be acquired by the closest study and thought.'[28] The problem was raised once more in 1911, with the report commenting:

I can only once more express my earnest conviction that no stone should be left unturned to afford our higher leaders the utmost opportunity to acquire the requisite knowledge, and that no general or other officer should be allowed to retain his command who shows any lack of the most necessary qualifications.[29]

But, constrained by the immutable problems of lack of space and shortage of funds, there was relatively little the army could do to address the problems. Thomas Snow

HM King George V. (Library of Congress, Harris and Ewing Collection)

Kaiser Wilhelm II of Germany, in Russian military uniform on the left and Tsar Nicholas II of Russia on the right, in German military uniform, 1905. (Library of Congress, George Grantham Bain Collection)

Emperor Franz Josef of the Dual Monarchy, Austria and Hungary. (Library of Congress)

British Prime Minister at the outbreak of war, the Rt. Hon. H. H. Asquith MP. (Library of Congress, George Grantham Bain Collection)

British Foreign Secretary at the outbreak of war, the Rt. Hon. Sir Edward Grey, MP. (Library of Congress, Harris and Ewing Collection)

German Chancellor at the outbreak of war, Theobald von Bethmann-Hollweg. (Library of Congress, George Grantham Bain Collection)

General Count Franz Conrad von Hotzendorf, Austrian Chief of Staff during the crisis in June–August 1914. (Library of Congress, Harris and Ewing Collection)

The Rt. Hon. Winston S. Churchill, MP, British First Lord of the Admiralty at the outbreak of war. (Library of Congress, George Grantham Bain Collection, photograph dated 1908)

The Rt. Hon. David Lloyd George, MP, Chancellor of the Exchequer at the outbreak of war. (Library of Congress, George Grantham Bain Collection)

Field Marshal Lord Kitchener, brought into the British War Council as Secretary of State for War by the Prime Minister at the outbreak of war. (Library of Congress, George Grantham Bain Collection)

Admiral of the Fleet Sir John Fisher, 1st Sea Lord, 1904–10, responsible for the construction of the *Dreadnought* and general modernisation of the Royal Navy, and, having retired in 1910 at the age of 70, recalled as 1st Sea Lord in November 1914. (Library of Congress, George Grantham Bain Collection)

Lord Haldane, Secretary of State for War, 1905–12, the man responsible, with others, for pre-war reform of the British Army. Raised to the Peerage as Viscount Haldane in 1911, he was Lord Chancellor at the time of the July 1914 Crisis. The photograph shows him in the back seat of a car with General Clarence Page Townsley, commander of West Point, during Haldane's visit to the U.S. Military Academy, West Point, New York State, 30 August 1913. (Library of Congress, George Grantham Bain Collection)

Sergei Sazonov, Russian Foreign Minister at the outbreak of war. (Wikimedia Commons)

Nikola Pašić, Prime Minister of Serbia at the outbreak of war. (Wikimedia Commons)

The Rt. Hon. John Redmond, MP, Irish Nationalist politician. (PD, UK, unknown)

The Rt. Hon. Sir Edward Carson, Irish Unionist politician, inspecting men of the Ulster Volunteer Force. (The Irish Volunteers Commemorative Society)

The Mayor of Richmond reads out the 'Declaration of War' in Richmond Market Place on 5 August 1914, followed by the playing of the National Anthem, at which soldiers from the Green Howards Depot present arms. (Museum of the Green Howards, Richmond, North Yorkshire)

Recruitment poster for the Green Howards in Scarborough. (Museum of the Green Howards, Richmond, North Yorkshire)

The foundering of HMS *Aboukir*, 22 September 1914, gouache, by Charles Dixon. (National Museum of the Royal Navy)

The wounded *Lion*, oils, by W. I. Wylie. HMS *Lion* was severely damaged at the Battle of Dogger Bank, 24 January 1915. This painting of her was commissioned by Earl Beatty and shows her approaching Rosyth. Having been patched up there, she was repaired fully in Newcastle. (Courtesy of Nicholas Beatty, temporarily on loan to the National Museum of the Royal Navy)

SMS *Königsberg* grounded in the Rufiji River following shelling by the monitors, HMS *Severn* and HMS *Mersey*, 11 July 1915. (National Museum of the Royal Navy)

Field Marshal Sir John French. (Spencer Jones)

An artist's impression of a British rearguard in August 1914. (Spencer Jones)

A crowd of volunteers waiting to enlist at the Central London Recruiting Depot, Great Scotland Yard, in 1914. (IWM Q 81797)

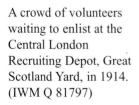

Recruits of the Sheffield City Battalion (12th Yorks and Lancaster Regiment) drilling at Bramall Lane, Sheffield, September 1914. (IWM HU 37016)

The railway bridge at Nimy, held on 23 August 1914 by Private Sidney Frank Godley. (Matthew Richardson)

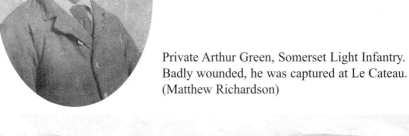

Private Arthur Green, Somerset Light Infantry. Badly wounded, he was captured at Le Cateau. (Matthew Richardson)

German soldiers sweep across a French cornfield in August 1914, a sight which must have been experienced by those at Le Cateau. (Matthew Richardson)

An aerial view of the Ypres battlefield as it appeared in 1914. (Matthew Richardson)

Captain Mark Haggard, 2nd Battalion Welsh Regiment, killed at the Battle of the Aisne. (Matthew Richardson)

The German writer, Paul Oskar Hocker, a captain in a reserve regiment. (Matthew Richardson)

Gheluvelt village in 1914. (Matthew Richardson)

complained after the war: 'We had none of us [*sic*] the practice in handling such large bodies of troops, and the restrictions placed on the manoeuvre of troops in England had taught me many false lessons.'[30] Therefore, although Sir John French had the most combat experience of any commander on the Western Front in 1914, he also had the least experience of pre-war manoeuvres.

The BEF of 1914 was thus an army of certain contrasts. It had a battle-hardened officer class who drew upon a common ethos of personal courage and initiative that would prove of great value in the chaotic fighting that was to follow. They embodied the skills of leadership as expressed by Sir Michael Howard:

> Leadership is the capacity to inspire and motivate; to persuade people willingly to ensure hardships, usually prolonged, and incur dangers, usually acute, that if left to themselves they would do their utmost to avoid. It is essential at the lower levels of command, where danger and hardship are at their greatest, but the need for it does not diminish at higher levels.[31]

Yet, at the same time, the officers of the BEF had relatively little experience of handling large formations and the problems that this entailed. In this sense the skills of leadership were not matched by a thorough understanding of what John Pimlott has termed 'the management of command', defined as 'the assessment and dissemination of information needed to direct military force'.[32] This inexperience would prove dangerous and sometimes costly in 1914. It would be up to, in Snow's words, 'the grit of the officers and men' to see the army through the campaign.

* * *

At the outbreak of the conflict, the Secretary of State for War, Lord Kitchener, was cautious about deploying the army. He anticipated a long, costly struggle and was wary about wasting the highly-trained manpower of the BEF in the opening weeks of the war. His concerns were embodied in his instructions to Sir John French at the outset of the campaign, which stated:

> . . . while every effort must be made to coincide most sympathetically with the plans and wishes of our Ally, the gravest consideration will devolve upon you as to participation in forward movements where large bodies of French troops are not engaged and where your force may be unduly exposed to attack . . . In minor operations you should be careful that your subordinates understand that risk of serious losses should only be taken where such risk is authoritatively considered to be commensurate with the object in view.[33]

These orders required the British commander-in-chief to walk a tightrope between honouring the needs of the French whilst simultaneously retaining an independent role that stressed the need to avoid casualties. These conflicting duties would have been onerous at the best of times, but in 1914 they proved almost impossible. Against pre-war expectations, the BEF found itself involved in a life-or-death struggle against the main thrust of the German invasion. Its opponent, for the early part of the campaign, would be Alexander von Kluck's First Army, which outnumbered Sir John's force by more than three to one. Compounding the danger, and greatly increasing the risk of encirclement, was the fact that relations with the French were at best frosty and at worst adversarial.[34] Initially, little information was shared between the two armies and when cooperation did occur it tended to be local.

The combination of the vast weight of the German attack and the lack of firm links with the French, immediately took the initiative from the BEF and robbed Sir John of his freedom of action. His army was too small to maintain an independent role without being annihilated and thus he was forced to conform with French movements, although this was a confusing process given the lack of cooperation between the two forces.

The situation required cool heads and steely determination, attributes described by the army of the day with a single word – 'grip'. Unfortunately, British commanders struggled to meet the challenges. Indeed, the great problem of the campaign, and the factor that made it the 'badly bungled affair' of Snow's recollection, was the dislocation of British command organisation. This was most apparent at GHQ. Sir John had gone to war with the unusual arrangement of having two chiefs of staff. The men selected for these posts, Murray and Wilson, were strikingly dissimilar and, while there might have been hope that the contrast would produce sparks of imagination, it only resulted in friction and disarray. Hampered by lack of experience and under immense pressure from the pace and ferocity of the campaign, GHQ came close to collapse. An exhausted Murray suffered a physical breakdown on 26 August and at the same time Wilson's morale plummeted to the point that he considered the BEF to be beaten.[35] Both men recovered but GHQ remained disorganised and prone to sudden alarm throughout the weeks that followed.[36] Given the problems apparent at GHQ, Sir John French can perhaps be forgiven for his erratic conduct of the campaign.[37] Nevertheless, his peculiar decision to absent himself on the eve of the Battle of Mons, his failure to manage the retreat during its critical moments and his lack of drive at the Battle of the Marne and the Battle of the Aisne, all combine to paint an unflattering portrait of the commander-in-chief.

The problems of organisation were not unique to GHQ. The BEF's Cavalry Division had not been permanently constituted in peacetime and its staff was hastily assembled on the outbreak of war. Some impression of this process may be gained by the fact that its commander, Edmund Allenby, recruited his chief of intelligence, the highly able George Barrow, through a chance meeting in a War Office corridor.[38] However, this scratch staff proved unable to handle the over-strength division, which consisted of four brigades rather than the more usual three.[39] By 26 August, a combination of the friction of war, the breakdown of communications and the controversial actions of the disobedient Hubert Gough, commanding 3rd Cavalry Brigade, had caused the division to splinter into its component parts. The failure to train the division as a whole in peacetime had reaped its deleterious rewards in war.[40]

Despite these difficulties, the BEF survived and ultimately succeeded in 1914. Several factors contributed to this result. First, as Sir Michael Howard has noted, the mistakes of commanders can sometimes be remedied by the quality of their soldiers: 'Like well trained horses, they can carry even indifferent and incompetent riders.'[41] A comparatively small proportion of the men of the BEF had combat experience but their training and the iron bonds of regimental loyalty contributed to a stoic endurance of the trials of the Great Retreat. This was greatly complemented by the leadership of their immediate officers. C. R. Ballard, who had served as a staff officer in 1914, recalled that the relatively successful engagements at Mons and Le Cateau 'led to mutual confidence between officers and men; officers knew that any order would be obeyed without hesitation; men had none of the feeling that someone had blundered'.[42] Nevertheless, Ballard admitted that the efforts involved meant that 'the battalions did not look pretty, and the march discipline appeared to be so bad'.[43] Straggling was endemic, particularly amongst the recently-recalled reservists who lacked the fitness of their regular comrades. Many reservists were also hampered by newly-issued boots which inflicted agonising blisters. It was in these circumstances that the powers of the junior officer and NCO were put to the test. Captain Tudor St. John of the Northumberland Fusiliers remembered being disgusted by the sight of dejected men at the roadside:

> This was not to happen in the ranks of the FIFTH. March discipline was maintained by the unfailing efforts of the officers and N.C.O.s, urging and persuading their men on and when needs be, kicking them and pulling them up, to continue the march when they sank to the ground exhausted.[44]

Battalions took pride in retaining their composure during this trying time. Major George 'Ma' Jeffreys of the Grenadier Guards noted with satisfaction that his battalion did not lose a single man through straggling, although he took delight in recording the apparently sloppy march discipline of the nearby Coldstream Guards![45] The full extent of straggling is difficult to gauge. Casualty figures for August and September 1914 are unreliable as paperwork was, understandably, poorly kept during the retreat. Undoubtedly a proportion of men, too exhausted to keep moving, fell into German captivity. Nevertheless, the BEF as a whole kept moving, largely driven on by the combination of tenacity of the soldiers and the unsung work of company and battalion officers.

The one occasion when this system failed is worthy of mention here as an illustration of what might have been, had the 'grit' of the British Army failed. On

27 August, Lieutenant Colonel A. E. Mainwaring, 2nd Royal Dublin Fusiliers, and Lieutenant Colonel J. F. Elkington, 1st Royal Warwickshires, were persuaded by the mayor of St. Quentin to sign a document that surrendered both their battalions.[46] The officers had lost contact with their brigade and their battalions were hopelessly jumbled following the Battle of Le Cateau. Mainwaring was a sick man and should never have travelled to France, and Elkington had simply reached such a point of physical and mental exhaustion that his resolve failed him. Ultimately, the timely arrival of Major Tom Bridges, 4th Dragoon Guards, saved the day. Bridges learned of the surrender document and resolved to circumvent it by rallying the men through the improvisation of a marching band using instruments acquired from a nearby toyshop.[47] This inventive method worked and both battalions marched south rather than into German captivity. The incident, although atypical, provides a stark illustration of what might have befallen the BEF if discipline were to have given way.

Senior commanders also played their part in sustaining the BEF on the retreat. The force was sufficiently small that it was possible, in the terminology of the day, 'to get around the army' and speak with the soldiers. Although Sir John French has been criticised for abnegating his role as a battlefield commander,[48] his efforts to sustain the morale of his army are often neglected. French was a 'soldiers' general who was much loved by the men. He spent 28 August on the road, delivering short speeches to weary troops, writing later: 'These glorious British soldiers listened to the few words I had to say to them with the spirit of heroes and the confidence of children.'[49] C. D. Baker-Carr, who served as Sir John's chauffeur in 1914 and later became a brigadier general, commented: 'Sir John French may not have been a great soldier in the modern sense of the word, but he was a great leader of men.'[50] Sir William Robertson confirmed the opinion, writing after the war:

> Sir John was extraordinarily popular with the troops, and I doubt if any other General in the Army could have sustained in them to the same extent the courage and resolution which they displayed during the trying circumstances of the first six months of the war.[51]

French was not alone in 'getting around the army'. Smith-Dorrien carried out similar work with II Corps, remembering that on 28 August: 'I was able this day to see a lot of the troops on the march, and talked to them, and tell them that the true reason for retirement was not that we had been beaten.'[52] Corporal John Lucy of the Royal Irish Rifles was one of the soldiers Smith-Dorrien met that day. Lucy recalled: 'He [Smith-Dorrien] did not wear the hard and sometimes haughty look of other generals, and we liked him for it . . . He was our man.'[53]

Divisional commanders carried out similar morale-boosting work. George 'Ma' Jeffreys encountered Charles Monro, commander of 2nd Division, in late August and recorded the exchange: 'General Monro was just sitting down to dinner, and the dear old man said, "Hullo Jeffreys, what do you want? Have something to eat." I told him I'd got a starving battalion outside and that I wanted rations.'[54] Monro immediately despatched his divisional quartermaster-general to deal with the problem and the men were fed.

But sustaining morale was only half of the campaign. The BEF also had to fight several fierce engagements against a numerically superior opponent in conditions of acute danger. The constant fear that the small British Army would be encircled by the German onslaught coloured the thinking of senior officers.[55] However, the tactics, training and tenacity of the BEF proved their value. The army was not immune from mistakes. For example, the mistimed cavalry charge at Audregnies on 24 August and the careless deployment of the 1st Kings Own at the Battle of Le Cateau resulted in needless casualties. In other cases, the collapse of battlefield communication led to battalions becoming isolated, and in some cases, destroyed.[56] However, for the most part the BEF fought well and earned the grudging respect of its German opponents.[57] British cavalry proved especially adept at blinding German reconnaissance and screening the retreating footsloggers.[58] Smith-Dorrien was impressed by the 'shooting power' of his infantry and even the self-critical Thomas Snow noted that at Le Cateau 'nothing could shake the defence' and that his men 'mowed down the attacking Germans literally in thousands'.[59] Junior officers kept their men fighting even when communications broke down and they became isolated from brigade or divisional control. The sheer determination of individual formations to 'hold on' is a striking feature of the Great Retreat. Sometimes this resulted in the tragic loss of units, such as the 2nd Munster Fusiliers at Etreux, who never received orders to withdraw and refused to give ground. A similar fate befell the 2nd Suffolks at Le Cateau. However, this steely resolve to fight to the end imposed serious delays on the German pursuit, and, at Le Cateau, played a critical role in allowing the remainder of II Corps to retreat without interference.[60]

Furthermore, the 'man on the spot' generally got the key decisions of the campaign correct. The most important of these was Smith-Dorrien's famous decision to disregard GHQ's orders and turn and fight at the Battle of Le Cateau. Although certainly a grave gamble, it achieved its objective of halting the German pursuit and allowing the BEF to break contact. Furthermore, although less widely recognised, the decision of Quartermaster-General William Robertson to abandon War Office supply protocol in favour of improvised roadside supply dumps was inspired and played a huge role in keeping the BEF moving and fighting.[61]

The final factor that allowed the BEF to survive was a certain element of luck. It has been said that war is a contest of mistakes, and that whomsoever makes the least, is usually victorious. On the opposite side of the lines, German commander Alexander von Kluck made a number of serious errors. The inability of his inefficient cavalry to break through the screen of British horsemen forced him to operate in an intelligence vacuum, and, as such, he never truly grasped the vulnerability of the BEF. At both Mons and Le Cateau, he allowed his forces to attack piecemeal and missed the opportunity to encircle the isolated British. Despite being stalled at Le Cateau, von Kluck came to the erroneous conclusion that he had destroyed the entire BEF and several French divisions. The sudden appearance of British forces at the Battle of the Marne in early September surely came as a rude shock.

In conclusion, it is important to remember that successful retreats do not win wars, but disastrous ones can certainly lose them. The Great Retreat had been, respectfully to paraphrase the Duke of Wellington, a damned near-run thing. Snow's assessment that the operation was a 'badly bungled affair' remains debateable, but his assertion that it was 'grit' that saved the day is correct. The importance of this factor is often overlooked. Echoing Carl von Clausewitz's idea that war was primarily a contest of wills, prominent soldiers, including Lord Moran and Field Marshal Lord Wavell, identified that morale was the final arbiter of success in battle.[62] Soldier turned historian John Baynes noted correctly, that tactics are relatively less important because if morale is absent then troops will simply not march or fight.[63]

Fortunately for the BEF, it was uniquely equipped by experience and culture to sustain its morale and endure the hardships of a difficult campaign. Even highly-trained armies are not perfect instruments, and there were moments of panic and acts of indiscipline and desertion, but, as a whole, the morale of the army stood the test.[64] Much of this success can be traced to the unsung leadership of junior officers and the tenacity of the men they commanded. Although written in broad terms, James Edmonds's summary of the Great Retreat remains a fitting conclusion:

> [The BEF was] hastened forward by forced marches to battle, confronted with greatly superior numbers of the most renowned army in Europe, and condemned at the very outset to undergo the severest ordeal which can be imposed upon an army. They were short of food and sleep when they began their retreat, they continued it, always short of food and sleep, for thirteen days; and at the end of the retreat they were still an army, and a formidable army. They were never demoralized, for they rightly judged that they had never been beaten.[65]

Notes

1. James Edmonds, *Official History of the Great War: Military Operations France and Belgium 1914*, Vol. 1 (London: MacMillan, 1933), p. 10 [hereafter *Official History*. All references are to 1914, volume 1].
2. Richard Meinertzhagen, *Army Diary 1899 – 1926* (Edinburgh: Oliver & Boyd, 1960), p. 80.
3. Holger Herwig, *The First World War: Germany and Austria-Hungary, 1914-1918* (London: Arnold, 1997), p. 116. Herwig characterised First Ypres as a 'military debacle' for Germany.

4. The original BEF – 1st to 6th Division and the Cavalry Division – had numbered 120,000 men. The higher figure includes colonial garrisons and British soldiers in India.
5. I owe this information to Professor William Philpott.
6. For a summary of recent historiography of the BEF, see Spencer Jones (ed.), *Stemming the Tide: Officers and Leadership in the British Expeditionary Force 1914* (Solihull: Helion, 2013), pp. 19–20.
7. Edmonds, *Official History*, p. 284.
8. Much of this criticism is veiled and between the lines. On this point, see Andrew Green, *Writing the Great War: Sir James Edmonds and the Official Histories, 1915 – 1948* (London: Frank Cass, 2003), p. 55.
9. This argument is put forward most strongly in Nikolas Gardner, *Trial by Fire: Command and the British Expeditionary Force 1914* (Westport: Praeger, 2003).
10. The National Archives UK [hereafter TNA], CAB 45/129, 'Account of the Retreat of 1914' by General T. D'O. Snow, p. 1
11. Mark Pottle and Dan Snow (eds.), *The Confusion of Command, the War Memoirs of Lieutenant General Sir Thomas D'Oly Snow, 1914-1915* (London: Frontline, 2011), p. 5.
12. Byron Farwell, *Queen Victoria's Little Wars* (Barnsley: Pen & Sword, 2009), p. 1.
13. Leo Amery, *The Times History of the War in South Africa*, Vol. 2 (London: Sampson Low, Marston & Company, 1904), p. 26.
14. France could draw upon combat experienced units of the *Armée Coloniale* in 1914 but the bulk of its forces were of the Metropolitan Army and had not seen action. Russia had the experience of the Russo-Japanese War to draw upon but veteran soldiers made up a small proportion of its vast army. In 1914 the only military with a comparable level of combat experience to the BEF was that of Serbia, which had recently fought in the First and Second Balkan Wars.
15. W. N. Nicholson, *Behind the Lines: An Account of Administrative Staffwork in the British Army 1914-1918* (London: Cape, 1939), p. 146.
16. Peter Hodgkinson, 'The Infantry Battalion Commanding Officers of the BEF' in Jones (ed.), *Stemming the Tide*, p. 299.
17. For full details, see *The Quarterly Army List, April 1914* (London: HMSO, 1914).
18. Gary Sheffield, 'The Making of a Corps Commander: Lieutenant-General Sir Douglas Haig' in Jones (ed.), *Stemming the Tide*, p. 113.
19. Spencer Jones and Steven J. Corvi, 'A Commander of Rare and Unusual Coolness: General Sir Horace Lockwood Smith-Dorrien' in Jones (ed.), *Stemming the Tide*, pp. 153–4.
20. John Bourne, 'Major-General Sir Archibald Murray' in Jones (ed.), *Stemming the Tide*, p. 54; Brian Curragh, 'Henry Wilson's War' in Jones (ed.), *Stemming the Tide*, p. 73.
21. For full details of these reforms, see Spencer Jones, *From Boer War to World War: Tactical Reform of the British Army 1902 – 1914* (Norman: University of Oklahoma Press, 2012).
22. Hodgkinson, 'Infantry Battalion Commanding Officers', pp. 299–300.
23. *Field Service Regulations Part I 1909: Operations* (London: HMSO, 1909), pp. 27–8.
24. For example, see Hodgkinson, 'Infantry Battalion Commanding Officers', pp. 307–9.
25. For a discussion of the problems of pre-war manoeuvres, see Mark Connelly, 'Lieutenant-General Sir James Grierson' in Jones (ed.), *Stemming the Tide*, pp. 140–4.
26. The 1898 manoeuvres were a chaotic affair. See D. M. Leeson, 'Playing at War: The British Military Manoeuvres of 1898', *War in History* 15(4) (2008).
27. Connelly, 'James Grierson', p. 148.
28. TNA WO 163/16, Inspector General of Forces Report for 1910, p. 219.
29. TNA WO 163/17, Inspector General of Forces Report for 1911, p. 473.
30. TNA CAB 45/129, 'Account of the Retreat of 1914' by General T. D'O. Snow, p. 1.
31. Michael Howard, 'Leadership in the British Army in the Second World War: Some Personal Observations' in G. D. Sheffield (ed.), *Leadership and Command: The Anglo-American Military Experience since 1861* (London: Brassey's, 1999), p. 117.

32. Quoted in Sheffield, *Leadership and Command*, p. 1.
33. Quoted in Edmonds, *Official History*, pp. 499–500.
34. For an evocative description of the fraught state of Anglo-French relations at the outset of the war, see John Terraine, *Mons: The Retreat to Victory* (London: B. T. Batsford, 1960), pp. 36–53.
35. Bourne, 'Archibald Murray', p. 64.
36. For detailed and contrasting studies of this, see Bourne, 'Archibald Murray', Curragh, 'Henry Wilson's War' and Gardner, *Trial by Fire*.
37. This view has been advanced by John French's most recent biographer. See Stephen Badsey, 'Sir John French and Command of the BEF' in Jones (ed.), *Stemming the Tide*, pp. 27–51
38. Spencer Jones, 'Scouting for Soldiers: Reconnaissance and the British Cavalry, 1899–1914', *War in History* 18(4) (2011), p. 510.
39. The reasoning that lay behind the unusual size of the Cavalry Division remains open to debate but was most likely due to budgetary concerns. On this, see Stephen Badsey, *Doctrine and Reform in the British Cavalry 1880 – 1918* (Aldershot, Ashgate, 2008), pp. 191–238.
40. Nikolas Gardner, 'Command Control in the "Great Retreat" of 1914: The Disintegration of the British Cavalry Division', *The Journal of Military History* 63(1) (1999). It should be noted that Gardner's view is challenged by Badsey, *Doctrine and Reform*, pp. 242–8
41. Howard, 'Leadership in the British Army', p. 120.
42. C. R. Ballard, *Smith-Dorrien* (London: Constable & Company, 1931), p. 185.
43. Ibid, p. 186.
44. Quoted in John Mason Sneddon, *The Devil's Carnival: The First Hundred Days of Armageddon, 1st Northumberland Fusiliers August – December 1914* (Brighton: Reveille Press, 2012), p. 109.
45. Michael Craster (ed.), *Fifteen Rounds a Minute: The Grenadiers at War 1914* (Barnsley: Pen & Sword, 2012), p. 50.
46. For a detailed discussion of this notorious incident, see Peter T. Scott, *Dishonoured: The 'Colonels Surrender' at St. Quentin, The Retreat from Mons, August 1914* (London: Tom Donovan, 1994).
47. Ibid, pp. 54–9.
48. On this point, see Badsey, 'Sir John French', p. 48.
49. Viscount French of Ypres, *1914* (London: Constable & Company, 1919), p. 88.
50. C. D. Baker-Carr, *From Chaffeur to Brigadier General* (London: E. Benn, 1930), p. 27.
51. William Robertson, *Soldiers and Statesmen 1914–1918*, Vol. I (New York: Charles Scribner's Sons, 1926), p. 71.
52. Quoted in Jones and Corvi, 'Smith-Dorrien', p. 168.
53. Quoted in ibid, p. 144.
54. Quoted in Craster (ed.), *Fifteen Rounds a Minute*, p. 57.
55. On this point, see Sheffield, 'Douglas Haig', pp. 118–26.
56. On this point, Niall Barr, 'Command in the Transition from Mobile to Static Warfare, August 1914 to March 1915' in Gary Sheffield and Dan Todman (eds), *Command and Control on the Western Front: The British Army's Experience 1914 – 1918* (Staplehurst, Spellmount, 2007), pp. 13–39.
57. Paddy Griffith, *Battle Tactics of the Western Front: The British Army's Art of Attack 1916–1918* (London: Yale University Press, 1994), pp. 51–2.
58. Badsey, *Doctrine and Reform*, p. 244.
59. CAB 45/129, 'Account of the Retreat of 1914' by General T. D'O. Snow, p. 21.
60. Spencer Jones 'The Battle of Le Cateau, 26 August 1914' in Mungo Melvin (ed.), *The First World War Battlefield Guide: The Western Front* (Andover: Army Design Studio, 2014), pp. 15–19.
61. John Spencer, '"The big brain in the army": Sir William Robertson as Quartermaster

General' in Jones (ed.), *Stemming the Tide*, pp. 96–7.

62. John Baynes, *Morale: A Study of Men and Courage* (London: Leo Cooper, 1967), pp. 92–3
63. Ibid, p. 93.
64. Alexander Watson has argued that the large number of BEF soldiers who were captured in 1914 is indicative of low morale within the army. This view stems from a misunderstanding of the conditions of the opening months of the war. The relatively open, fast-paced campaigns of 1914 meant it was far easier to be cut off and fall prisoner than in the trench battles of 1915–17. However, Watson also notes that indiscipline rose to record levels in the winter of 1914–15, largely due to losses amongst seasoned officers. On both points, see A. Watson, *Enduring the Great War: Combat, Morale and Collapse in the German and British Armies, 1914–1918* (Cambridge: Cambridge University Press, 2008), pp. 142–3.
65. Edmonds, *Official History*, p. 284.

Suggested Further Reading

Ascoli, David, *The Mons Star* (Edinburgh: Birlinn, 2001).
Ballard, C. R., *Smith-Dorrien* (London: Constable & Co., 1931).
Barrow, George, *The Fire of Life* (London: Hutchinson & Co. Ltd, 1942).
Bird, Anthony, *Gentlemen, We Will Stand and Fight: Le Cateau, 1914* (Ramsbury: Crowood Press, 2008).
Bloem, Walter, *The Advance from Mons 1914* (Solihull: Helion & Co., 2011 reprint).
Bridges, Tom, *Alarms and Excursions: Reminisces of a Soldier* (London: Longmans, 1938).
Cave, Nigel, and Jack Sheldon, *Le Cateau* (Barnsley: Pen & Sword, 2008).
Craster, J. M. (ed.), *Fifteen Rounds a Minute: The Grenadiers at War 1914* (London: MacMillan, 1976).
Edmonds, James, *Official History of the Great War: Military Operations France and Belgium 1914*, Vol.1, (London: Macmillan, 1933).
Gardner, Nikolas, *Trial by Fire: Command and the British Expeditionary Force 1914* (Westport: Praeger, 2003).
Haldane, Aylmer, *A Brigade of the Old Army 1914* (London: E. Arnold, 1920).
Hamilton, Lord Ernest, *The First Seven Divisions* (London: Hurst & Blackett, 1916).
Hamilton, Richard F., and Holger Herwig, *War Planning 1914* (Cambridge: Cambridge University Press, 2010).
Herwig, Holger, *The Marne 1914* (London: Random House, 2009).
Holmes, Richard, *The Little Field Marshal: A Life of Sir John French* (London: J. Cape, 1981).
Holmes, Richard, *Riding the Retreat: Mons to the Marne Revisited* (London: J. Cape, 1995).
Jones, Spencer, *From Boer War to World War: Tactical Reform of the British Army 1902–1914* (Norman: University of Oklahoma Press, 2012).
Jones, Spencer (ed.), *Stemming the Tide: Officers and Leadership in the British Expeditionary Force 1914* (Solihull: Helion & Co., 2013).
Jones, Spencer, *The Great Retreat of 1914: From Mons to the Marne* (London: Endeavour Press, 2014).
Kluck, Alexander von, *The March on Paris and the Great Battle of the Marne 1914* (London: E. Arnold, 1920).
Lucy, John, *There's a Devil in the Drum* (London: Faber & Faber, 1938).
Murland, Jerry, *Retreat and Rearguard 1914* (Barnsley: Pen & Sword, 2011).
Richards, Frank, *Old Soldiers Never Die* (London: Faber & Faber, 1933).
Scott, Peter, *Dishonoured: The Colonels' Surrender at St. Quentin 1914* (London: Tom Donovan, 1994).
Sneddon, John Mason, *The Devil's Carnival: 1st Battalion Northumberland Fusiliers August – December 1914* (London: Tommies Guides, 2012).
Spears, Edward, *Liaison 1914: A Narrative of the Great Retreat* (London: W. Heinemann, 1930).
Terraine, John, *Mons: The Retreat to Victory* (London: MacMillan, 1960).

Chapter 7

The Raising of the New Armies: Some Further Reflections

* * *

Peter Simkins

Of all the multitude of events, campaigns and battles, and individual deeds and stories which we shall no doubt seek to commemorate as we reach the Centenary of the Great War, very few – if indeed any – are, in my view, more worthy of consideration than the raising of Britain's New Armies during Field Marshal Lord Kitchener's tenure of office as Secretary of State for War. The statistics which this process generated were, by themselves, staggering and, for the British army and the society from which it sprang, unprecedented. By the end of 1915, in response to Kitchener's successive appeals for recruits, 2,466,719 men had voluntarily enlisted in the army. This was a higher total than the country was able to obtain by conscription in 1916 and 1917 combined, while the number of men secured by compulsory means in 1918 was only 30,000 more than the number of volunteers attested in September 1914 alone.[1] That month, 462,901 had joined the army. The highest weekly returns for the whole of the war were recorded between 30 August and 5 September 1914, when nearly 175,000 were attested. The peak figure for a single day – 33,204 – was reached on Thursday 3 September 1914, this number being bigger than the average *annual* intake for the Regular Army in the years immediately prior to the First World War.[2]

These returns enabled Kitchener and the War Office to create thirty divisions for five so-called 'New Armies', with each 'New Army' duplicating the six infantry divisions of the original and existing British Expeditionary Force (BEF). Twenty-eight of those New Army divisions would see active service on the Western Front at various stages of the war.[3] At the same time, the Territorial Force (TF) was permitted to expand, to raise new second- and third-line formations and to undertake active service abroad. Fourteen second-line TF divisions were thereby created, of which seven fought, at some stage, in France and Belgium.[4] Quite apart from the artillery, engineer, medical and other ancillary units needed to complete each division, 994 infantry battalions were formed during Kitchener's period of office. Of the 557 'Service' and reserve battalions formed for the New Armies between August 1914 and June 1916 – excluding new Territorial battalions – 215, or 38 per cent, were locally raised by bodies other than the War Office.[5]

Despite all previous shortcomings in experience and preparation, this colossal national effort provided Britain with its first-ever mass army and one which not only ultimately proved capable of fighting a modern industrial war on a continental scale but also played a key role in defeating the formidable main enemy in the main theatre of operations. The recruits attested in 1914 and 1915 constituted the second-largest volunteer army in history (the biggest being the Indian Army of 1939–45).[6] It was also the largest and most complex single organisation created by the British nation up to that time.[7] In the sense that, in 1914–15, it was raised, to a considerable extent, with practical and widespread support from civilian committees and *ad hoc* voluntary organisations all over the country, this was probably the nearest thing to a true citizen army that Britain has ever produced. For good or ill – depending upon one's standpoint in the debate – the raising of the New Armies determined the nature and scope of Britain's subsequent commitment to, and participation in, the war for the next four years, an involvement which eventually touched every household in the land in some way.

It is, of course, impossible to recount the whole saga of the raising of the New Armies in the space available to me, or to review fully all the scholarly research which has been undertaken and published in this general subject area since my own work, *Kitchener's Army*, first appeared in 1988.[8] However, a number of such studies surely do deserve special mention. They include, for example, three outstanding works which analyse and reassess the extent of popular support for the war in Britain – namely Adrian Gregory's *The Last Great War*, Catriona Pennell's *A Kingdom United* and David Silbey's *The British Working Class and Enthusiasm for War, 1914-1916*.[9] Important work on the complicated topic of Ireland's response to the conflict and contribution to recruiting has been carried out by, among others, Timothy Bowman, Terence Denman, Myles Dungan, David Fitzpatrick, Richard Grayson, David and Josephine Howie, Eric Mercer and Michael Wheatley.[10] Similar studies have been made of the response in Scotland and Wales.[11]

In addition, the past two decades or so have witnessed the production of a prodigious number of new unit histories, not least the series of Pals battalion studies published by Leo Cooper and Pen and Sword since the mid-1980s. Again, space limitations prevent me from naming them all individually, but the series has encompassed books on locally-raised battalions from Accrington, Barnsley, Birkenhead, Birmingham, Bradford, Durham, Hull, Kensington, Leeds, Liverpool, Manchester, Salford, Sheffield and Tyneside, as well as slightly less localised units such as the Sportsman's Battalion of the Royal Fusiliers and the 16th (Public Schools) Battalion of the Middlesex Regiment.[12] Other New Army battalion histories which have been produced by other publishers, or which fall outside the 'Pals' category, are Matthew Richardson's *The Tigers*, on the 6th to 9th Battalions of the Leicestershire Regiment; Jack Alexander's *McCrae's Battalion*, on the 16th Royal Scots; Derek Clayton's book on the 9th King's Own Yorkshire Light Infantry; and John Stephen Morse's history of the 9th Sherwood Foresters.[13] Scholarly studies of Territorial battalions have also emerged in this period, including Bill Mitchinson's book on the London Rifle Brigade, the late Jill Knight's work on the Civil Service Rifles and Helen McCartney's splendid analysis of the Liverpool Rifles and Liverpool Scottish in the Great War.[14] All this excellent scholarship notwithstanding, I am somewhat relieved to find that many of my earlier conclusions about the raising of the New Armies seem to remain fundamentally valid. Nevertheless, perhaps I may be permitted to venture a few further reflections of my own, and, in those cases where my judgements have been challenged, or even misinterpreted, to fire a few gentle shots in reply.

Scholars now generally agree that there was no immediate 'rush to the colours' at the outbreak of hostilities and that the recruiting surge – which was of relatively short duration – occurred somewhere between three to five weeks after Britain had declared war. Opinions still differ, however, as to the precise date when the recruiting boom began and the factor, or factors, which gave it the greatest impetus. David Silbey, for example, contends that 'historians' – though he cites *my* book as his sole reference – have wrongly suggested that a four-week delay in the recruiting surge was the result of hesitation stemming from 'intellectual or moral' misgivings 'on the part of British men'. In fact, in my book *Kitchener's Army*, I devote the best part of a chapter to an examination of the host of different motives for enlistment and merely state that for 'some' (not 'all', 'most' or even 'many' – an important distinction) the reason for initial hesitation was an intellectual or moral one.[15] Silbey also asserts, on more than one occasion, that the principal and decisive cause of the boom in enlistments was an article by Arthur Moore which appeared in *The Times* on 30 August and which shocked the nation into action with its news of the retreat from Mons and the recent setbacks suffered by the BEF in Belgium and France. Referring to 'terrible losses', the report stated that the BEF required instant and immense reinforcement. 'The British Expeditionary Force', it continued, 'has won indeed imperishable glory, but it needs men, men, and yet more men'. What Silbey fails to mention is that F. E. Smith, then Head of the Press Bureau, confessed to having suggested the insertion of the passage calling for more recruits.[16] He (Silbey) is, of course, quite right to point out that the recruiting returns climbed steeply after this article had appeared in *The Times*, as they topped 20,000 on 31 August and rose to 31,947 two days later.[17] However, one might reasonably argue that, in several respects, the seeds of the recruiting surge had really been sown in the week before Moore's piece was published.

As Catriona Pennell has observed, it was difficult for a man to volunteer if the necessary machinery was not yet in place at a local level to process recruits.[18] It was not until the second and third weeks of August that the true potential of the voluntary system began to be realised as civilian effort became more fully mobilised in support of the recruiting campaign. Civilian recruiting committees were being organised during this period, while town halls, schools and other public buildings were made available, on an increasing scale, to serve as recruiting stations or as venues for patriotic meetings. In London, the mayors of twenty-eight metropolitan boroughs offered to place not only their town halls but also their staffs at the War Office's disposal.[19] Such practical, and growing, support undoubtedly made it easier for men to enlist and had the appropriate machinery not been in place by late August, the high recruiting totals of the following fortnight would probably have proved much more difficult to achieve.

Another fact which might lead one to qualify the significance of *The Times* report of 30 August is that the latter was *not* the first bad news from France to appear in the national press. *The Times* of 25 August had carried a report on the Battle of Mons under a headline referring to the 'British Army's Stern Fight'. This article admitted that the 'battle is joined and has so far gone ill for the Allies'. In the same issue a leader urged that it was now vital to cut through the 'excessive regard for red tape in accepting recruits'. This earlier article too seems to have a direct impact on recruiting figures. On 25 August, 10,019 men enlisted, the first five-figure total to be recruited in a single day. The daily recruiting returns then rose steadily, if unspectacularly, nearing 13,000 within four days.[20] Admittedly these figures did not match the impressive enlistment returns of the first week of September, but they were certainly not insignificant in the context of the recruiting campaign as a whole.

A third factor which partly pre-dated Arthur Moore's article was the formation of the Parliamentary Recruiting Committee (PRC), which – potentially at least – provided the government with much of the machinery it required to pull together the diverse strands of the recruiting drive and to direct and monitor civilian effort more effectively at a local level. The creation of the PRC similarly signalled that responsibility for the administration and direction of the recruiting campaign was beginning to shift from the War Office to politicians and to local civilian bodies.[21] Catriona Pennell writes that the PRC did not have its first meeting until 31 August.[22] This is not strictly true. Although the PRC was *officially* constituted on that date, preliminary meetings had already been held on 27 and 28 August at which some of the foundations for the future activities of the body were laid. By the end of the third meeting it had been decided that, in any given area, the work of the political party organisations and the recognised recruiting authorities should be co-ordinated, with the PRC helping local civilian committees to find distinguished speakers for public meetings. A fair amount of latitude was granted to local political associations, which could determine whether a few large meetings or a series of smaller ones were more likely to be productive in their own individual constituencies. General agreement was also reached concerning the importance of keeping the press properly informed about the PRC's work and of producing recruiting literature to supplement that issued by the War Office. To orchestrate recruiting propaganda throughout the country, a special Publicity and Publications Sub-Department was formed.

These were not the only steps taken by the PRC in late August. A scheme was devised whereby local party activists would canvass for recruits in much the same fashion as they traditionally canvassed to secure votes. In each constituency party agents were to organise their sub-agents, canvassers and other volunteers to deliver recruiting circulars to all males on the electoral register. Every circular would be accompanied by a stamped, addressed card, upon which the elector was invited to enter details of his age and marital status, to indicate his willingness to enlist if called upon by the War Office and, alternatively, to state any 'qualifications or reservations' which might deter him from joining up. The canvassers would then call on householders again within three to five days to check whether or not the cards had been posted. The project was discussed in some detail on 31 August although, in the event, it was decided to keep it in reserve 'until Lord Kitchener deemed such action necessary'.[23]

The latter decision may help to explain why the PRC's overall campaign did not begin to get properly into gear until October–November 1914, when national enlistment totals were themselves showing distinct signs of decline and giving the government some grounds for concern.[24] Catriona Pennell, indeed, claims that the PRC was 'inactive during the biggest surge in recruitment'.[25] This suggestion is, I believe, misleading, since it tends to obscure the extent to which the party organisations were already deeply embedded and integrated into local society and to understate the contribution of MPs, elected councillors and party volunteers in facilitating the September recruiting boom. For example, Montague Barlow, the Conservative MP for South Salford, played a prominent role in the raising of the 1st Salford Pals (15th Lancashire Fusiliers). At the crucial recruiting meeting on 3 September which first established the Salford Pals battalions, the speakers included Sir George Agnew and Sir William Byles, the Liberal MPs for West and North Salford. These local MPs were also to serve on the raising committee.[26] In Sheffield, where the local City battalion (12th York and Lancaster Regiment) commenced enlistment on 10 September, forty volunteer clerks had been organised by the Conservative and Liberal Parties. Meanwhile, in Durham in the early days of September, a committee, chaired by the Earl of Durham and given the task of overseeing the raising of the first Durham Pals battalion (18th Durham Light Infantry), numbered among its members Herbert Pike Pease, the Unionist MP for Darlington, and Colonel Rowland Burdon, the former Conservative candidate for South-East Durham. Burdon generously donated £1,000, and H. Pike Pease £50, towards the costs of raising the battalion.[27] And one should not forget that Lord Derby, a figure of considerable influence in the political life of the north-west, had a leading role in the raising of the Liverpool and Manchester Pals. All this evidence hardly indicates 'inactivity' during September.

It should be noted, too, that the preliminary moves towards the creation of locally-raised or Pals battalions were made – in the form of offers to Kitchener, newspaper appeals or exploratory public meetings – in Bristol, Birmingham, Hull, Liverpool, Manchester and Newcastle, all between 25 and 29 August.[28] The Pals movement swiftly gathered momentum as community and civic pride and local loyalties and rivalries came into play, fostering what was almost a sense of competition between different towns and cities, particularly in the north of England. There is certainly evidence to show that Lord Derby's proposal to form a battalion of non-manual workers in Liverpool quickly inspired both prominent citizens and potential recruits in other cities to follow his lead. On 31 August, the *Yorkshire Evening Post* called for the formation of a 'Leeds commercial battalion', while a correspondent who signed himself 'Willing' wrote to the *Yorkshire Observer*: 'Is there no influential citizen of Leeds who will come forward and call a meeting re the Earl of Derby's scheme for a battalion of "pals" for this district ?'[29] In the West Midlands, J. E. B. Fairclough, who went on to enlist and later wrote a history of the 1st Birmingham Pals, wrote to the *Birmingham Daily Mail*: 'I notice that a battalion of clerks, etc., is being raised in Liverpool. Why not one in Birmingham?'. Henry Gibbons, another potential volunteer (who was killed on the Somme in 1916), also saw this idea as 'a most useful one'.[30] Such sentiments and rivalries seem to have been as great an incentive to raise or join local battalions – and possibly an even bigger spur – as bad news from France. The Pals movement did much to give the recruiting campaign of the first half of September its character, substance and impetus, but it originated *before* 30 August.

One more factor needs to be taken into account when debating the influence which Arthur Moore's report in *The Times* exerted on recruiting. On 28 August, Kitchener had issued an appeal for a further 100,000 men. The upper age limit was now extended from thirty to thirty-five for new recruits, forty-five for ex-soldiers and fifty for some former non-commissioned officers. At the same time, it was pointed out that married men with children would be accepted and would draw separation allowances at army rates.[31] Both the extension of the upper age limit and the confirmation that separation allowances would be paid undoubtedly enlarged the potential pool of volunteers, thereby contributing to the subsequent surge in enlistments. In making this point and the others discussed above, one is *not* seeking to underplay the importance of *The Times* article, for it clearly did help to prompt the recruiting boom of the following fortnight. However, as I trust I have demonstrated, there were several other developments involved, most of which can be traced back to the five or six days which preceded the report in question.

David Silbey further contends that some 'histories' – this time citing Keith Grieves as well as myself as the authors responsible – have stated that the recruiting system was badly organised and inefficient in its execution. This assertion, he writes, does not stand up to 'close scrutiny'.[32] Again, I beg to differ. There are multiple indications that Kitchener and the War Office lost their grip on the recruiting campaign in late August and early September 1914, thereby generating both short-term and long-term problems for themselves *and* for the volunteers they drew into the army.

It soon became apparent, in the opening two weeks of the war, that the existing War Office recruiting machinery was unable to deal with even the relatively modest numbers of volunteers then coming forward. It was also recognised that better results could be obtained by making more extensive use of the apparatus of local government and by securing the co-operation of local politicians and businessmen who possessed precisely the kind of knowledge and experience of conditions in their areas that the War Office lacked. At that stage, if the army were to be expanded significantly, it seemed vital to harness civilian drive to recruiting over the whole country and, since the War Office system was already creaking under the strain, to decentralise, where possible, the task of processing recruits.[33] The trouble was that, having let the genie out of the bottle, Kitchener and the War Office, in late August and early September, signally failed to impose a ceiling upon enlistments, to regulate the flow of volunteers or to predict the problems which such unrestricted recruiting would cause. They were therefore caught in something of a vicious circle, for as more and more men were persuaded to join up, the harder it became to cope with them.[34]

For a while, especially in early September, the recruiting surge defeated almost all attempts by the War Office to restore order to the situation. Regimental depots which had been designed to house between 250 and 500 men at most were now swamped with newly-enlisted volunteers. At least six depots contained more than 2,000 recruits each and the depot of the Cheshire Regiment at Chester bulged with as many as 3,052.[35] The recruits themselves paid a stiff price for this rapid and haphazard expansion and, on every side, there were acute shortages of accommodation, uniforms, weapons, personal equipment, blankets, bedding, toilet facilities, eating utensils and even rations. Not surprisingly, the growing congestion at the depots prompted a lengthy attack on the recruiting policy of the government in the House of Commons on 9 September, when Major-General Sir Ivor Herbert, the Liberal MP for Monmouthshire South, accused the War Office of lack of foresight: 'If this is to be an example of the organisation now at the War Office', he complained, 'it is time that the Secretary of State, who has the reputation of being a good organiser, should vindicate that reputation'.[36]

To be fair, the War Office tried to tackle the accommodation crisis with commendable speed, once it was appreciated that the scale of the problem had been seriously underestimated. The machinery for the quartering of troops, under the Quartermaster-General's Department, was streamlined and, as early as 2 September, training centres for the six divisions of the Second New Army (15th to 20th Divisions) were earmarked, these being confirmed on 11 September.[37] However, attempts to ease the chaos and congestion at the regimental depots by sending men to the new training centres merely transferred the problems from one place to another. If anything, because of the continuing absence of basic facilities, the conditions which recruits encountered at the training centres were worse than those they had faced at the depots. Matters were not helped by the fact that the sites of some training camps – such as those at Codford, Sherrington and Chiseldon – were badly selected and prone to flooding.[38]

In a belated attempt to stem the flood of volunteers and apply a brake to recruiting, on 11 September the War Office announced that the minimum height requirement for recruits would henceforth be raised from 5ft 3in to 5ft 6in, while the minimum chest measurement was increased from 34in to 35.5in.[39] Despite this measure, the unrestricted recruiting of late August–early September 1914 had important 'knock-on' effects in the longer term. For example, the efforts of recruiting staffs to clear bottlenecks and speed up the enlistment process at the height of the surge in August and September almost inevitably resulted, in some places, in a lowering of standards, especially on the medical side. These shortcomings were not immediately evident but became increasingly apparent in the following weeks, as the numbers of unfit men being discharged grew progressively larger. Indiscriminate enlistment in the opening weeks also had serious implications for industries which were essential to the war effort, as the many skilled men who joined the army at that time could not easily be replaced later in the conflict. As a case in point, this even affected the War Office's own hutting programme, which ran into difficulties in the autumn of 1914, not only because of poor weather but also because unrestricted recruiting had led to a shortage of skilled building workers.[40] In fact, the accommodation problem was only really eased when the War Office decided to billet some 800,000 troops on the civilian population in the winter of 1914–15 – yet another sign of how dependent Kitchener and the War Office had become on civilian goodwill and support to compensate for the deficiencies in the recruiting organisation.[41]

None of this supports the idea that Kitchener and the War Office were fully in control of the recruiting process in the crucial weeks of August–September 1914, being often reactive rather than proactive. The evidence suggests to me that, by the beginning of September, Kitchener saw the offers by local authorities to raise Pals battalions both as a means of relieving the pressure on the War Office recruiting organisation and of ameliorating some of the short-term financial problems created by the sudden expansion of the army. He therefore resolved to sanction local battalions only when the raisers were prepared to bear the bulk of the initial expenses incurred. On 4 September the War Office informed the regional commands of Kitchener's hope that 'those large cities and private committees which are now raising or contemplate raising complete battalions will be able to make arrangements in connection with [TF] County Associations to find training grounds and housing or tentage and to clothe and feed the men on a contract scale fixed by the War Office, until they can be taken over by the military authorities'.[42] This, in essence, marks the point at which the shift from the War Office system towards locally-raised units actually occurred, for, from October 1914 onwards, only nineteen 'Service' battalions were raised by the War Office through traditional channels, while eighty-four locally-raised battalions were formed.[43]

Silbey takes issue with me once more by arguing that I have 'somewhat overstated' the case in claiming that, in the opening months of the war, the private citizen was subjected to 'an unrelenting barrage of recruiting propaganda'. Citing a complaint by the *Daily Mail* on 5 November that, so far, there had been only an 'occasional poster', he asserts that, up to that point, the campaign of recruiting propaganda had been 'a sporadic effort'.[44] He goes on to say that the advertisements in the first few months of the war were small and restrained and that Kitchener 'would not, in fact, allow the War Office to change the one-eighth of a page advertisement that they had mocked up early on'. Silbey observes that a concerted campaign of government recruiting propaganda did not begin until late 1914 and remained *ad hoc*, decentralised and ultimately chaotic until the final year of the war.[45] I would strongly contend, however, that this line of argument overlooks a number of important points and tends to conceal certain key facts which, together, might lead to a different interpretation.

The first of these crucial points is that, during the recruiting boom of late August and early September, when many of the Pals battalions were being formed, a large proportion of recruiting appeals, and associated information about public meetings and the location of recruiting offices, appeared in the *local* rather than the *national* press. How else, in an age before radio and television, were potential recruits going to learn about the raising of units in their own area? In their own newspapers the big cities and towns possessed an effective means of focusing attention on local affairs and enterprises. Reproductions of such local press appeals and advertisements can be found in several of the recently-published studies of Pals battalions.[46] Nor was the campaign restricted to newspaper appeals. In Birmingham, by late August, a huge barometer outside the Town Hall registered the numbers of recruits enlisting there, while illuminated tramcars adorned with recruiting slogans nightly toured the streets of Glasgow and Leeds.[47] This localised recruiting effort in August and September can scarcely be described, with any accuracy, as 'sporadic' and, in any case, it sufficed to bring in unprecedented numbers of recruits. In September 1914 it was simply unnecessary for the newly-created PRC to launch an intensive poster campaign. As Nick Hiley remarks, the PRC's Publications Sub-Department, at its first meeting in September, cautiously agreed to produce nothing more than a simple Union Jack poster for announcing local meetings. Only at the start of October 1914, when recruiting began to slow down – partly as a result of the War Office's decision to raise the minimum physical requirements – was the PRC 'asked to help restore the previous level of enlistment'.[48] From then on, the recruiting campaign was more centralised, and increasingly co-ordinated and orchestrated by the PRC, which used its extensive network of local party organisations to help individual communities and civilian committees, in every corner of the land, to make their own efforts more effective. Thus one can, I feel, justifiably maintain that recruiting propaganda was already fairly intense by late August, even if much of it, over the following few weeks, was concentrated at a local level, and also that the PRC then assumed a greater role *nationally* in the recruiting campaign from October–November 1914. If there *were* a hiatus in the 'barrage' of recruiting propaganda, then I submit that it was a rather short one.

The myth of Alfred Leete's iconic 'Your Country Needs You' poster (and of the alternative design 'Kitchener Wants You') has long since been exposed. The original design first appeared on the front cover of *London Opinion* on 5 September 1914 and was not issued as a poster, in either form, until the end of that month, by which time the peak recruiting figures had already been passed. Nick Hiley's research suggests that its subsequent appearance on London hoardings in September and October 1914 was a 'purely private venture'. There is no evidence, he states, to show that it was in any sense an official design. Neither version of the poster carries a PRC serial number or a Stationery Office imprint; neither is mentioned in the PRC minutes or the official summary of its work; neither was included among the many posters which proudly hung on the walls of the PRC's Publications Sub-Department office at 11 Downing Street; and there are no references to Leete's design in the published accounts of the wartime work of the printers David Allen and Sons.[49]

If, in fact, the famous Kitchener poster had little real influence on recruiting, there can be no doubt about the scale of the PRC's activity or its enormous output once it truly got going in October–November 1914. Its own records reveal that its campaign involved the production of more than 5.7 million full-size posters in over 140 different designs, as well as 550,000 smaller strip posters for taxicabs, railway carriages and trams, and some 450,000 show-cards for display in public buildings, shops, offices and houses.[50] The PRC also helped to organise public recruiting meetings throughout the country. Although it was hoped to use unpaid speakers whenever possible, the PRC's Finance Committee paid fees of up to two guineas a day if required, while up to £15 would be granted to defray the costs of advertising and printing for a mass meeting in a large town. In January 1915 it was reported that over 3,000 meetings had been held to date and more than 6,000 speakers provided.[51] In November 1914, the PRC's deferred 'Householder's Return' canvassing scheme was finally launched in the area of south-east England covered by Eastern Command, then extended to other Commands. By 12 December, 4,400,000 households had received the forms.[52]

The trouble was that all this expenditure of time, money and effort did not halt a marked decline in recruiting returns. In October 1914, 136,811 men joined the army, a huge drop from the September figures. The enlistment totals fell again to 117,860 in December and 87,896 in February 1915, the first month since the outbreak of war in which the returns were below 100,000.[53] It has been calculated that, by the summer of 1915, almost six PRC posters were needed in order to bring forward a single volunteer.[54] The PRC's 'Householder's Return' canvassing scheme also failed to produce the desired results. Arthur Henderson, leader of the Parliamentary Labour Party, admitted in July 1915 that, of the eight million householders who had received the forms, less than half had bothered to reply, and the government as yet had no means of ensuring that those who promised to enlist would actually do so.[55] As the recruiting returns dropped, so some aspects of the PRC's campaign became more strident, coercive and manipulative, resorting to what almost amounted to moral blackmail. A well-known example of this is Savile Lumley's design 'Daddy, what did YOU do in the Great War?', which the PRC issued as Poster No.79 in March 1915. 'I tried to stop the bloody thing, my child' was the reported answer of Robert Smillie, the Scottish miners' leader.[56] There were, indeed, distinct signs that the PRC's campaign was becoming counter-productive and beginning to alienate the British public. By the end of July 1915, official confidence in the PRC's campaign had evaporated to such an extent that the War Office begged the PRC to suspend activities as people were 'sick of posters and recruiting meetings'.[57] Nick Hiley is careful to emphasise that some of the more 'bullying' images produced during the PRC's campaign were uncharacteristic, had entirely private origins and were designed not by government officials but by commercial advertisers and graphic artists who wished to demonstrate their patriotic credentials.[58] However, the caveats offered by Hiley do not completely absolve the PRC of responsibility for incorporating such designs into its official campaign.

The complex questions of motives for, and patterns of, volunteering in 1914–15 have been analysed in detail by various scholars and do not need to be re-examined here.[59] However, I *will* venture a few additional observations about the middle-class contribution to recruiting as, before August 1914, many men from this social stratum would probably never have given serious consideration to joining the army. It might also be apposite to say a little more on this topic because a fair sprinkling of the locally-raised Pals battalions initially contained a sizeable proportion of middle-class volunteers, and some of these units – following their sacrifice on the Somme on 1 July 1916 – have accumulated the same sort of myths and semi-romantic overtones as, for example, the Anzacs.

In his fine study of working-class enthusiasm for the war, David Silbey states that the overall working-class enlistment total of 1,358,848, as estimated in August 1915, is reached by adding 1,267,500 industrial workers to 91,348 from the agricultural sector, though he adds that this is only 'a rough approximation'. He goes on to offer the tentative conclusion that, in the first year of the war, 67.4 per cent of volunteers were working-class, while the remaining 32.6 per cent probably came from the middle and upper classes 'with some unaccounted-for unemployed men and agricultural workers thrown in the mix'. Silbey then suggests that the approximate percentage of middle and upper-class men who joined up in the first twelve months is higher than their percentage of the population, while the working-class figure is lower. However, he is careful to point out that, almost inevitably, the numbers of rejections on medical grounds were far higher among working-class men and that this 'would go a long way towards explaining the disparity between the enlistment rate of the social classes'. Numerically, working-class men still constituted both the largest pool of military manpower and the largest section of Britain's fighting forces'.[60] In commenting upon Silbey's findings, Adrian Gregory reasserts that if the majority of the army obviously came from the majority of the population (the urban working class), yet the barriers of health and the exclusion of vital war workers meant that the proportion of middle-class men in the army 'was even higher than in the population as a whole – a significant over-representation'.[61] When writing my own book, I looked at the response of different occupations in terms of numbers enlisting between August 1914 and February 1916 and discovered that the higher percentages of enlistments over the whole period were registered by the entertainment industry (hotels, restaurants, theatres, cinemas, etc.) at 41.8 per cent, the professions at 41.7 per cent, and finance and commerce at 40.1 per cent, as against manufacturing industries at 28.3 per cent, mining at 24.7 per cent and transport at 22.4 per cent. One must, of course, bear in mind that the professions, commerce and service and distribution trades had a more flexible workforce than heavy industry and that a male employee in a shop or hotel could more easily be replaced by a female worker than a man in shipbuilding. Many men from the professions received commissions while the commercial classes became a particular target for the raisers of some Pals battalions.[62]

Like Territorial Force 'class' battalions in, for example, London and Liverpool, there were locally-raised Pals battalions which sought a measure of exclusivity from the outset. As Adrian Gregory neatly puts it, some Pals units 'were actually less about who you served with, but much more obviously about who you didn't serve with'.[63] Lord Derby's preliminary appeal on 27 August, which led to the formation of four City battalions in Liverpool, was clearly aimed at men, 'such as clerks and others engaged in commercial business, who wish to serve their country and would be willing to enlist . . . if they felt assured that they would be able to serve with their friends and not be put in a battalion with unknown men as their companions'.[64] Commenting on the proposal in Birmingham to raise a battalion of non-manual workers, Alderman W. H. Bowater, the Deputy Mayor, also stressed that this offered such men a good opportunity to serve their country 'among those of their own class'. On 31 August, under the heading 'The Turn of the Middle Class', an article in the *Birmingham Daily Mail* expressed the hope that 'shopmen, accountants, bank clerks, etc.' would come forward to 'prove the boast that the strength of Britain lies in the middle class'.[65] In Sheffield, appeals for the 'University and City Special Battalion' were 'intended primarily for Professional and Business Men and their Office Staffs' but also embraced lawyers, teachers, journalists and shop assistants.[66] Referring to what became the Hull Commercials (10th East Yorkshire Regiment) as the 'black-coated battalion', the *Hull Daily Mail* argued – a trifle defensively and patronisingly – that: 'It must not be thought there is a desire for class distinction but just as the docker will feel more at home amongst his every day mates, so the wielder of the pen and drawing pencil will be better as friends together'.[67] Inevitably, this policy aroused criticism. The Leeds Pals were described as the 'Feather Bed Battalion' by one correspondent who wrote to the *Yorkshire Evening Post*, while A. W. Humphrey, in the socialist *Labour Leader*, complained that: 'the middle-class and professional classes form exclusive companies, they do not hasten away to the nearest recruiting office, for fear they should rub shoulders with their less polished fellow-beings. Their patriotism does not run to that'.[68]

Recent painstaking research by Joe Devereux into the personal backgrounds of the officers and other ranks of the Liverpool Pals who were killed on 1 July 1916, or died of wounds received on that day, indicates that some of these Pals battalions still retained a fair proportion of their original members, as well as much of their local identity and ethos, at least until that fateful first day of the Somme offensive. Joe Devereux arrives at an overall total of 257 officers and men of the four City battalions – 17th, 18th, 19th and 20th King's (Liverpool Regiment) – who were killed on 1 July or who later died of wounds. He estimates that, of the 182 officers and men with known occupations, 127 (or 69.7 per cent) were clerks.[69] The heaviest toll of fatal casualties among these four battalions was incurred by the 18th Battalion (2nd City) which, according to Devereux's figures, lost ten officers and 184 other ranks, although he gives the names and personal details of only 181 of the other ranks in question. Of the 181 men of the 18th Battalion named, 129, or 71.2 per cent, enlisted between 31 August and 7 September 1914 and can therefore be described as original Liverpool Pals. Again, of those named, 110, or 60.7 per cent, were clerks; a further forty-two (or 23.2 per cent) were in other non-manual jobs, ranging from salesmen and shop assistants to teachers; two (or 1.1 per cent) were classed as engineers; and seventeen (or 9.3 per cent) were in manual occupations and included labourers, miners, plate layers, painters and builders. Most of the latter working-class recruits enlisted in the first half of 1915.[70]

Even so, one should not assume that all locally-raised or Pals battalions maintained their original composition to the same extent as the 18th King's. The granting of commissions to potential officers was one cause of dilution. The 1st Birmingham Battalion (14th Royal Warwickshire Regiment) lost 302 other ranks in this manner up to the end of 1915 and nearly half of the men of the Leeds Pals (15th West Yorkshire Regiment) appear to have become officers before the unit left England.[71] Of the 1,028 officers and men on the nominal roll of the Leeds Pals just prior to their departure for Egypt in December 1915, only six officers and 534 other ranks were original volunteers who had joined the battalion in early September 1914.[72] Laurie Milner has estimated that, although nearly 250 officers and men of the Leeds Pals died at Serre on 1 July 1916, less than 10 per cent of the original September 1914 volunteers were among the fallen.[73]

More recently, Tim Lynch has posed some interesting and thought-provoking questions about the social, geographical and occupational composition of Pals battalions and about the nature of the society that produced them. He points out, for instance, that the towns and cities of the industrial north, in particular, experienced a huge growth in population in the second half of the nineteenth century, meaning that volunteers in 1914, born largely between 1874 and 1895, were thus mainly the children of first-generation migrants to an area 'rather than from long-established communities'. Lynch goes on to argue that home ownership among the lower classes was comparatively rare, that homes were often rented from employers or private landlords, and that moves were frequent. Men did not always join the army from the address where they were born or from the address recorded in the 1911 census. 'The romantic notion of Pals growing up together in close knit supportive communities', Lynch writes, 'is simply not supported by the emerging evidence.' Taking Accrington as an example, Lynch states that 'local legend' has it that the town's losses on 1 July 1916 were such that no family in Accrington was spared. He observes, however, that, based on a pre-war population of 45,000 – and even if every man of the Accrington Pals killed on that day came from the town (which they did not) – it would have been necessary for each family to have consisted of almost 200 people for the legend to be true. In fact, Tim Lynch contends, 'losses impacted on both relatively small geographical and, more importantly, social and occupational groups', the impact on the town itself being 'not as great as imagined but considerably focused within sections of the town's workforce'.[74]

The details provided by Joe Devereux, as noted above, would seem to back Tim Lynch's various points for, while the dead of the 18th King's on 1 July 1916 were predominantly clerks from the business and commercial houses and firms of Liverpool and Merseyside – and while as many as 92.8 per cent appear to have lived in the city or the surrounding area – it is difficult to discern any pronounced pattern of shared residential backgrounds. Having analysed the information presented by Devereux, I could detect just seven cases in which two of the fatal casualties of the 18th Battalion on 1 July came from the same road or street and, in one of these seven cases, the men were brothers.[75] Only in two other cases can the men be described as near neighbours.[76] Although this sample is admittedly narrow, the evidence it offers seems to undermine the popular perception that whole streets were plunged into mourning as a result of the sacrifice of the Pals battalions on 1 July.

The 30th Division, of which the four Liverpool City battalions formed part, actually did well on 1 July, helping to capture Montauban and the key German observation post at La Briqueterie. Moreover, the casualties of these battalions on 1 July were not the heaviest they would suffer on the Somme, an estimated 450 officers and men being killed in the attempt to take Guillemont on 30 July.[77] As I have written elsewhere, my own analysis of the performance of the New Army divisions on the Somme suggests that those of the Fourth and Fifth New Armies (30th to 41st Divisions), which contained a large proportion of the locally-raised or Pals battalions, collectively had a lower success rate in attacks than the War Office-raised formations of the First, Second and Third New Armies (9th to 26th Divisions). This might, in turn, indicate that strong social, geographical or community links were *not* (contrary to the expectations of the original raisers of Pals battalions) a guarantee of success in battle – though, of course, the highly-localised character of many of these battalions was inevitably, and increasingly, diluted by losses and replacements as the Somme offensive progressed.[78]

The massive and rapid expansion of the army, almost from scratch, in less than two years – and while fighting a brutal industrialised war against a skilful and implacable enemy – was, I repeat, a colossal *national* achievement, even if, at times, the process was haphazard and dependent upon many acts of improvisation. Again, it was, in my view, only made possible by a huge and almost immeasurable surge of civilian support. But there is still much about this multi-faceted process that we do not know – the influence of social, geographical or occupational factors upon the combat performance of units being just one of many aspects which require deeper examination. The story of the raising of Britain's New Armies is still, 100 years on, a subject which is eminently worthy of further study.

Notes

1. *Statistics of the Military Effort of the British Empire during the Great War, 1914-1920* (London: HMSO, 1922), p. 364.
2. Monthly recruiting figures, September 1914–February 1915, *Statistics of the Military Effort of the British Empire*, p. 364; Daily recruiting returns submitted to the Adjutant-General, 30 August–5 September 1914, The National Archives (TNA), WO 162/3; Daily recruiting returns, August–December 1914, TNA, NATS 1/398; Weekly returns of recruits for Regular Army and Territorial Force, 4 August 1914–22 May 1915, TNA, WO 159/3.
3. Major A. F. Becke, *Order of Battle of Divisions, Part 3A: New Army Divisions (9-26)*, and *Part 3B: New Army Divisions (30-41) and 63rd (R.N.) Division* (London: HMSO, 1938 and 1945).
4. Becke, *Order of Battle of Divisions, Part 2B: The 2nd Line Territorial Force Divisions (57th-69th) with the Home Service Divisions (71st-73rd) and 74th and 75th Divisions* (London: HMSO, 1937); Ian F. W. Beckett and Keith Simpson (eds), *A Nation in Arms: A social study of the British army in the First World War*, Appendix I, Infantry Divisions of the British army, 1914–18 (Manchester University Press, 1985), pp. 235–6.
5. Becke, *Order of Battle of Divisions, Parts 1-4* (London: HMSO, 1933–45); Brigadier E. A. James, *British Regiments, 1914-1918* (London: Samson, 1978), pp. 41–118.
6. Adrian Gregory, *The Last Great War: British Society and the First World War* (Cambridge University Press, 2008), p. 73 and p. 316, fn. 12.
7. Correlli Barnett, *Britain and her Army, 1509-1970: A Military, Political and Social Survey* (London: Allen Lane, 1970), p. 392.
8. Peter Simkins, *Kitchener's Army: The Raising of the New Armies, 1914-16* (Manchester University Press, 1988: reprinted Barnsley: Pen and Sword, 2007).
9. For details of the work by Adrian Gregory, see above (note 6). See also David Silbey, *The British Working Class and Enthusiasm for War, 1914-1916* (Abingdon: Frank Cass, 2005), and Catriona Pennell, *A Kingdom United: Popular Responses to the Outbreak of the First World War in Britain and Ireland* (Oxford University Press, 2012).
10. Timothy Bowman, *The Irish Regiments in the Great War: Discipline and Morale* (Manchester University Press, 2003); 'Composing Divisions: The Recruitment of Ulster and National Volunteers into the British Army in 1914', *Causeway*, No.1 (1995), pp. 24–9; and 'The Irish Recruiting Campaign and Anti-Recruiting Campaign, 1914-1918', in Bernard Taithe and Tim Thornton (eds), *Propaganda: Political Rhetoric and Identity, 1300-2000* (Stroud: Sutton, 1999), pp. 223–38. See also Terence Denman, *Ireland's Unknown Soldiers: The 16th (Irish) Division in the Great War* (Dublin: Irish Academic Press, 1992); Myles Dungan, *They Shall Grown Not Old: Irish Soldiers and the Great War* (Dublin: Four Courts Press, 1991); David Fitzpatrick, 'The Logic of Collective Sacrifice: Ireland and the British Army, 1914-1918', *The Historical Journal*, Vol. 38, No.4 (1993), pp. 1017–30; Richard S.

Grayson, *Belfast Boys: How Unionists and Nationalists Fought and Died Together in the First World War* (London: Continuum, 2009); David and Josephine Howie, 'Irish Recruiting and the Home Rule Crisis of August-September 1914', in Michael Dockrill and David French (eds), *Strategy and Intelligence: British Policy during the First World War* (London: Hambledon, 1996), pp. 1–22; Eric Mercer, 'For King and Country and a Shilling a Day: Recruitment in Belfast during the Great War', MA, Queen's University, Belfast, 1998; and Michael Wheatley, *Nationalism and the Irish Party: Provincial Ireland, 1910-1916* (Oxford University Press, 2005).

11. See, for instance, Derek Rutherford Young, 'Voluntary Recruitment in Scotland, 1914-1916', PhD, University of Glasgow, 2001, and Robin Barlow, 'Some Aspects of the Experiences of Carmarthenshire in the Great War', PhD, University of Wales, 2001.

12. It would be tedious indeed to attempt to list all the titles in the series, but good examples of this genre are: Jon Cooksey's *Pals: The 13th and 14th Battalions York and Lancaster Regiment* (1986); Laurie Milner's *Leeds Pals: A History of the 15th (Service) Battalion (1st Leeds), The Prince of Wales's Own (West Yorkshire Regiment)* (1991); Graham Maddocks's *Liverpool Pals: A History of the 17th, 18th, 19th and 20th (Service) Battalions, The King's (Liverpool Regiment), 1914-1919* (1991); Geoff Inglis, *The Kensington Battalion: 'Never Lost a Yard of Trench'* (2010); and Michael Stedman's *Salford Pals: 15th, 16th, 19th and 20th Battalions, Lancashire Fusiliers. A History of the Salford Brigade* (1993).

13. Matthew Richardson, *The Tigers: 6th, 7th, 8th and 9th (Service) Battalions of the Leicestershire Regiment* (Barnsley: Leo Cooper/Pen and Sword, 2000); Jack Alexander, *McCrae's Battalion: The Story of the 16th Royal Scots* (Edinburgh: Mainstream, 2003); Derek Clayton, *From Pontefract to Picardy: The 9th King's Own Yorkshire Light Infantry in the First World War* (Stroud: Tempus, 2004); John Stephen Morse, *9th (Service) Battalion, The Sherwood Foresters (Notts and Derby Regiment)* (Eastbourne: Tommies Guides, 2007).

14. K. W. Mitchinson, *Gentlemen and Officers: The Impact and Experience of War on a Territorial Regiment, 1914-1918* (London: Imperial War Museum, 1995); Jill Knight, *The Civil Service Rifles in the Great War: 'All Bloody Gentlemen'* (Barnsley: Pen and Sword, 2004); Helen B. McCartney, *Citizen Soldiers: The Liverpool Territorials in the First World War* (Cambridge University Press, 2005).

15. Silbey, *The British Working Class and Enthusiasm for War*, p. 112 and p. 168, fn. 99; Simkins, *Kitchener's Army*, pp. 165–87, particularly pp. 169–70.

16. *The Times*, 30 August 1914; *Parliamentary Debates, House of Commons, 1914* (31 August 1914), LXVI, cols. 494–8.

17. Silbey, *British Working Class*, pp. 23–4; Simkins, *Kitchener's Army*, pp. 65–6; Daily recruiting returns submitted to the Adjutant-General, 30 August–5 September 1914, TNA, WO 162/3.

18. Pennell, *A Kingdom United*, p. 156; Barlow, 'Some Aspects of the Experiences of Carmarthenshire in the Great War', p. 27.

19. Simkins, *Kitchener's Army*, pp. 49–56; L. S. Amery, *My Political Life*, 3 vols (London: Hutchinson, 1953–5), II, pp. 26–8 (Amery was appointed Director of Civilian Recruiting for Southern Command); *The Times*, 16 and 18 August 1914; George F. Stone and Charles Wells (eds), *Bristol and the Great War* (Bristol: Arrowsmith, 1920), pp. 108–9; *Western Daily Press*, 13 August 1914; Minutes of the Executive Committee of the Bristol Citizens' Recruiting Committee, 20 August 1914, Bristol Central Library.

20. *The Times*, 25 August 1914; Daily recruiting returns submitted to the Adjutant-General, 23 to 29 August 1914, TNA, WO 162/3.

21. Simkins, *Kitchener's Army*, pp. 61–2; Roy Douglas, 'Voluntary Enlistment in the First World War and the Work of the Parliamentary Recruiting Committee', *Journal of Modern History*, Vol. 42, No. 4 (1970), pp. 564–85.

22. Pennell, *A Kingdom United*, p. 144.

23. Minutes of Preliminary Meeting of the Parliamentary Recruiting Committee, 27 August 1914, and Minutes of Meetings of the Parliamentary Recruiting Committee, 28 and 31 August 1914, British Library (BL), Add.Mss. 54192.

24. Simkins, *Kitchener's Army*, pp. 104, 121–2; Monthly recruiting figures, September 1914, *Statistics of the Military Effort of the British Empire*, p. 364. In October 1914, a total of 136,811 enlistments was recorded, a huge drop from the figure of 462,901 registered in September.

25. Pennell, *A Kingdom United*, p. 144.

26. Michael Stedman, *Salford Pals* (Barnsley: Leo Cooper/Pen and Sword, 1993 and 2007), pp. 17, 25–6.

27. Paul Oldfield and Ralph Gibson, *Sheffield City Battalion: The 12th (Service) Battalion, York and Lancaster Regiment* (Barnsley: Wharncliffe, 1988), p. 26; John Sheen, *Durham Pals: 18th, 19th and 22nd Battalions of the Durham Light Infantry in the Great War* (Barnsley: Pen and Sword, 2007), p. 23.

28. Minutes of the Meeting of the Executive Committee of the Bristol Citizens' Recruiting Committee, 27 August 1914, Bristol Central Library; *Birmingham Daily Post*, 28 August 1914; *Birmingham Daily Mail*, 29 August 1914; J. E. B. Fairclough, *The First Birmingham Battalion in the Great War, 1914-1919* (Birmingham: Cornish, 1933), pp. 1–4; Terry Carter, *Birmingham Pals: 14th, 15th and 16th (Service) Battalions of the Royal Warwickshire Regiment. A History of the Three City Battalions raised in Birmingham in World War One* (Barnsley: Pen and Sword, 1997), pp. 35–8; Captain C. I. Hadrill (ed.), *A History of the 10th (Service) Battalion, The East Yorkshire Regiment (Hull Commercials)* (London and Hull: A. Brown and Sons, 1937), p. xv; David Bilton, *Hull Pals: 10th, 11th, 12th and 13th (Service) Battalions of the East Yorkshire Regiment. A History of 92 Brigade, 31st Division* (Barnsley: Pen and Sword, 1999), p. 19; *Liverpool Daily Post*, 27, 28 and 29 August 1914; Graham Maddocks, *Liverpool Pals: A History of the 17th, 18th, 19th and 20th (Service) Battalions, The King's (Liverpool Regiment), 1914-1919* (London and Barnsley: Leo Cooper/Pen and Sword, 1991), p. 24; Arthur Taylor to Lord Derby, 29 August 1914, Derby papers, Liverpool Record Office (LRO), 920 DER(17) 14/2; Captain C. H. Cooke, *Historical Records of the 9th (Service) Battalion, Northumberland Fusiliers* (Newcastle and Gateshead Incorporated Chamber of Commerce, 1928), p. 1 and *Historical Records of the 16th (Service) Battalion, Northumberland Fusiliers* (Newcastle and Gateshead Incorporated Chamber of Commerce, 1923), pp. 1–2.

29. *Yorkshire Evening Post*, 31 August 1914; *Yorkshire Observer*, 31 August 1914; Milner, *Leeds Pals*, p. 20.

30. *Birmingham Daily Mail*, 29 August 1914; Terry Carter, *Birmingham Pals*, p. 37.

31. Minutes of Meeting of the Military Members of the Army Council, 27 August 1914, TNA, WO 163/44; *The Times*, 28 August 1914; Simkins, *Kitchener's Army*, p. 60.

32. Silbey, *The British Working Class and Enthusiasm for War*, p. 27 and p. 147, fn.90. See also Keith Grieves, *The Politics of Manpower, 1914-1918* (Manchester University Press, 1988).

33. Amery, *My Political Life*, II, p. 28.

34. Simkins, *Kitchener's Army*, pp. 53, 63.

35. Note of the strength of Infantry Depots, according to returns submitted to the Adjutant-General's Department, 29 August 1914, TNA, WO 162/4; Statement showing the strengths of Infantry Depots, 12 September 1914, TNA, WO 162/24.

36. *Parliamentary Debates, House of Commons, 1914* (9 September 1914), LXVI, cols. 607–615.

37. Major D. Chapman-Huston and Major Owen Rutter, *General Sir John Cowans: The Quartermaster-General of the Great War*, 2 vols (London: Hutchinson, 1924), II, pp. 21–2; Minutes of the Meeting of the Military Members of the Army Council, 1 September 1914, TNA, WO 163/44; Circular from Adjutant-General's Department to GOCs-in-C of Commands, 2 September 1914, TNA, WO 32/11341; Army Order XII of 11 September 1914 (AO 382 of 1914).

38. Colonel H. H. Story, *History of the Cameronians (Scottish Rifles). 1910-1933* (Aylesbury: Hazell, Watson and Viney, 1961), p. 241; Lieutenant-Colonel C. Wheeler (ed.), *Memorial Record of the Seventh (Service) Battalion, The Oxfordshire and Buckinghamshire Light*

Infantry (Oxford: Blackwell, 1921), p. 3; C. T. Atkinson, *The History of the South Wales Borderers, 1914-1918* (London: Medici Society, 1931), p. 61. For a detailed discussion of the accommodation problem, see Simkins, *Kitchener's Army*, pp. 231–52.

39. Telegram from Adjutant-General's Department to OCs Districts, 11 September 1914, TNA, WO 159/18; *The Times*, 12 September 1914; Recruiting Memorandum, No.72, 17 September 1914, TNA, WO 159/18.
40. S. Higenbottam, *Our Society's History* (Manchester: Amalgamated Society of Woodworkers, 1939), pp. 191–2.
41. General Sir John Cowans, 'Supply Services during the War, Part I: Quartering', published in *Statistics of the Military Effort of the British Empire*, pp. 833–4; Simkins, *Kitchener's Army*, pp. 244–52.
42. Telegram from Adjutant-General's Department to GOCs-in-C of Commands, 4 September 1914, TNA, WO 159/18; Minutes of Meeting of the Military Members of the Army Council, 12 September 1914, TNA, WO 163/44.
43. Becke, *Order of Battle of Divisions, Parts 1-4*; James, *British Regiments, 1914-1918*, pp. 42–118.
44. Silbey, *British Working Class*, pp. 29, 118; Simkins, *Kitchener's Army*, p. 186; *Daily Mail*, 5 November 1914.
45. Silbey, *British Working Class*, p. 118; Eric Field, *Advertising: The Forgotten Years* (London: Ernest Benn, 1959), p. 29; Gerard DeGroot, *Blighty: British Society in the Era of the First World War* (London: Longman, 1996), p. 175; Gary S. Messinger, *British Propaganda and the State in the First World War* (Manchester University Press, 1992), p .33; David Sweet, 'The Domestic Scene: Parliament and People', in Peter H. Liddle (ed.), *Home Fires and Foreign Fields: British Social and Military Experience in the First World War* (London: Brassey's, 1985), pp. 9–20; Cate Haste, *Keep the Home Fires Burning: Propaganda in the First World War* (London: Allen Lane, 1977), p. 50.
46. See, for instance, Stedman, *Salford Pals*, p. 33 and *Manchester Pals*, p. 37; Carter, *Birmingham Pals*, p. 42; Milner, *Leeds Pals*, p. 21; Oldfield and Gibson, *Sheffield City Battalion*, p. 25; and William Turner, *Pals: The 11th (Service) Battalion (Accrington), East Lancashire Regiment. A History of the Battalion Raised from Accrington, Blackburn, Burnley and Chorley in World War One* (Barnsley: Wharncliffe, 1987), p. 52. See also Simkins, *Kitchener's Army*, pp. 82–6.
47. *The Times*, 21 August 1914; Milner, *Leeds Pals*, p. 19; Thomas Chalmers, *An Epic of Glasgow: History of the 15th Battalion The Highland Light Infantry (City of Glasgow Regiment)* (Glasgow: McCallum, 1934), p. ix.
48. Nicholas Hiley, '"Kitchener Wants You' and "Daddy, What did YOU do in the Great War?": The Myth of British Recruiting Posters', *Imperial War Museum Review*, No. 11 (1997), p. 41; Parliamentary Recruiting Committee, Minutes of Meeting of the Publications Sub-Department, 3 September 1914, BL Add. Mss. 54192.
49. *London Opinion*, 5, 12 and 26 September 1914; Parliamentary Recruiting Committee, Publications Sub-Department Report, circa May 1916, TNA, WO 106/367; Hiley, '"Kitchener Wants You"', pp. 42, 44–5, 47; Simkins, *Kitchener's Army*, pp. 122–3.
50. PRC Publications Sub-Department Report, c. May 1916, TNA, WO 106/367, p. 3 and Appendix, 'Numbers and Cost of Publications'; Douglas, 'Voluntary Enlistment in the First World War and the Work of the Parliamentary Recruiting Committee', pp. 564–85; Hiley, '"Kitchener Wants You"', p. 40. See also Philip Dutton, 'Moving Images: The Parliamentary Recruiting Committee's Poster Campaign, 1914-1916', *Imperial War Museum Review*, No. 4 (1989), pp. 43–58.
51. Minutes of Meeting of the Finance Committee of the Parliamentary Recruiting Committee, 18 October 1914, BL Add. Mss. 54192; *The Times*, 6 January 1915.
52. Minutes of Meetings of the General Purposes Committee of the Parliamentary Recruiting Committee, 21 and 26 October 1914, BL Add. Mss. 54192; Douglas, 'Voluntary Enlistment', p. 572; 'The Householder's Circular', *The Times*, 6 January 1915.

53. Monthly recruiting figures, September 1914–February 1915, *Statistics of the Military Effort of the British Empire*, p. 364.

54. Hiley, '"Kitchener Wants You"', p. 50; PRC Publications Sub-Department Report, c. May 1916, TNA, WO 106/367, p. 2; 'Notes from an Interview with Colonel Gossett', 22 May 1916, TNA, WO 106/364.

55. *Parliamentary Debates, House of Commons, 1914-1915*, LXXIII, col. 146; Simkins, *Kitchener's Army*, p. 122.

56. PRC Recruiting Poster No. 79, Imperial War Museum DA/0311; Arthur Marwick, *The Deluge: British Society and the First World War* (London: Bodley Head, 1965), p. 52.

57. Hiley, '"Kitchener Wants You"', p. 50; PRC's Publications Sub-Department Report, c. May 1916, TNA, WO 106/367, p. 2; 'Notes from an Interview with Colonel Gossett', 22 May 1916, TNA, WO 106/364; *General Annual Reports on the British Army, 1 October 1913 to 30 September 1919* (London: HMSO, 1921), p. 60.

58. Hiley, '"Kitchener Wants You"', pp. 54–5.

59. See, for instance, the works by Adrian Gregory, David Silbey, Catriona Pennell, Timothy Bowman and Richard Grayson cited above. See also Simkins, *Kitchener's Army*, pp. 49–75, 79–100, 104–33 and 165–87.

60. Silbey, *British Working Class*, pp. 42–7; 'Estimate of the Condition of the Industrial Population of the United Kingdom', August 1915, TNA, CAB 27/2.

61. Gregory, *The Last Great War*, p. 317, fn. 29.

62. Board of Trade, 'Enlistment from the Industrial Classes and the State of Employment in Government and other Work in mid-February 1916', Reconstruction papers, TNA, RECON 1/832; P.E. Dewey, 'Military Recruiting and the British Labour Force during the First World War', *Historical Journal*, Vol. XXVII, No. 1 (1984), pp. 210–11; J. M. Winter, *The Great War and the British People* (London: Macmillan, 1986), p. 34; Simkins, *Kitchener's Army*, pp. 109–10.

63. Gregory, *The Last Great War*, p. 78.

64. *Liverpool Daily Post*, 27 August 1914; Brigadier-General F. C. Stanley, *The History of the 89th Brigade, 1914-1918* (Liverpool Daily Post, 1919), pp. 3–4.

65. *Birmingham Daily Post*, 28 August 1914; *Birmingham Evening Despatch*, 28 August 1914; *Birmingham Daily Mail*, 29 and 31 August 1914; Carter, *Birmingham Pals*, pp. 36–9.

66. Oldfield and Gibson, *Sheffield City Battalion*, pp. 22–5; *Sheffield Daily Telegraph*, 4 September 1914.

67. *Hull Daily Mail*, 1 September 1914; Bilton, *Hull Pals*, p. 20; Hadrill (ed.), *History of the 10th (Service) Battalion, East Yorkshire Regiment*, p. 1; Peter N. Farrar, 'Hull's New Army, 1914', *Journal of Local Studies*, Vol. 1, No. 2 (1981), pp. 32–3.

68. *Yorkshire Evening Post*, 8 September 1914; Milner, *Leeds Pals*, p. 25; *Labour Leader*, 29 October 1914.

69. Joe Devereux, *A Singular Day on the Somme: The Casualties of the Liverpool Pals, 1 July 1916* (Cheltenham: Promenade Publications, 2013), pp. xvi, 14, 22.

70. These figures and percentages have been extrapolated from the information provided by Joe Devereux in his book *A Singular Day on the Somme*, pp. 1–169.

71. Sir William H. Bowater (ed.), *Birmingham City Battalions: Book of Honour* (London: Sherratt and Hughes, 1919), pp. 23–9; W. H. Scott, *Leeds in the Great War, 1914-1918* (Leeds: Libraries and Arts Committee, 1923), p. 113.

72. These figures have been compiled by comparing the names and regimental numbers of the men listed on the battalion's Nominal Roll in late 1915 with the names of the original volunteers which were published in the *Yorkshire Post* on 6, 7, 8 and 9 September 1914. A copy of the Nominal Roll, printed by John T. Turner of Pontefract in 1915, was located in the Local History Department of the Leeds City Library. I am indebted to my friend and former IWM colleague Laurie Milner for pointing these sources out to me.

73. Milner, *Leeds Pals*, p. 165.

74. Tim Lynch, 'Draft Issues', undated letter via email (2014), *Stand To! The Journal of the Western Front Association*, No. 100 (June 2014), p. 7.

75. Privates Herbert and Frank Prescott of Melling Lane, Maghull; see Devereux, *A Singular Day on the Somme*, pp. 100, 166–7. Herbert, aged 26, was killed on 1 July 1916. Frank, aged 25, died of his wounds on 25 July.
76. Private Robert Griffiths of No. 24 and Private Charles Gastrell of No. 26 High Park Street; and Private Frank Miller of No. 49 and Private Hugh Jones of No. 55 Faraday Street, Everton. See Devereux, *A Singular Day on the Somme*, pp. 37, 42, 61, 85–6.
77. Captain Wilfrid Miles, *Military Operations: France and Belgium, 1916, Vol. II* (London: Macmillan, 1938), pp. 163-6; Devereux, *A Singular Day on the Somme*, p. v.
78. See Chapter 3, 'The Performance of New Army Divisions on the Somme, 1916' in Peter Simkins, *From the Somme to Victory: The British Army's Experience on the Western Front, 1916-1918* (Barnsley: Pen and Sword, 2014).

Suggested Further Reading

The most detailed survey of the topic remains my *Kitchener's Army: The Raising of the New Armies, 1914-16* (Manchester University Press, 1988; reprinted by Pen and Sword, 2007). In addition to a lengthy examination of voluntary recruiting in Britain and Ireland in 1914–15, it contains chapters on experiences of enlistment, officers and NCOs, and the arming, equipping, housing and training of the New Armies. Much helpful information about the infantry divisions of Britain's first mass citizen army, including the New Army formations, can be found in Martin Middlebrook's *Your Country Needs You: From Six to Sixty-Five Divisions* (Barnsley: Leo Cooper/Pen and Sword, 2000). There is also a useful chapter by Clive Hughes on 'The New Armies' in *A Nation in Arms: A Social Study of the British Army in the First World War*, edited by Ian F. W. Beckett and Keith Simpson (Manchester University Press, 1985; reprinted by Pen and Sword, 2004). Charles Messenger's *Call to Arms: The British Army 1914–18* (London: Weidenfeld and Nicolson, 2005), which is the best recent study of the overall organisation of Britain's expanded army in the Great War, similarly contains highly relevant observations on the new formations raised by Kitchener, the War Office and local bodies in 1914–15. The creation of an often overlooked, but essential, component of British infantry divisions is covered, in his customary thorough fashion, by K. W. Mitchinson in *Pioneer Battalions in the Great War: Organized and Intelligent Labour* (Barnsley: Leo Cooper/Pen and Sword, 1997).

Three very fine scholarly works which consider the nature and extent of public support for Britain's role in the conflict are David Silbey's *The British Working Class and Enthusiasm for War, 1914-1916* (Abingdon: Frank Cass, 2005); Adrian Gregory's *The Last Great War: British Society and the First World War* (Cambridge University Press, 2008); and Catriona Pennell, *A Kingdom United: Popular Responses to the Outbreak of the First World War in Britain and Ireland* (Oxford University Press, 2012). The latter book includes a particularly valuable discussion of Ireland's response to the war. In this connection, Richard Grayson's *Belfast Boys* (London: Continuum, 2009) is likewise recommended. Richard van Emden presents interesting evidence about under-age volunteers for the New Armies in his *Boy Soldiers of the Great War* (London: Headline, 2005). For a recent study of the locally-raised Bantam units, see my chapter '"Each One a Pocket Hercules": The Bantam Experiment and the Case of the Thirty-Fifth Division' in Sanders Marble (ed.), *Scraping the Barrel: The Military Use of Substandard Manpower, 1860-1960* (New York: Fordham University Press, 2012).

Chapter 8

First Clash of Arms in the West: British and German Soldiers in Action, 1914

* * *

Matthew Richardson

The period of the First World War on the Western Front between August and December 1914 exerts a special fascination. It was a page turn in history, a brief period of just over four months which began with mass movement of troops over open country, gallant cavalry charges and gaudy uniforms. However, in this same arena of combat, motorcycles, armoured cars and aircraft were beginning to make their presence felt, and by the end of 1914 both sides were bogged down in the deadlock of trenches, barbed wire and No Man's Land.

The almost Napoleonic character of the campaign had rapidly given way to a very different form of warfare. Leaving aside for the moment the French, this first campaign was fought by two armies raised on almost diametrically opposed principles. The Germans had compulsory military service, and their war was fought by a mass army of conscripts – some of them the unwilling members of subject peoples – and almost all of them with just a basic two years of training. The huge number of this conscript force was, in the autumn, augmented by the injection of a flood of volunteers thrust into battle virtually untrained. The British, by contrast, had a small, highly professional army, based on a long-service principle, in which every man was a volunteer. These differing characteristics would shape the coming conflict.

The campaign is worthy of study for another reason – the fact that it is extremely well documented. The actions made a striking impression upon those who lived through it on both sides, in some cases more than any other period of their war service, the experience deeply embedded in their memory. Thus there is a rich body of literature – published and unpublished, British and German, officer and enlisted man – upon which the historian can draw.

The soldier of the British Expeditionary Force (BEF) of 1914 was often from the lowest stratum of society, but the army none the less encouraged pride and self-worth among its men. It was said that the army tamed lions, such was the raw material it had to work with, but the sharp lessons of the Boer War of 1899–1902 had led to improvements in fieldcraft, tactics, and above all, marksmanship. Edward Packe was unusual in that although educated at public school, he served in the ranks. He tells us:

> The Pre-war soldier had little to learn. He had to be fit and keep himself and his kit immaculate. He had to know his Drill and be able to use his Rifle and Bayonet and he had to do what he was told instantly.[1]

Captain Thomas Burke, meanwhile, was in the almost unique position of being a British officer who had also served in the German army. This gave him an unrivalled insight into the German military machine, and the differences from its British counterpart. He draws our attention to the fact that, unlike the British, the regular German army had almost no experience of colonial warfare or even overseas garrison duty in countries like India to sharpen its fieldcraft. In spite of the fact that in many cases he was drawn from more promising raw material than the British recruit, and standards of basic education were higher in Germany at this time, the German soldier was neither encouraged nor expected to show any initiative, indeed this was almost frowned upon. In particular, Burke highlights the lack of fellowship between German officers and men, and between old and new hands. He tells us:

> [A] reason for the lack of camaraderie is that the men are not, like the British Tommy, professional soldiers, but are birds of passage, serving only two or three years, and longing to be free. You will even find, on stable doors and elsewhere in the barracks, chalked inscriptions stating the number of days between soldiering and freedom . . .[2]

The British began the campaign of 1914 as the junior partner of the French, and the BEF took up its position on the extreme left flank of the French army, as they moved forward into Belgium to meet the wheeling German army. On 22 August, Trooper Ernest Thomas, of C Squadron of the 4th Royal Irish Dragoon Guards, fired the first shot from a British soldier in the First World War:

> I could see a German cavalry officer some four hundred yards away standing mounted in full view of me, gesticulating to the left and to the right as he disposed of his dismounted men and ordered them to take up their firing positions to engage us. Immediately I saw him I took aim, pulled the trigger and automatically, almost instantaneously, he fell to the ground, obviously wounded . . . at the time it seemed to me more like rifle practice on the plains of Salisbury. In one respect, however, and within a second or two, it was mighty different. From every direction, as it seemed, the air above us was thick with rifle and machine gun bullets . . .[3]

A day later, a much larger clash took place at the Belgian town of Mons. By the later standards of the First World War, the Battle of Mons was no major action. There were only about 4,000 British casualties, and the fighting lasted just two days. However, it has largely overshadowed the much greater battle fought subsequently at Le Cateau, for the real importance of the battle was psychological. Here in the Belgian coalfields, the first British blood was spilled in Western Europe since the Battle of Waterloo almost a century earlier. For this reason, the battle still looms large in British consciousness. Even those with scanty knowledge of military history will probably have heard of the Retreat from Mons, though perhaps not entirely sure when, where and why it took place.

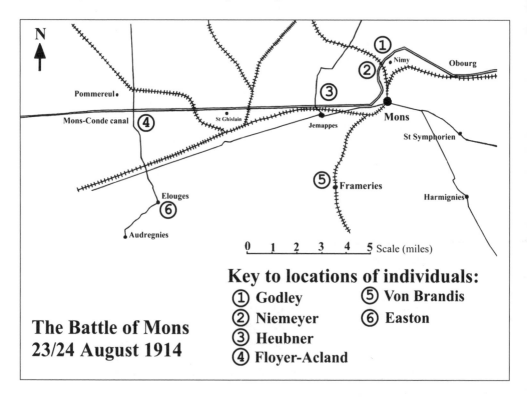

Several roads and railways diverged from Mons, heading north-east and north-west. The bridges by which the roads traversed the major water obstacle of the Mons-Condé canal were to be the focal points of the battle. Field Marshal Sir John French, commanding the BEF, told General Sir Horace Smith-Dorrien of II Corps that he believed only one or at most two enemy corps would be encountered. In fact seven enemy corps were on their way. By early afternoon of the following day, two German corps were actually engaged, with a third entering the fray and a fourth about to do so; indeed a feature of the battle was to be the piecemeal way in which the German units involved came into action. To some extent this negated the overall superiority in numbers enjoyed by the Germans, for the British were thus able to deal with each attack as it developed, before turning to the next.

Lieutenant Maurice Dease and Private Sidney Godley of the 4th Royal Fusiliers were to be awarded the Victoria Cross for their heroism on 23 August in defending the Nimy Bridge, holding it with a single Maxim machine-gun, and thus allowing their comrades a breathing-space in which to escape. Dease was to be killed that day, his award a posthumous one. However, Godley survived, and a remarkable recording of his voice, with gruff working-class accent, exists within the archives of the BBC. Originally broadcast on 4 August 1954 to mark the 40th anniversary of the outbreak of the Great War, it adds priceless detail to the bare bones of his citation:

The Germans came over in mass formation and we opened fire. The British troops, this great volume of fire, this fifteen rounds rapid fire what we'd been highly trained in was very effective which halted the German's advance and we held them during the whole of the day.[4]

Reckless bravery was also shown by the Germans in attempting to cross the canal. The book *Die Schlacht Bei Mons* was written shortly after the battle by two German staff officers who were present. In it they state:

It was almost 2.30 in the afternoon before the enemy, under the weight of our artillery fire, gave up the canal bank. Patrols following soon after found the railway bridge west of Nimy blown up, and the swing bridge to the northwest had been opened by the local inhabitants on the south bank. Unflinchingly, Musketier Niemeyer, from the patrol of Sergeant Rower of number 8 company jumped into the water, swam across the canal and brought a barge back, over which the patrol crossed despite heavy fire. Whilst Sergeant Rower and his men drew the fire of the enemy, Niemeyer managed to close the bridge once again, so that the following soldiers could cross. In performing this brave act, Niemeyer died a hero's death.[5]

Tremendous heroism was shown at other points along the canal, as the Royal Engineers worked frantically in the face of heavy German shelling and small arms to demolish as many crossing points as possible. A sapper officer summed up the attitude of those responsible for these demolitions:

One point I think should be emphasized about hasty demolitions in the face of the enemy. Beware of calculations. I gave an order to my people not to fuss over calculations but to cover the girders with all the stuff they could tie on, and let it go. The result was we never failed through lack of power but we burnt a hell of a lot of powder! My view was that my first job was to demolish and do it thoroughly and quickly and certainly. Replacement of explosives I am afraid I did not look upon as my funeral.[6]

As the morning progressed, the German attack also began to spread westwards along the line of the canal. Around 11 a.m., the blow fell against the British positions in front of Jemappes, held by the 1st Battalion Royal Scots Fusiliers. German shells fell mainly in the village itself, in the rear of the positions held by the Fusiliers along the canal. Consequently, when the Germans advanced in dense lines, they were met with a withering fire emanating from rifles and machine-guns. Taking heavy casualties, the Germans were forced to pause, before approaching more cautiously using cover. A German officer, Heinrich Heubner, left a graphic account of the fighting at this point in the line. He wrote:

> We steeled ourselves and crossed the canal, over which our brave pioneers had thrown a superb bridge. On the other side of this waterway stood the shattered and burning railway station. In a small square, like dogs against a house wall, squatted the first English prisoners we had seen so far in the war. There was an old corporal, with about eight men. In a wider semicircle around them stood some of our enlisted men, astonished by the defenceless British soldiers. I must confess that they made a very good impression upon me, almost all deeply suntanned, well-clothed people.[7]

This sneaking admiration for the British soldiers encountered occurs again and again in German accounts from this period. It stands in strange contrast to the almost casual brutality which the Germans also routinely handed out to their captives. The last word on this first day's fighting goes to the adjutant of the Duke of Cornwall's Light Infantry, away on the western edge of the battlefield, Lieutenant Arthur Nugent Floyer-Acland:

> I can't quite describe my feelings through this show, but I somehow don't believe it dispelled the old idea that we were on some big sort of manoeuvres, which had idiotically been with me since we started from the Curragh. The burst and hum of the shrapnel surprised me, and the bullets made me duck my head! It interested me, I think, when a bullet flicked the ground just in front of [my horse] as I was riding along a road to get more ammunition. I won't say I was not frightened, I'm sure I was, but I don't think I knew it. We got away well, and without much loss, and with a somewhat poor opinion of the German's rifle shooting.[8]

The following day, at Frameries, the Germans followed up by closely pressing the British rearguard. A remarkable account of this action again came from *Leutnant* Cordt von Brandis, who painted a vivid picture of his regiment advancing into battle following their standard, which had previously been borne in the Franco-Prussian War, and with their buglers playing a traditional Prussian battle song:

With our flag flying we stormed out on to the sun drenched field. Far before us, 800 meters or more, lay the edge of the village. Each wave struck out across fields of stubble and clover, devoid of cover. Right and left, as far as the eye could see, reinforcements hurried forward, with flashing bayonets, wave upon wave. Everywhere sounded the bugles: 'Kartoffelsupp – Kartoffelsupp' their incomparable, rousing attack signal. The blazing August sun burned down on this marvellous battle scene. What worry to us were the shells, the whistles and the bangs; what did it matter that some men sank with a loud groan to the hot ground . . . Tommy seemed to have waited for the moment of the assault. He had studied our training manuals well, and all at once, when we were still in the open without cover, turned his machine guns on, 'Like the very Devil!' Everywhere the gunners sprayed fire over us, right and left the bullets whistled and banged. In the corn stooks they rustled, as if they were mice. Wounded who had hidden behind them, huddled together. [9]

When at last they reached the village, they found it abandoned:

And our enemies? Their many bush wars had taught the veteran English soldiers cunning, and at Frameries they knew brilliantly what was the right time to make off. They played their machine guns as the last trump card to delay us, for as long as possible, whilst they themselves disappeared.[10]

On the other side of the battlefield, the BEF had bought itself time – and a breathing space – with a dramatic cavalry charge at Elouges. One of the members of the 9th Lancers who charged here was Trooper Harry Easton from Canterbury. He had enlisted in the regiment in 1906, and was thus, like most of his fellow troopers, a highly-competent horseman. However, as he remembered many years later, one of the finest cavalry regiments in Europe was brought to a halt not by enemy fire, but by the unexpected feature of a barbed wire fence; the lancers galloped up and down the length of it like rabbits, unsure of what to do next. Enemy fire was intense, and Easton's horse fell under him. Even after seventy-five years his memory of the events was vivid:

About one or two hundred yards [on we] found ourselves confronted with a huge brick yard surrounded by a 12 foot high barbed wire fence. We were in to it very close when my horse fell and threw me – I'm not sure whether she had been hit or had stumbled although the ground I remember was flat, slightly downhill & a small bump here & there. The CO signalled 'Troops Right Wheel' but it was not possible because we were in total confusion. There was no room left in front for such a move to be made by mounted men. There was a terrible mix up of Hussars and Lancers trying to extricate themselves.[11]

Two days later, 26 August marked the anniversary of the Battle of Crécy in 1346. The weather was hot and misty, much as it had been 850 years earlier. The similarities did not end there, for once again a small force found itself in a desperate situation, faced by a confident and numerically superior foe. The majority of the men of the BEF who had reached Le Cateau on the night of 25 August were exhausted, and although the original intention had been for them to continue to retire, in the early hours of 26 August General Smith-Dorrien's headquarters issued an order to them to stand their ground instead. The contrast between the Mons battlefield, and the countryside which was about to bear witness to the battle of Le Cateau, could not have been greater. Unlike the sprawling industrial townships of the Mons salient, the country around Le Cateau was predominantly rural, characterised by open rolling fields offering no cover for advancing troops.

Captain Cecil Brownlow served with a Brigade Ammunition Column of the Royal Field Artillery. His unit had already begun retiring early that morning, but had halted to replenish ammunition when a staff car pulled up, the officer within telling them to turn around at once. Brownlow's account of the battle is one of the most evocative:

> Nosebags were whipped off the horses' heads, limber lids were shut with a clang, amid curses and imprecations the wagons were reversed on the road, and, with every vehicle bumping and rattling, we trotted as fast as we could towards the sound of the guns, which every moment grew louder and louder. Owing to the distance we had to go and to the exhaustion of the horses, it was necessary to march by alternate periods of trotting and walking, but even so the horses were soon black with sweat and flecked with foam . . .[12]

Under cover of mist and the steep sides of the Selle valley, German troops had penetrated Le Cateau and emerged from the town to attack the foremost British units, which had had no time to prepare their positions or indeed to choose their ground. Among the German soldiers in action here was a reservist named Karl Storch. He recalled some weeks later:

> Surrounded, we held the 'Tommies' in an iron grip; stubbornly they fought their weapons, but their trenches had become graves for them. One always looks during such important times for some memento, by means of which in later times the events are more clearly recalled. So it was with me. There lay the paybook of an Englishman: 'Soldiers Small Book. Alfred Stratton, Corps Middlesex' was written on it. I took this with me. Maybe someone will take it carefully from my trunk in 50 or 100 years, and say, 'this was brought home from the Battle of Saint Quentin, by my dear great great uncle, what times they must have been!'[13]

Private Arthur Green from Bath was a regular reservist, who had enlisted after the Boer War. Green's published memoir of the First World War, entitled *The Story of a Prisoner of War*, is a striking tale. Simply educated, Green's writing is full of colloquialisms and quaint turns of phrase, which reinforce its authenticity. He writes powerfully of the fighting on 26 August:

> We could see the enemy in thousands. Well, we let them have it hot and holy for a few minutes; then the order came to retire, and just as I was getting up I got one through the hat, hitting it off. Near shave, I thought. We retired about 100 yards at a rush, seeing nothing, as we were over a bit of a ridge. We had to rush back about twenty yards. It was then that I ran to the wrong place, as me and Jonnie Ashment ran in the way of a machine-gun. I got mine in the thigh. I thought I'd been kicked by an elephant. It hit me sickey, I can tell. I riggled [*sic*] my straps off, drank all my water, tried to get up, thinking I could run; but I found my leg would not let me go. But I managed to get 100 yards back behind a hedge. Here I seen the two captains, Captain Jones Mortimer and Captain Watson, in my company, with about thirty men of different corps. Only two Somersets were with them. Jones Mortimer said: 'Well, hard luck, Green. Buck up. Keep up courage, and lie low. Perhaps you'll get picked up later.'[14]

Despite having held on all day, and having given the Germans a bloody nose, the fight at Le Cateau was only ever intended as a holding action, and as evening drew on it became necessary for those units still in contact with the enemy to try to extricate themselves. In some cases this was harder than in others. Captain James Jack was a staff officer but, giving the lie to a hoary old First World War cliché, he was neither callous nor incompetent. His diary was published after his death, and in it he describes how he risked his life to get word to withdraw, to a body of men placed by him earlier in the day:

> Being now most anxious for the safety of the troops recently placed by me . . . I ran forward along the outskirts of the village to warn our friends to retire. Presently a tremendous crash of musketry fire broke out in front. Following a hedge which obstructed the view I came on the Argylls just below me, manning the bank of a road at the south-eastern corner of Reumont. They were firing hard at the Germans whose advancing lines were flooding all over the ground from the direction of St Benin, the closest being some four to six hundred yards distant.
>
> A fusillade of bullets was skimming the road bank and a wire fence stood between me and the Highlanders. Expecting to be hit at any moment, I called to the men to tell their colonel to retire at once; then to their kindly warnings 'Be careful, Sir', climbed the fence, slid down the track, and hastened crouching along . . .[15]

Jack notes that in spite of the heavy rifle and shellfire to which they were exposed as they ran back, he believed that not a single man was lost in this affair. Other stragglers from the Le Cateau battle continued to fight on, and the following day, 27 August, Karl Storch was involved in mopping up British rearguards still holding their ground. He offers an interesting insight into the mind-set of the average German soldier at the time. He was a refined and well-read man in civilian life. The war had already begun to brutalise him, as he himself admitted:

> We attacked [*and*] overran their firing line, and within half an hour we had captured 400 Englishmen. They all held up their hands and had suffered many dead and wounded in such a short space of time. A 'New Testament' had fallen out of an English backpack; I turned the leaves inside. There was a dedication written on the first page. I snapped the black book shut again and flung it at a wounded Englishman among the turnips, who cried and whined. I had no more compassion, at that time everything within me had turned to stone, and now when I remember it I regard myself as brutal, because I called to him, 'Look at here, old fellow, that's a praying book [*sic*].' Others may talk in such cases of mercy, but there are times in war when one is taken over by the other side of one's nature, by the hatred for these island people who have caused so much untold grief, such sadness and misery in the world.[16]

The most famous minor action of the Retreat was probably the clash at Néry on 1 September 1914, when the Germans, having initially surprised a mixed British force of artillery and cavalry at rest in its bivouac area, were eventually driven off with great loss. A remarkable and rare German account of the Néry action exists, in the form of a diary kept by a soldier who was present with the *Husaren-Regiment Königin Wilhelmena der Niederlande (Hannoversches) Nr.15*, a man named Gustav Ostendorf:

> We took cover in the oats field as our artillery roared, this artillery fire had already destroyed seven enemy field guns. One enemy gun [pulled by horses] came out at the gallop from the village, it had hardly been touched whilst at the factory, but then this also was hit by two shell bursts together. Thus we did not have much more trouble from hostile shells, however at the same time, our guns had been reduced just to four, partly by barrels exploding. Suddenly we heard the Englishmen shouting to the left of us, they were quickly halted [by artillery], but they had already taken prisoner ten or fifteen men from the left wing.[17]

Trooper William Clarke served with the 2nd Dragoon Guards (Queen's Bays) and was also present at the action at Néry. He wrote many years later of his memories of that misty morning which were still remarkably vivid, adding that the fog had delayed the Bays from saddling up, and they were having breakfast when the first shells struck. His testimony as well as being a valuable account of the battle offers an insight into the calm stoicism – and the high degree of training – of the British regular:

When the battle had ended, somewhere about 10am we helped to collect the wounded and cleared up, collecting bits and pieces of useful equipment. It was my first sight of multiple deaths in battle. Many men and horses, both German and British, dead and abandoned . . . Everything seemed to happen so quickly, events were out of our control. I know that I felt frightened and excited at the same time. We were a very highly trained and efficient regiment, and we did as we were trained to do, responding quickly to a situation without question. And if you wanted to live you had to kill.[18]

By early September the German advance had begun to run out of steam. Just as with the men of the BEF, the constant marching had taken its toll of the German soldier. Furthermore, as in almost every case when an apparently victorious army follows on the heels of a defeated enemy, the latter is able to fall back on supplies and reinforcements, whilst the advancing force finds itself at the end of ever longer and more precarious supply lines. Remembering this phase of the campaign, *Hauptmann* Walter Bloem wrote:

The most depressing factor . . . was our own exhausted selves: we were all literally done in. For exactly two weeks since August 23rd, we had been in constant touch with the enemy, and lately had had minor encounters with him daily. If this was modern warfare we had not been trained, nor were we prepared for it . . . At this early period . . . our ideas of war . . . were based entirely on the 1870 campaign. A battle, according to that, would begin at 6am and end, victoriously of course, at 6pm . . . But this was something entirely different, something utterly unexpected. For a month now we had been in the enemy's country, and during that time had been on the march incessantly . . . without a single rest-day. We were astonished at our own powers of endurance.[19]

As the German First Army and Second Army swung around to face southwards, the garrison of Paris advanced to meet them. Von Kluck, commanding the First Army, peeled off to meet the threat, in the process creating a gap between his army and that of his opposite number, Von Bulow. This precise moment gave birth to the legend of the 'Miracle of the Marne.' Winston Churchill would later identify it as the critical juncture at which the Germans came closest to winning the war but instead, let the opportunity slip through their fingers. As the BEF (which had now grown in strength to three corps) halted its retreat, and began to advance into the gap, Von Kluck realised almost too late that he had thrust his head into a giant bag which was in danger of closing. It was now the turn of the Germans to begin retreating, and Walter Bloem was among those soldiers providing the rearguard in La Ferté-sous-Jouarre. He wrote a graphic description of the state of the town, and offers a vivid insight indeed into the outlook of the German officer at this time:

I was so impressed by the sight that, when we halted just after crossing back over the Marne, I made my company a small speech: 'You see that, men, 'I said, pointing back at the town, 'that's what they hoped to do to us, and now we've done it to them. You can understand now why we are here: so that that should take place in this foreign land and not in our own homes. That is why we have had not a minutes rest for the past four weeks, that is why you have marched the soles off your feet, that is why we have fought in a dozen engagements, and it is for that, too, so many of our friends have given their lives. Think that over, men, and be proud and thankful that it is you, you yourselves, who have spared your homes such a fate!'[20]

There were instances of brutality on both sides during the campaign of 1914, and often little evidence of the camaraderie between opposing frontline soldiers which was supposedly a feature of the Great War. Prisoners of war fared particularly badly in many cases. However, there were occasional instances of humanity between enemies. Writing to his regimental journal in 1934, Major E. D. Martin described the comradeship which developed between him and a German officer:

Lieut Baron von Bischoffshausen of the Jager battalion was wounded in the advance of the 5th Dragoon Guards at Sablonnieres on the Petit Morin on the 8th September 1914. We were both wounded very near each other; perhaps he got me – I certainly did not get him as I was hit before I really saw anything. We spent that day in an ambulance together, then two days in a train to St Nazaire, and two more on the Carisbrooke Castle coming home to Southampton. There our ways parted. He asked me to try to get word home to his mother through the Chilean Embassy. As his brother had already been killed he knew she would be in great anxiety about himself as missing.[21]

Back on the battlefield the Allied advance continued, and on the evening of Sunday 13 September, the leading elements of the British Expeditionary Force crossed the Aisne. Early next morning, the men had dug themselves in well up on the farther slopes. British engineers were busily strengthening the new bridges and repairing some of the old, which the Germans had partially destroyed, so as to enable them to bear the weight of heavy traffic. A general advance was now begun along the whole western section of the Allied front, and along the whole frontage of the BEF. September 14th was a day of general attack. The 2nd Battalion Welsh Regiment had to clear the crest of the hill behind which lay the village of Chivy. Among them was a young officer, fresh from Sandhurst, experiencing war for the first time. His name was Second Lieutenant C. A. B. Young, and he recalled what to modern readers may seem to be the archaic instructions of his commanding officer in the face of modern weaponry:

Our objective . . . was the ridge of the Chemin des Dames. The approach to it was up about 600 yards. A grassy slope with no cover, even a hillock. Absolutely open. There was no possible chance of taking the position because it was too far and there was no cover. We had no artillery worth having . . . [we advanced] in extended open order. The colonel's order: officers to the front, drawn swords. [There was] heavy fire coming from the German position . . . rifle fire and some machine gun fire . . . Mark Haggard of course, was one of the famous characters of that [incident] . . . he was hit and couldn't move and he kept shouting out, 'Stick it Welsh!' but he died poor chap. A fellow went out and picked him up and got a Victoria Cross for it. Brought him back. [But we] hadn't gone more than about forty yards before we all came to a halt . . . We all saw that it was impossible and started to come back . . . [it was] not more than a quarter of an hour, before everybody realised it was an impossible job.[22]

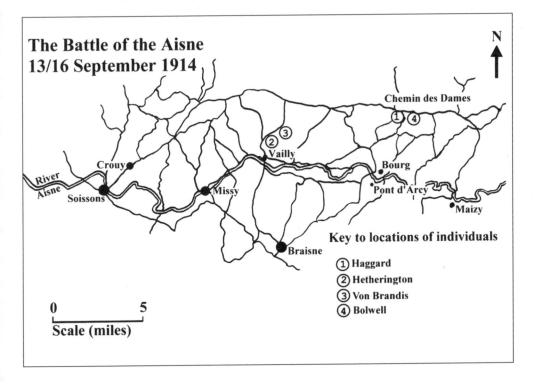

The Battle of the Aisne 13/16 September 1914

N

Chemin des Dames

① ④

② ③

Vailly

Crouy

Bourg

River Aisne

Pont d'Arcy

Soissons

Missy

Maizy

Braisne

Key to locations of individuals

① Haggard
② Hetherington
③ Von Brandis
④ Bolwell

0   5

Scale (miles)

Captain Mark Haggard, a nephew of the author Sir Rider Haggard, was a company commander in Young's battalion. He had attempted single-handed to capture a Maxim gun, but just before he reached it, he was struck by several bullets and fell to the ground mortally wounded. His reckless bravery was typical of that of young aristocratic British officers in this phase of the war. One of the best accounts by an enlisted man of this day of bitter fighting on the Aisne comes from Frederick Bolwell, who expertly captures the mood of this rain-soaked battle, fought on wooded slopes against an often invisible enemy. Describing the fighting near Troyon he paid an uncommon tribute to his enemy:

> It had been a most awful and bloodthirsty day, with two of the finest bodies of men that ever faced each other opposed to one another. There was bound to be a good fight, and it was the cleanest and most sporting day's battle I have ever fought.[23]

Several battalions now tried to force the passage of the Aisne over the hastily-constructed pontoon bridge at Vailly. The 1st Battalion Northumberland Fusiliers, fighting its way uphill through thick woodland soaked by recent rain, suddenly emerged into open country in full view of the Germans. Lance Corporal Fred Hetherington described the ensuing melee in another good contemporary account:

> We were so near the German trenches that we got the order to charge. When they saw the steel glittering on our rifles they squealed like rats and bolted from the trenches. To escape us they had to get over other trenches behind, and some of them were not quick enough. One fellow scrambled out just in front of me. He may have had a mother living, a wife, children, a sweetheart. I cannot say; I did not stop to think of that, but while I ran blindly towards their fire, I just thought of our fellows lying dead and wounded in the trenches. As I struck, I tripped and fell right over him. By the time I had picked myself up, the charge was practically over. . . . Yes, it's a bit vivid, perhaps, but it is war – real war. To live in it is to go through purgatory on earth.[24]

The following day at Rouge Maison Farm, about a mile north-east of Vailly, the 4th Battalion Royal Fusiliers were heavily attacked by the Germans, who tried to wrest the farm from them. An account of the fighting here survives from one member of the opposing German forces, Cordt von Brandis. He called to his men:

> 'Forward, at them, at the Englishmen, at these damned island pigs who are guilty of starting the war!' First we were fifty, then thirty of us as we approached their raised earth defences. There the foremost ones jumped up, with hands held high! One ran towards me, quite a young fellow, saying 'Sir Sir, don't kill me'. The second line defended itself, a wounded

Briton who had been shot flung his clasp knife, blade outstretched, against the cartridge pouches of a corporal; it stuck there, shaking.

It was with this great 'hurrah', this roar of courage, that our people attacked the mercenaries of 5 Company Royal Fusilier Regiment. It was a terrible eruption of the courage with which the men had borne the retreat, and revenge upon those responsible for our strain. Across the battlefield, Khaki clad men lay crumpled, felled by spades and rifle butts, but in death still the features of their clean-shaven, tough faces looked relaxed.

They were manful opponents, the experienced colonial warriors of the first English army. The officers, the captain and the second lieutenant who also both lay dead in the firing line, proved this.[25]

Again, we see this odd mixture of contempt and admiration for the British expressed by a German officer. The fighting thus far had been merely a curtain-raiser for what was to follow in the next four years, but already the strain was beginning to tell on some. One British officer on the Aisne wrote of his personal sense of desolation, but at the same time of his respect for his men and their endurance. This was to be a defining characteristic of the British officer in the Great War:

I have never spent and imagine that I can never spend a more ghastly and heart-tearing 48 hours than the last. Not a moment in which to write a word in my diary. We have been fighting hard ever since 8am on the 14th and have suffered much . . . However, we have done and shall continue to do, please God, what we have to do and that is all about it. The sights were ghastly . . . absolutely ghastly, and whoever was in the wrong in the matter which brought this war to be, is deserving of more than he can ever get in the world. Everyone very cheery and making the best of things. Men of course wonderful, as T. Atkins always is.[26]

The focus of the war on the Western Front, however, was now shifting northwards. The conflict was entering a new phase, the so-called 'Race to the Sea', as each side sought to out-manoeuvre the other by finding an open flank.

In order for the BEF to be closer to its supply chain, the decision was taken to withdraw it from the Aisne, and it entrained for the north, in order to resume its position on the French left flank once more, between La Bassee and the Belgian city of Ypres.

The pivotal position in the La Bassee sector was the village of Neuve Chapelle, and both sides battled desperately for control of the ruins. Here on 23 October an Irish regular soldier by the name of John Lucy crouched with his comrades under a devastating German barrage, as the enemy tried to wrest the village from them. He wrote:

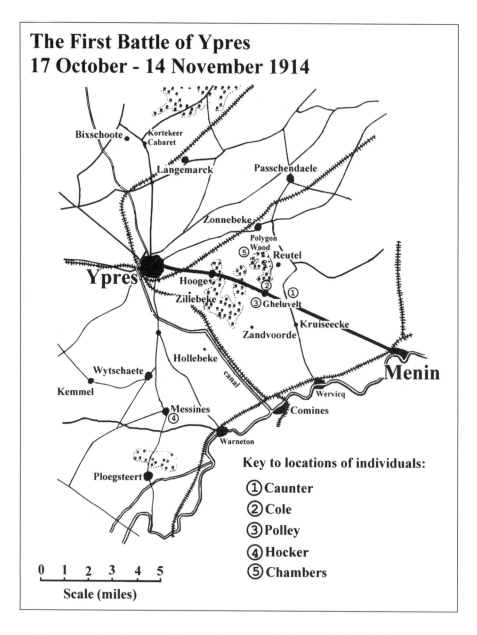

The First Battle of Ypres
17 October - 14 November 1914

Bixschoote

Kortekeer Cabaret

Langemarck

Passchendaele

Zonnebeke

Polygon Wood

⑤

Reutel

Ypres

Hooge

②

①

Zillebeke

③ Gheluvelt

Kruiseecke

Zandvoorde

Hollebeke

canal

Wytschaete

Menin

Kemmel

Wervicq

Messines

Comines

④

Warneton

Ploegsteert

Key to locations of individuals:

① Caunter

② Cole

③ Polley

④ Hocker

⑤ Chambers

0 1 2 3 4 5

Scale (miles)

the enemy found our position, and we crouched wretchedly, shaken by the blastings, under a lasting hail of metal and displaced earth and sods, half blinded and half choked by poisonous vapours, waiting for the enemy infantry . . . Time seemed to stand still; an hour was a day under this torture. We smoked nervously, lighting up and passing cigarettes with trembling fingers. The battle smoke killed the taste of the nicotine. As the day grew on we felt hungry, but we had no desire to eat. Our mouths were parched by the poisonous vapours, and with the thought that we would have to stand up to the German infantry attack any moment, we had no saliva.[27]

In spite of the devastating fire they were under, Lucy noted proudly that the line held. Frank Richards' 2nd Battalion Royal Welsh Fusiliers, was in the trenches south west of Armentières, near Laventie. On 24 October his battalion too was heavily attacked, but Richards was confident that the line here also could be defended. Like that of Lucy and his men, the training of these regulars stood them in good stead, and more than made up for any inferiority in numbers:

> Shells began bursting all along our front . . . Some of the enemy had now come out of the trees and no doubt intended to advance a little way under cover of their barrage. But the shelling was not severe enough to prevent us opening out rapid fire at them. I don't think any one of them ran twenty yards before he was dropped. To good, trained, pre-War soldiers who kept their nerve, ten men holding a trench could easily stop fifty who were trying to take it, advancing from a distance of four hundred yards.[28]

The avowed intention of the German high command to break through on this front had been thwarted partly by the determination of British regular soldiers such as Richards and Lucy to stand their ground, but also by the timely arrival of the Indian Corps as reinforcements.

Already by late October the German commanders were shifting their heavy artillery to the north, away from the La Bassée sector, in order to give all the weight that they could to their offensive at Ypres, which was also now reaching its nadir. The Ypres battlefield of 1914 was almost totally obliterated (both physically and in the nation's collective memory) by the later battles which took place over the same ground. The Ypres Salient in 1917 was a shell-scared waterlogged moonscape, but in 1914 it was very different. The countryside to the south east of Ypres was dotted with woods, forming an almost continuous chain from Zonnebeke to Wytschaete. As well as mature trees they contained dense undergrowth, altogether providing a good deal of cover for the movement of troops and for attacking formations to assemble. In this final phase of the 'Race to the Sea', the objective of the Germans was to smash through the BEF line between the Belgians on the Yser and the French further south, and to reach the Channel coast. Faced with the German juggernaut bearing down on them, the objective of the BEF became simply to hold on.

October 31st was to be the critical day of the battle for Ypres, vital in determining the outcome of the 1914 campaign, and in fact one of the most critical days of the entire war for the British. It dawned unusually warm and clear, and for the first time in Flanders the Germans were able to use a balloon to direct the fire of their heavy artillery. It was to be with devastating effect. On this day, Lieutenant J. A. L. Caunter, of 1st Gloucesters, was taken prisoner in a sunken road immediately north of the Menin Road, 800 yards east of Gheluvelt. He left the following account of his treatment at the hands of his German captors:

> We fired at [the enemy] as hard as we could, and while I was firing at one column about 100 yards off I heard a yell from one of my men, 'Here they are, sir'. It was another German column coming up a ditch. They were upon us before I knew that they were there. I dived into a hole. About a company of them came along and pricked us out of our holes with their bayonets. I counted our men afterwards by Menin church. There were about 13, four or five of them not of my company. There were no officers with the Germans at first, and the German men stood around us yelling like a crowd of pariah dogs. A private, who spoke English, prevented them from bayoneting me. They were Westphalians, an Ersatz regiment, number one hundred and something. They began tearing me to pieces. They tore off my equipment and in doing so tore my coat. One man hit me on the head with a gun.[29]

By midday, the weight of the German attack against the British here had begun to tell. Gheluvelt was lost around 1 p.m. and a sizeable gap had been driven into the British line. Unless that gap could be closed, the BEF was in danger of being cut off from the coast. It was ordered that the 2nd Worcestershires should make a counter-attack to try to recover the lost ground. Private John Cole was serving with the battalion, and afterwards wrote an account with the authentic ring of a British regular:

> We go into reserve but these days there is no rest as we are urgently needed to stop another breakthrough this time along the Ypres-Menin road. Fed up to the teeth we go forward led by our CO Major Hankey when out of the forest country come the grey hordes of Germans. At Major's command, charge! Our troops spreading out bayonets fixed and spreading out leaving it to luck how many come out alive. The German reaction was swift. A thunder of artillery burst among troops, gaps appeared but the waves of bayonets went on. More than a hundred of the battalion were killed and many wounded. These unshaven haggard men of the 2nd Worcs came face to face with the fresh faced Germans of the 244th and 245th regts tough youngsters with the swearing tommys [*sic*] in khaki with their remorseless cold steel stabbing, the heart went out of the Germans. They fled in a grey mass.[30]

Late in the afternoon of 31 October, on the 7th Division front south of the Menin Road, another remarkable counter-attack was organised. Among the British soldiers was Private H. J. Polley, one of the survivors of the 2nd Battalion

Bedfordshire Regiment. He wrote later of how the intensive pre-war training of the British swayed the balance here:

> Never, during the whole of the war, had there been a more awful fire than that which we gave the Germans. Whenever we got the chance, we gave them what they call the 'Englishman's mad minute' that is, the dreadful fifteen rounds a minute rapid fire. We drove it into them and mowed them down. Many a soldier, when his own rifle was too hot to hold, threw it down and snatched the rifle of a dead or wounded comrade who had no further use for it, and with this fresh, cool weapon he continued the deadly work by which success could alone be won.[31]

By nightfall an eerie calmness had descended on most of the battlefield, both sides having fought themselves to a standstill. At Bethlehem Farm, near Messines, the German writer Paul Oskar Höcker, captain in a *Landwehr* infantry battalion, was attempting to get some rest, after what must have been an exhausting day. As might be expected from a professional writer he paints a vivid picture of the situation, and the significance of the date was not lost on him:

> Nearby in a village the chimes of midnight can be heard. I hear quiet mooing of cattle, whilst chickens cackle. In the firing line an order is passed along, about the importance of keeping a close watch out, although we want to sleep. But it is unpleasantly cold. I am lucky, in that the Grenadiers have left a couple of overcoats behind in the trench. One has bullet holes in it. It is a dead man's coat. Suddenly Rochlitz draws our attention to the bank in front of us. In the moonlight there are visible six or seven figures. 'Engländer!' he whispers tersely. Yes, they are English. But they will carry out no more raids. They are dead. The brown shadows appear eerie now in the cold moonlight . . It is All Souls Day . . .[32]

The fighting of 11 November around Ypres was probably the second most critical day of the entire battle, after 31 October (though on this occasion there was not the same sense of crisis as that day when Gheluvelt was lost). Though the Germans did not break through the British lines, they did in fact penetrate at a number of points, most notably at Nonnen Boschen, and there was certainly the potential to roll the BEF back into the sea. Any and all reserves the British army had, were thrown into the front line. A letter survives from a young German guardsman who was present that day in the *3. Garde-Regiment zu Fuß* (3rd Foot Guard Regiment). The account is full of the usual Teutonic bravado, but is valuable none the less. It reads:

> You will have read of the battle, because the English were overwhelmed by this massive attack. There were some sights to see here, like how the

rifle butt was used as a weapon; we advanced too slowly using the bayonet, so we removed them. Then we could reverse our rifles, and as a result advanced much faster. We were so far forward, that we held a fire trench with the English, we were separated from them only by a breastwork; so we remained for three days, friend and foe in the same trench.[33]

The British unit which faced them was the 1st Battalion King's Liverpool Regiment, which recorded sardonically in its War Diary that it was '[now] supported on the right by the Prussian Guard'[!][34] The King's soon received reinforcements from the 5th Field Company, Royal Engineers. There were no 'second line' troops that day – all fought as infantry, engineers included. Corporal Arthur Chambers was a member of the 5th Field Company, waiting in reserve on the western side of Polygon Wood. His diary for 11 November records:

We blaze away & many fall at such close range. Lieut Collins falls mortally wounded. The air is humming with bullets. The Germans, who are enormous men enter the wood on our right and we fear a surprise rush from there, a farm in the wood catches fire, and the smoke is blinding us. We continue to fire all day & pick off a great number of them. One big fellow got to very close quarters, but he had to give best to 303 at 20 yards' range. We hang on till 2.30pm & hold up the attack & learn that reinforcements are coming up on the right – the Black Watch, Ox & Bucks and the Irish Guards are advancing in skirmishing order on our right towards us. When they get level with us we all charge. I shall never forget the sensation, but it certainly isn't fear. The Germans broke and ran for it, but we captured a good many.[35]

The final *vale* to the men of the BEF who stood their ground here must go to a German soldier, the editor of the *Berliner Tageblatt*, who was serving as a Reserve *leutnant* in Flanders at this time. After the battle he wrote a telling – and surprisingly candid – piece about the soldierly qualities of the British Tommy in his newspaper. In it he said:

They soon gave us practical proof that they could shoot, for in the first few engagements our battalion was reduced to about half . . . we were at once struck with the great energy with which their infantry defended itself when driven back and by the determined efforts made by it at night to recover lost ground. In this it was well supported by its field artillery which . . . is at least as good as ours . . . The main strength of the British undoubtedly lies in the defence and in the utilization of ground. Their nerves undoubtedly react better than those of the Germans, and their sporting instincts render them easier than our men to train in shooting, and in the use of ground and patrolling. The hardiness of their infantry was very apparent near Ypres. The shelter trenches were so well constructed that they could not be discovered with the naked eye . . . my own observation shows me that the British are excellent at patrol work, which I cannot say of our men.[36]

High praise indeed, from one who had nothing to gain by such public admiration of his opponents.

Thus, in a space of just four and a half months, some of the most critical battles of the First World War had been fought. They were clearly battles of the machine age, in which artillery and machine-guns were used to grind down the opposition, yet they were also battles in which individual tenacity, training and courage still had a part to play, and indeed could prove decisive. Comparing and contrasting German accounts of these critical days with those of their British opponents offers us valuable insights into the campaign and the differing ways in which it was perceived by those who took part in it. More than this, I would argue that it is essential for an understanding of what actually happened on the Western Front from the first clash of arms between British and German units at the end of August to November, 1914, and the onset of deadlock.

Notes

1. Edward Packe, unpublished memoir (Courtesy of Jo Edkins).
2. Thomas Burke, *The German Army from Within* (London: 1914), p. 83.
3. Ernest Thomas, 'I Fired The First Shot!', in Sir John Hammerton (ed.), *The Great War . . . I Was There!* (London: nd), p. 41.
4. Sidney Godley interview, BBC Radio (recorded 15 April 1954); British Library Sound Archive, reference 1CDR0001911.
5. Raimund von Gleichen-Ruszwurm and Ernst Zurborn, *Die Schlacht Bei Mons* (Oldenburg: 1919), p. 30.
6. Quoted in Sir Reginald U. H. Buckland, 'Demolitions Carried Out at Mons and During the Retreat', *Royal Engineers Journal* (March 1932), p. 23.
7. Heinrich Heubner, *Unter Emmich vor Lüttich, unter Kluck vor Paris* (Schwerin i. Mecklb.: 1915), p. 70.
8. Arthur Nugent Floyer-Acland, unpublished typescript diary, Liddle Collection, University of Leeds.
9. Cordt von Brandis, *Die Stürmer von Douaumont: Kriegserlebnisse eines Kompagnie führers* (Berlin: 1917), p. 19.
10. Ibid.
11. Harry Easton, manuscript recollections, Liddle Collection, University of Leeds.
12. Cecil A. Brownlow, *The Breaking of the Storm* (London: 1918), p. 79.
13. Karl Storch, *Vom feldgrauen Buchhändler: Stimmungsbilder, Briefe und Karten von Karl Storch* (Magdeburg: 1917), p. 38.
14. Arthur Green, *The Story of a Prisoner of War* (London: 1916), p. 3.
15. Quoted in John Terraine, *General Jack's Diary* (London: 1964), p. 38.
16. Storch, *Vom feldgrauen Buchhändler*, p. 39.
17. www.stadt-land-oldenburg.de/i-weltkrieg.htm (author's translation).

18. William Clarke, unpublished typescript recollections, Liddle Collection, University of Leeds.
19. Walter Bloem, *The Advance from Mons* (London: 1930), p. 152.
20. Ibid, p. 167.
21. *Journal of the 5th Inniskilling Dragoon Guards* (1935), p. 127.
22. C. A. B. Young, tape-recorded recollections, Liddle Collection, University of Leeds.
23. Frederick Bolwell, *With a Reservist in France* (New York, 1917), p. 47.
24. *Isle of Man Times*, 24 October 1914.
25. Von Brandis, *Die Stürmer von Douaumont*, p. 36.
26. WO95/1280, The National Archives, London.
27. John Lucy, *There's a Devil in the Drum* (London: 1938), p. 223.
28. Frank Richards, *Old Soldiers Never Die* (London: 1933), p. 35.
29. WO 161/96/19, 637-45, The National Archives, London.
30. John Cole, manuscript recollections, Liddle Collection, University of Leeds.
31. Quoted in Walter Wood, *In the Line of Battle* (London: 1916), p. 281.
32. Paul Oskar Höcker, *An der Spitze meiner Kompagnie* (Berlin: 1915), p. 211.
33. Quoted in Joachim von Delbrück, *Der Deutsche Krieg in Feldpostbriefen* Vol III (Munich: 1915), p. 306.
34. Quoted in James E. Edmonds, *Military Operations France and Belgium 1914*, Vol II (London: 1922), p. 436.
35. Arthur Chambers, typescript diary, Liddle Collection, University of Leeds.
36. Quoted in Edmonds, *Military Operations France and Belgium 1914*, Vol II, p. 456.

Suggested Further Reading

Brownlow, Cecil, *The Breaking of the Storm* (London: Methuen, 1918).
Edmonds, Brigadier General Sir James E., *Military Operations France & Belgium 1914* (2 vols) (London: Macmillan, 1929).
Höcker, Paul Oskar, *An der Spitze meiner Kompagnie* (Berlin: Ullstein, 1915).
Huebner, Heinrich, *Unter Emmich vor Lüttich, unter Kluck vor Paris* (Schwerin i. Mecklb.: F. Bahn 1915).
Lucy, John, *There's a Devil in the Drum* (London: Faber & Faber, 1938).
Richards, Frank, *Old Soldiers Never Die* (London: Faber & Faber, 1933).
Richardson, Matthew, *1914: Voices from the Battlefields* (Barnsley: Pen & Sword, 2014).
Terraine, John, *General Jack's Diary* (London: Eyre & Spottiswoode, 1964).
Von Brandis, Cordt, *Die Stürmer von Douaumont: Kriegserlebnisse eines kompagniefübrers* (Berlin: August Scherl, 1917).

PART TWO

Chapter 9

The Green Howards and Corporal Tom Riordan at the First Battle of Ypres

* * *

Roger Chapman

The attractive and evocative names or nicknames of the county regiments mean a lot to the officers and men of the British infantry. It was particularly so for the Green Howards – the Regiment of the North Riding of Yorkshire. It was the nickname given to the regiment at a time when regiments were named after their colonels. As the colonels changed so did the name. So, in 1738, when the Honourable Charles Howard – the son of the 3rd Earl of Carlisle, of Castle Howard in North Yorkshire – was made colonel of a regiment, they were called 'Howard's Regiment of Foot'. They had green facings on their red infantry coats.

The nickname came from when there was confusion on the battlefield some six years later. The Regiment was ordered to France to fight in the War of the Austrian Succession and found itself fighting alongside a similarly-named regiment – that of Lieutenant General Thomas Howard. The easiest way to tell them apart was by the colour of their facings. Charles Howard's Regiment became known as the 'Green Howards' and Thomas Howard's regiment the 'Buff Howards', the latter shortened later to 'The Buffs'.

So, the Green Howards was the nickname for The Yorkshire Regiment or to be more correct 'Alexandra, the Princess of Wales's Own Yorkshire Regiment', during the Great War. With a history and tradition going back to the seventeenth century there was an almost fanatical family *esprit de corps* with generations of families serving both as officers and enlisted men.

It was a typical county infantry regiment, drawing most of its young soldiers from the towns, ports, villages and hamlets in the north of the county and officers from the land owning or professional class. By the end of the war, there were twenty-four battalions each consisting of over 1,000 men. Ten of these battalions fought on the Western Front in Belgium and France, continually reinforced by trained recruits. Of the 68,000 men who wore the Green Howards' cap badge in the war, over 25,000 were wounded and 8,500 killed. In addition, we should be mindful of the 2,800 taken prisoner. Fifty-six Battle Honours were awarded to the regiment and twelve Victoria Crosses were earned by officers, NCOs and men of the regiment. However, in August 1914, as a result of the Haldane Reforms, there were only two regular battalions – the 1st Battalion based in British India, and the 2nd in the Channel Islands – with a 3rd Battalion for recruiting and basic training, and a 4th and 5th Battalion as part-time Territorials, based in North Yorkshire.

Most soldiers recruited from Yorkshire have a dour toughness, leavened by a sense of humour, which manifests itself in stoic pride in the battalion they serve and for those men that fight alongside them. To illustrate this characteristic, I have chosen to write about Tom Riordan, a 22-year-old NCO in the 2nd Battalion, The Yorkshire Regiment (The Green Howards). Tom wrote a memoir which covers the dramatic events of the First Battle of Ypres, but does more than this, revealing the essence of the Regular soldier and, I like to think, the Yorkshire soldier.

Riordan had joined the Green Howards in 1908 as a drummer boy at the age of 16. His father, Sergeant Major Thomas Mortimer Riordan, was equivalent to the Regimental Sergeant Major in the regiment at the time. Hence, Tom had a lot to prove. His strong personality, smartness and marksmanship soon singled him out for promotion to Lance Corporal and, by 1912, he was a Corporal knocking on the door of the Sergeants' Mess.

In August 1914, the 2nd Battalion was stationed in Guernsey at St Peter Port. However, 'B' Company – in which Tom was a Section Commander – was detached to Fort Albert on the island of Alderney some 50 miles to the north. His memoir sets the scene:

Our posting to Alderney proved to be a real cushy station. We were accommodated in Fort Albert with a Battery of Royal Garrison Artillery, who had two guns mounted on the highest point of the fort. From their observation platform you could see the whole of the island and on a clear day we could see France.

We had a very easy time there and parades usually finished at about 12 noon. We occasionally did a route march around the island, but this was only 6 miles. We did no more, otherwise we would have gone dizzy going round and round.

At the end of July, as the crisis in Europe worsened and war suddenly appeared imminent, life on Alderney changed.

On the 1st August we were ordered to pack our kit, keeping out only the articles required for active service, and we were sent out to put the island in a state of defence. We did continuous guard on the beaches. I think we were delighted when war was declared on Germany. The general opinion among the troops was that it would be over in a few months.

Then, war was declared on 4 August and Captain Walker, the Alderney detachment Company Commander, received a telegram at 5.00 a.m. on the following day to act on what was called the 'War Book' locked in his Company safe. More accurately this book was a mobilisation encyclopaedia. It ran to several million words giving detailed instructions for action to take on the declaration of war. Captain Walker's first task was to secure the island, inform the inhabitants and hand over responsibility to the local Territorial commander and then stand by to move to Guernsey to join the rest of the Battalion.

Immediately war was declared all soldiers under the age of 19 were posted back to England and replaced with reservists, who were immediately called up. This left me with only one regular soldier in my section – Private Harry Tandey. Many of the reservist[s], who joined us in Guernsey, were almost at the end of their commitments and were not too happy about being 'called up'. They were a tough crowd who took some handling, but soon proved to be fine, dependable soldiers.

It had been planned that the 2nd Yorkshires would remain in Guernsey for the duration of the war, but a telegram marked 'Top Secret' arrived at Battalion Headquarters on 20 August, stating that the battalion was to proceed at the earliest opportunity to Southampton and join the 21st Brigade of the newly-formed 7th Division.

On the 28th August, the battalion was relieved by the 3rd Battalion, The North Staffordshire Regiment. We paraded at 10.00am and marched behind the Guernsey Militia Band to two steamers: the 'Sarnia' and the 'Vera'. We reached Southampton at 6.00pm the same day to find we were the first unit to arrive of the newly formed 7th Division.

The battalion had moved into a tented camp, erected near Lyndhurst in the New Forest, in the south of Hampshire. There were thirty-two regular officers under the command by Lt Colonel Charles King, many of the officers having served in the Tirah campaign on the North West Frontier of India and in the 2nd Boer War in South Africa. Fuelled by tales of the retreat from Mons and news of the Battle of the Marne, crossing the Aisne and attempting to capture the heights beyond the far bank in September, the battalion trained hard. Lord Kitchener had warned off the 7th Division, now fully formed in the New Forest, to join the British Expeditionary Force (BEF) in France and sent instructions about their behaviour in a foreign country. They were also sent a soldier's prayer to peruse.

Riordan and his section in B Company, under the command of now Major Walker and his platoon commander 2/Lt Brooksbank, spent most of their days on the ranges firing their Short Magazine Lee-Enfield rifles, while Lt Legard led training with the two Vickers machine-guns in the Medium Machine-Gun Section.

> The grapevine proved to be correct, and on Sunday 4th October we marched into Southampton where we embarked on a boat named: 'The Californian'.

There was a sweepstake on board as to their destination. Was it to be Calais, Ostend, Boulogne or Dunkirk? Only Major General Thomas Capper, commanding 7th Division, knew it was to be Zeebrugge. The Germans had diverted from their original invasion plan – the Schlieffen Plan – and were aiming for Antwerp. The 7th Division was to land and defend Antwerp from the approach of the Imperial German Army.

> Early next day we landed at Zeebrugge in Belgium. I have never seen so many boats in such a small harbour. We had to cross two boats to get onto the quay We marched to Bruges and my company was sent on outpost duty near Ostend that night. It was rather an eerie experience for we were told nothing and did not know if the Germans were close to us or miles away.

The battalion then marched to Ostend in order to cover the landing of 3rd Cavalry Division at the port. It was during this march that the men heard the sound of heavy artillery for the first time. The roads were choked with Belgium refugees and the remnants of the Belgium army. It took two days for the Cavalry Division to offload all their horses and equipment. Once the cavalry was safely ashore, the battalion was told to march back to Bruges where they took over the same billets as before.

News had reached 7th Infantry Division and 3rd Cavalry Division that the Germans had taken Antwerp. It was now decided, as Antwerp was lost, that the Division must march to Ypres and link up with the British I Corps under General Sir Douglas Haig, part of General Sir John French's BEF, making their way north to the same city.

At that time, although the infantry was used to marching long distances, they had not done so on Belgian roads. The rough cobbled surface soon took their toll. Many men got blisters. To make things worse, on 13 October, there was a marked drop in temperature and torrential rain. The march from Bruges to Ypres was far from pleasant, although the villagers turned out to greet them with fruit, cigarettes, sweets, beer and wine. The men were carrying 150 rounds of ammunition, their rifles and equipment, a total weight in the area of 60–80lbs. The Green Howards had been ordered to act as the advance guard for the whole Division.

> We arrived in Ypres on or about the 14th October and must have marched half way round before entering the town for we saw signposts with Ypres

on them showing first 10 kilometres, then 5 kilometres. We were billeted for the first night in a small house on the south east side of the town.

The first person to see action in the Division, Captain (QM) Edward Pickard DCM – he had won the Distinguished Conduct Medal in the Boer War as a Sergeant – was looking for billets for the soldiers in a small village called Kruisstat, to the south-east of Ypres, along with his Regimental Quartermaster Sergeant and Billet Sergeant. A small boy ran up to Captain Pickard, who was on his horse, shouting out '*Uhlans', Uhlans'*. Captain Pickard dismounted, grabbed a rifle from a Sergeant Bell – as officers were only equipped with a revolver and sword at that time – and he and his Regimental Quartermaster Sergeant aimed in the direction where the boy was pointing. Eighty yards away there were two *Uhlan* cavalrymen on horseback making a reconnaissance.

The Quartermaster and the Quartermaster Sergeant both fired two shots and hit the Germans in the back as they spurred on their horses. The *Uhlans*, although wounded, made their escape but fortunately a Commander Sampson was in an armoured car close by and gave chase. A short while later, a triumphant Sampson returned with two prisoners: an '*Uhlan*' officer and warrant officer, who were returned to Ypres for interrogation. So, the first shots of what was to be the First Battle of Ypres, had been fired on 14 October 1914.

The Division no longer acted on the orders of the War Office in London. It now came under the command of Field Marshal Sir John French with the rest of the BEF trying to outflank the German Army in what has been dubbed the 'Race for the Sea'. Sir John ordered Major General Capper to start planning a move east from Ypres towards Menin. The interrogation of the *Uhlans* cannot have been significantly revelatory because French was still unaware that the Germans were simultaneously amassing troops and artillery in vastly superior numbers in and around Menin to make an assault on Ypres.

General Sir Henry Rawlinson, commanding IV Corps, wrote his operational orders on Friday 15 October and for the first time mentioned the recently-formed 7th Division. He had ordered the division to advance eastwards the next morning from Ypres and take up a position about 9 kilometres from Ypres close to Gheluvelt, so setting the scene for one of the most numerically mismatched battles of the war to date, a battle from which the 7th Division was to earn the title 'The Immortal 7th Division'.

It had taken General Capper and his staff almost 18 hours to manipulate the three brigades of the division into position for the advance. At 4.00 a.m. on 16 October, with 2nd Yorkshires in the vanguard of 21 Brigade, they advanced east using the Menin Road as the centre line.

We had been advancing for some time when suddenly a rifle shot came from our front. We were crossing a turnip field at the time and I do not think I have seen anyone dive for cover behind turnip tops as we did at that moment.

When I looked up I saw three strange soldiers on horses going away from us along the road as fast as their horses could go, while the company on the right was firing at them. They got away all right. We then moved forward with more alertness but nothing happened and we arrived at Gheluvelt.

'A' Company had captured eight German hussars and the battalion had suffered no casualties. The inhabitants of Gheluvelt quickly told the Green Howards that the Germans had moved out the evening before and were a mile further to the east at a crossroads in a hamlet called Nieuwe Kruiseke. Looking eastwards there was a pitiable sight. The road was packed with people from the nearby villages trying desperately to flee from German soldiers massing around Menin. Some seemed to have all their worldly possessions in carts drawn by ponies or dogs, others were pushing wheelbarrows loaded with all they could carry. Everyone had a look of terror in their faces as they hurried madly to safety, spurred on by the memory and sight of the burning villages behind them.

It took the 2nd Battalion almost an hour to cover the remaining mile to its objective at Kilometre 9 on the Menin Road, a small cluster of houses, a location later known as the Menin Crossroads. The battle which was about to take place at the crossroads was commemorated in a 1925 painting by Fortunino Maturio. Tom Riordan is in the painting and can be seen with his section moving out to a new position to the north of the main road to Menin protected by Lt Legard with his sword and the two Vickers machine-guns pointing towards Becelaere. The man carrying the wounded soldier is the same Private Harry Tandey from Tom's section who survived the war to win the VC, DCM, MM and five mentions in dispatches – the most highly-decorated private soldier in the British Army.

Here the battalion was to dig in and defend the position. Trenches were dug in the wet earth. It did not take too long for the men to make themselves as comfortable as possible. Wire was sent up from the rear but the Brigade was not properly equipped for this 'new' type of warfare. There were of course as yet no steel helmets or periscopes to look over the parapet so the men were subject to sniper fire and artillery from German positions overlooking them at Becelaere. Soon camp stoves were sent up to provide hot meals to the men digging the trenches. As yet, the officers and men were unaware of the mighty forces being drawn up in front of them

The German High Command had been quick to realise the threat posed by the appearance of a fresh division in the area of Ypres and the decision was taken at once to send the new XXVI and XXVII Reserve Corps, recently arrived by train, to stem the British advance from Ypres. Their training had been minimal, some had not been equipped with full uniforms and the majority had only just received their rifles. By 21 October their numbers had swollen to a staggering 175,000 men with further seasoned troops moving north from the Aisne to support them. (A certain Corporal in the 16th Bavarian Reserve Regiment was to get his baptism of fire opposite the Yorkshire Regiment in the battle to come – Adolf Hitler.) Also arriving, to make the German force more powerful still, were the artillery units, which so effectively destroyed the defence of Antwerp. Their task was a simple one: 'To smash through and sweep away this contemptible little British army at Ypres and secure the Channel Ports.' The 7th Infantry Division and 3rd Cavalry Division, unknown to them, were to be outnumbered by over 8:1.

As the 7th Division feverishly prepared its positions, the Germans were deploying from the area around Roulers and Menin their recently formed Fourth Army under General the Duke Albrecht of Württemberg. Advancing west from Menin on a direct line to the Green Howards came XXVII Bavarian Reserve Corps, over 75,000 strong but consisting of 75 per cent volunteers (university students in the main, under 23 years of age) and the remainder fully-trained reservists. The students' military preparation had consisted of only fourteen days basic training, ten days platoon training and seven days of company training. These inexperienced soldiers, many of whom still wore their University of Munich caps, advanced west with boundless enthusiasm and seemingly total disregard for their own safety, but it could not make up for their lack of training.

The German infantry attacked in force on 20 October. For the first time the 2nd Yorkshires were in the thick of the fighting. Surprisingly, the casualties in the Division were light, mostly from artillery fire, the trenches not yet being completed. After repeated German attacks, at 5.00 p.m., the machine-gunners got a good target as the inexperienced German soldiers massed together in their forming-up position just below Becelaere and were mown down. The German command had not realised that their left flank was visible to the Green Howards and used open ground to assemble, just to the north of the Cross Roads. Over 2,000 troops were concentrated and visible in an area not much larger than a football stadium. The official German casualty figures for that day on that front were 937 dead. The total of wounded was not recorded.

Of this stage of the battle, Riordan wrote:

> After that attack we saw or heard nothing that evening or night to think the Germans were anywhere near us. We were therefore very surprised when we 'stood to' at dawn to see a line of trenches about 100 yards in front of us. They must have dug it during the night and we had heard not a sound. I decided to put up a trip wire as far forward as possible in front of our trench. As soon as it was dark, I went with two men and fixed it. We were not disturbed although we did make some noise fixing the tins.

During the night, six horse-drawn ammunition carts came up and 96,000 rounds of ammunition were distributed to the forward trenches and the two medium machine-gun detachments.

> The next day the Jerry snipers got to work and we had three or four men killed by them. They also started shooting artillery that day but their range

was bad and most of the shells fell short or went over the top of our trench. Their snipers were well hidden and we were ordered not to expose ourselves during the daylight.

It was on 22 October that the Green Howards found they had a serious problem developing on their left flank. The first they knew about it was when bullets started to fly over the heads of 'B' and 'C' Company from the rear. The Germans had managed to make a thrust between the 2nd Wiltshires and 2nd Royal Scots Fusiliers. 'D' Company, on the left of the Yorkshire's position, had peeled back during the massed attack and the survivors had taken up a position behind 'B' Company. Major Walker, with 'B' Company, held his ground and ordered every alternate man in the trench to face to the rear.

The battalion's commanding officer, Charles King, receiving news of this impending disaster, moved the machine-guns, 'A' Company and men from Battalion HQ to fill the gap. Meanwhile the Adjutant was sent to rally the men of 'D' Company, who had retired, and urge them to return and fill the gap. There was savage hand-to-hand fighting. Lt Legard was killed charging the enemy, firing one of his Vickers machine-guns from the hip – no mean feat as the gun weighed 60lbs. Captain Jeffries, 'D' Company Commander, called for reserves from what remained of 'D' Company and charged the enemy with fixed bayonets. He, himself, was carrying a revolver and brandishing his sword. The gap was retaken but Jeffries was mortally wounded.

As this counter-attack on the left flank was in progress, 'B' and 'C' Companies were attacked by over 2,000 German infantrymen. The enemy was driven off, suffering appalling casualties yet reappearing again and again in increasing numbers. Each attack was met by a hail of accurate rifle fire and eventually the Germans were forced to fall back.

They made several attacks against our trenches during the next week too. They came in droves or masses and we could not miss them as they were so tightly packed. We saw a great number fall but for some odd reason they always retired when they got within 20 yards of our trenches. They made night attacks as well but never came close enough for us to see them.

The Green Howards had held their position. By mid-afternoon on 24 October, the fighting had died down and commanders were able to take stock of the situation. All the units in 21 Brigade had taken heavy casualties. Of the 2nd Wiltshires, there was little trace. It was as if they no longer existed – of the 1,100 men of that Battalion, who had left Southampton twenty-two days before, only eighty were fit to fight next day. So hard pressed were 2nd Yorkshires that they were unaware of the disaster that had overtaken their sister unit on their left flank.

Of Sunday 25 October, Tom Riordan wrote:

Looking back on those three weeks I can never understand why the Germans did not overcome us when they attacked, for we could not have held them. There were long gaps between sections without a man in them. For instance, the next section on my right was at least 20 to 30 yards away and to my left the same distance. They could never have guessed we were so thin on the ground.

Sunday 25 October had seen 7th Division's most heroic stand during the First Battle of Ypres. Direct help had arrived at last in the shape of 1st and 2nd Divisions. They, with the French division attached to the BEF, arrived in Ypres from the south. The 7th Division no longer had to hold and defend single-handedly a seven-mile front.

However, it was not until two days later that the 7th Division was relieved. In incessant rain, 21 Brigade had to beat off two more German assaults using the Menin Road as the axis. The Germans now had observation balloons to direct their artillery. The final attack came at 1.30 p.m. on the 26th when the Germans renewed their efforts to force a passage by sending in another fresh Reserve Brigade of some 5,000 men. The weather had improved slightly allowing the artillery more accuracy but once more the German soldiers were caught in their assembly area by machine-gun and artillery fire. They reached no further than 200 yards from Tom Riordan's section's trench. This was the last serious attack before the 2nd Yorkshires were relieved by troops from 1 Brigade of 1st Division.

We were relieved by the Coldstream Guards during the night and we made our way back towards Ypres. We halted in a field just before dawn and had breakfast. Later we were told we were going back for a short rest. We were marched into a large wood and told to make ourselves comfortable. There was a deserted farmhouse nearby with plenty of straw and hay in the barn. We collected a lot of this to make a bed. There was plenty of water and we had a good wash and shave, the first for more than three weeks.

As Tom and the remains of the battalion were resting in the woods, the German General Fabeck, not deterred by the failure of his Reserve Corps, was reorganising and preparing for the next phase of the battle. His heavy artillery was first to arrive and took position in woods around Wervik, so that they could not be observed by aerial reconnaissance.

Tom Riordan had just nicely settled in to make himself comfortable for his first good night's sleep for a while, when a whistle blast for Orderly Sergeants to report to the Regimental Sergeant Major Hatton, was heard. Tom had been made the Orderly Sergeant for 'B' Company and when he met the RSM he was told to prepare the Company to move at once. At 5.00 p.m. the Company was ready to move back up the Menin Road to the frontline for the second and, for many, the last time.

Marched up the Menin Road. We soon realised that we were going back to that hell on earth, but when we reached Gheluvelt we turned right and then left. Soon after we entered this road, a salvo of three shrapnel shells burst high on our left flank and as it was very dark I clearly saw hundreds of red hot small balls running across the road in front of me. Had the shells burst a few yards nearer to us, I am sure many men would have been killed. The only casualty I heard was that one fellow had the heel of his boot knocked off.

The 7th Division was now positioned to the south of the Menin Crossroads, with 3rd Cavalry Division on its right and the 2nd Division on its left. The Green Howards were positioned opposite Kruiseke with the Bedfords on their left and Scots Fusiliers on their right. Tom Riordan was with 'B' Company initially in reserve to the rear of the Scots Fusiliers. Still exhausted after three weeks of marching and fighting, the Green Howards reoccupied previously dug trenches on their right.

We went to some trenches which, when it got light, we found must have been occupied by The Black Watch for we found pieces of equipment etc. marked BW. When fully daylight came the Jerries opened up heavy shellfire on our trenches but my platoon were lucky as we were in a sort of close support trench about 50 yards back from the front line. The front line was almost completely flattened and there were many killed and wounded.

Thursday 29 October would prove a hard day for the battalion. Major Walker was killed and Captain Broun took over 'B' Company. The battalion had now been fighting for ten days and they had been far from fresh at the start. After a massive artillery bombardment, the enemy broke through the Scots Fusiliers and, as a result, two Green Howard Companies were sent forward from the reserve to support the Scots.

Captain Broun who was now in command came back and called for NCOs. I seemed to be the only one there. He told me we would go forward in bounds towards the front line.

I jumped up and shouted 'Advance'. I must have been 10 yards in front of the others when I heard a whistle of a shell. It proved to be shrapnel and I saw it explode but I must have got only the blast. That shell must have killed about 20 men.

On reaching the edge of the wood I told the men to spread out along the edge of the wood. It was suddenly very quiet with no sound of shooting. I therefore told the men that I would dash across the field. If I was fired upon they should get further back in the wood and work their way to the right and so get to the farmhouse from the other side of the wood.

Off I went and was about half way across when a machine gun opened up from my left. I could see bits of earth thrown up just in front of me. I must have got out of sight of the gunner for the gun stopped and I fell down exhausted by a man lying there. It turned out to be the CO, Colonel King, who told me I was a fool to have crossed the field. I told him that the second in command, Major Alexander, had been severely wounded. He seemed quite upset about this but smiled when I told him that the Brigadier had got lost trying to find our position.

Once he had joined up with the rest of 'B' Company at the farm close to the front line, Tom saw that his greatcoat had bullet holes in the flaps at the back. He also saw that a bullet had ripped his puttee on the outer side of his left leg. He had been very lucky. It had been the last time he would speak to his commanding officer, because the next day Colonel Charles King, the Adjutant and Captain Broun were all killed by artillery fire in a trench during an 'Orders Group'.

The evening of Thursday 29 October, found 7th Division holding only a fraction of the original line, with a frontage of a mere 3,000 yards. As a thick fog descended, so the enemy barrages ceased. Most of the men were able to get a few hours of sleep, huddled in the bottom of their trenches.

The next day, the 30th, the Germans continued the pressure. Major General Capper withdrew the battalions, to the left and right of the Scots Fusiliers and Green Howards, to form a new line of defence 2,000 yards to the rear. Once this line was established, orders were given for 21 Brigade to withdraw at 11.45 a.m. However, the message did not reach the Green Howards until well after 2 p.m. and did not reach the forward trenches of the Scots Fusiliers at all.

Somehow, the two battalions held off attack after attack, although the enemy had managed to get into the woods behind them. Captain Moss-Blundell, who had taken over command of the remains of the battalion, began the withdrawal at 3.30 p.m. Corporal Tom Riordan was in a trench with seven other men to the far right of the Company position. They had been fired at from the rear and had engaged a group of Germans going across the front from right to left, had engaged them and saw them go down. There was then a lull in the firing.

I had no orders to retire and it was beginning to get dark. I sent my two flank men to the right and left to see if they could get in touch with anyone for no firing now came from either side of us. I decided it was time we retired and gave the men a rough idea how to get back to Hooge, but it was now a case of everyman for himself. I sent them back one at a time and I followed the last man. I was making for the wood from where a machine gun opened up on me. There was a hedge and ditch to my right, which would have given me cover from view until I got into the wood. As I got to the end of the small wood on my right someone called 'Come here Corporal'.

It was an officer in the Royal Scots Fusiliers with an arm in a sling. He had about twenty Scots in a trench with him and told Tom to drop into the trench. The officer, Captain Burgogne, had not received any orders to retire and did not believe Tom when he told him that it was a general order until a Scots Corporal arrived telling everyone to retire. Captain Burgogne decided that they should all go back together. 'Follow me' he ordered.

> We had only gone about 20 yards when a line of Germans rose up a few yards in front of us and fired a few rounds over our heads shouting 'Halt. Halt'. We all halted in our tracks as they had bayonets fixed and were coming for us. I was therefore in the bag. For me the war was over, but how I wish we had made a fight for it.

All the battalions in 21 Brigade had been shattered during the Germans' final thrust. Out of a battalion of 1,000 men landed at Zeebrugge, the Green Howards only had one Captain, three 2nd Lieutenants and 320 men left. Ten of the officers had been killed and eighteen wounded, and 655 other ranks had been killed or wounded. Six days later, the remains of 21 Brigade were withdrawn from the line.

Riordan spent four grim years as a prisoner of war in Germany, returning to England to learn that it seemed but a handful of the original 2nd Battalion had survived the four years of war. Perhaps his captivity had saved him. Furthermore, there was sunshine on the horizon. He was promoted to the rank of RQMS in 1919 and in the same year married and in due course was to have five sons and three daughters. As with his father, he was to be promoted to RSM and appointed a Member of the British Empire, and two of his sons were commissioned into the Green Howards. One of those sons, Major Jack Riordan, was both an RSM and appointed MBE, making him the third generation of Riordans with these twin distinctions.

If you were to walk into the Medal Room of the recently renovated Green Howards museum, you would find yourself surrounded by over 3,500 medals won by men of the regiment in various campaigns since the Crimean War. It is at such a time you might reflect about the infantrymen, who once proudly wore these medals and what it meant to them belonging to such a regiment.

A regiment is essentially a large family, and an hierarchical one at that. Like most families there are characters, some weak, some strong, with the strong often helping the weaker to conform and appreciate how the family should behave. There is a code of conduct, if not honour, which expects the individual to perform at his best, whatever the conditions. Soon, this is manifested in a form of pride in belonging to what is perceived as 'the best'. (Yes, it must be accepted that this positive quality can have a reverse side – suspicion of outsiders bordering on disdain.)

The size of the battalion within the Regiment is usually such that the commanding officer knows every man by name and often his wife and family too. In many cases the commanding officer and most of the company commanders joined as very young second lieutenants, whose sergeants took them in hand and taught them what was expected of them in peace and war.

The platoon sergeant would take his newly-joined officer aside and tell him that it his duty 'to serve to lead'. He must look his men in the eye and by his example, leadership and man-management, make his platoon the best in the whole battalion. As his sergeant, he will help him to do it. The mutual respect that the subaltern has for his sergeant grows as both gain promotion in their respective ranks. Sometimes, as a company commander, his old sergeant is his company sergeant major. Occasionally a commanding officer is lucky enough to have his former platoon sergeant as his regimental sergeant major many years later.

The British infantryman is never lacking in fighting ability, as many a bar-room brawl displays, but ultimate success in battle lies in persuading the man to fight to the last, whatever the odds. The paradox is that he seldom finds his inspiration in profound belief in a cause. Nor does patriotism or *la gloire* hold much appeal. His strength lies in simpler things: his sense of duty, his confidence in his mates, his knowledge of his craft and weapons, his trust in his leader, but possibly, most important of all, is his belief in himself that he will behave in a certain way in the eyes of his friends fighting alongside him. This is engendered from what is called the regimental system.

Life in the small, rather enclosed world of a regiment breeds mutual knowledge and trust that makes for solidarity and courage in war. Tom Riordan found this. Even when his battalion was shattered, he and the men around him fought on for over three weeks against overwhelming odds. If asked why, the question might well have been thought unnecessary but the answer would have been: 'Because I was a Green Howard.'

In the final resort it is the duty of a Green Howard soldier to face death without flinching. He must do so, if at nothing more, because it lessens the chances of death for his friends; men who wear the same cap badge, come from the same county, support the same football team, and who, he knows, will never let him down. It is family and friendship that promote valour. Here lay the strength of the Green Howards in the Great War and, for that matter, all subsequent wars, campaigns and engagements, where the Regiment fought with the same valour as it did at the First Battle of Ypres in 1914.

I would like to record my boundless appreciation of the Riordan family's trust in making Tom Riordan's memoir available to me for the preparation of this chapter.

Roger Chapman.

Chapter 10

Britons in Berlin: Ruhleben
– the Internment of British Civilians

* * *

Peter Liddle

Few British people in 1914, even in an awareness of Anglo-German rivalry in numbers of areas, saw any reason to feel concern about their reasons for employment in Germany, business in Germany, cultural enrichment in Germany, or plans to holiday in Germany that year. There is little evidence that the July Crisis following upon the assassination of Archduke Franz Ferdinand led to any Britons scurrying for home or cancelling plans to travel there. There are diaries which record quite the contrary.

After years of tracking down men who experienced civilian internment in Germany, ultimately finding sixty, interviewing many of them, respectfully soliciting their 1914–18 diaries, letters, photographs and ephemera for study and conservation, the newest discovery, in 2014, thanks to the son of the internee in question, has diary entries which confirm this point to perfection.[1]

Thomas Wyndham Richards, an elementary school teacher in Cardiff, planning to improve his German on a language cramming course in Berlin, wrote in his diary for 24 July 1914: 'Leave for Berlin'. He was bound for Tilley's Cramming School, where on arrival he was tested for his competence and assigned to a class. His diary records 'terrific excitement in the streets' but without further comment, and he went sailing at Potsdam that weekend. He saw soldiers mobilising but, when he went for his class on Monday 3 August, he was clearly surprised that his tutor had not turned up. The following day, with Britain's Declaration of War, a telegram arrived from home and we may reasonably guess that it instructed him to come home immediately.

Whatever may have been the case, Richards decided to walk the streets and his diary tells us he was 'arrested by three soldiers with loaded rifles and fixed bayonets', marched to a police station, held for two hours, and then released. He lived up to the image Britons like to think they uphold: 'Was not frightened. Amused.'

He and other students attempted to get police passes to leave for home. They were not granted and they were told they would have to stay till the end of the war. There is no evidence of optimism in the Richards diary on that issue. 'All very down about it,' he wrote, adding that most of them feel sure they are destined for jail. However, having registered with the Police, the classes continue while the students grumble that the British Government was doing absolutely nothing to help them by negotiating for an exchange of civilians. Quite apart from the more important business pre-occupying the British Government, this was wishful thinking with a number approaching 60,000 enemy aliens in Britain while the British male civilians in Germany totalled something under 5,000.

On 21 September, a special train conveyed many British women and children, the elderly men, and the sick, out of the country – not all the women I should add: some, like Mrs Alec Lloyd, stayed in her flat in Ludwigshafen while her husband, a research assistant, was detained in the factory where he was employed.[2]

Earlier in September, about forty British male civilians, considered by German authorities 'suspects', had been transferred from the City Jail in Berlin to what had been the place of captivity for Russian and Polish POWs, Ruhleben, six miles west of the city. The forty men were to be the first of many. With the British decision in September to intern their enemy aliens, the German Press had called for reciprocal treatment in Germany. On 6 November, all the registered men were instructed to report to the local town hall or police station, where they were arrested and escorted under guard, on foot, by vehicle or by train, as their location determined, to join the 'suspects' in Ruhleben, yes, a district, but really known for the Trotting Course which bore the district's name.

The Trotting Course was a ten-acre site, had three grandstands, horse-boxes, ancillary buildings and a central open area for the racing. It was within these parameters that British civilian internees were to spend their war. If one were to picture a racecourse, but with a shortened track, or an agricultural showground with one much elongated ring, three grandstands, next to each other down one side, lines of stables and stalls and separate administrative buildings, that would give a good idea of the camp's general appearance. The internees were going to live in the two-story stables, as barrack blocks.

For some months from their November arrival, weather conditions and the failure to secure use of further roofed accommodation beyond their stable blocks, limited to some extent what activities could be pursued, but diary records refute the observation sometimes made that it was not until the warmer weather of spring and the relaxation of German restriction of use of potential facilities that the inmates really stirred themselves into action. Just three days after internment, the Welsh schoolmaster, Richards, captained a football team of students from Tilly's which beat a team of British jockeys, caught in Germany by the racing season. Two days later, he captained a team of public schoolboys, playing under the name of Oldham Athletic, against a so-called West Bromwich Albion team in the first round of what was being called the Ruhleben Cup, with sixteen teams entered. His team got to the final before being thrashed 9-2 by a team calling itself Tottenham Hotspur, containing six professionals, all coaching in Germany.

There were other positive developments from the earliest days – a library was established in one barrack, thanks to the generosity of the American Ambassador; Protestant services were held in the Grandstand on the second Sunday of internment; a Dr Cimino set up a School of Languages; a meeting of University graduates established an Arts and Science Union; a Literary and Debating Society was founded; and recitals and concerts were held. Fittingly to cap that list, on 25 December, a choir of 100 with three soloists and an orchestra of twenty-five, performed Handel's *Messiah*.

Nevertheless, the location was Central to Eastern Europe with temperatures set to plunge – chilblains, colds and sore throats were common. Cramped in the stables, frayed tempers were frequent too. In such circumstances it is nice to see the humour of a few, giving amusement to many, as for example heavy rain leaving flooded areas and British notices appearing, sanctioning fishing but banning mixed bathing.

An extraordinary letter survives documenting living conditions in the camp that winter. A student named Vincent, much later Professor E. R. Vincent, a Bletchley Park cryptographer, wrote in response to a strange letter from his father which on close examination showed key words after any punctuation mark. The letter, by such means, invited him to report on conditions. Vincent replied using that basic code: 'Very bad food, insufficient bread, only one blanket provided, sanitary conditions filthy, lights are needed.'[3] From the following spring, with sport and general recreation sanctioned by the Germans in the open area in front of the grandstands and the area under the stands cleared to give space for indoor group activities, expansion of opportunities for leisure certainly did proceed apace.

But first to the accommodation, the horseboxes, now barracks. Initially there were eleven, separate, cold, draughty stable blocks, ten constructed of brick and concrete, one of timber and brick. They were two-storied. The ground floor space was about eleven feet square. Six men with their personal possessions slept in that space, initially on straw. There was a central corridor within each barrack, linking the line of horseboxes. In the dark, low-ceilinged, unpartitioned hay-loft above, more men were crammed, 200 to a barrack. The hay-lofts were reached by an external staircase and, in a sense, life for men in the loft was only linked to the men below by the downstairs door being slid open and shut, rumbling on its wheel-track suspended as it was along one side of the loft, inches from sleeping or resting heads. Of course shouted rows or carousing below was within the hearing of the 'lofters', but this was scarcely a link to cherish.

In due course, straw sacks and then plank beds – in tiers on the ground floor – provided some improvement in comfort and more space. New latrines were installed by June 1915 at either end of the camp, soon directionally-named Spandau and Charlottenburg, but on breakdown in their efficiency the result was atmospherically disastrous. The internees themselves, led by the civil engineers and practical men among them, were responsible for critical areas of improvement in their environment – drainage, walkways raised above the mud, and furniture fabrication from wood salvaged or bought.

More barracks were built but from the earliest days each block had its own social character as men gravitated towards those with whom they felt naturally associated – men with public school and university backgrounds, seamen, non-white seamen, ship's boys, for example. It was a German decision to accommodate separately those Jews who accepted such an arrangement on the grounds of the preparation of *Kosher* food. Perhaps seventy Jews identified themselves for such a move out of the 300 estimated to be in the camp.

It was not just a question of the necessary building of additional barracks to avoid over-crowding as more men came in batches to the camp, but the adaptation of existing ancillary buildings for Ruhleben's new purpose. A YMCA hut for church services, quiet reading, letter writing and the sale of basic commodities – cigarettes, chocolate, writing materials – was a tremendous asset recorded in many letters and diaries.

An area under a grandstand to house a postal service and one for a parcels office were also of major importance in terms of the efficient distribution of letters and Red Cross parcels with their massive influence on morale – 40,000 parcels in the month of January 1917, as the British blockade bit into German capacity to feed its own people, provides an indication of the fundamental significance of food parcels to the internees. It was not merely an issue of physical welfare but spiritual too, enabling the internees to strengthen the element of independence wrought from the German authorities by administrative, social, sporting, cultural, intellectual, practical skill and trade enterprise.

Among other features of the Ruhleben landscape were the well-patronised cinema and the café that were established, but an extraordinary phenomenon was the growing of flowers and cultivation of vegetables. Until March 1916, the German authorities had banned the receipt in parcels of the means of such horticultural enterprise, but with this ban then lifted, 'Forget-me-Not', the horticultural correspondent of the Camp Magazine encouraged readers to make their surroundings more like home. A positive response ensued and in due course flowers flourished in newly-dug borders or window boxes. In the letters of a man called Turner, there is an illustration of pride in gardening success as he states with tongue in cheek that his block's flowers were drawing so many admirers that he feared the shade from the crowd might be to the flowers' detriment.[4]

Of course, much more useful than colourful blooms were the vegetables cultivated in designated plots and, in September, the Ruhleben Horticultural Society was established. An appeal for help, made from the new 'offspring' to the parent body, the Royal Horticultural Society, led to the sending of seeds, bulbs and published guidance. The Ruhleben Society, with its one German Mark membership fee, soon attracted not far short of a thousand members. offered winter lectures, engaged in landscaping and set up a plant nursery (somehow with cold-frames and glasshouses), and this even became profitable.[5] Anyone familiar with flower and produce shows today and throughout time will feel no surprise on learning that competition for the best Barrack garden and in the September 1917 Flower and Vegetable Show, was fierce.

Certainly a dominant feature of the outdoor Ruhleben scene from the spring of 1915 was sports-clad figures competing on marked-out playing fields. Football may have led the way, but rugby and hockey were soon to follow. There were a few excellent tennis players, one a Davis Cup player, who always drew a crowd if he were playing in a competition on one of the seven courts marked out in front of one of the grandstands. Cricket had its star players too, one, T. H. Turner, left a nice record in a letter home, of the innocent schoolboy vanity of the sportsman: 'I got 50 with two or three sixes and hit the last four balls, 6, 4, 4, 4, 4.'[6]

Probably the most attractive sporting story to come out of Ruhleben followed the opening of a five-hole – what would now be called 'pitch and putt' – golf course. Two old seadogs – Master Mariners – decided to learn the game, paid for coaching from two golf pros interned with the numbers of professional sportsmen caught in Germany at the outbreak of war, and in time beat them. For all the sports – the indoor ones too like boxing – crowds came to watch skilled exponents and the best teams.

Notices, advertisements, posters for concerts or dramatic productions, shoe-cleaning stands, improvised stalls for the sale of something marketable, queues for hot water, or tickets for some performance, were part of a busy outdoor scene. Indoors, under the grandstands, posted alongside 'through' routes, were timetables for this and that activity, lists and instructions specific to various classes, and, making use of every space, art and sculpture groups, classes undergoing teaching, committee meetings, table tennis, gymnastics, boxing, music and drama rehearsals. So successful was an art exhibition that a separate art studio was built at the west end of the camp from which work for ten further exhibitions was in due course produced.

In the summer, everything, everywhere, was dusty; in the autumn and early winter, rain, chilly winds, and mud, were common; then, early in the New Year, hard frost, ice and snow and for all except the athletically nimble, there was a perilous passage to the latrines with the ship's boys armed with snowballs making the journey a misery.

Can we make generalisations about the men in the camp? Perhaps a third was of working-class seamen with but basic education. Among them were men from wide-ranging ethnic backgrounds, and many young lads, ship's boys. There were also, by definition, ship's officers and Master Mariners. Outside this Mercantile Marine category – these men having been caught in German ports at the outbreak of war – occupation and trade would be an appropriate classification: jockeys, football and golf professionals, painters and decorators, circus performers, barbers, gardeners, tailors, craftsmen, cobblers.

Professionals in another sense could be grouped too: lecturers, teachers, doctors, dentists, clergymen, accountants, lawyers, scientists, musicians, but then it becomes more difficult. How does one classify businessmen, bankers, actors, clerks, and where do journalists, and students fit in? There were even some Army officers or cadets on leave as civilians. Every occupation and profession seem to have been represented, men from every educational and social background. It could be said that here were all the ingredients of British society thrown into a small cooking pot. Would the resultant stew be generally acceptable?

Some form of organisation would be the key to ensuring general welfare. The German authorities set this in train by requiring each barrack to elect an interpreter. These interpreters became recognised by the internees as their captains with responsibilities beyond that of interpreting for the German authorities. The captains formed a Captains' Committee and it was the task of these men formally to require the leaders of all sporting and educational provision in the camp to regulate their activities. The authority of the captains was reinforced by the parallel establishment of an internee police force and, in turn, in September 1915, the Germans recognised the responsibility exercised by these men.

In a paradoxical way, the closed community of Ruhleben was now being structured into an open but disciplined society. People with skills, talents, interests, enthusiasms and needs, all had opportunities for fulfilment. The captains elected as Captain of the Camp, a strong, determined character, European manager of a film company, A. J. Powell. He was not to everyone's taste, in particular that of the intellectuals who did not share his social, educational or business background, and thought him irascible and dictatorial, but his record of independent judgement stood the test of time. With a revised constitution in the summer of 1918, he still defeated his opponent for re-election by over a thousand votes. Although he had the advantage of being the incumbent, one might have thought that a history of disputes over his authority – something he guarded with zeal – combined with boredom encouraging an appetite for change, would have won support. That it did not, may be taken as an endorsement of his pursuit of the welfare of the whole community.

Morale throughout the camp was being raised during 1915 by the sheer range of activities which could be pursued. Apart from the crucial absence of women, everything was there – shoe repair, a haircut, a classroom teacher, an entertainer, a sports team to watch or play for, a choir or a chess club, and bookies for what became almost universal – betting. There were other helpful factors. The internee's, own language was all around him, perhaps even his own accent; certainly his own values and national identification. A throughway was soon Bond Street and where it met a junction, Trafalgar Square or Piccadilly Circus. There may have been German-uniformed guards, wire and watchtowers, but there was much that was altogether familiar in so many ways, from clothing worn to pipe-tobacco smell. There were jobs for those who would do labouring and get paid for it. Of perhaps a slightly different nature, there is a nice illustration of payment in kind – a cobbler repairing and re-studding a pair of football boots in return for being allowed to borrow them.

With a view toward widening educational provision beyond the elitist range of the Arts and Science Union, the Captains' Committee selected an Education Committee in January 1915, formally to establish a Camp School bringing all the *ad hoc* teaching within its ambit. After issuing a questionnaire inviting the men to list what they would like to study, the responses led to the drawing up of a curriculum of about fifty subjects, with scholars, teachers and some students now able to offer tuition, with official approval. There were about 200 teachers, their areas ranging from the basic – reading, writing and arithmetic – to general school subjects and then to the more specialist. The school prospectus holds detail to be applauded by the most forward-thinking educationalist today – from Hotel Management, (including Menu Writing), to the teaching of Welsh and Irish; from Law, Accountancy, Stock Exchange and Salesmanship, to Agriculture, Electrical Engineering, Navigation, Painting, Musical Appreciation, Handicrafts and Bookbinding. A total of 1,400 students was enrolled.

Ultimately, examinations were initiated and even externally assessed by Examining Boards in the United Kingdom, the Board of Trade, the Royal Society of Arts and the London Matriculation Board. This formal provision of education introduced an element of routine which was beneficial to all so engaged because, otherwise, the ordered established way of life which to some extent frames most people's lives, would have been absent. It is of some note that the later distinguished atomic scientist James Chadwick, an internee, was engaged in experimental research and teaching at the school. A tremendous asset to teaching, for research and for purposeful leisure, was the establishment of a library, founded by the generosity of an internee and materially expanded by the British Board of Education.

A leading teacher at the school, and in course of time Head of Britain's Double Cross counter-espionage system in the Second World War, was John Masterman, who bestrode Ruhleben intellectually and athletically. An exchange lecturer at Freiburg University in 1914, Masterman was Ruhleben's leading athlete, outstanding at cricket, tennis and hockey. He played a full part administratively as well as in teaching. If Masterman were noteworthy for exceptional all-round talent, and as a leading contributor to intellectual life at Ruhleben, another clever man, the philosopher and art historian Matthew Prichard, made his mark in people's memories through highbrow conversational eccentricity. He had a strangely magnetic personality attracting admiring acolytes by reason of provocatively challenging questions like that to one of his disciples complaining of agonizing toothache. 'Toothache, toothache, what is toothache?' In common with the serious purposes of the Camp School, there were parallel coaching developments in all the sports: gymnastics, boxing, and athletics for example, and competitions, leagues and cups too.

There were, it must be said, adjustments to make for all those who, unlike the seamen, had no experience of communal life. For those who had been educated at boarding school then, yes, this would have given them some preparation for life within Ruhleben, with its total lack of privacy in answering nature's needs, in washing, showering, eating, sleeping, being alone for quiet solitary reflection. Such was life in Ruhleben.

Of the cultural, and sporting roles to be filled – producers, directors, managers, secretaries, conductors, captains of teams – all were needed and were there, or would be discovered. Specific locations had then to be found and booked, facilities likewise. Managers or secretaries might readily gather others with skills and enthusiasm related to a particular activity but the group had to be sufficiently large to sustain the activity with loyalty and staying power against the onset of disinterest or competition from another group.

A dramatic society would need a place for rehearsal and performance, have to choose a play, and find a producer/director and actors. Scripts would need to be obtained from somewhere or written, and costumes produced. Scenes would need designing, painting, erecting. Lighting would have to be acquired and set up, make-up prepared, and men skilled in these areas found or trained. Then posters, programmes, tickets for admission, would have to be designed and printed. It would be no small undertaking to initiate this and bring a production to fruition. Perhaps the prize in respect of bringing things together is due to those involved with production of Gilbert and Sullivan's *Mikado*, even the score having to be put together from memory.

From the challenge of Thespian problems to those of sport. Surely the prize here must be with regard to cricket. One cannot imagine the benevolence of the American Ambassador or any ready cooperation of the German authorities being able to provide the needs of this alien game – stumps, bails, pads etc! They were clearly in evidence at Ruhleben and certainly must have been sent out from England.

The appeal of attending – and for some, performing – in plays, music hall, concerts, recitals and lectures, was widespread. With time on one's hands that may be considered scarcely surprising but attendance and performance were certainly good for individual and general morale.

Amid these positive factors it should be registered that there were internees with German identification because of the strict German interpretation on entitlement to nationality. Readiness to serve in the German armed forces could circumvent questionable entitlement to German nationality but Ruhleben had some particularly unfortunate internees, the 400 or so who identified with the German cause but even if accommodated in separate barracks, were still cooped up in the camp with great numbers thinking of them as the enemy and who found them an easy target for exclusion or taunting.

Observation must be made about two elements in the life of anyone incarcerated long-term in wartime – homesickness and the uncertainty of how long current circumstances would last? As in a POW camp, men simply had to deal with the absence of their loved ones and while there was no easy answer to this beyond the link of letters – something which in fact did not invariably bring the comfort sought – in the case of Ruhleben it could well be that more than love was at stake. The businessman, with his affairs in Germany, in all likelihood had lost everything quite beyond hope of recovery, a pretty hopeless situation from which to recover morale. Additionally, war news from German newspapers was of course generally depressing too and even if discriminating British readers could judge where it were exaggerated or simply not true, reports of strikes in the South Wales coalfields or German victories at sea and on land, were less than uplifting.

There was for long a quite general hope that an exchange of civilians would take place. Rumour, in ample supply in camps of all sorts, was in abundance at Ruhleben. Some men, on grounds of age or sickness, had reason buttressing their hopes and a few had their yearnings fulfilled; far more were to be disappointed. Speculation over when the war would end led one internee into trouble. Lewis Widdowson had written home that only 'JC' knew when the war would end.[7] He had difficulty in persuading the German censor that 'JC' was not a secret, all-knowledgeable informant, but Jesus Christ, the writer's respectful variant on 'God only knows when this bloody war will be over'.

Still on the subject of erosion of morale, a Ruhlebenite, who had been an electrical engineer in Germany with many German friends and homes where he was welcome, received a letter from one of those friends. The impact of its receipt is not known but from its contents it was not calculated to cheer him.

England has shown herself in every way unworthy – not only has she trampled on moral values, disregarded them, played them false, not only has she allied herself with the decadent French who can hatch up such trials as the Panama and Dreyfus scandals and are syphilitically rotten to the bones – in Germany we had to provide special camps for them – no, England, the free country, has allied herself with barbarians like the Russians whose semi-culture knows no equal, where the knout [knotted rope], the oppression of and ignorance of rotten Grand Dukes prevail – all this to get rid of an unfortunate competitor.[8]

It is idle to pretend that Ruhleben, with its array of intellectual and sporting pursuits, kept frustration and impatience completely at bay. Close juxtaposition, day after interminable day, was going to make habitual behaviour – the hyena laugh, the smoker's cough, nose-picking, repetitive, boring stories – more and more infuriating,

Naturally there were mood swings. Wyndham Richards, second in command at the ever busy Parcels Office, captain of his barrack football team, selected for representative football and rugby teams, playing tennis, attending concerts, lectures and plays, still penned this diary entry for 31 August 1916: 'Oh I'm sick of things in general. I've a good mind to go to bed again and stop there for several weeks. Am absolutely sick of the War, of my Box mates, of myself, of everything.'[9] More dramatic than Richards' short-lived depression was the derangement of a man called Buckley who rapped the table at an Old Etonian dinner to introduce, as at the 'Congress of Vienna', 'My Lords, Ladies and Gentlemen, His Grace the Duke of Wellington'. In due course Buckley was to be removed from the camp to a private sanitorium where an internee visitor found him alert and ready to repel entry by the Kaiser and General Ludendorff.

Economic deprivation clearly added to the morale-sapping effect on a Nottingham painter and decorator's homesickness. His diary has quite pathetic entries about not being able to afford extras to supplement the basic and inadequately nourishing food supplied by the German authorities. 'I have written several cards to my wife and relatives but have had no reply. I often think the authorities do not allow my cards to go through. There is a relief fund subscribed for by the prisoners who have money to help those in need. I have signed my name for relief. I hope I shall be thought of.' As it happened his firm, Waring and Gillow, sent him some clothes.[10] Further evidence of frustration at straitened personal circumstance was expressed by George Merritt, who was to become a celebrated actor. Many years after the war, bitterly he recalled his fury at his appeal within the camp for charity, leading to his receiving a pack of broken biscuits.[11]

Relatedly, it is interesting that in diaries, letters and recollections, there is very little evidence of reported theft or violence but one internee did record hiding his Red Cross food tins in a window box to frustrate hungry German guards. He had good reason so to do. When the Berlin Fire Brigade had to be called out to deal with a serious fire, internees recorded in letters and diaries that the firemen had 'rescued' and kept tins of food they found, leaving the internees to deal with the blaze. It had started early in the morning of 14 July 1917, in a shed holding horses and a few cows. Quickly it spread to the boundary fence and ancillary buildings, threatening nearby barracks. Buckets of water and even the tennis hose were used by the internees before three fire engines arrived, the internees connecting the hoses which finally dowsed the flames. Soldiers had arrived but were there it seemed to frustrate escape rather than in any fire-fighting role.

On the question of the German issue of food and its inadequacy, it is worth relating that, for some internee offence, the Germans imposed a ban on recreation and entertainment, whereupon in retaliation, instead of relying on 'home production', Red Cross or family food parcels, the Barrack Captains ordered everyone to queue for his German allotment. The ban was lifted immediately, indicative that the Germans simply had not the food for the number of internees they held. The men did not always win their conflicts with German authority and some paid the price for infraction of regulations or insolence with solitary confinement in prison in Berlin or in the harsher environment of the POW camp at Havelburg.

Slight reference has been made to illness within the camp but there was to be a serious epidemic of diarrhoea in 1917, dealt with, in so far as this was practicable, by the hospital block staff just outside the camp. It requires mention that three internees – Stanley Lambert, in command, and two seamen, Albert Smith and John

Bean, in support – had taken over and transformed this dirty, overcrowded, virtually unstaffed and inadequately-equipped 'facility', making it immeasurably safer for internees who had fallen ill and did not need to fear disastrous consequences. However, sadly beyond their remit, there was an individual tragedy when a man expired in agony overnight. The cause, it seems, was ptomaine poisoning, the unwholesomeness of the German-issued food being suspected. The German authorities, at internee urging because of the man's terrible pain, notified the camp doctor immediately, but his reply that his hours did not cover a night visit left the sufferer without treatment. The circumstances of his death gave rise to bitter resentment. To move from this deeply-felt tragedy to a shared delight, the flooded central area in front of the grandstands froze one winter, actually serving as an ice rink for hosts of keen amateurs with a variety of footwear attempting to emulate the performance of an expert admired and envied by all.

With regard to an activity of year-round significance in the camp – music – its sheer variety is stunning. There were, as might be expected, professional musicians with their instruments and music readily available to take a lead in this, like F. Charles Adler, the distinguished conductor. The Bayreuth Festival, as it happened, had been responsible for trapping numbers of British music-lovers and performers in Germany. However, the provision of musical entertainment and employment was by no means exclusively classical. There is a complete list of all the music performed in the camp in 1918, the categories including symphonies, concerti, intermezzi, choral and vocal works, overtures, waltzes, and then, within the category 'Songs, Rags and Character', appear *Chatterbox Rag*, *Hitchy Coo* and *The Mississippi Two-step*. For all the stimulus, fun, fellowship, and one imagines consolation, it was certainly serious too. Amongst the papers of a man called Douglas Jones there is a note for him to appear at a practice of Verdi's *Requiem*, '**Sharp**, at 11.30.'[12]

The popularity of Music Hall further indicates that entertainment was not all highbrow. A Music Hall programme features turns which include a contortionist, a knife manipulator, a dancer, a comedian, a coster dialogue, and something called an 'eccentric act'. There was indeed something for everybody, but the circus wild animal trainer – stage name, Gypsy Jupp – convincingly depicted in some collections of photographs, must surely have struggled to put on an exciting act without his animals.

High standards were aimed for in all public performances, that is ticketed concerts, dramatic productions, shows and suchlike, performed before internees, the Camp Commandant, his officers and guests, or anyone visiting the camp in an inspection or supervisory role. With regard to attendance from outside the camp, a diary reference has this to record of a gala performance of *The Mikado*: 'About sixty people from the American Embassy and Consulate attended, occupying all stall places and front rows of the Circle. Was sitting in second row of the Circle, just behind three fair damsels. Quite exciting perfume.'[13]

Dramatic productions were occasionally reviewed acerbically in the Camp

Magazine, no matter how diligently all concerned had striven for perfection. *The Speckled Band, Lady Windermere's Fan* and a *Shakespearean Tercentenary Celebration* were among the special successes but the actor, George Merritt, in a performance of *The Knight of the Burning Pestle*, notable for its racy, not to say blue, language, was quite up to dealing with a restless audience. Lewis Widdowson, a member of that audience indicating its disapproval, recorded in his diary that Merritt stopped the dialogue, came to the front of the stage, had himself spot-lit, and declaimed: 'If you don't like it you can bugger off then.' The play proceeded with no further interruption.[14] As a point of interest concerning Merritt himself, the significance attached to distinction on the stage, and the perilous prevalence of gambling, Merritt, after performing fifty dramatic roles, received an illuminated address and a sum of money. He promptly loaned the money to a friend to set up a roulette wheel. The venture failed, leaving Merritt with but his illuminated address.[15]

The parallel existence of serious study, pre-occupying recreation and commercial enterprise is captured in some of the societies and business enterprises in almost any random list of activities – the Italian Circle, the Technical Circle, the Bridge and Chess Clubs, the Ruhleben Camp Magazine, with its delightful sub-title, 'All the World's a Cage', and the issue of News Bulletins. However, many of the activities drew competitively on the same talented people and the same audience pool. There was competition for facilities, and in advertising too. Tom Marshall, an educationalist and talented violinist, wrote home in January 1917, that: 'It would amaze you to see the numbers of little plots and intrigues and squabbles that go on in this camp, chiefly between Societies', and later captured the stresses exhibited among the cultural hierarchy: 'The orchestra is getting ready to play during the performance of "The School for Scandal" next week. It should be an interesting object lesson to this camp to which the name might well be applied.'[16]

It is predictably difficult to find evidence of homosexual activity within the camp, social convention and legal proscription being as they were, but with the diverse nature of man, the enclosed circumstance and, one may presume, the absence of women, it must have been practised. Interview enquiry on the matter led to a general response that, by choice aided by coercion, those so drawn gathered themselves into an area of a particular barrack. Heterosexual activity, for the determined man with funds to sustain his appetite, could be engineered. A diarist marks Friday 15 December 1916 as: 'An Event of Great Importance.' With advance information obtained, and arrangements made accordingly, he obtained a pass to leave the camp with a colleague to attend the sanatorium, some distance away, to visit a sick internee. Instead, a rendezvous was kept for them by two compliant girls. 'Had a simply gorgeous time. Oh it was grand to kiss again. Promised to go again. Next time was promised something better. Got back pretty drunk, believe me. Cost me 45 Marks all told. Immediately wrote home for more money.'[17] Propriety precludes the revelation of more detail on this matter but, as might be expected, the price goes up and there were certain medical consequences.

Nevertheless, the sense of freedom, the excitement of using the Berlin underground, walking the streets, going to a public cinema and shopping, may be added to the fulfilment of the diarist's central aim. In the case of a group of eight who received permission to go out of the camp to buy a piano, it seems that their principal purpose had been a drunken orgy with girls involved. This was achieved and, additionally, somehow, they got back to the camp with a piano, though one not fit for re-tuning.

It has been observed that close examination of the faces in photographs of internees does not reveal the strain as in those of prisoners of war. One could hardly suggest that there might be general explanation of this in the two incidents just described but it is surely appropriate to link those escapades to the thoughtful reflection of the ex-internee, psychologist and historian of the camp, D. J. Ketchum, who wrote in his study of Camp Society, that 'the paradox of Ruhleben was that many Ruhlebenites found freedom for the first time in their lives – conventional schoolmasters, strait-laced churchgoers, dutiful sons, hen-pecked husbands'.[18]

In conclusion, something must be put forward with regard to escapes and escaping activity. There were many attempts, usually caught early, in one instance, scandalously by internee betrayal. For failure, the prison in Berlin, or the nearby POW camp at Havelburg was the punishment. Some escape endeavours were without any serious pre-planning and they were doomed from the start. Some men tried again and again, one making five or six attempts. However, a few achieved success, like Wallace Ellison in October 1917. It was on his third attempt. In July 1915, he was within ten minutes of the border with the neutral Netherlands when he was caught; his penalty was 113 days of solitary confinement in Berlin's city prison. An attempt the following year also ended in narrow failure, but in 1917, disguised as a German businessman, after four weeks at large, he carefully planned and skilfully executed the border crossing. He celebrated with a lecture tour of Britain recounting his experiences and followed this with a published memoir.[19] Ellison and the men who made it home were meticulous in their preparations. It is touching to learn that Edward Morris Falk, who was successful in 1915, was materially assisted in his essential purchases by a Grimsby sailor who handed over £5 earned in performing menial tasks in the Camp. Falk, on an approved visit for some society purchasing in Berlin, bought all he needed from a city store!

Of course for anyone considering such dangerous excitement there was the logistical deterrence of Berlin being so far by land from any neutral country, the Netherlands or Switzerland, though by sea, Swedish ports presented some possibility. For those so minded, it must be said that there was the further deterrent of the German authorities, embarrassed by their being apparently so lax in preventing escape attempts, decreeing that anyone attempting to escape would be shot. There was potentially another discouraging element, the loss of the would-be adventurer's contribution to some team or society, indeed his own loss too in this respect, by departure.

There is so much more to the story of Ruhleben: the mock Parliamentary by-election, the Great World Fair staged, the question of the resilience of Christian faith in the camp, the smuggling-in of English newspapers and liquor, the smuggling-out of food to those wives who had chosen to remain in Germany, the rat hunt, the personalities and conduct of the German Camp Commandant, Graf von Schwerin, his second-in-command, Baron Taube, the German officers and guards, the hypothetical question as to how much longer could morale have been sustained into the following year if the war were not to have ended, more particularly after the release in January 1918 of 370 older men – many of them leading lights in significant activities. Perhaps it should be noted here that fourteen of those men were listed as insane!

There are other psychological issues which might be considered too. Did the young internees become aware, as they learned more about the fighting fronts, that they were safer in Ruhleben and so, were secretly thankful, if perhaps in a sense, embarrassed by this reality? There is evidence in Wyndham Richards' diary of the fury of frustration at not being able to play his part – but such entries diminish as the years roll on.

The story of the last days of the camp has its comic side, with the internees being asked to assist in the making and professional hoisting of a red flag for the now revolutionary camp guards in the chaos of Berlin, and also being largely responsible for dealing with their own immense administrative problem of evacuation and transportation home. However, in recognizing the excitement of those days for the internees, we should not overlook the anxiety. Walter Swale in his recall of seeing the German officers leaving their headquarters stripped of their badges of rank and his wondering what would happen next, illustrated two significant developments of which to be mindful. They are certainly part of the Ruhleben story.

First, in the fear of the camp being over-run by hungry revolutionaries, the internees raised a squad of ex-soldiers and cadet officers, special constables too, to aid in the defence of their food stocks and personal property. Second, that though the ship which took many of them to Hull from Denmark was greeted rapturously in the port, they were taken first for interrogation to a camp in Ripon. Swale called this procedure 'Mental Decontamination' relating it to the perception that the ex-internees might have been infected by the communist bug rife in Berlin and more particularly because some had souvenir copies of the leaflet first read out from the Head Office of the camp and then issued as a leaflet – Peace and Reconciliation – 'Forgive and Forget',[20] the text of which does indeed seek to stimulate kindred revolutionary sympathy.

The efficiency with which the evacuation and continental part of the homeward journey was planned and carried out, compels admiration. The first train left for Denmark on 22 November, but then perhaps after all that had been achieved, such enterprise and efficiency were to be expected.

A British identity had been upheld, a controlled detachment from the enemy maintained, positive goals had been pursued, the very best made from the misfortune of being in Germany when war broke out. Quite deliberately, scarcely any comparison has been made between life in Ruhleben and that in camps holding servicemen – other ranks or officers – as prisoners of war. The comparative comfort and relatively self-governing nature of the internees' circumstance make such comparisons inappropriate, but the collective achievement of the Ruhleben men is perhaps under-sung and is really quite remarkable.

Notes

The abbreviation LC is for the University of Leeds, Brotherton Library, Liddle Collection of First World War Archival Materials.

1. *Wyndham's War*, being the Diaries of Thomas Wyndham Richards, 1914–18, pp. 21ff (see bibliography). I am tremendously indebted to the son of this diarist, Derek, who generously made available to me the material for his book as it was developing and patiently answered innumerable questions relating to his contextual research on Ruhleben Camp.
2. Lloyd, J. A., letters and diaries, Liddle/WW1/RUH/30 LC.
3. Vincent, E. R., letter, Liddle/WW1/RUH/56 LC.
4. Turner, T. H. letter, Liddle/WW1/RUH/55 LC.
5. A very interesting article by Mark Griffiths, 'The Other RHS', in *Country Life* (August 2014), provides the remarkable information that the Ruhleben Horticultural Society sent dahlias and chrysanthemums to London for sale, and the German authorities bought vegetables and provided pig slurry for fertilizer due to the shortage of horse manure.
6. Turner, T. H., letter, Liddle/WW1/RUH/55 LC.
7. Widdowson, L. J., papers and recollections, Liddle/WW1/RUH/58 LC.
8. Letter in the papers of W. E. Swale, Liddle/WW1/RUH/52 LC.
9. *Wyndham's War*, p. 247.
10. Widdowson, L. J., letter, Liddle/WW1/RUH/58 LC.
11. Merritt, George, recollections, Liddle/WW1/RUH/34 LC.
12. Jones, D., papers of, Liddle/WW1/RUH/01 LC.
13. *Wyndham's War*, p. 271.
14. Widdowson, L.J., diary, Liddle/WW1/RUH/58 LC.
15. Merritt, George, recollections, Liddle/WW1/RUH/34 LC.
16 . Marshall, T. H., letters, Liddle/WW1/RUH/33 LC.
17. *Wyndham's War*, p. 269.
18. J. D. Ketchum, *Ruhleben, A Prison Camp Society* (University of Toronto, 1965), p. 56.
19. Ellison, Wallace, Liddle/WW1/RUH/20 LC.
20. A copy of this leaflet is held with the papers of W. E. Swale, Liddle/WW1/RUH/52 LC.

Suggested Further Reading

Bury, Bishop Herbert, *My Visit to Ruhleben* (London: A. R. Mowbray, 1917).
Cohen, Israel, *The Ruhleben Prison Camp* (London: Methuen and Co, 1917).
Ellison, Wallace, *Escapes and Adventures* (Edinburgh: Blackwood, 1929).
Gerard, James W., *My Four Years in Germany* (London: Hodder and Stoughton, 1918).
Ketchum, J. D., Ruhleben, *A Prison Camp Society* (University of Toronto, 1965).
Keith, Eric A., *My Escape from Germany* (Nisbet, 1918).
Powell, A. J., and F. Gribble, *The History of Ruhleben* (London: Collins, 1919).
Pyke, Geoffrey, *To Ruhleben and Back* (London: Constable, 1916).
Richards, Derek, *Wyndham's War, being the diaries of Thomas Wyndham Richards* (Newport, South Wales: The Vine Press, 2014).
Stibbe, M., *British Civilian Internees in Germany* (Manchester University Press, 2008).

Chapter 11

The Torment of Captivity: Germans, Austrians and Turks Interned on the Isle of Man

* * *

Matthew Richardson

During the Great War, both sides interned enemy civilians who were living or working in their territory upon the outbreak of hostilities. For the British part, the idea that civilians might be partisan (and therefore must be controlled) first gained ground during the South African War of 1899 to 1902, when members of the Boer civilian population were held in concentration camps. At the start of the First World War, there were approximately 60,000 Germans living in Britain. On 5 August 1914, the day after war was declared, the Aliens Restriction Act was passed by the British Government. The Act allowed the Government to control the movement of 'enemy aliens', and to regulate where they could live and what they could do. Following the outbreak of war, the notion that all such people could potentially be acting as enemy agents developed into a veritable 'spy-fever'. The initial decision to intern enemy aliens was made on 7 August 1914, and by 23 September 10,500 civilians had been arrested. The Home Office in London, through the Destitute Aliens Committee, proposed the opening of a camp on the Isle of Man and the first group of 200 internees arrived on 22 September 1914, just over six weeks after the outbreak of war.

Ultimately up to 29,000 Germans, Austrians, Hungarians and Turks would be interned on the Isle of Man. Many of them were merchant sailors, others had been waiters, barbers, small tradesmen or servants. In smaller numbers were businessmen or clerks. There were also what might be termed 'quasi-military' prisoners, such as army reservists, and colonial troops captured on the high seas going to or from Africa. A certain number of those interned had been resident in England since early childhood, and when they entered internment camps some of them could not actually speak German.

The first internment camp on the Isle of Man was the Douglas Holiday Camp (also known as Cunningham's Camp), a large tented holiday complex above Douglas Promenade. However, even at this early stage it was clear that Cunningham's Camp alone could not accommodate the number of prisoners which mass internment could potentially produce. A new camp was built on farmland known as Knockaloe Mooar near Peel, a site which had been used before the war as a camping ground for Territorial troops, and one of the few locations on the Island which possessed an adequate water supply for a large number of men. However, it would be some months before Knockaloe could receive its first prisoners, and at Douglas Camp on 19 November 1914, a combination of poor winter weather, overcrowding (there were over 3,000 internees housed in the camp by that stage, instead of 2,400 as suggested) and complaints about the food, led to a riot. After dinner, the prisoners refused to disperse, and, instead, began hurling plates and cutlery at the guards. The atmosphere turned violent as – ignoring the pleas of their more peaceable compatriots – some internees advanced towards the kitchens brandishing broken chair legs. The women in the kitchens became hysterical and the guards, after first shooting over the heads of the rioters, fired directly into their number. Five internees died, some in the resulting stampede. One member of the guard, a National Reserve soldier named James Bailey, told the subsequent inquest that the soldiers had stood the barrage of plates, knives and furniture for about ten minutes, receiving not just splatters of soup and jam but also cuts to their hands and faces, before opening fire:

[I] aimed for the gallery, at one man I had been watching for several minutes, firing all sorts of missiles . . . He seemed to be a ringleader . . . I aimed at the main part of the body. We haven't much chance to aim at any particular part of the body. [I] then fired at the body of prisoners formed in mass before the guard. The row continued, and they were still coming forward, [I] and the others considered it necessary to fire again. [I] only fired twice [and] could not tell what effect the second shot had; four or five of [us] fired together. After that, the prisoners cleared out of the dining room. [Then] the guard got the word to double round through the kitchen to the other side of the dining room, as the prisoners had gathered there, but they found it a false alarm, as the prisoners had got back to their tents . . . It was [my] firm opinion that we were justified in firing, otherwise something much more serious would have happened.[1]

The inquest found that the guards had acted lawfully, both in self-defence, and also because if the prisoners had managed to seize their rifles, a breakout might have followed. As a result of the riot, the transfer of prisoners to the new purpose-built camp at Knockaloe was speeded up. Douglas Camp, however, remained open, containing a Privilege Camp (for those internees with money), a Jewish Camp (for those with special dietary requirements), and a camp for the residue of ordinary prisoners. Dr Charles L. Hartmann, a 59-year-old author, scholar and former

German honorary consul in Japan, arrived in the Privilege Camp in November 1915. He left a fascinating portrait of the extraordinarily luxurious lifestyle of its inmates. In his diary he wrote:

> The Privilege Camp, in which I find myself, is home to about four hundred people. A part of them are housed in tents, the rest in newly built huts, for three to four men. The huts mostly have a small garden planted in front of them, and depending on how they are furnished, are more or less comfortable. There are carpenters, upholsterers, and furniture makers available to work on them. A few of the huts are even luxurious with curtains, pictures, vases, good lights and are equipped with portable paraffin heaters. The walls and roofs of the huts are covered with asbestos sheets, so they grant considerably better protection than wooden barracks against the cold . . .[2]

For these prisoners, internment presented none of the hardships which characterised life at Knockaloe. Alcohol was permitted, in the form of wine and beer. Furthermore, Hartmann tells us:

> The catering for these 400 privileged prisoners is cared for by a restaurateur who is under the control of the kitchens committee. Three tables have their own waiter, all qualified fellows and with a quite excellent Head Waiter in charge, who had worked for years in Paris and London. Many, who were quite unnoticed outside of the camp, here play swanks, and order extra luncheons for four or five invited guests, or extra food for themselves, so that they alone take up three quarters of the time of our waiters. Because they have no interests other than food, drinking, blethering and boasting, the torment of captivity barely enters their consciousness . . .[3]

Also in Douglas Camp around the same time was Frederic Dunbar-Kalckreuth, a German of Scottish and American descent. He also wrote of his experiences at Douglas where, being from an upper-class background, he too was accommodated in the Privilege Camp. In December 1915, a month after his arrival, Dunbar-Kalckreuth noted how the approach of Christmas, as well as stirring the emotions of those prisoners who had families (and particularly children) still in Germany, was a particular source of irritation:

> I went into our hut, where a few Chinese lanterns were giving an illusion of 'merry Christmas'. Hot wine bubbled away on the paraffin stove. It gave off a nice scent of cloves and cinnamon. Everyone was given over to his own thoughts . . . Here, where every day is a day off work, and where the same daily routine dominates, I find the official days of celebration

particularly oppressive. I'm not surprised that people take to drink and that Mr Slyshanks' wine canteen makes a roaring trade as a result.[4]

'Slyshanks' was the nickname (a play on his surname) given by the prisoners to Joseph Cunningham, the owner of the camp; who they viewed as profiting doubly from their misfortune, both through the rent he received for his holiday camp from the British Government, and also through the sale of provisions to the prisoners. Religious celebrations, however, were not confined to the Christian element of the camp. The Jewish portion was also highly organised in this respect. Maurice Jeger, an Austrian Jew who had worked in Cardiff as a printer, remembered that the Passover story of the Hebrew slaves in Egypt had added resonance in the circumstances of captivity on the Isle of Man:

Again the Passover holidays had arrived, for the second time in our captivity, and even though many expected to be freed, nevertheless, we put all our energy into preparations for this holiday. The Jewish committee, which had been formed from representatives of the Jewish barracks, uniformly took the decision to celebrate the Passover in the traditional way, and immediately began its preparations . . . they had access to 'Kosher' meat here, and a separate kitchen for which they had to pay the small amount of 1 shilling weekly. The spiritual head of the Jews was an interned Rabbi named Silberman, a Hungarian who had also spent some years in Vienna . . . The commandant now promised to provide everything which the religion requires, and also agreed to provide financial help . . . 650 Jews assembled, all looking their smartest in their best clothes, from all areas of Austria, Germany and Turkey, in the decorated barrack hall, to mark the Exodus from Egypt and to celebrate freedom from slavery . . .[5]

Conditions at Knockaloe Camp contrasted greatly with those at Douglas. Knockaloe was originally built to accommodate 5,000 internees, but finally it was extended to 23,000 prisoners, making it the second-largest settlement on the Isle of Man. Among the earliest occupants was Karl Berthold Robert Schonwalder, a 32-year-old German who had been resident in Birmingham since 1900, and who had married an Englishwoman. Schonwalder kept a meticulous diary of day-to-day events in Knockaloe, and his notes reveal the severe hardship experienced in the depths of a Manx winter. In November 1915, he wrote:

It is very cold and wet & [we] are walking about in the house [hut] with an overcoat on. This afternoon we have 2 stoves put in, to warm 2 huts or 6 rooms & me being in the middle hut which has no stove the fire makes no difference . . .[6]

Later that month he added:

. . . here at Knockaloe up to date a great many sleep on a mattress or rather a straw sack which lies on the floor the damp penetrating, not one has a Govt. Bolster & only 3 blankets are allowed & no more fires have been put in our huts. As regards clothing I myself have been waiting and am on the list ever since I have been here for a pair of pants, vest & clogs (boots we don't get) but have not seen any, nor anyone else . . .[7]

Knockaloe had a reputation as an unpleasant location not only at Douglas Camp, but also among Germans and Austrians interned in England. Even two years later, conditions were still harsh. Major Paul Stoffa, an officer in the Austro-Hungarian army, was transferred there from Alexandra Palace Camp. In his published memoirs he wrote:

I soon discovered why the camp at Knockaloe inspired such dread amongst the inhabitants of the Alexandra Palace. Here internment was reduced to its simplest elements: barbed wire, huts and mud. There were no 'frills', no panorama of London stretching for miles, which in itself was an element of qualified freedom, no permanent buildings and no visitors, it was the home of make-shift, grim, cold and monotonous. The incessant drizzle outside supplied the key-note of our existence . . . it gave one the . . . feeling of utter isolation, a complete severance from the outside world. No wonder that so many men degenerated here by degrees into something near a state of savagery: the decent majority struggled hard to keep afloat in a sea of hopeless despondency – many went under, insanity claiming not a few.[8]

In 1932, Paul Cohen-Portheim published his memoir of Knockaloe, *Time Stood Still*. His view of the camp was more benign, but he acknowledged that much of this was down to his personal outlook. He wrote of his arrival there:

. . . my first impression on seeing Knockaloe Camp in daylight was one of delighted surprise . . . Stepping out of the hut I found radiant sunshine, marvellously pure and bracing air, and a panorama of turf clad hills. That is how, in spite of all that was to follow, Knockaloe has remained in my mind, for I am what the French call a *type visuel*, which means that the look of a thing, place, or person matters most to me. When choosing a house or flat I have always been apt to consider the view from the window more important than more practical matters, and if I had to choose an internment camp – which I hope to God I shall never have to again – I should be guided by similar considerations. This is apt to annoy other people a good deal. Knockaloe was considered the most distasteful of all camps, the one where hardships were worst and conditions most unpleasant, that is why I feel apologetic to my fellow-prisoners when I state that I rather liked being there. It is only fair, however, to add that my stay there was short and that we had marvellous summer weather. The case of the men who were there for years . . . is, of course, a very different one.[9]

His induction consisted of a speech from the commandant, translated afterwards into German:

And that ended the ceremony. And now, what next? Now there was nothing to do, nothing at all, nothing whatsoever, nothing – for how long? There was a sort of shanty called a canteen, standing just outside the wire, with its counter open to the camp, where one might try to buy something. No matter what, one had nothing one needed, so everything would be welcome. Hundreds were waiting already; I waited for about two hours and everything had been sold out when my turn came.[10]

Herein lay the problem. Although some internees were hired out to farmers for labouring purposes during the war, many refused, perceiving this as co-operation with the enemy. With so little to do, time hung heavy on men's hands, and much of the illness suffered by the internees was psychological rather than physical. Boredom was a serious problem, and it is hardly surprising that gambling was prevalent. George Kenner, a German artist previously resident in London, was granted a transfer to be in a hut with his brother, but:

Unfortunately I learned here were many gamblers. They gathered up to 20 and 30 round the table in our hut, and sat together by candle and petroleum light (smoke hung in blue clouds). Long ago the electric light had been turned out for the nights rest, yet, under such circumstances one could not think of sleep. Several times the enclosure sergeant had rebuked them by taking away all the money, but now they put out spies to betray his approach. All this, through years, made a bad influence upon the mind of my young brother. It required great perseverance to lift him upon a higher plane.[11]

Many prisoners developed a listlessness as the weeks of internment turned to months, then years. One laconic guard officer, talking to a journalist, neatly summed up the whole situation in one line when he commented: 'You must either give 'em something to do, or let them go "dotty".'[12]

In order to combat this problem, the Society of Friends (Quakers) established workshops for the internees, in which to produce goods for sale outside of the camp. In 1915, work also began on improving living conditions by making equipment for games, libraries, gardening and by building camp theatres. J. T. Baily of the Society of Friends was invited to become involved in the setting-up of workshops and occupational activities in a number of internment camps. In October 1915 he came to Knockaloe. He observed:

> Probably the worst disease to be combated in a civilian internment camp came to be known as 'barbed-wirelitis'[*sic*]. It could soon develop into incipient insanity; prisoners of war who were readily subject to it were those who felt most acutely the injustice of their incarceration, particularly when they had adopted Britain as their home by having been resident over many years . . . The symptoms of the disease were moroseness, avoidance of others, and an aimless promenading up and down the barbed wired boundary of the compound . . . if this could not be stopped insanity would follow and probably suicide . . . the surest way to prevent and cure the disease – while the war continued – was occupation and it was to the provision of this in every possible form that the Friends Relief Service . . . gave every attention and to the promotion of which I was called to organise. That such provisions were effectual was proved by the fact that where the disease developed it was among those who stubbornly refused to engage in any activity.[13]

In spite of his efforts, Baily was viewed with suspicion by both sides; the camp authorities questioned the motives behind his sympathy for enemy prisoners, whilst many of the internees, at first at least, believed that he was some sort of spy. To his credit he persevered, and by 1916 the American Embassy in London was able to report that:

> Nearly 72 per cent of the interned men in the camp are at work. Many of the men were employed as bootmakers, tailors, joiners, cap workers, plumbers, woodworkers, gardeners, latrine men, police, coal and railway workers, quarry workers, post-office workers, and parcel-post workers, etc.[14]

Much of the recognition for this must go to the Friends' Emergency Committee, a Quakers' organisation, which helped to provide books, tools and equipment for the internees to work with and to start workshops in the camp. Nevertheless, an appeal from Baily appeared in *The Friend* of 16 November 1917 in which he stated:

> The Industrial Committees of all four [sub]camps, together with myself, are viewing with much anxiety the prospect of another winter for the interned spent under trying conditions of camp life and Manx weather. To many men it means a fourth winter of internment . . . there are now large numbers seeking occupation who have hitherto held indifferently aloof, and even those who opposed all such efforts from a mistaken idea of being patriotic to Germany are now co-operating in these efforts.[15]

The physical hardship of daily life in a camp comprised of wooden huts, in a climate as harsh as that of the Isle of Man in winter, can be imagined. One internee who found it particularly difficult was Otto Schimming, a missionary from Togoland who was of course more used to the heat of West Africa:

The life in the hut compartments with at most thirty inhabitants has a more comfortable character than in the large halls of the Alexandra Palace[,] if it were not for the adverse climate and the mud. Our hut floor was always damp. The sun warmed only the 'B' huts, they have the windows facing the south. 'A' huts have the windows to the north, and the sun's rays never fall through them. In December and January the sun only comes out from behind the mountains after 9 o'clock in the morning and at 3 o'clock is already disappearing again. I felt certain that I could not for long bear it in this damp hut, in mud and slush and storms of snow and rain. In the last week of January I was struck down with a fever. First I believed it was an attack of malaria, but quinine did not help. I became more and more wretched, but hoped for improvement and refused to call the doctor. After five days other prisoners brought the doctor, as I could no longer get up . . . My temperature was 106 degrees . . . he had me taken to the hospital. I had pneumonia with an almost intolerable headache.[16]

It is also an often-overlooked fact that the camps contained numbers of subjects of the Ottoman Empire, Germany's ally with which Britain was at war in the Middle East. The voices of Turkish internees are seldom heard when internment is discussed, but we are fortunate in that we have at least one source upon which to draw. Mustapha Shefket, who gave his address as Camp 3, Compound 2, Hut 5a at Knockaloe, wrote in September 1917 to a Swedish diplomat about the various hardships which he was experiencing:

I am a Turkish subject and 17 months ago was arrested by the British at the Isle of Chios where I had lived since a very long time, and, together with German and Austrian Consul I was brought to this country. Being 56 years of age and having passed all my life in a hot country, I find it very difficult to stand the hardships of an internment in a northern country. I am especially afraid of the coming autumn and winter and, once again, beg you to endeavour to get me exchanged, liberated or, at least, sent to a place more suited to my condition of health.[17]

The special dietary requirements of Muslim prisoners in Knockaloe must have presented some challenges to the camp authorities, but it should not be forgotten that a number of the Ottoman subjects who were interned on the Isle of Man were actually Jews, hailing from present-day Israel, and would have been accommodated in the Jewish compound at Douglas. During the First World War, the Right Reverend Herbert Bury was given responsibility for religious matters throughout the prisoner of war camps of the British Isles. He visited the Isle of Man in 1916, and reported not just upon the Jews but also the inhabitants of Knockaloe, whom he perceived as being largely pro-British:

> One's sympathy could be given to those – far and away the greater number of them – who have loved England, and all things English, and never wished to leave, nor thought of leaving, it again. Some have sons fighting for us in France and some of their sons have died for us. But still I said to them frankly . . . that though it was an embittering thing to feel that because some were suspected, and rightly, of being spies, and some were evil and treacherous, so many of the innocent had to suffer, yet they must bear the burden their nationality had laid upon them, and suffer with their country-men. They were quite sensible about it, and said afterwards: 'We don't know ourselves, though here with them, who the spies and undesirables are, and it must be still more difficult for the authorities to track them out.'[18]

There were nonetheless many within both camps who vigorously and vociferously identified with the German cause. Pastor Rudolf Hartmann, in a sermon given in Knockaloe in November 1915, stressed the part being played by the internees in a greater German struggle, and urged them to remember the sacrifices being made on the battlefields of Europe:

> Our dead – in this hour, we remember in particular those, both young and old, who have been taken from our midst and will never see the homeland again, because they have been brought over to the greater homeland. Our dead – for whom we should see it today as our solemn duty to provide a worthy place of burial. Yet those who have died in Knockaloe are but a few among the thousands who will return to the homeland, who will once more be able to serve life.[19]

The same month, Schonwalder, in his diary, describes the sullen and truculent anti-British mood in the camp. He noted that:

> It is getting a bit weary here they don't seem the same sort of chaps as at Wakefield if you speak English to anyone they don't answer you or tell you that this is a German camp.[20]

Later he seemed to take positive delight in the difficulties which Britain was experiencing, commenting:

I don't think [the war] will last much longer the English have this time what they have been asking for[.] this is no Boer War . . . they are on the road to Bankruptcie [*sic*].[21]

In June 1916, Schonwalder gleefully recorded the names of the British ships lost at the Battle of Jutland, the news of which was clearly common knowledge in the camp, adding: 'This will take the swank off John Bull.'[22]

He also records numerous escape attempts by his comrades including trying to cut the wire, construction of a tunnel, and a party of sailors who managed to get as far as Peel with the intention of securing a boat for return to Germany; Schonwalder, who had lived in England for many years and thus might be expected to be pro-British, added that he wished the participants the best of luck in these attempts. Overall, these were hardly the actions of prisoners who loved England and all things English, as the Rt Reverend Herbert Bury had reported. Protest and patriotic expression took whatever form it could. Schonwalder recorded on 1 May 1916:

In Comp[ound] I they have been upholding May Day making a procession headed by theyr [*sic*] band with the red flag & a green one for Ireland the Sub. Com. came in with a few soldiers and told them to stop which they did but boot [booed] him out of it loud enough for us to hear & then they shouted 3 cheers for Little Willy [Crown Prince Wilhelm].[23]

Not surprisingly, growing frustration and resentment in Knockaloe led to violence, as it had at Douglas. In October 1916, Schonwalder wrote:

When the sub com[mander] came in [compound] IV this eve he ask [*sic*] one officer what was the matter & he told him they want their liberty, he gave them a speech & after he had gone they broke the canteen open, 2nd time this week & practically cleared it. Its only 5 yards from our wire & the chaps in [compound] V watched them carry the stuff away. I heard tonight that they want the soldiers from the other camp drafted up here & then they start in other camps they been talking about setting the hall on fire. I trust they will do nothing of the kind, but you cannot blame them giving trouble after 26 months behind wire.[24]

This incident was followed the next day by a proclamation informing prisoners that combining together to cause trouble amounted to mutiny, for which they were liable to be court-martialled and shot.

Matching the anti-British sentiments expressed within the camps, there was a considerable amount of hostility directed <u>towards</u> the incarcerated enemy aliens, much of it from the English press. Based it seems on the Isle of Man's pre-war reputation as a place for fun and frolics, the idea grew up in some quarters that the internees were somehow on holiday. Under the heading 'The Huns Paradise', in May 1915 the populist weekly *John Bull* took an ill-informed swipe at both the internees and the Manx authorities:

> Some of the newly-interned aliens are said to be destined for the Isle of Man, and they are probably congratulating themselves on securing such pleasant quarters. The place has been made very comfortable for them – almost, in fact 'a home from home' . . . Certainly for some weeks past the Isle of Man has been a pleasant sojourn for Germhuns [*sic*], who have been permitted, encouraged and assisted to have a good time.[25]

However, there were many within the Manx population who held similar anti-German views. Mary Faragher, a Douglas woman who had gone to Vickers in Barrow to undertake war work, wrote to her mother in April 1918 about a German aristocrat who, due to his rank, was allowed special privileges whilst interned:

> I . . . read in the paper about Baron von Bissing being over on the Island I must say we have the elite of German society there now it is disgusting such vermin as Von Bissing are allowed to pollute the earth he ought to be transported to Germany . . . interned is too good for the likes of him.[26]

The same year, Douglas Councillor, Knox, objected to the use of alien labour on the roads, stating:

> As long as he was a member of the Council he would never agree to a halfpenny of the ratepayers' money being spent in employing Huns. He had come to the conclusion that alien labour was only justified when it was employed within barbed wire, and certainly it should not be utilised by the Council.[27]

Section 5 of the Regulations governing internee labour stated that:

> A farmer employing an Alien will be required to give an undertaking . . . that he will not permit him to have any communication with any person other than himself or his authorised agent.[28]

Yet in spite of the attempts by the authorities to prevent (as far as possible) contact between the internees and the local civilian population, it was inevitable that such interaction would occur, particularly as the war went on and internees were increasingly used for labour outside of the camps. This of course coincided with the disappearance of a large portion of the local population of young males, now in uniform elsewhere. In November 1918, Alice Kerruish, a forty-year-old married woman from Kirk Michael was charged with communicating with an Alien prisoner, contrary to camp regulations. In her statement she said:

> Two aliens named Willy and Harry from Knockaloe Camp were working for my husband John R. H. Kerruish . . . in the harvest, putting in corn, when I got on friendly terms with them. I wrote on two occasions and I sent a shilling's worth of sweets on two occasions to Willy and the last time I sent a shillings worth of sweets to Harry. Willy, when working in the stackyard, got in conversation with ____, and he asked me if I would see her and ask her to write to him.[29]

The High Bailiff clearly believed that in Mrs Kerruish's case matters had gone beyond 'friendly' to 'extremely intimate relations', and furthermore she was attempting to induce other women to behave similarly. We cannot know the full extent of her relationship with Harry, but in the circumstances it is not wholly surprising that such liaisons occurred, and Mrs Kerruish was by no means the only Manx woman charged with communicating or 'trafficking' with aliens. Tom Lilley of Castletown was perhaps better qualified than most to understand the impact of the war on personal beliefs, having one son in the army and another in prison as a conscientious objector. Writing in 1917 he recorded:

> There has just passed the house under escort between 30 & 40 aliens from Douglas who are working at Scarlett breaking stones for the Highway Board. They are singing and marching in tune as if they were happy as the customary trippers that pass through here in normal times. They are mostly young fellows . . . they appear to be inoffensive, good looking and by their actions, good natured lot of young fellows; they are followed night & morning by a crowd of children boys & girls who march behind them during their holidays. Until recently they have been in the habit of regaling the children at the Railway station on their return to chocolate and sweets, bought at the automatic machines, out of their scanty earnings, and even bringing sweets from Douglas to them . . . But latterly the Police have prevented the children from gaining access to the Railway station and consequently the little kiddies are despondent. I suppose the authorities were afraid if this sort of thing continued the children would begin to love the aliens, instead of hating them as they are taught to do.[30]

Within the camps of Douglas and Knockaloe there were also printing presses, upon which the prisoners could produce their own German-language camp magazines. Numerous issues of the various titles which were published by civilian prisoners during their internment have survived. Whilst the short-term objectives of the camp authorities, in allowing the internees to produce such magazines, were focussed upon the maintenance of morale and of their mental well-being, the longer-term value of the magazines to historians is incalculable in reflecting both everyday activities, and the hopes and concerns of those interned. Two of the longest-running magazines were *Knockaloe-Lager-Zeitung* and *Lager-Echo*. An early issue of *Knockaloe-Lager-Zeitung* did not refer at all to hope or to the future, instead there was a sense of despair, bitter irony and the fear of being interned for an indefinite period:

> We are still interned: Our acute wailing over the loss of freedom has changed into chronic resignation . . . One year ago when we started our career in journalism, a joker suggested that we should not forget the words 'volume one' under the title of the magazine. We did what he wanted, though we would never have thought it possible that there would be a 'volume two'. However we were wrong and today we wonder if there will be a third volume?[31]

The censorship of personal letters was the subject of satirical commentary in *Knockaloe-Lager-Zeitung* in July 1917:

> Three weeks ago I was called to go to the censor. I went there. The stern man showed me a letter and asked me in English if I was the author. After I agreed he wanted to know why I had rubbed something out. Immediately I remembered that ages ago I had made an inkblot on a sheet of paper which I wanted to remove with soft rubbing. I took the letter and examined it with great interest. Only with every effort did I find the scene of the crime.[32]

The magazine mocks the efforts of the camp censors, but control of information passing in and out of the camp was taken very seriously. Archibald Knox, the Isle of Man's greatest artist, worked as a parcel censor at the camp, one of many civilian staff in Knockaloe and Douglas. After the war he wrote to a friend:

> Our business was to intercept communications: there was always some new trick – an epidemic of the same trick; but for the last 13 months we had comparative peace: they must have admitted defeat for we seldom found anything. At one time for several months there were tins of preserved meat – according to the label assurance also it was made in a neutral country: for 'meat' would have been comforting if they had got it for it was a fortnight's newspapers rolled and folded and packed and sealed to deceive even a censor. Those were specially prepared for PsOW [*sic*] parcels but the same game was tried in all sorts of amateur ways, baked in loaves, in tins of fat, sewn up in a chest protector, sewn in pieces of cabbage leaf and buried in a tin of sauerkraut, cuttings fitted in medical [globules] packed in an [odour] bottle and so on.[33]

Opportunities for work have already been discussed, but theatre, film, music, art, sport and lectures on different subjects also offered the possibility of occupying the mind. In the printing office of Camp IV were produced not only the *Knockaloe-Lager-Zeitung*, but also almanacs and Christmas and Easter cards for the camp, as well as various theatre programmes, and it is these which reflect the importance of cultural life within the camp. Every issue of *Knockaloe-Lager-Zeitung* and *Lager-Echo* reported on theatre productions and concerts in the different compounds and also about lectures and seminars on different topics. Acting in plays was popular. Camp IV at Knockaloe had a theatre in each of its seven compounds and in six months the theatres put on 113 comedies, forty-two plays, fifteen dramas, twenty-one variety shows and a pageant. The men also had to play female roles, which sometimes caused difficulty: 'The association had to struggle a little with the lack of suitable ladies' players.'[34] However, this challenge also seemed to encourage some actors:

We wanted to highlight the extraordinary portrayal of the character of Gertrud Gronau whose actor (Mr. Ehlers) not only distinguished himself because of his pleasant voice and female appearance but also because of his sensitive appreciation of this role.[35]

Indeed, some of the actors even specialised in female roles: 'Mr Buerkle is one of our best ladies' actors but he is more suited to playing the intriguing woman in her mid thirties.'[36]

The extent to which some prisoners seem to have immersed themselves in an adopted female persona – a persona which seems to have extended in some cases far beyond the boundaries of the theatre – has led to speculation as to whether or not they had fully adopted the role of women in a closed all-male society. Cohen-Portheim tells us:

The first and obvious conclusion anyone considering the matter dispassionately would arrive at is this: when you lock up thousands of men between eighteen and fifty years for a very prolonged period and prevent any intercourse with the opposite sex, you inevitably drive them, indeed almost force them into homosexual intercourse. As this conclusion would have been considered painful and not good for the ears of the public, the matter was never discussed or even alluded to in the papers, and the whole problem was ignored, but it can and should not be ignored by any writer on the subject of prison life . . . Such acts were, I should say, extremely infrequent, and personally I know of none at all. This may seem improbable, and would be more than improbable if there was not one most important point to be considered: The camp offered no possibility of isolation . . . there was no possible privacy for anybody, and such intercourse would have had to be conducted within hearing (if not seeing) of others, and therefore to the general knowledge . . .. As to their committing sexual acts of any kind whilst under observation – as they always were – that was almost unthinkable.[37]

The case of Alice Kerruish discussed earlier also demonstrates that if prisoners were determined enough, contact with females was not entirely beyond their reach. Undoubtedly a well-executed play made it possible to forget about camp life for a short time as the *Knockaloe-Lager-Zeitung* commented in July 1917:

> There is an amazing tension in the air. The tension of a premiere. The lights in the audience hall are going out, the last acts of the overture are gone. The bell is ringing for the last time, the curtain is raising – and we are looking forward to forgetting for a few hours that we have been prisoners of war for three years.[38]

Besides the theatre, music provided a diversion. In Camp IV at Knockaloe there were four string orchestras, three choirs and a military brass band which put on eighteen general concerts, twenty-two classical, five open-air and eight zither concerts in six months. Many prisoners also tried to occupy themselves with reading, which caused some trouble as the *Lager-Echo* reported in July 1917:

> Reading and always reading is one of the best possibilities for diversion. In the first days of our arrest we were always occupied with finding a book, it didn't matter if it was a detective novel or a little girl's novel, and then we absorbed it line by line as a narcotic against all senseless brooding over events which have taken place. Unfortunately, our private stocks were not very large in the beginning, when the connection to the homeland was still present, so we had to go all around the houses to get any book. Really good books could only be received from best friends and only after passionate persuasion.[39]

In December 1916, in order to try to end the shortage of quality literature (which was a problem in every compound), the *Knockaloe-Lager-Zeitung* published a call for the donation of books to the library of Camp IV, which already possessed some 8,000 titles. It is perhaps surprising that the internees were missing scientific books, rather than fiction, but the magazine explained:

> After two years of internment some of us do not feel like being shown the pleasures of freedom in novels and novellas. We prefer practical lectures which could be necessary for the future.[40]

One year later the magazine again emphasised the importance of reading in order to gain the stimulus which, under ordinary circumstances, would be provided by the natural world:

> The internee is virtually cut off from the whole wide world of nature, the plants, animals and free living and unrestricted men, the beautiful, colourful world is somewhere outside behind the wire, and nearly every impulse we need in order not to become intellectually stunted we have to obtain from books. The book is of great importance to us, and the ones who don't want or aren't able to read in the camp are poor ones, very poor.[41]

Those who wanted to widen their horizons could join numerous classes and lectures about different topics. In a single camp at Knockaloe, there were eleven different schools in operation in June 1917. Seven general schools provided lessons ranging from popular arithmetic and three types of shorthand, through to ten different languages, electro-mechanics and hotel book-keeping. Three advanced schools specialised in preparation for matriculation exams and a preparatory class for army service and nautical school. The seminar programme of the literary-scientific association of Camp IV offered a wide variety of topics including the work of medieval poet Walther von der Vogelweide, the production of gunpowder, the mining of gold in the Transvaal and wireless telegraphy, to name just a few. As the annual report stated, the association intended to:

> bring some diversion amid the monotony of camp life and to show that we will not lose our confidence, even under difficult conditions, and that we aspire to the cultivation of the mind. In our hearts we hope that the voice of peace will soon drown the sound of the weapons in the world and open the gates. Until that time we must follow our own path.[42]

Those who were more interested in sport were able to compete at football, boxing, gymnastics, tennis and cricket. One young man, whose career as a professional boxer began in Knockaloe, was Hans Breitensträter, who remembered:

> No one can understand what it means as a young man to spend so many years behind barbed wire, if they have not experienced this themselves. In the camp, sport became our only salvation . . . [our sports were] football, baseball and tennis, but primarily boxing . . . Courage, however, was not my companion when in the end I had to climb the ropes into the ring. The referee was the lightweight champion of the British Army, Fitzpatrick. The spectators were our fellow internees, almost all the English officers and many soldiers. Everyone believed that the fight would be over very quickly, and indeed it did not last long. The match was to be over 20 rounds, but no one had foreseen what would happen.[43]

Against his own expectations, Breitensträter triumphed against his heavier and more experienced opponent, adding:

> The cheering of my companions was indescribable. They carried me on their shoulders to my barrack, and I was the champion and the darling of the whole camp.[44]

As well as the applause of his peers, Breitensträter received a significant purse of prize money, which he recalled was useful in purchasing additional food supplies.

Away from the boxing ring, many internees occupied themselves with gardening and a horticultural competition was held on 24 August 1916. The judges were the owner of the Knockaloe farm and the head gardener of Kershaw Nursery at Douglas. The internees were very creative, especially in the category of gardening tools. One of the winners was awarded a prize for his watering can made from corned beef tins. The results of the competition were applauded in the *Knockaloe-Lager-Zeitung*:

> More than 55,000 cabbage plants have been planted, which will provide a full harvest, as well as the usual useful plants like peas, beans, carrots, different sorts of salads etc., which will provide a pleasant diversion in the internees' diet. The camp itself contains many garden plots of a decorative nature which we like to see. When we have portions of vegetables at lunch in the vegetable season we will remember our gardeners thankfully and in our imagination we will shake their hands.[45]

But even this plethora of activities ultimately could not make the internees entirely forget their internment. In September 1917, when many had been imprisoned for three years, the *Lager-Echo* commented:

> How many men are able to occupy themselves still! Not everybody is educated or young enough to work intellectually, to learn languages, to study mechanical engineering, to read a chemical book or something similar [. . .]. The average one is only suited for manual crafts: fretsawing, wood and bone carving, painting, knotting and things like that. The ones who really felt like working have tried all possible crafts. But after three years of internment and all the attendant circumstances even the most eager person is fed up with carving vases from bones or making wooden frames en gros.[46]

The editors of the magazines, in spite of their efforts to draw the attention of their readers outside of the camp through reports about flora and fauna, or philosophical debates, inevitably held up a mirror to the captive population. If one were to take their articles as a barometer of the mood of more than 20,000 men in

The 2nd Battalion The Yorkshire Regiment, march through St Peter Port, Guernsey, behind band and drums, to embark on troopships to join the newly-formed 7th Division encamped near Southampton. (The Museum of the Green Howards, Richmond)

RQMS Tom Riordan on his wedding day, 2 November 1919. Note the medal ribbons on his tunic. (The Museum of the Green Howards, Richmond)

Lt Colonel C. A. C. King and officers of the 2nd Battalion The Yorkshire Regiment, at a training camp on Blackdown Heath whilst waiting to join the BEF in Belgium and France. (The Museum of the Green Howards, Richmond)

Lieutenant F. C. Legard, who was to be killed in action near Ypres on 23 October 1914, is here photographed in England with his Vickers Medium Machine-gun Section, prior to the move to Belgium in September. (The Museum of the Green Howards, Richmond)

The Menin Cross Roads occupied by the 2nd Battalion The Yorkshire Regiment (Green Howards) during the First Battle of Ypres, October 1914, painted in 1925 by Fortunino Matania. The figure in the foreground is Private Henry Tandey carrying a wounded comrade. During his service, Tandey was to be awarded the VC, DCM and MM. He survived the war. His section commander, Corporal Tom Riordan, is at the rear of the column of 'B' Company soldiers. (The Museum of the Green Howards, Richmond)

The acting Commanding Officer of the 2nd Yorkshires (Green Howards), Captain B. H. Leatham, visits 'B' Company trenches accompanied by the Intelligence Officer and the Medical Officer after the First Battle of Ypres. (The Museum of the Green Howards, Richmond)

Life in Ruhleben Internment Camp, near Berlin: outside one of the stable blocks now being used as barracks. Note the commercial business of a shoe shine. (Liddle Collection, University of Leeds)

Kindred companions, Box 23, Barrack X1, Ruhleben. As on the label of the original photograph, 'Back Row, l to r, Michael Pease, Geneticist, Cambridge, Schlesinger, fine Cellist, London. Second row, Douglas Doyle Jones, Barrister and fine Illuminator, London, FC Milner, schoolmaster, Halifax. Front row, WE Swale, Engineer, Tonbridge, M Perrot, Student born in France'. (W. E. Swale, Liddle Collection, University of Leeds)

An artist's impression of life in one of the Ruhleben stable boxes of a 'barrack'. Six men with their belongings in an eleven-foot square space. More men were accommodated in the shallow hay-loft space above. (W. E. Swale, Liddle Collection, University of Leeds)

The freezing of the flooded central area of the Trotting Course at Ruhleben offered an opportunity for ice skating. Note the chimneys of the Spandau Munitions Works in the background. (Liddle Collection, University of Leeds)

Prizewinners, surely, at a Ruhleben vegetable show! The growing of flowers and vegetables was hugely assisted by the foundation of the Ruhleben Horticultural Society benefiting from its officially established association with the 'other' RHS – The Royal Horticultural Society – which sent seeds and bulbs from England. (Liddle Collection, University of Leeds)

Ruhleben Dramatic Society's production of *A School for Scandal*, a play the title of which was thought by one internee at the time to be symbolic of the gossiping rivalry between societies in the camp. The photograph shows some very pretty 'girls' and splendid costumes. (Liddle Collection, University of Leeds)

Steve Bloomer (left) of Derby County Football Club, and Fred Pentland of Queens Park Rangers, Middlesbrough and Blackburn Rovers. They were among the football coaches engaged by German clubs and consequently interned at Ruhleben. Pentland had been in charge of the German Olympic team. After the war, both went on to have outstandingly successful coaching careers in Spain. (Liddle Collection, University of Leeds)

An internee's sketch of the riot at Douglas Camp,
November 1914. (Courtesy of Manx National Heritage)

Frederic Dunbar-Kalkreuth,
a wealthy German, interned
at Douglas Camp.
(Matthew Richardson)

Jewish internees at Douglas Camp. (Courtesy of Manx National Heritage)

Paul Stoffa, a Hungarian who wrote in vivid terms of his internment at Knockaloe. (Matthew Richardson)

Hans Breitenstrater, a German for whom boxing was his salvation in Knockaloe Camp. (Matthew Richardson)

Maschinengewehr 08, the German Army's standard machine-gun. (Infantry and SASC Weapons Collection)

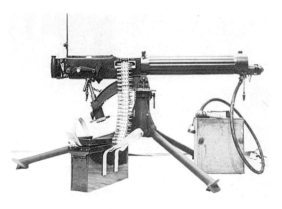

The Vickers gun, the British Army's standard machine-gun. (Infantry and SASC Weapons Collection)

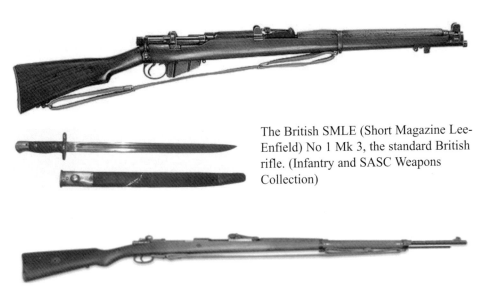

The British SMLE (Short Magazine Lee-Enfield) No 1 Mk 3, the standard British rifle. (Infantry and SASC Weapons Collection)

Gewehr 98 rifle, the standard German rifle. (Infantry and SASC Weapons Collection)

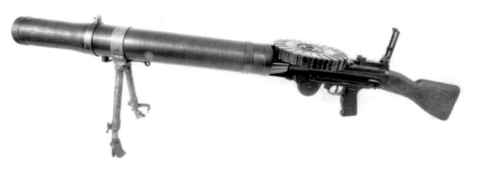

Lewis Gun, British light machine-gun. (Infantry and SASC Weapons Collection)

MG 08/15, the German light machine-gun. (Internet Public Domain)

Stokes Mortar, British trench mortar. (Internet Public Domain)

G 98K. The rifle for German snipers. (Infantry and SASC Weapons Collection)

MP 18. German sub-machine-gun. (Infantry and SASC Weapons Collection)

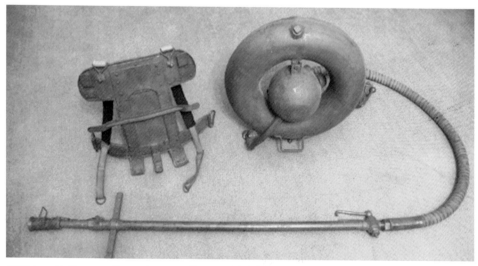

WEX small German flamethrower. (Internet Public Domain)

Knockaloe, one would find quite differing emotional reactions. Resignation, defiance, irony, hope, pride, sadness, rage and ridicule are all to be found in the magazines, which incorporate in their variety the different personalities of their authors. Numerous articles, however, reflect despair and hopelessness. In a November 1916 piece, there was an admission that theatres or orchestras provided merely a temporary distraction from reality:

> We can see on the left fellow prisoners going to and from the wire, driven by their inner restlessness . . . Whatever you do is characterised by nervousness. Nothing seems to succeed, nothing can satisfy us . . . Those who can practise their professions, even in a very moderate way, are luckier than others . . . The shrill laughing which is heard sometimes coming from our lips now, has nothing in common with the hearty laughter of freedom. It is a discharge of the permanent tension we are living with. One can't strike the right note in the confusion of the wire. Our ambitious theatre associations and brave musicians try sometimes to cheer us up and sometimes they really succeed in relaxing our strained faces. But when the game is over and the music has faded we are even more imprisoned by the feeling of loneliness.[47]

There can be little doubt that internment caused serious mental health problems, on a scale perhaps not previously understood. Ballamona Mental Hospital records show that for the period from November 1917 to May 1919 some sixty-six internees were admitted with a variety of mental health conditions. A typical example is perhaps that of Ludwig Albach, admitted to Ballamona in July 1918 with Melancholia. In his admission notes, Dr George Kelman stated:

> This p/w was a very good athlete in the camp, being the best high jumper in it, he was also a very successful theatrical manager, but within the last year, he has gradually gone down, become morose & keeping away from people, getting into dark corners, hiding away from the light with sudden attacks of crying & wringing his hands, of late he has not slept well & has been secreting pieces of rope, necessitating constant watch being kept on him, also breaking out at night to catch the train home.[48]

As an indication of how serious this situation was, by contrast, in the same period, some forty-five civilians and three guards were admitted to the hospital. Given that the internee population was perhaps half the size of the civilian population of the Isle of Man, then an internee was almost three times more likely than his civilian counterpart, outside of the wire, to develop mental health problems. Of course, there were as many different reactions to internment as there were internees. R. F. Koch, writing of his time in Knockaloe, stated:

I consider myself lucky to have been there, it was not so bad, after all, we had our school and our football grounds and that was the most important thing at that time . .. at that time I spoke English and my best friends were the 'sentries' marching along the barbed wire, I often talked with them, they were all rather elderly men and they brought me in some chocolate, woollen socks, fresh collars for shirts and many other little things that really were not allowed to come in, but they were kind to me.[49]

Koch was aged twenty, and as has already been stated, it was those older men longer established in England who perhaps found internment hardest to cope with. As the war drew to a close, concern grew among them over what the future held for those who had been interned in the Isle of Man for the duration of hostilities. How would they be perceived in a post-war Germany? Would they be shunned for not having played their part on the battlefields? This concern is clearly evident in a paragraph in the *Knockaloe-Lager-Zeitung* in the final months of the war:

We are not deserters, and he who dares to deny our right of public work after the war, because fate has banished us to this island, is out of his senses. We would give him the correct answer: [. . .] Every conscientious and honest man has his civil rights, and on the Isle of Man we didn't gain those rights spectacularly, but instead with patient study.[50]

For many in the post-war years, internment was a chapter of history that they wished to forget. It was certainly a chapter which relatively few who were interned wished to talk about – the number of published memoirs or monographs which describe life in Douglas or Knockaloe camps can almost be counted on the fingers of one hand. There was no glory to be won in an internment camp, and no medals to be awarded except those which the internees made themselves. When such souvenirs of internment do survive, and are passed down through families, often they pose more questions than answers, for 'grandfather never spoke about it'. Little wonder then, that for so long, internment has been one of the untold stories of the First World War.

Notes

1. *Isle of Man Weekly Times*, 28 November 1914.
2. Charles L. Hartmann, *Kriegsgefangener auf Gibraltar und der Insel Man* (Bern: P. Haupt, 1918), p. 181.
3. *Op cit*, p. 188.
4. Frederic Dunbar-Kalckreuth, *Die Manner Insel* (Leipzig: Paul List Verlag, 1940), p. 186.
5. Maurice Jeger, *22 Monate in Englisher Kriegsgefangenschaft – Aus den Internierungs-lagern Shrewsbury, Handforth, Knockaloe, Douglas (Insel Man)* (Vienna: Max Pöck, 1917), p. 67.
6. Manx National Heritage, Schonwalder papers, 10 November 1915, MS 12028.
7. *Op cit*, 24 November 1915.
8. Paul Stoffa, *Round the World to Freedom* (London: 1933), p. 230.
9. Paul Cohen-Portheim, *Time Stood Still* (London: Duckworth, 1932), p. 32.

10. *Op cit,* p. 36.
11. Manx National Heritage, Kenner memoirs, MS 11425.
12. *Manx Quarterly* Vol 3 No 17 (October 1917), p. 71.
13. Manx National Heritage, J. T. Baily papers, MS 10417.
14. HMSO, *Reports of visits of inspection made by officials of the United States Embassy to various internment camps in the United Kingdom* (London: 1916), p. 21.
15. Manx National Heritage, J. T. Baily papers, MS 10417.
16. Otto Schimming, *13 Monate hinter dem Stacheldraht* (1919), p. 15.
17. Ottoman archives, Istanbul, HR.SYS.2203/20.
18. Herbert Bury, *Here and There in the War Areas* (London: 1916), p. 143.
19. Manx National Heritage, Rudolf Hartmann papers, MS 12779.
20. Manx National Heritage, Schonwalder papers 18 August 1915, MS 12028.
21. *Op cit*, 2 December 1915.
22. *Op cit*, 3 June 1916.
23. *Op cit*, 1 May 1916.
24. *Op cit*, 1 October 1916.
25. *Isle of Man Examiner* 29 May 1915.
26. Manx National Heritage, Mary Faragher papers, MS 13141.
27. *Isle of Man Examiner*, 16 March 1918.
28. *Ramsey Courier*, 8 March 1918.
29. *Peel City Guardian*, 9 November 1918.
30. Manx National Heritage, Lilley papers, MS 12840.
31. *Knockaloe Lager Zeitung*, 7 October 1916.
32. *Knockaloe Lager Zeitung,* 4 July 1917.
33. Manx National Heritage, Archibald Knox letter 26 October, 1919, MS 09954/2.
34. *Knockaloe Lager Zeitung,* 7 October 1916.
35. Ibid.
36. *Knockaloe Lager Zeitung*, 6 February 1918.
37. Cohen-Portheim, Time Stood Still, p. 128.
38. *Knockaloe Lager Zeitung*, 4 July 1917.
39. *Lager Echo*, 28 July 1917.
40. *Knockaloe Lager Zeitung*, 22 December 1916.
41. *Knockaloe Lager Zeitung*, 29 December 1917.
42. *Knockaloe Lager Zeitung*, 25 May 1917.
43. *Der Querschnitt*, Vol 1 (1921).
44. Ibid.
45. *Knockaloe Lager Zeitung*, 7 October 1916.
46. *Lager Echo*, 15 September 1917.
47. *Knockaloe Lager Zeitung*, 18 November 1916.
48. Isle of Man Public Record Office, Ballamona Hospital Casebook, C17/1J.
49. *Isle of Man Examiner*, 24 January 1963.
50. *Knockaloe Lager Zeitung*, 27 June 1918.

Suggested Further Reading

Cohen-Portheim, Paul, *Time Stood Still* (London: Duckworth, 1932).
Cresswell, Yvonne, *Living with the Wire* (Douglas: Manx National Heritage, 2010).
Dunbar-Kalckreuth, Frederic, *Die Manner Insel* (Leipzig: Paul List Verlag, 1940).
Hartmann, Charles L., *Kriegsgefangener auf Gibraltar und der Insel Man* (Bern: P. Haupt, 1918).
Jeger, Maurice, *22 Monate in Englisher Kriegsgefangenschaft – Aus den Internierungs-lagern Shrewsbury, Handforth, Knockaloe, Douglas (Insel Man)* (Vienna: Max Pöck, 1917).
Richardson, Matthew, *This Terrible Ordeal: Manx letters, diaries and memories of the Great War* (Douglas: Manx National Heritage, 2014).

Chapter 12

From Cricket Whites to Khaki – Sport and the Great War

* * *

Clive Harris

Come, leave the lure of the football field
With its fame so lightly won,
And take your place in a greater game
Where worthier deeds are done.
No game is this where thousands watch
The play of a chosen few; But rally all!
If you are men at all, There's room in the team for you.
A. Lochhead

There is no doubt that the Great War, despite being primarily, and often erroneously, remembered for mud, gas, incompetence and more mud, brought about such seismic social change that its impact still ripples across society today. Regardless of social standing, political leaning or regional identity, the effects and by-products of a conflict that took place a century ago have shaped and changed our nation.

As we delve deeper into our past, history has never been a more popular pastime, in a pattern similar to that seen during the centenary of the American Civil War, the number of memorials commemorating the Great War at home and on the fields of France look set to double.

Nowhere is the renewal of interest more prevalent than in the sports clubs of today. Among the massed ranks of football clubs poppies now adorn shirts in November, and Leyton Orient, West Ham, Reading and Charlton have all unveiled war memorials in recent years at their stadiums. Watford, Millwall and Raith Rovers have played in commemorative strips and match day programmes across the land contain regular articles on players who served in the Great War.

Not to be outdone, the leading rugby and cricket clubs have published histories and visited the battlefields of France and Flanders. Stories of Wimbledon champions and Grand National winners have been told in the national media, the

Tour de France was even re-routed to pass Ypres and Verdun as the sporting world remembers. There have been strong links between sport and war for a century now but where and how did it begin; to find the answer we need to return to the summer of 1914.

It is fair to say that football was already at war when Sir Edward Grey announced 'The lamps are going out all over Europe. We shall not see them lit again in our time', if only at war with itself! The emergence of public holidays and the population explosion of our cities had led to the game being played by the masses for the masses. As new super clubs raced towards professionalism there remained a desire to retain the amateur status that had prevailed for the previous four decades.

Accusations such as 'overpaid, underworked players' and 'players today have lost touch with reality and the working man' were commonplace in the football periodicals of 1914, but more worrying was the situation that the game found itself in when war was declared in August. Fixtures had been arranged, contracts signed and in some cases stadium leases had been agreed. It just wasn't as simple as the opening verse of the Lochhead poem quoted at the start of this chapter suggests.

For many people, cricket also had its role to play in the upcoming war. The apocryphal Wellington quote that 'The battle of Waterloo was won on the playing fields of Eton' resonated within the higher, more traditional echelons of the sport. Indeed, reference to the war 'being fought with a straight bat' or that Britain should be 'playing the game', were frequently used in the newspapers when commenting upon the opening phase of the war. Cricket, or the perceived image of cricket, was felt by some to sum up our national identity and spirit. In reality, growing professionalism, especially among the elite northern leagues if not at county level, presented a similar if not smaller problem than that facing football. One area not so complicated for cricket was the timing of the outbreak of war. By August the season was coming to a close, players could be released for military service, grounds could be offered for the war effort and life could return to normal should it actually 'be all over by Christmas'.

To demonstrate a truly remarkable response to a sense of 'duty & sacrifice' we must turn to Rugby Union. First-class players flocked to the colours in such numbers that the sport could boast that 90 per cent had enlisted by 1918. One club, Roslyn Park, lost seventy-two of its members. Alongside this tragically lengthy roll of honour stands the award of two Victoria Crosses, eleven Distinguished Service Orders (two with Bars) and no less than sixty-three Military Crosses, a war record not unlike that of an infantry battalion.

One aspect that united all three sports was their usefulness as recruiting tools. The clubs understood this, the authorities realised and encouraged it and the idea of marching alongside your idols from the terraces to the trenches soon caught the imagination of the public, filling the ranks of Territorial and New Army battalions across the land in the autumn of 1914. With the numerical advantages that sports club recruiting could provide (not to be underestimated in a conflict where mass mattered), sport also had a critical role to play within the army itself.

'No efficient army ever underrates the value of personal fitness, and sport, in various form, has always helped to this end.' General Sir Charles Harrington opened the pamphlet of the newly-formed Army Sport Control Board (ASCB) with these words in 1918. As early as 1860 the British Army had opened its first 'School of Army Physical Training'. This was a direct result of the Crimean War where, in founder Major Frederick Hammersley's own words, 'the general health and fitness of recruits and soldiers left a good deal to be desired'.

The Great War presented an even bigger challenge for the British Army as the need for men, combined with such an effective recruiting campaign as Lord Kitchener's 'Your Country Needs You', led to the stretching of minimum physical requirements to accommodate so many willing volunteers. Records show that men were joining up younger, older, thinner, fatter and shorter than the pre-war Regular Army. The 170-strong Army Gymnastics Staff would not be able to remedy this alone through the use of dumbbells, route marches and lots of imagination. Inter-company and battalion sports were therefore more important than ever as the New Armies took shape and the Territorial Force geared up for overseas service. Fitness concerns were not purely the domain of the newly-emerging units within the British Army. It is now widely stated that almost 40 per cent of the British Expeditionary Force were reservists recalled to the colours. Many had been in civvie street for over two years and lacked the physical edge that full time soldiers possessed.

It is equally important to remember the situation at the front by early December 1914. The retreat from Mons and mobile warfare had ended on the Aisne and the so-called 'race to the sea' had stagnated at Ypres. Trench warfare set in for the winter, a monotonous routine for manning static positions was emerging and men were being fed a high calorific diet in excess of that of home. Were it not for filling a soldier's time by keeping them both active and stimulated when out of the line, the British Army would face a future of fatness over fitness. Never had the participation of organised sports played a more vital role in both the physical standard and morale of the British Army. The sports club recruitment consequence of the introduction into the army of professional and first-class amateur athletes was to be a cornerstone in raising the level of physical fitness in the army.

War hangs like a deathly pall over the land of golf, on the eastern seaboard of Britain the peaceful resorts are largely in the hands of the military authorities, vast entrenchments have been constructed and the adjacent ground turned into tented fields. It is no purpose of ours to discuss the cause or significance of the terrible campaign. Those of us who have travelled in Germany have had graven into the mind, the all-pervading worship of the military spirit, the joy of the people of the Fatherland in the rattle of the scabbard and the clank of the soldiers step. (*Golf Monthly*, 1914)

The long-established pastime of golf was flourishing in the years immediately leading up to the war. Yet, like every other aspect of British life, the conflict would threaten, shape and ultimately change the sport forever.

Few readers of *Golf Monthly* could have envisaged the impact on their courses and clubs in the summer of 1914. By October, the R&A had requested that clubs cancel the membership of German- and Austrian-born members within their ranks (a decision not finally reversed until 2004 by one West Country club). The wide-open fairways and rough links were coveted by newly-raised units for training areas. Woking Golf Club was approached to give up its course for artillery training (that was until the Divisional staff were offered complimentary seven-day membership) and many courses were adapted to nine holes, alternate tee positions being utilised as vegetable plots in the original 'Dig for Victory' campaign.

Around the courses lots of changes were apparent, the first use of female green keepers among them, but perhaps the biggest threat caused by the war was the fast-rising price of rubber. The need for rubber for military use in a rapidly-expanding army led to the price of a golf ball increasing tenfold. The problem reached its height when New Scotland Yard was forced to form a special squad to combat organised criminal gangs from stealing balls off the courses at an alarming rate.

As more and men of service age enlisted in the colours, membership levels dropped and when the golfing authorities suggested every club purchase a war bond of several hundred pounds, numbers faced insurmountable financial problems and were forced to close. Damage to courses was not restricted to training. One Derbyshire course was damaged in an air raid, prompting the R&A to issue a rule change that any bomb craters on a course were to be treated as 'ground under repair' and a free drop was to be allowed.

The Lutyens-designed Knebworth Golf Course was not alone in being converted into a VAD hospital as Britain adapted to war but it was not only the courses that were affected. What became of many of the golfers too? A founding member of the Professional Golfers' Association (PGA), Albert Tingey, had his own successful golf school in Paris and managed the Fontainebleau Course in 1914. On the declaration of war he returned to the UK via Dunkirk and immediately made contact with fellow PGA member Charles Mayo. Mayo was the course professional at Burhill Golf Club in Surrey. This course was owned by the Guinness family who had also planned to open a new course at nearby Bramley designed by Charles Mayo. The guest of honour was to have been Prince Albert of Schleswig-Holstein but events in Europe at the time, not long before the outbreak of war, overshadowed the planning and the project was put on hold. (Despite this the club has now celebrated its centenary, though never having been formally opened.)

Prompted perhaps by the words of the influential Harold Hinton, the 1913 Amateur Champion, 'No caddie between the ages of 19 & 35 should be given a single job or the slightest encouragement to be about the links, my advice to golf clubs is to assist these young fellows to get to the nearest recruiting station,' Tingey and Mayo set about the raising of a new 'Pals' battalion made up of golfers and their caddies to serve side by side in the New Armies. The idea was given full support by the PGA and initially nicknamed 'The Niblick Brigade'. Among the early men to offer their assistance, were William Robertson Reith, Wilfred Reid and George Duncan. The latter would go on to win the British Open in 1920. This little band decided that further applicants should be single with no children but the new rule meant that Robertson Reith himself was excluded from joining, though he did eventually serve with the Royal Sussex Regiment in 1916. Word was put out looking for further volunteers.

In early September 1914, the first wave of men to try and enlist met at Gattis Italian Restaurant in White Cross Street. Twenty-six new volunteers then met the golfing press and photographers at the base of Nelson's Column in Trafalgar Square before attending a nearby recruiting office. With spaces in London's new army battalions filling quickly, the group caught the train to Winchester where they were able to secure places in the 13/Rifle Brigade. For them the experience of recruitment in Winchester is well-described in the history of the battalion:

> Day after day in the late summer of 1914, hundreds of men pressed up the High Street of Winchester to the arched west gate of the Rifle Brigade Depot. All sorts and conditions of men, navvies, stockbrokers, artisans, clerks, miners, golf professionals, artists and students, they besieged the barrack square and waited long hours until the harassed staff could enrol them. At last they were sorted out and some of them eventually became the 13th (Service) Battalion of the Rifle Brigade.

The desire to serve together placed the golfers in 'B' Company and issued service numbers beginning S/44.

Golfers were not alone in the battalion to boast sporting prowess: a group of semi-professional football players from Stockton was joined by Captain Arnold Strode Jackson. Strode Jackson had triumphed in the 1912 Stockholm Olympics winning a gold medal in the 1,500 metres, entering as an independent after not being selected by his country. He broke off a fishing holiday in Norway to participate. The event, dominated by the USA, included seven Americans in the final, three of whom deliberately blocked the path of anyone attempting to take the front of the field. Strode Jackson was forced to run wide but still posted an Olympic Record of 3 minutes 56.8 seconds. He took the lead on the final bend and won by a photo finish leading to the race being dubbed the 'Greatest Race Ever Run'. Strode Jackson, who held blues at Oxford for hockey, rowing and football, would end the war as a 27-year-old Brigadier with three wound stripes and four Distinguished Service Orders to his name.

As the battalion prepared for war, Albert Tingey provided regular updates on life in Khaki via a column for *Golf Monthly*. Though rumoured to be destined for the Dardanelles by the end of April 1915, overseas service finally arrived in late

July when *Monas Queen* slipped out of the Solent on route to France. The first golfing casualty in the unit came in early 1916 when William Eastland described in a letter from the front the following incident:

> Rifleman Herbert Line, formally assistant at le Touquet, has been struck in the face by a bullet which ricocheted off the ammunition pouch of another recruit. Another rifleman went to Line's assistance but was hit through the lung and died before reaching hospital but Line himself was able, with the help of stretcher bearers, to walk to the dressing station. We are happy to say that he is already on the fairway to recovery.

Trench life was interspersed with periods of rest. During one spell at Auxi le Chateau, the 'Niblicks' arranged putting and driving competitions, a popular offer for many of the officers of the battalion to learn from the professionals in the ranks. Going one better, Ramsey Ross, a course designer serving in the Honourable Artillery Company, actually built an eighteen-hole golf course in the Ypres Salient complete with barbed wire marking fairways and shell holes forming bunkers and water hazards. He was not alone and by the end of the year a second course was built close to the firing line by Scottish professional, Tom Fernie, of the 9/Highland Light Infantry. Before long, staff officers were spending so much time playing golf that the General Staff at St Omer made the decision to build a nine-hole course within their grounds to solve the problem. Sports journalist Allan Gardiner, of the 12/Royal Irish Rifles, designed the course and *Golfing* magazine appealed for old clubs and unwanted balls to be donated for men to use at the front.

The Somme fighting, notably at Contalmaison on 10 July 1916, was greatly to affect the Niblicks, Sergeant Jimmy Scarth, the Doncaster professional, and Sergeant Fred Jolly, the Beckenham professional, both being wounded. As sportsman, the chances of a career being ended by a minor injury were higher than for many peacetime tradesman serving in the trenches. Jolly was to return to the Battalion and was awarded a Meritorious Service Medal for gallantry in June 1918. By the end of the Battle of the Somme, Harry Towlson from Thorpe Hall Golf Club, Alfred Seward from Beckenham and a colleague of Jolly's, Claude Macey, the Littlehampton professional, had all been wounded. Worse still, William Eastland, who had written the letter about Herbert Line's wounding, had been killed in late November on the Ancre. The former Surrey golfing professional is buried in Contay Commonwealth War Graves Cemetery.

The following year saw the battalion serve in the Ypres Salient. Whilst billeted at Dead Dog Farm near Hill 62, the original 'Niblicks' were thrilled to meet none other than Charles Mayo, by now an officer in the Tank Corps. A memorable evening celebration was enjoyed as stories of the links and golfing memories were exchanged long into the night. However, the sound of the guns was ever-present and the news that the talented Maurice Henment of Sevenoaks Golf Club had been killed nearby was to cast a shadow over the occasion.

The final year of the war saw the 13/Rifle Brigade heavily engaged. By late May, an action in Bucquoy saw two Victoria Crosses awarded to the Battalion. The advance to victory continued and of a curious incident in late October, one of the last surviving 'Niblicks', Sergeant Harry Shoesmith, was to recall that when moving through a damaged building he realised that he had just passed a German patrol moving through the next room. Shoesmith, Jim Scarth and Claude Macey were the only men of the original group which dined at Gattis to return to the post-war professional game. One of those too badly injured to play again was Lance Corporal Ernest Jones. Jones, having lost a leg, moved to the United States where he became a golfing coach. His training there, alongside the losses in our own professional game, were direct causes of the shift in golfing power from Great Britain to the USA, a legacy that would continue for the next eighty years.

Without doubt one of the most colourful sporting characters before the war was the heartthrob of the tennis world, Anthony 'Tony' Wilding. Blond and standing six foot two inches tall, women had flocked to see him on court in the Wimbledon Men's Final of 1913. Played in scorching heat, stringent security checks (as a result of the threat of Suffragette arson attacks) led to a number of his admirers fainting towards the climax of the match and having to be laid out, courtside, to recover.

Described in the national press as 'dashing', 'handsome' and 'gentlemanly', Wilding had begun life in Opowa, Christchurch, New Zealand in 1883 where his father was a partner in a leading law firm. He grew up in the comfortable surroundings of the family home, 'Fownhope', named after the West-Country village the family had left in 1879. Key to Tony's development as a first-class athlete were the presence of a tennis court, croquet lawn, cricket wicket and a freshwater swimming pool, along with two brothers and two sisters to foster healthy competition. A keen horseman, he would often ride fifty miles a day on his favourite pony 'Jack' and his eccentric habit of shooting birds that landed on his lawn enabled him to become an accomplished shot with both rifle and shotgun at a very early age.

Keen to further his education, he left New Zealand in 1902 to study law at Trinity College Cambridge. Privately, he also hoped to become a professional cricketer whilst in Britain having represented New Zealand at junior level some years previously. It soon became obvious, however, that tennis was his main talent. During his summer break in 1903 he emerged as a prospect on the tour circuit, but continued to study hard for his law degree, eventually being called to the Bar in 1906. In due course he became a solicitor and barrister for the New Zealand Supreme Court and would voyage regularly between his two adopted countries, perfecting his backhand stroke and service on deck during the long crossings.

His first appearance at the All England Club came in 1904 where he played H. Maloney, a man he had watched from the stands only a year earlier and commented on his unfashionable attire of 'ill-fitting Blazer and odd socks'. By now Wilding was appearing in competitions in France, Norway, Serbia, Hungary and Germany. He represented Australasia in the International Lawn Tennis Challenge (later renamed the Davis Cup after its founder Dwight Davis) and 1906 saw him achieve his first major victories, taking both the men's singles and men's doubles titles at the Australian Open. By 1913, championship wins had followed at Wimbledon, Melbourne, Johannesburg, Bad Homburg, Nice, Christchurch, Prague and Brussels.

During this period he developed a fascination with motorsports and would often arrive at tournaments with a suitcase strapped to the back of his Bat Jap motorcycle. One summer he entered and won a race between Land's End and John o'Groats, his attachment to mechanical petrol-driven machinery leading to an unlikely role in the war.

A thing that marked Wilding out among his rivals was a revolutionary training regime where he would daily, run, distance walk, skip and use a punch ball to improve core fitness whilst concentrating on weaknesses in his game. He had the ability to pick his shots carefully, was an expert at the lob, and displayed excellent pace, but was also able to slow the game down and dictate the pace, much to the frustration of his opponents.

One daring exploit in his pre-war life came when he decided to learn to fly in 1907. He employed a French instructor at Mourmelon le Grand, near Rheims, who spoke no English other than to say 'Good bye' in different tones. Despite this language barrier, an engine failure mid-flight and several bumpy landings, he described his first experience of flight as being 'very fine'. He also noted at the time 'a good deal of German trainee pilots at the school'.

By 1910 he was unstoppable and was crowned Wimbledon Men's Champion in 1910, 1911, 1912 and 1913. By now his sporting, academic and social standing was further enhanced by the publication of his autobiography, *On the Court and Off*. His engagement to the Broadway actress, Maxine Elliot, described as the most beautiful woman in America, only added to his public appeal and he began to endorse various products including 'The Wilding' tennis racquet made by leading manufacturer, Ayres.

The story of Anthony Wilding's last competitive match is so compelling it is worthy of note. During a Davis Cup match for Australasia alongside his long-time playing partner Norman Brookes, the son of a rich gold miner, and someone who would serve in the Red Cross during the war, their opponents were Otto Froitzheim and Oskar Kreuzer representing Germany. The match was staged in Pittsburgh, USA. Whilst the result, a victory for Wilding and Brookes was a formality, the date 1 August 1914, was, to say the least, of historical significance. Midway through the match the organiser heard news of Germany declaring war on Russia and he promptly cut the telegraph wires to the stadium so that the game would not be disrupted. After the match, the German duo rushed for home aboard a cruise ship which, however, was intercepted by a Royal Navy warship. The German and Austrian passengers, including the tennis players, were to be interned for the duration of the war. The crowd at that tennis encounter could not have given any thought to the fact that they had seen Wilding play his last match.

On his return to the United Kingdom in early September it was not a question of whether to enlist but how quickly could it be done? Using his social influence, he canvassed the opinion of his friend Winston Churchill who facilitated a swift and smooth passage into the Royal Naval Air Service Armoured Car Section with a commission in the Royal Marines. This fledgling unit was being established at Wormwood Scrubs Prison.

Equipped with a variety of different machines the group was effectively a pioneer of armoured warfare. Popular were the Rolls-Royce Silver Ghost Armoured Cars, capable of a speed up to 45mph. They were equipped with a .303 machine-gun fitted in a revolving turret and they made use of boilerplate armour. Wilding was given command of the experimental Seabrook Armoured Lorry, looking more like a boat than a land vehicle. It was equipped with both a machine-gun and a 3pdr gun.

In less than six weeks from his enlistment, Lt. Wilding was in France and wrote home in late October 1914 that he was 'motoring as close as possible to the German Lines to report all information to Headquarters'. His knowledge of the European road network, gained during his days on the tennis circuit, was proving invaluable to the higher command. He also commented on shooting at aircraft as 'I find it the most intensely interesting work I have ever done. I am afraid the war will be a big business'.

His unit, not the most popular among the more traditional naval commanders, was described by Commander Charles Risk in April 1915 as: 'From their appearance, their apparent discipline, and the variety of so-called uniform as worn by both officers and men, and their unshaven appearance, I am not surprised to learn that the Armoured Car Force is still known as "The Motor Bandits".' Wilding was fully suited to military life, however, and had risen rapidly to the rank of Captain. He was keen to get to grips with the enemy and was given command of two Seabrooks and thirty crew and almost immediately motored straight to the front and fired some 500 rounds at a house containing a German machine-gun crew. Realising the potential of these new weapons, the Indian Corps requested twenty-four of them to be attached. Wilding volunteered. He found the Indian Army officers 'thoroughly agreeable' and messed with them wherever possible.

It was just weeks later, on 9 May 1915, that he lost his life, serving alongside General Willcocks' Indian Corps near to the crossroads at Neuve Chapelle known as Port Arthur. He was positioned with his 3pdr trailer gun just behind the British breastworks. Only a day earlier, he had annoyed a staff officer who kept ducking behind a trench wall and using a periscope whilst Wilding stood boldly upright to view the enemy positions. We know he spent his last hours writing to both his mother and his ex-commander, Chilcott, The letters had a very different tone. To his mother he described what was to be his final meal as 'the best I have had at the front, Pea soup followed by Roast Lamb, fruits and white wine'.

The following day saw his fiercest battle experience yet, despite the attack ending in a dismal failure. Wilding's crew fired like demons: by 16:45 they had fired over 400 rounds and Wilding stated he was going to take a short nap before continuing the fight. Fellow tennis player Don Pretty was waiting for him at his dugout. They entered and shortly afterwards a heavy burst of laughter was heard from within: whatever the punchline was, is lost to time, as almost simultaneously a shell hit the roof with a tremendous explosion. Despite men digging furiously to rescue them, it was in vain. Wilding's body was identified by his monographed gold cigarette case Pretty, though still alive, succumbed to his wounds two days later.

The Wilding family received hundreds of letters of condolence in the coming weeks. The Duke of Westminster wrote: 'he was one of my finest officers and had done very fine work'. The Viscountess Grosvenor wrote: 'he was so loved and spent many happy days in England with his friends and now he is among the bank of heroes who have paid the great sacrifice and that will be your comfort dear Mrs Wilding.'

Perhaps for the most fitting tribute to such an iconic character as Anthony Wilding, we need to return to his gold cigarette case, presented to him after a tennis victory on the French Riviera in the summer of 1914. He never smoked but carried cigarettes for those who did.

Of less wealthy upbringing was Colin Blythe of 78 Evelyn Street, Deptford. With unemployment, pre-war, running at 30 per cent in his area, little time could be spent on recreation or sport. Growing up in this deprived area of Southeast London, Blythe entered into an engineering apprenticeship at the Woolwich Arsenal. The hard manual labour involved caused a deterioration in his health, leading his doctor to prescribe as much open-air exercise as possible. As was to be learned later, this was an initial bout of epilepsy which was to blight his very promising sporting career.

In July 1897, Colin walked to nearby Rectory Field, Blackheath, to watch the final day of a Kent versus Somerset cricket match. As he watched Kent all-rounder Walter Wright, warming up in the nets, he was asked to 'bowl him a few'. Doing as he was asked, Blythe's raw talent was soon obvious and he was invited for a trial in Charlton Park and then at Tonbridge. Despite having only a few coaching sessions, Colin Blythe was invited to join the playing staff of Kent for the following season. Kent's pioneering academy, known as the 'Tonbridge Nursery', led to a period of dominance in the game. Blythe's emergence was rapid and in his first season guesting for local clubs he took 105 wickets for an average of 13 runs; his county debut was to come in the following year.

For the twenty-year-old there could have been few tougher opponents against whom to take your bow than Yorkshire, on a run of fourteen straight wins and widely regarded as English cricket's top side. A local reporter described the action:

> Towards the bowling crease stepped Blythe, as innocent looking as a babe. The ball pitched just off the wicket, the burly Yorkshireman played forward, but the leg bail fell, and Blythe had phenomenally taken a wicket – and a good wicket too – from the first ball he ever bowled for his county.

By the end of his first season he was described in *Wisden* as a 'new and promising bowler' but few could have predicted the season that was to follow. He finished with the outstanding figures of 232 maiden overs and 114 first class wickets for an average of 19, including his destruction of a much-fancied Lancashire side where he took all 10 wickets for just 72 runs. So impressed was the watching Canterbury crowd that they passed a hat around and raised £7-1s-6d for their new hero. Throughout this period Colin continued to work at the Woolwich Arsenal to supplement his meagre cricketing income. He was also attracting wider renown when he bowled nine touring South Africans out in an exhibition game whilst the Boer War was raging in their homeland. He was chosen to tour Australia in 1901/2 and enjoyed the distinction of being awarded man of the match in one game, taking seven wickets for England, an honour that resulted in the presentation of a gold pocket watch. There was still more to his credit: winning a gold medal representing an England XI in a football match against Freemantle.

Perhaps the most memorable description we have of Colin's natural cricketing ability was provided by journalist G. D. Martineau:

> As he trod his measure to the wicket, it was as though he stepped to a tune played on his own violin. Then the left arm whipped around behind his back and came up and over in a curve as beautiful as the swoop of a gull. The ball seemed to float for an instant, then struck down and upwards – a thing of beauty.

His South London character and dialect added to his popularity among teammates and opponents. Nicknamed 'Charlie', he once applauded Reggie Spooner for hitting him for six before remarking: 'Oh, Mr Spooner, I'd give all my bowling to bat like that.'

Kent were crowned county champions during this period and Blythe was regarded as being among the sports elite. In 1907 he set a long-term record with his bowling figures of 17 wickets for 48 runs in a first-class game against Northamptonshire.

His penultimate season, 1913, saw Kent again crowned champions and his final match was fittingly at Lords, in a defeat against Middlesex in the summer of 1914. By now however, like so many of his cricketing contemporaries, thoughts turned from cricket whites to khaki and by the end of August he had enlisted in the Royal Engineers where his No.1 Fortress Company specialised in light railway construction and bridge building. Whilst going about his military business, he kept tabs on the sport he loved and even made post-war plans by accepting Eton College's offer to be head cricketing coach at the cessation of hostilities, a role fate decreed he was never to fulfil.

In August 1917, Sergeant Colin Blythe was part of a draft which joined the 12/Kings Own Yorkshire Light Infantry, a pioneer battalion made up of West Yorkshire miners tasked with light railway construction in the Ypres Salient. When not working within the range of the guns his hutted camp to the east of Ypres was subjected to regular air raids. There was little time for rest and no time for cricket. As the ANZAC Corps prepared for the battle of Menin Road Ridge and the assault on Polygon Wood, Colin and his men were building the Cambridge Spur line, a job that required skill and nerves of steel working almost entirely at night and right up to the trench lines. By November, he was still engaged in railway construction when on the 8th, just south of the Ypres-Wieltje road, a shell exploded above the heads of his working party. Colin Blythe received a mortal wound that ripped through the leather wallet containing the portrait of his wife Janet. He died shortly afterwards. He is buried in Oxford Road Cemetery alongside three Kent comrades killed by the same shell. His grave is often bedecked in cricketing tributes. The current England side have visited the site as once again the modern game stopped to remember the Great War.

By May 1915, over 2,000 MCC members had enlisted and during the war the Old Trafford and Trent Bridge grounds were converted into hospitals, Leicestershire's pavilion was turned into an indoor rifle range and many well-known cricketers were to lose their lives. Perhaps the final cricketing word should go the largely unknown Arthur Collins. A regular officer in the Royal Engineers, he was killed at Black Watch Corner in the First Battle of Ypres in November 1914. As a thirteen-year-old boy playing for Clifton College in 1899 he scored an incredible 628 not out. Despite this record-breaking achievement he never played a first class match choosing a life in the army as a career.

> The word was passed along 'London Irish lead on to assembly trench'. The assemble trench was in front, and there the scaling ladders were placed against the parapet, ready steps to death, as someone remarked. I had a view of the men swarming up the ladders when I got there, their bayonets held in steady hands, and at a little distance off a football swinging by its whang from a bayonet standard. (Patrick Macgill describing the Battle of Loos.)

To say that men flocked to the colours across the footballing community is not entirely correct. A trickle of professionals enlisted in the first days. Donald Bell, then on the books of Bradford Park Avenue, was one of the very first, if not the first, to request a termination of his contract to enlist. This was duly granted and he found himself in the ranks of the King's Own Yorkshire Light Infantry within weeks. A chance meeting with his old school chum, Archie White, led to a commission in the 9/Yorkshire Regiment where Donald immediately became a popular figure among fellow officers and those in the ranks. Bell was to serve at Loos and on the Somme including a notable action at Horseshoe Redoubt on 5 July 1916.

He described the action in the last letter he wrote home to his father later that evening:

When the battalion went over, I, with my team crawled up a communication trench and attacked the gun and the trench and I hit the gun first shot from about 20 yards and knocked it over . . . The G.O.C. has been over to congratulate the battalion and he personally thanked me. I must confess it was the biggest fluke alive and I did nothing. I only chucked one bomb but it did the trick. The C.O. says I saved the situation for this gun was doing all the damage . . . I am glad I have been so fortunate for Pa's sake, for I know he likes his lads to be at the top of the tree. He used to be always on about too much play and too little work, but my athletics came in handy this trip . . . do not worry about me, I believe that God is watching over me and it rests with him whether I pull through or not.

This action, and those that followed a few days later, led to the award of a Victoria Cross:

For most conspicuous bravery. During an attack a very heavy enfilade fire was opened on the attacking company by a hostile machine gun. 2nd Lt. Bell immediately, and on his own initiative, crept up a communication trench and then, followed by Corpl. Colwill and Pte. Batey, rushed across the open under very heavy fire and attacked the machine gun, shooting the firer with his revolver, and destroying gun and personnel with bombs. This very brave act saved many lives and ensured the success of the attack. Five days later this very gallant officer lost his life performing a very similar act of bravery.

Donald Bell was the first professional footballer to receive this supreme award. He sadly became the only professional footballer to hold the VC and to be killed in action. Today he lies in the immaculate Gordon Dump Cemetery but his sacrifice and sense of duty was soon followed by supporters of Newcastle United, Crystal Palace and Bradford Park Avenue for whom he had played. The high profile of footballers at the front was undoubtedly an important recruiting tool and within the game the speed of those joining up began to gather pace.

Both north and south of the border, battalions were raised with footballing links; the 16/Royal Scots, led by the charismatic Lt Colonel George McCrae, was formed from sixteen players and 500 season-ticket holders of league leaders Heart of Midlothian. They were joined by over a hundred supporters of Edinburgh city rivals, Hibernian, alongside players from Falkirk, Raith Rovers and Dunfermline Athletic.

The battalion was not restricted to footballers alone, with Scottish rugby international, John Dallas, serving, and the secretary of the Scottish Rugby Union too, Arthur Fluett, who fell at Arras in 1917. Hockey was represented by Scottish goalkeeper, Finlay MacRae, who received a Military Medal and Bar before meeting his fate in August 1917. Murdoch McLeod, who today would have been called a bodybuilder, reputed to be 'the strongest man in Scotland', may be chosen to represent a minority sport. Murdoch was killed on the Somme and is buried close to Donald Bell in Gordon Dump Cemetery.

In London, the 17/Middlesex was also raised as a footballer's battalion. *The Sportsman* published an article on 16 December 1914, announcing that 400–500 men connected with the game had met at Fulham Town Hall and among them were players from Clapton Orient, Chelsea, Tottenham Hotspur, Millwall, Brentford, Brighton and Luton Town, whilst some men came from as far away as Bristol Rovers, Sheffield Wednesday and Aston Villa.

Such was the popularity of the unit that a second 23/Middlesex was raised largely from within the game, the battalion serving in both France and Italy. Across the country supporters and players were enlisting side by side. West Ham United could claim links with 13/Essex and 179 Howitzer Brigade whilst Charlton Athletic filled the ranks of the 20/Londons and the 8 Howitzers from Plumstead. A particularly fascinating footballing character to serve was Alex 'Sandy' Turnbull. From a tough background in Ayrshire, Sandy had lost his father in a mining accident when he was just 16, leaving him to become the family breadwinner. When not working at the pit, he began to make a name for himself playing in local amateur leagues. Bolton Wanderers were the first to attempt to lure him south with a professional contract, but he declined the offer. A year later, in 1902, Manchester City made him an offer he could not refuse.

Manager Tom Maley built a side around Turnbull, fellow striker Billie Gillespie and Welsh international Billy Meredith which won the Second Division Championship at the first time of asking. The following year, they finished runners up to Sheffield Wednesday, courtesy of twelve Turnbull goals, and won the 1903 FA Cup Final. The meteoric rise led to suspicion among the authorities regarding illegal payments and bonuses. The matter was dropped in time for the 1904/05 season with Turnbull scoring twenty goals and again the team finished narrow runners up in the First Division. After the last game of the season, the opposing captain, Alec Leake of Aston Villa, claimed he was offered a bribe to throw the game. The City captain, Billy Meredith, was found guilty and suspended for a year. Meredith, in turn, blew the lid off to the Press on what payments were being made. The resulting fine imposed on the club forced a fire sale in which 'Sandy' Turnbull moved across the city to join Manchester United. He had scored 53 goals in 110 games, won an FA Cup medal, the Second Division title, and twice ended as runners-up in the First Division during his short spell with the blue half of Manchester.

Whilst playing in a United shirt, both glory or controversy were never far away. After his teammate Thomas Blackstock collapsed and died during a reserve game, Turnbull, outraged at his club's handling of the matter, vowed to establish a players' union. Frowned upon by many in the sport, the idea of a union was so popular among the players that games were almost cancelled until the union was formally recognised. The 1907/08 season saw Turnbull score twenty-five goals in thirty appearances and Manchester United swept to their first ever League Championship. He scored a hat trick against Liverpool but also became the first player ever to be sent off in a Manchester derby.

The following year he achieved every schoolboy's dream when he scored the winning goal in the FA Cup Final win over Bristol City. Celebrations that evening were led by the comedian George Robey at the Alhambra Theatre. The following morning when the players woke with sore heads, the lid from the trophy was missing. Only after a lengthy search was it found, in Alex Turnbull's jacket pocket.

A further title winner's medal followed in 1910, again with Turnbull's goals assisting. It was in this season that he scored the first ever goal at the club's new ground, Old Trafford. Unlike Donald Bell, Turnbull's footballing career was not cut short by the war but by his alleged involvement in a match-fixing scandal in 1915. Losing the game 2-0 to Liverpool itself raised suspicion but when it was discovered that a number of bets at the odds of 7-1 had been placed predicting the score, Turnbull was one of seven players given a lifetime ban.

To escape the controversy, he journeyed to enlist in the 17/Middlesex. His overseas service was, however, with the 8/East Surreys, a unit already famed for its footballing exploits when Captain Billie Nevill led them over the top, kicking footballs towards the German lines. By May 1917, Alex had reached the rank of sergeant when he was killed in the attack on Cherisy.

The Great War has been described as being fought by ordinary people in an extraordinary time. The sporting world, however, showed that it was also an extraordinary war fought by extraordinary people. A century on, their service and sacrifice is not being forgotten.

Suggested Further Reading

Anon, *The Last Post – Death Roll of Sport* (The Field Press, 1919).
Belton, Brian, *War Hammers* (Tempus Publishing, 2007).
Concannon, Dale, *Spitfire on the Fairway* (Aurum Press, 2003).
Harris, Clive, and Julian Whippy, *The Greater Game* (Pen & Sword Books, 2007).
Jenkins, Stephen, *They Took the Lead* (DDP One Stop, 2005).
Macgill, Patrick, *The Great Push* (Herbert Jenkins, 1916).
Mortimer, Gavin, *Fields of Glory* (Carlton Publishing, 2001).
Oldfield, Lt Col E., *The History of the Army Physical Training Corps* (Gale & Polden, 1955).
Riddoch, Andrew, and John Kemp, *When the Whistle Blows* (Haynes Publishing, 2008).
Wisden's Almanac 1918, 1919, 1920.

Chapter 13

Infantry Weapons of the Great War

* * *

John Whitchurch

At the beginning of the First World War most major European armies had fought in conflicts at some time in the previous half-century; either against each other or in conflicts of a colonial nature. These conflicts had of course an influence on the arms and equipment used by the infantry; particularly the Franco-Prussian War of 1870–1, the Second Boer War of 1899–1902 and the Russo-Japanese War of 1904–05.

During the Franco-Prussian War, use of breech-loading rifles meant soldiers could lie down and take up prone firing positions. They no longer needed to stand in ranks and volley fire. The Boer forces during the Second Boer War were good shots and well-armed with the German magazine-fed bolt-action 7mm Mauser rifle. Individual shooting standards in the British Army at that time were not good; skills such as judging distance and effective use of cover, both important for survival on the battlefield of the day, were not taught to individuals. The Boer War had a profound effect on the weapons and shooting standards of the British Army. The first use of machine-guns in both defence and attack featured in the Russo-Japanese War. Also during the Russo-Japanese War, massive and effective use of grenades and mortars in the defence of entrenched camps was commonplace. Most European Powers had military observers present during the war and as a result the Germans, in particular increased the manufacture and issue of machine-guns while the British ignored the reports of their Military Observer!

The British Infantry Platoon, 1914

By 1914 the British Expeditionary Force infantryman was a highly-trained individual with many years service in either the Regular Army or as a reservist. Each man was armed with either a .303in Lee-Enfield No.1 Mk1 Rifle or a Short Magazine Lee-Enfield (SMLE) and the Platoon Commander with a .455in Webley revolver and a sword. The infantry platoon was fifty-four strong. Each infantry battalion was issued with two Maxim or Vickers machine-guns.

The SMLE

The SMLE was a magazine-fed bolt-action rifle. The magazine held ten rounds of ammunition in staggered column form. On later versions a clip (charger) for rapid loading was introduced, and a rear receiver bridge with charger clip guides was added to the design. Fully to load the magazine required two standard five-round clip although loading by loose rounds was still an option. Prior to 1916, all SMLEs (and earlier Long Lee-Enfields) were issued with so-called 'magazine cut-off' – a simple device, located at the right side of the receiver and intended to cut off the cartridge supply from the magazine to the action when engaged, so the rifle could be used as a single-loader and ammunition in the magazine could be saved for the most intense moments of combat.

The Lee bolt action was the most famous feature of the SMLE. The locking action and bent-down bolt arm lent itself to quick reloading. The combination of the relatively high-capacity magazine, fast clip reloading and rapid action enabled the SMLE to produce one of the highest practical rates of fire amongst contemporary designs. One notable feature of the Lee bolt action was that the bolts were not interchangeable between different rifles of the same mark. Each bolt had to be fitted to its respective action, thus making the production and in-field bolt replacement more complicated.

A Mk VII bullet fired from an SMLE could reach in excess of 2,000 yards. The performance of the .303in was roughly equalled by other cartridges such as the German 7.92mm and French 8mm Lebel. The *Government Manual of Small Arms* (1911) stated that a .303in bullet at 200 yards could penetrate 38 inches of hardwood, 58 inches of softwood, 14 inches of lime-mortared brickwork, 18 inches of packed sandbags and 60 inches of clay. Each rifleman carried 150 rounds in his webbing.

The .455 Webley Pistol

The first top-break revolvers were developed by the Webley & Son Company (Webley & Scott Co. from 1897) of Great Britain in the 1870s. The first Webley revolver had been officially adopted for Royal Navy and Army service in 1887, as the Webley Revolver, .455, Mark I. It was a break-top, six-shot double action revolver, chambered for black powder .455 British Service cartridge, officially known as Cartridge .455 revolver, Mark I. This cartridge launched a heavy, 18-gram (265 grains) lead bullet at the relatively slow muzzle velocity of 180 metres per second. All Webley revolvers were Double Action or Double Action Only, with very distinctively-shaped barrels. The Webley revolver, .455, Mk 6, adopted in 1915, was the 'ultimate' Webley .455 six-shooter. The Mk 6 featured a redesigned squarer pistol grip, a 6in barrel and a removable front sight. Officially superseded in 1932, with the adoption of the Enfield No.2 .38 calibre revolver, it nonetheless remained in wide use by British troops during the Second World War.

The Maxim machine-gun

The original Maxim machine-gun was developed by an American, Hiram Maxim, who became a British citizen in 1900.The weapon relied on one of the first uses of recoil operation known, with patents appearing as far back as 1883. The Maxim machine-gun was a short-recoil operated, water-cooled, fully automatic only, belt-fed machine-gun. Water jackets were made from sheet steel. The trigger was located between the dual spade grips attached to the back plate of the receiver and was operated by the gunner's thumbs.

The feed system for the Maxim used non-disintegrating belts, made from cloth or tarpaulin, with metallic struts. Feed was from the right side only and the feed system was operated through the horizontally pivoting pin/levers system by the recoiling barrel. The gun, weighing just over 27 kilograms, had a rate of fire of 500 rounds of .303 ball ammunition a minute and was operated by a crew of four.

The German Infantry Platoon, 1914

The German army of 1914 went to war with a reputation and confidence born of 60 years of victorious campaigns. Each infantryman was armed with a 7.92mm Mauser 98 Rifle and the Platoon Commander with a 9mm P08 Luger pistol and a sword. The platoon was thirty-nine strong. Each three-battalion regiment had a machine-gun company armed with six MG08 Maxim machine-guns.

7.92mm Gewehr 98 Mauser Rifle

The Model 98 rifle was a magazine-fed, bolt action rifle. The magazine and the bolt action were the two most famous features of the Model 98. The magazine was a two-row integral box, with quickly detachable floor plate. The magazine was filled by hand through the receiver top opening, either with single rounds, pushed in one by one, or via stripper clips. Each clip held five rounds, enough to fill the magazine, and was inserted into the clip guides, machined into the rear receiver bridge. The Mauser bolt was a simple, extremely strong and well thought-out design. The bolt arm was rigidly attached to the bolt body and, on the original Gewehr 98 rifles, the bolt arm was straight and located horizontally when the bolt was in the closed position.

9mm P08 Luger Pistol

The Parabellum pistol was developed by Georg Luger in Germany in 1898. The name Parabellum was derived from ancient Latin saying *Si vis Pacem, Para bellum* – 'If you want Peace, prepare for War'. The Luger design was based on an earlier idea, but Luger improved it and substantially reduced its size. Lugers were adopted by many countries and were still in use in the 1950s. They were all recoil-operated, locked-breech, semi-automatic handguns. Some early Lugers featured an automatic grip safety at the rear side of the grip. Lugers were manufactured with different barrel lengths ranging from 98mm up to 350mm (14in), some in 'carbine' versions, with an additional forward handguard and detachable butt stock. All Lugers were very well built and accurate pistols, especially for the period. However, they were all too sensitive to fouling as well as too pricey, when compared to more modern designs, such as the Browning High-Power or Walther P38.

Kugelhandgranate 1913

After shrewd observation of the 1904–05 Russo-Japanese War, several European armies, including France and Germany, recognized the need to pay some interest to hand grenades. The *Kugelhandgranate* 1913 was a first development of the previous century's ball grenades. These cast-iron spheres were machined with outside deep fragmentation grooves (for the production of 70 to 80 pieces), drilled with a threaded hole designed to receive a transportation plug; replaced by a fuse, once primed, ready for use. The fuse, a traction igniter, was a hollow bronze tube, filled with compressed black powder (giving a 7-second delay, or 5 seconds for the red-painted igniters) and triggered by pulling a brass wire attached to a friction block dipped in a mixture of glass, manganese bioxyde and potassium chlorate. The German troops entered the war in 1914 with reasonable quantities of such grenades, relatively modern, with their fragmentation design and their igniter, which was quite unresponsive to humidity. This large grenade, weighing a kilogram would have needed considerable strength and technique from the soldier for it to reach its projected 15-metre range.

MG08

This gun, developed from an earlier 1901 model, was a belt-fed, water-cooled, fully automatic weapon based on the Maxim 'toggle lock' system. After cocking and firing the first shot, the mechanism would continue to operate as long as the trigger was operated, there was ammunition and the weapon didn't jam. Fed from 250-round belts, its cyclic rate was about 400 rounds a minute, though it was more economical and less prone to overheating when fired in shorter bursts. Its basic mount was the *Schlitten* or 'sledge', a steady, versatile but heavy platform. Carried on the march in carts, the gun and mount could be moved like a stretcher on the battlefield, dragged or dismounted and carried over the shoulders. It was manned by a crew of six men.

7.85cm Lichte Minenwerfer (leMW)

Along with the effective use of hand grenades, the Russo-Japanese War had shown the value of mortars against modern fieldworks and fortifications and the Germans were in the process of fielding a whole series of mortars before the beginning of the First World War. Their term for them was *Minenwerfer*, literally mine-thrower; they were initially assigned to engineer units in their siege warfare role. In common with Rheinmetall's other *Minenwerfer* designs, the *leMW* was a rifled muzzle-loader that had hydraulic cylinders on each side of the tube to absorb the recoil forces and spring recuperators to return the tube to the firing position. It had a rectangular firing platform with limited traverse and elevation. Wheels could be added to ease transportation or it could be carried by at least six men.

Minenwerfer/Light Trench Mortar
A revised wheeled carriage for the 7.85cm *leichtes Minenwerfer n/A* was adopted in 1918 to allow a flatter trajectory (and greater accuracy) for anti-tank action. The accurate range of these weapons was 500 metres. In September 1918 an instruction was issued to the effect that half of every battalion's light trench mortars should be dedicated to anti-tank work. The 192nd Division of the German Army had already pioneered this approach in August 1918. They proved very effective but were restricted in use by a shortage of horses for the transport of ammunition. During this trial, British tank crews had described the use of light trench mortars in this role and from September onwards German light trench mortar crews reported that tank gunners were paying them particular and unwanted attention. With their relatively short range if operating in the mobile anti-tank role (in the open) they were highly vulnerable to machine-gun fire from tanks.

By 1918, after four years of war, the weapons and the organisation of the infantry had changed considerably. Warfare on the Western Front on the Allied side had become an all-arms battle with integration between the infantry, the artillery, tanks and close air support, whilst on the German side new tactics bred new weapons. There was less reliance on the individual skills of the soldier and more reliance on equipment to overcome the shortfalls in training time.

Machine-guns

During the Great War, the rise of the machine-gun as a crucial weapon of war was a spectacular one. It entered the war as a backup weapon for the rifle firepower of an army battalion, but rose to the status of Queen of the Battlefield and in the British Army the basis of a self-contained Machine-Gun Corps under the direct command of the higher echelons by the end of 1918. Whilst it is true that artillery fire inflicted many more casualties on the combatants overall, the machine-gun proved to be a deadly weapon and the outcome of many actions was determined by its destructive firepower.

Machine-guns of the Great War were either water or air cooled. Each form of cooling had its advantages and disadvantages. Water-cooled guns made use of a water-filled cooling 'jacket' fitted around the barrel. This jacket helped to dissipate the heat generated as a result of firing. Typically in water-cooled guns the water in the jacket would start to evaporate after roughly 750 rounds had been fired. This method of cooling proved more efficient than air-cooling, but it carried with it some inherent disadvantages. A fresh water supply was as necessary as an ammunition supply to replenish the water jacket once the local supply had evaporated. This required additional crewmembers as water carriers. Also, the water added significantly to the weight of the system. It was not uncommon to need up to four men to move and serve the weapon. In air-cooled machine-guns the barrel was cooled by the air around it. While effective to an extent, it forced the gunner to fire the weapon using short, controlled bursts of fire, thus avoiding overheating by allowing cooling of the barrel between bursts. Additionally, a spare barrel was necessary to enable barrel changes to keep the gun from overheating during prolonged, rapid firing and this often proved a time-consuming affair and introduced problems associated with handling an extremely hot barrel under fire. Water-cooled machine-guns eventually gave way to air-cooled machine-guns by the time of the modern age of warfare.

Vickers Machine-Gun

Like most other medium support machine-guns born around the turn of the century, the British Vickers Medium Machine-Gun originated from the revolutionary Maxim series of 1889. The Vickers was essentially an improved Maxim, primarily differentiated from the original in its inversion of the toggle locking action. Vickers also took to reducing the overall weight of the original weapon, introducing aluminium to replace steel where possible. The British Army adopted the new Vickers design in 1912 as the 'Gun, Machine, Vickers, .303 inch, Mk 1' and it became the standard support machine-gun thereafter. The gunner traversed and fired the gun holding a pair of spade grips fitted at the rear of the receiver. The Vickers fired the .303in round from a 250-round canvas belt. The cartridge was developed in 1888 and first adopted in the Lee-Metford service rifle series before becoming the standard British and Commonwealth cartridge around the world. The cartridge itself was a rimmed design with a noticeable bottleneck and the bullet was a proven manstopper. Due to all the components that made up the weapon system, at least three personnel were required. The gunner carried and fired the gun while the No. 2 carried the tripod and managed the ammunition supply and feed while helping to clear jams as needed. The No. 3 carried and managed the critical water supply during combat, giving assistance to the gunner and No. 2 when required. For transportation the weapon system was broken down into gun, mounting, ammunition and water supply. The Vickers was a cumbersome and heavy weapon but this was somewhat offset by its reliability and sustained firepower, giving it real tactical value which was well appreciated. While the weapon could be traversed from left to right in the normal sense, it could also provide plunging arc (indirect or semi-indirect) fire as an *ad hoc* light 'artillery' weapon when required. Furthermore, it was an effective offensive or defensive weapon. The Vickers proved so effective that it was adopted for use in all manner of aircraft, warships and vehicles. As a battlefield support weapon during the Great War the Vickers gave an excellent account of itself and, considered by many to be the best machine-gun of the conflict, was well-liked by its crews. Its rate of fire was from 450 to 500 rounds a minute and effective range from 2,000 metres but this range doubled using indirect fire.

The Browning M1917

The external appearance of the Browning M1917 was similar to the German

Maxim 08 and British Vickers although the internal Browning design has no relation to either weapon. John Browning developed his recoil-operated system to take advantage of the recoil force found in the expanding powder gasses of each successive shot. The working parts of the weapon were held in a rectangular receiver. Attached to the front of the receiver was the cylindrical water jacket with a portion of the muzzle extending from the front of the jacket. A carrying handle could be attached along the top of the water jacket to aid carriage. The trigger was part of a pistol grip assembly fitted to the rear of the body and proved an effective method of distinguishing the Browning design from both the German Maxim and British Vickers. The tripod was a heavy, tubular affair that provided the operator with both a swivel and elevation action to train effectively onto targets. Ammunition feed was situated along the left side of the body and utilized a fabric 250-round belt held in an ammunition box. The operator maintained a sitting or prone position behind the weapon. Due to its weight its use was mainly in defensive action. It required a four-man crew and its rate of fire and range were identical to the Vickers.

The Lewis Gun

The Lewis Gun, invented by an American, Isaac Newton Lewis, was probably the best of the light machine guns produced around the period of the Great War. He initially offered it to the US Army, but after they showed little interest, he moved to Europe, where his gun was quickly adopted by the Belgians and then, with the outbreak of war, by the British. The Lewis's air-cooled design meant it was light enough to be carried and used on the move by a single man. It held its ammunition in 47-round pan magazines, easier to use on the move than the non-disintegrating fabric ammunition belts of the time, which tangled round the gunner's legs as he moved. It was reasonably reliable, though rather complex and stoppage-prone by the standards of Second World War machine-guns. The gun's cyclic rate of fire was approximately 500–600 rounds per minute and it weighed 12.25kg.

By the time of the Third Battle of Ypres in August 1917, the British Army had integrated the Lewis Gun at platoon level within infantry battalions, in a specialised section containing the two-man gun crew, ammunition carriers and a pair of riflemen to act as scouts and provide local security. Lewis Gun sections were normally deployed in the second wave of an attack, so that they could deal with German machine-gun teams emerging from deep dugouts to defend pillboxes and shell holes after the moving 'creeper' artillery barrage had passed over them. The Lewis Gun section members were less burdened by consolidation stores than the standard infantrymen but made up for it with the extra ammunition drums carried in the circular webbing carriers on their equipment. The weapon was so popular that the Americans rechambered it to fire their 30-06 cartridge and the Germans rechambered captured Lewis Guns (over 100,000 by the end of the war) to fire their 7.92mm cartridge.

The MG08/15

Developed under the direction of Colonel von Merkatz, the new, portable, automatic weapon that emerged in the German Army was christened the *MG08/15*. This design paradigm, by which the standard heavy machine-gun was adapted so as to provide a portable version, was in marked contrast to the path taken by the Allies. The Allied armies adopted a number of light automatic weapons that were not at all adaptations of their heavy types. In doing so, they undoubtedly had much more efficient designs, but at the cost of overall production efficiency. The German decision to stay with the Maxim design simplified both production and training. This 'new gun' functioned the same in its firing cycle, provided the same rate of fire, used the same ammunition, belts and many internal parts and also maintained the same reliability as the older, heavier *MG08* and, therefore, required little extra retraining to operate it. The *MG08/15* was lightened to the extent where the gun could be advanced with attacking soldiers, but it had a number of key differences from the standard *MG08* including a new booster/flash hider, providing a far more positive recoil action and an attachment point for a 100-round ammunition drum to be hung on the side of the receiver. The gun crew was reduced from five to three and the gun could be carried and fired by one man. It was instrumental in the British punitive losses on the Somme and by the end of the war 130,000 *08/15s* had been produced. It is claimed that the *MG08/15* was singularly responsible for more casualties on the battlefield than any other weapon ever deployed, including the Atomic Bomb. If true, it deserves its nickname, the Devil's Paint Brush.

The *MG08/15*, being a 'light' mobile machine gun, needed the belt feed to be mobile. The solution was a drum with a removable spool in which a 100-round belt (cut from the standard 250-round belt) was wound. The drum was designed to open on a hinge to remove the spool and closed securely with a spring loaded latch. It slipped over a special hanger that mounted to the right side of the gun below the feed block. Spare drums were stored in pairs in wooden boxes that would be carried by the rest of the crew. Like the *MG08*, the *MG08/15* was water-cooled. The heat generated during sustained firing was more than sufficient to boil the water so the gun was equipped with a steam port. Although classed as a light machine-gun, the *MG08/15* was still a Maxim, so while it may have been one of the first 'light' automatic weapons, it was actually large, heavy, cumbersome, and even when new, required a lot of maintenance and care.

The Fusil Mitrailleur 1915 CRSG

The *Fusil Mitrailleur 1915 CSRG (Chauchat Sutter Ribeyrolles Gladiator)* was well ahead of its time. When finally deployed in useful numbers in the autumn of 1916, Col. Louis Chauchat's automatic rifle delivered a level of man-portable infantry firepower that was unrivalled in any other army. The *M1915 CSRGI* heralded a new era of automatic arms as it could be carried, loaded and fired by just one man. But the *Chauchat*'s story is an unfortunate one because Col. Chauchat's ingenious design, which in many ways was ahead of its day, was clearly let down by manufacturing standards that could be described as nothing short of criminally negligent and a cursory glance at a *Chauchat* would indicate that there was something very wrong with the weapon. The feed system used single-stack box magazines of semi-circular shape, necessary because of the severely tapered and rimmed cases of the French service rifle cartridge. The magazine had large openings in the right wall, probably designed to lighten it and allow an easy visual check of remaining ammunition. The trigger system was over-complicated as it required a special link to release the sear in automatic fire once the barrel was in battery. Basic furniture included a wooden butt, a separate pistol grip, and a vertical fore grip, located between the trigger guard and the magazine. A lightweight folding bipod was attached to the front of the trigger/magazine housing, below the barrel jacket.

Introduced into combat during the height of static trench warfare, the *Chauchat* suffered from the prevailing outmoded tactics of the time, as well as the harsh physical environment of the Western Front. One of the *Chauchat*'s greatest flaws was its flimsy magazine, which had a maximum capacity of 20 rounds of 8mm Lebel ammunition. Unfortunately, the magazine springs were not strong enough, so most *Chauchat* gunners 'short-loaded' their magazines for increased reliability. Even worse, the magazine was almost completely open on its right side (to provide gunners with a quick view of available ammunition), and this exposed the gun and its ammunition to all the mud, slime and grime that the trenches could provide. Also, the magazine feed lips were easily bent, and the entire magazine itself could be easily crushed or deformed. Canvas covers were eventually provided for the magazines, and while this helped a little, the disastrous magazine design was not corrected by the end of the war. While it may seem like an easy remedy to a completely predictable problem, it was not addressed in time to make the *Chauchat* a more dirt-proof design, and many French and American gunners paid for that fact with their lives.

It is estimated that 250,000 8mm *Chauchat*s were produced during the war using revolutionary new metal-stamping techniques – making it the most widely-manufactured automatic weapon of the war – and that 50,000 remained in operation within the French Army at the end of the war.

Rifle and Hand Grenades

Regarded as practical for siege operations only since Napoleonic times the grenade came to the attention of German army planners (notable among others) during the Russo-Japanese War of 1904–05. As with most things at the start of the war in August 1914, the Germans were ahead of the pack in terms of grenade development. Even as war began the Germans had 70,000 hand grenades in readiness, along with a further 106,000 rifle grenades. Curiously, when most people are asked to consider the means of trench attack most popular during the First World War, the rifle or bayonet is often suggested as the most likely answer. In fact both of these weapons were to be used chiefly to defend the grenadiers of the bombing parties; those men tasked with the bombing of trenches and positions using grenades of various types. Bombing parties grew in number and frequency as the war progressed and formed a major component of any infantry attack by the war's close (although US forces used them less, chiefly on account of supply shortages). The British bombing team usually consisted of nine men at a time: an NCO, two throwers, two carriers, two bayonet-men to defend the team and two 'spare' men for use when casualties were incurred. As an attack or raid reached an enemy trench, the grenadiers would be responsible for racing down the trench and throwing grenades into each dug-out they passed: this invariably succeeded in purging dug-outs of their human occupants in an attempt to surrender (often not accepted as they were promptly shot or bayoneted).

When Britain entered the war, it did so with just one type of grenade in its armoury (suitably named 'Mark 1'), and not very many of those. As with the machine-gun, the British high command could not see much use for the hand grenade. This situation soon changed however; indeed, within a year Britain was producing up to half a million hand grenades each week. Even so, British forces away from the Western Front, which was given first call on grenade supplies, were lacking in supplies of grenades until well into 1916. The French and Russian armies were rather better prepared than the British, since they fully expected to be in the position of besieging German fortresses: a task ideally suited to the grenade. Grenades, either hand- or rifle-driven, were detonated in one of two ways; either by impact (percussion) or by a timed fuse. Generally speaking, infantrymen preferred timed fuses (of whatever amount of time) to percussion devices, since there remained the constant risk of accidentally jolting a grenade while in a trench and setting it off.

The idea of using a pin, extracted by hand from a grenade, to set off a timed fuse quickly became commonplace and was a feature of later grenades. Another, earlier, method of igniting the fuse was via the so-called 'stick' grenade, where the fuse was lit when the grenade left the handle (stick) to which it was attached. Yet another type, cylindrical in shape and referred to as the 'cricket ball' grenade, was ignited by striking the grenade like a match before it was promptly despatched skywards. The first British grenade, the Mark 1 used in 1914, proved highly unpopular with soldiers. Forming a canister with a 16in cane handle, it was ignited by removing a safety pin through the top. When thrown, the handle (and attached linen streamers) ensured it landed nose-down so that the striker was forced into the detonator. However, the Mark 1 caused widespread distrust given that it was liable to explode prematurely if it came into contact with an object while in the act of being thrown, which was entirely feasible when throwing from a trench. Consequently, many British soldiers – and those based in Gallipoli who had no access to grenades of any type – resorted to the construction of home-made, or 'jam-tin' bombs, so-named because they were literally made out of jam tins, each packed with gun-cotton or dynamite, together with pieces of scrap metal. A length of fuse would project through the top of the tin, with each inch of fuse giving approximately 1.25 seconds delay. Other home-made grenades of differing designs were widespread and were seen on all fronts. Grenade development soon took off and, at least on the Western Front, *ad hoc* types dwindled in numbers as better models appeared.

Rifle grenades were simply attached to a rod and placed down the barrel of a rifle or, instead, placed in a cup attached to the barrel, and were launched by the blast of a blank cartridge. Such grenades were never popular, however, and were deemed (correctly) as inaccurate. The Germans ceased using rifle grenades in 1916, although they continued to experiment with revised models. The British and French, however, persisted with cup grenades. The British, who had pioneered their use, together with the French, improved the range of cup grenades from the average 180–200 metres to an impressive 400 metres (using finned grenades). The Germans belatedly restarted using cup grenades in 1918. The first truly popular British hand grenade – simply referred to as 'No. 15' – was churned out in huge numbers by the close of 1915, although its lack of performance in wet weather promptly led to a sharp downturn in its popularity. Whereas up to half a million No. 15s were produced in the autumn of 1915, they were seldom used at all beyond the turn of the year.

Sniping

The objectives of sniping were essentially the same as those of trench raiding: to gain mastery of No Man's Land, to wear down the enemy both numerically and morally, and to obtain information. Sniping was more than a century old in 1914, yet the skills were either poorly developed or forgotten in the major European armies. The first snipers were therefore French and German gamekeepers and foresters, Scottish deerstalkers and big game hunters, who transferred civilian techniques to the battlefield. It was a game in which the Germans achieved an early dominance, which lasted through 1915. The effect on the enemy, both physical and mental, was considerable.

Initially, equipment supply was problematic. In Germany the Duke of Raribor was credited with initiating the collection of sporting weapons for sniping use and the Bavarians are believed to have received their first 'scoped rifles in December 1914. Bavarian regiments were soon supplied at the rate of one sniper rifle per company, rising to three per company by 1916. From Britain and the colonies came game rifles like the Rigby, Jeffreys high-velocity .333in and Ross Model 1905. Yet at first Britain was seriously outmatched by the dominance of the German optics industry. An appeal in 1914 by Field Marshal Lord Roberts eventually netted 14,000 pairs of binoculars; but as far as sniper scopes were concerned, only 1,260 government orders had been placed by July 1915. By this time the Canadians were operating on a scale of four Ross rifles with telescopic sights per battalion, and Sir Max Aitken's *Canada, in Flanders*, claimed that a Native American, Private Ballendine, had already achieved a tally of thirty-six German kills. In the British Army, the efforts of individual enthusiasts like Major F. Crum of the King's Royal Rifles, Major T. F. Fremantle, and Lieutenant L. Greener of the Warwickshire's, bulked large. One officer, more than any other, has been identified with the systemisation of sniping and the establishment of army schools. Vernon Hesketh-Pritchard, a big game hunter and former Hampshire county cricketer, was at first turned down by the army on grounds of age, but succeeded in reaching the front, escorting war correspondents in 1915. In his luggage he brought 'scoped sporting rifles, and was soon preaching his creed 'to shoot but nor be shot'. His mission was, as he saw it, to 'invent ways to irritate Germans'. In July 1915 he conducted experiments with 'elephant guns' against the armoured shields which the Germans were already using to protect their firing loopholes, and by August was lobbying Generals Lynden Bell, Munro and others with a scheme to set up an official sniping establishment.

During early 1915, the British found themselves confronting German battalions with an official sniping establishment of twenty-four *Scharfschützen* (six per company) armed with *Gew'98I* rifles and telescopic sights from a variety of world-renowned German optical manufacturers. To counter the German sniping threat the British had virtually nothing and certainly no official service rifle with a telescopic sight. Copies of *The Field* from 1915 are full of pleading letters, written from officers in the trenches, to fellow sporting enthusiasts at home. The letters ask for sporting rifles to be sent to the front, particularly those with telescopic sights. There are also letters from enterprising officers who had privately purchased optical sights known as Galilean sights. These crude devices consist of two lenses, the larger of which is fixed near the front sight while the smaller is fixed on the rear sight, or in a fashion like the old A. J. Parker or Parker-Hale target sights. They were relatively cheap and required no special skills to set them up. They worked quite well, although they were fragile, with a magnification of about 2x power and narrow fields of view (about 5–7ft at 100yd). While outside the subject of this chapter, these Galilean sights nonetheless played an important role in the early days of British sniping. The War Office purchased three main makes and eventually 13,945 Lattey, Barnett and Martin sights were officially bought, to add to the thousands that were purchased privately. These sights helped hold the line alongside numerous sporting rifles, plus some early conversions of SMLEs by the trade which mounted various different types of scopes.

In July 1915, the first big War Office contract (1,120 sights) was placed with the Periscopic Prism Co Ltd (PPCo) for what was to become the most common sight used during the war (4,830 in total). In September and October of 1915, Holland & Holland and Purdey were contracted to fit Aldis scopes, each with their own design of fitting. These became the next most numerous type with over 1,700. At the same time, Whitehead Bros started to fit Winchester A5 scopes and this combination became the third most numerous with 907 made. Other scopes were used such as the Evans (about 120), the Watts (about 160 fitted in three different ways!), and there was one company, J. Bartle & Co, that was contracted to fit 2,000 Aldis scopes using the Bartle mount. Unfortunately, nobody knows what this mount looked like.

One unfortunate design fault of all the SMLE sniper rifles was the fitting of the scopes with side mounts, offset to the left. Officialdom decreed that this must be so – in order that the rifles could still be reloaded with five-round chargers! This made them far harder to use, particularly when a fast snap shot was required. It also meant that you had to cut a bigger hole in a loophole plate (making it easier for a German sniper to put a bullet through that hole). Only later in the war were some experimental overhead mounts developed. The Canadians, less constricted by officialdom, soon started to fit Winchester A5, PPCo and Aldis scopes on overhead mounts to their Ross Rifles and maybe also to some SMLEs. They used their own armourers to do this with some success, judging by the tallies that some of the Canadian snipers achieved. Cpl Francis (Peggy) Pegahmagabow MM and two Bars was the highest scoring sniper of the war with 378 confirmed kills. He was an Ojibwa Indian from Perry Sound Island, Ontario, Canada.

The first of the British Scouting, Observation and Sniping (SOS) schools was set up at Army level in December 1915 (Second Army) and the First Army SOS school, under the famous Hesketh-Prichard, was established in the summer of 1916. There had been unofficial schools at Corps level prior to this. Numbers of other schools were established later, including a Canadian school. Standards were high and snipers were expected to achieve headshots 50 per cent of the time at 400yds. Each of these schools had a slightly different syllabus and it was Major F. M. Crum who succeeded in writing a common syllabus. He also wrote the first official pamphlet SS 195 *Scouting and Patrolling* (Dec 1917). This was after he got into trouble for privately publishing a book called *Scouts and Sniping in Trench Warfare*. He even produced a film on sniper training and established a course at Aldershot to educate senior officers about the benefits of sniping. He was a pioneer of his time but has never received the same level of recognition as Hesketh-Prichard.

Trench Mortars

The rapid transformation of operations from a relatively fluid, fast moving conventional field war to the restrictions of trench warfare resulted in the quick and almost improvised development of trench artillery, whose task was to deliver as large and powerful as possible explosive charges onto short-range targets, following an almost vertical ballistic curve. These various and numerous weapons, sometimes called *Crapouillots* when French, 'Trench Mortars' when British, and *Minenwerfer* or *Ladungswerfer* when German, fired a variety of natures of ammunition at low muzzle velocity, producing far less stress than conventional shells due to the far lower pressures. These 'bombs' could be built with thin steel walls, allowing for more weight of powerful explosive charges that could represent up to 60 per cent of the total weight of the bomb. Such weapons were able to flatten tens of metres of trenches by a single hit, and destroy or terrorize the occupants.

Most of the trench artillery weapon tubes were not rifled, the in-flight stability being either non-existent, or controlled by fins; efficient enough at low velocity.

The bomb was either inserted entirely with its body and fins inside the tube, or a cylindrical tail welded to the bomb body was inserted inside the mortar bore (like the French 58mm *crapouillots* and their different ammunition). In other cases, like the powerful German regimental *minenwerfer*, the trench mortars' tubes were rifled like a conventional gun, and the ammunition's driving bands were pre-machined with the matching shapes, and introduced backwards by the gun muzzle. These weapons evolved all through the war, the final evolution being the famous British Stokes mortar, or the pneumatic mortars which used compressed air to propel the bomb instead of explosives.

The mortar proved to be an especially effective weapon during the war. This small, stumpy weapon was designed to fire at a steep angle – often 45 degrees or more – so that the projectile fell almost vertically onto the enemy position. As such, its capacity to drop into trenches made it much-feared among the troops. The other advantage of the mortar was that it could be fired from the relative safety of the trench, or a purpose-built mortar pit, avoiding exposure to direct small arms or artillery fire. The mortars were also considerably lighter than conventional artillery pieces with better mobility. Germany had a head start on the Allies at the beginning of the war, after they had witnessed its effects during the Russo-Japanese War. They began stockpiling mortars in readiness for use against France's fortresses, and had around 150 units by the start of the war. Both France and Britain were caught unaware by Germany's use of the mortar, causing France to dust off its own century-old Napoleonic-era devices. Britain, although slow to catch on to the idea, did eventually accept the weapon and improve its design. The smoothbore 3in Stokes mortar is generally regarded as the best of the mortars in use during the war.

Stormtroopers

The first official German stormtroop unit was authorized on 2 March 1915. The High Command of the Field Army ordered VIII Corps to form a detachment for the testing of experimental weapons and the development of appropriate tactics that could break the deadlock on the Western Front. It was considered a natural job for the Pioneers – the only element of the pre-war army experienced with hand grenades and trained for siege warfare. On 23 October 1916 General Ludendorff ordered all German armies in the West to form a battalion of stormtroops.

Stormtroopers were armed with a combination of weapons, modified weapons and new weapons produced specifically for them.

Karabiner 98k

The *Karabiner 98k* was a bolt-action carbine based on the *Mauser M98* system, adopted by the stormtroopers as it was handier than the *Gewehr 98*. The straight bolt handle found on the *Gewehr 98* bolt was replaced by a turned-down bolt handle on the *Karabiner 98k*. This change made it easier to operate the bolt rapidly, reduced the amount the handle projected beyond the receiver and enabled mounting of aiming optics directly above the receiver on the *Karabiner 98k*.

MP18

The *MP18* manufactured by Theodor Bergmann was the first practical submachine-gun used in combat. It was introduced into service in 1918 as the primary weapon of the Stormtroopers. The firepower of this new class of weapon, up to 500 rounds a minute, made such an impression on the Allies that the Treaty of Versailles specifically banned further study and manufacture of such light automatic firearms by Germany.

Flamethrowers

Berlin mechanical engineer and inventor Richard Fiedler was studying nozzle designs for spraying liquids when he realized that gasoline fired from a pressurised tank could be ignited and used as a weapon. On 25 April 1901, he patented his first flamethrower, a 'Method for Producing Large Masses of Flame'. That year he also approached the Supreme Army Command and was awarded funds to continue developing his prototype.

In 1905 Fiedler presented his flamethrower to the Prussian Engineer Committee on training grounds in Berlin. The Engineer Committee suggested several improvements, which Fiedler incorporated. In 1908 the Fiedler flamethrower was assigned to the Pioneer Experimental Company, the *de facto* 5th Company of the *Garde-Pionier-Bataillon*. The Pioneer Experimental Company tested a small, backpack model of flamethrower called the *kleine Flammenwerfer* or *Kleif* and a large apparatus called the *grosse Flammenwerfer* or *Grof*. Fiedler demonstrated both flamethrowers to representatives of the War Ministry, the General Staff, and the Engineer Committee in September of 1909. Flamethrowers were judged superior to the other major pioneer incendiary weapons.

The *Kleif*'s fuel was stored in a large vertical, cylindrical backpack container. High-pressure propellant was stored in another, smaller container attached to the fuel tank. A long hose connected the fuel tank to a lance tube with an ignition device at the nozzle. The propellant forced the fuel through the hose and out of the nozzle at high speed when a valve was opened. The igniting device at the nozzle set fire to the fuel as it sprayed out. The flamethrower was operated by two soldiers; one carrying the fuel and propellant tanks, the other wielding the lance. Its maximum range was 18 metres. The *Grof* was larger and could shoot about 36 metres. It could sustain flame for 40 seconds but needed more men to operate it. The Germans introduced another small flamethrower design in 1917 to replace the earlier *Kleif*. The *Wechselapparat* (*Wex*) had a doughnut-shaped backpack fuel container with a spherical propellant container in the middle. The French also used flamethrowers, and the British used some early ones but did not persevere with them.

Suggested Further Reading

Vickers Machine-Gun
Goldsmith, Dolf L., *The Grand Old Lady of No Man's Land* (Cobourg, Ontario, Canada: Collector Grade Publications Inc., 1994).

Maxim Machine-Gun
Goldsmith, Dolf L., *The Devil's Paintbrush* (Cobourg, Ontario, Canada: Collector Grade Publications Inc., 1993).

Browning Machine-Gun
Goldsmith, Dolf L., *The Browning MG Vol 1* (Cobourg, Ontario, Canada: Collector Grade Publications Inc., 2005).

Lee-Enfield Rifles
Skennerton, Ian, *The British Service Lee* (London: Arms and Armour Press, 1982).

Mauser Rifles
Walter, John, *The German Rifle* (London: Arms and Armour Press, 1979).

Sidearms
Myatt, Major Frederick, *The Illustrated Encyclopaedia of Pistols and Revolvers* (London: Salamander Books, 1989).
Wilson, R. K., and Ian V. Hogg, *Textbook of Automatic Pistols* (London: Arms and Armour Press, 1989).

Chapter 14

'Kettledrums of Death': Some Field Guns and Howitzers of the Great War

* * *

Philip Magrath

Artillery and its use changed radically during the course of the Great War. The weapons and therefore the tactics deployed during 1917 and 1918 were far more sophisticated than in 1914. Then, warfare featured a fast-moving contact battle involving infantry and cavalry, supported by artillery firing directly, that is, at targets visible to the aimer, much the same as it had for centuries. Three years later, the key to the change was effective indirect firepower, that is, fire delivered to a target unseen by the aimer. But to be successful it required intelligence about enemy dispositions using forward ground and aerial observation, fire-spotting and sound-ranging as well as any information that could be gleaned from enemy prisoners. It also required targeting involving fire-planning which was dependent on reliable communications, accurate mapping and a plentiful supply of reliable ammunition: this transformed artillery use into the modern style of warfare recognisable today – a Military Revolution, in the view of Jonathan Bailey.[1]

When the British Expeditionary Force took the field in August 1914, its artillery totalled 540 guns of five different types.[2] When the Armistice was signed, the Royal Artillery had 6,437 guns of fourteen different types in battery service in France.[3] If one were to add the numbers of guns that both the Germans and the French had in the field it is of little wonder that artillery dominated the battlefield. Clearly, in the confines of a chapter, it is not possible to mention them all and at the risk of alienating those devotees of super heavy and anti-aircraft artillery, this chapter will concentrate on the light field guns and the heavy field howitzers. Each section commences with the weapon I consider to be the best, detailing its characteristics and performance as well as comparing and contrasting these factors with the competition and recounting where possible recorded experience on the receiving end.

Additionally, no chapter on Great War artillery would be complete without a description of the barrage and no barrage would have been possible without the contribution of the horses, mules and donkeys – the silent volunteers – vital for gun movement and delivery of supplies.

Light Field Guns

It can be argued that each of the three light quick-firing field guns of the Western Front combatants in 1914 were three of the best artillery pieces of the entire war. These were the French *Canon de 75mm modèle 1897*, also known as the French 75, *Soixante-Quinze* or affectionately as *Mademoiselle Soixante-Quinze*: for the British, the 18-pounder; and the 7.7cm *Feldkanone* 96 for the Germans. But it was the French 75 that had the greatest impact, taking the artillery world by storm when it was introduced in 1898 as the first true quick-firing gun, later to be described as one of the most important military developments of the twentieth century.[4] What this amazing gun could do which had eluded the others was to deliver an incredibly high firing rate – as high as thirty rounds a minute from an experienced detachment – thanks to two unique features. First, its hydro-pneumatic recuperator could return a firing gun barrel to its pre-firing position undisturbed – once it had settled firmly onto the surface on which it was placed – and second the Nordenfelt eccentric screw breech mechanism. Its operation was simplicity itself – by the half-turn of a lever and back to open and close the breech – with the effect that ammunition could be fired as quickly as it was presented and loaded.[5] Such a high rate of fire when using the 7.2kg (16kg) shrapnel round – containing 290 lead balls – from a four-gun battery could saturate a forward area up to nearly 6,800m (4.4 miles) away with *rafales* or whirlwinds of fire and proving deadly to an advancing enemy. French artillery theorists believed that such fire would be far too damaging and demoralising for an enemy to offer any resistance thereafter to onrushing French infantry.[6] Also available was a particularly deadly 5.3kg (12kg) impact-detonating, thin-walled high-explosive shell with a time-delay fuze allowing the round to bounce forward and explode a fraction of a second later at head height and effective up to 8,851 metres (5.5 miles). This contained a number of chisel-edged fragments which were deadly within 20 yards of the bursting point. Additionally, the explosion seemed either to cause death by asphyxia or shock to the brain and spinal column. During the Battle of the Marne a French soldier wrote that 'what makes the strongest impression is the attitude of the men killed by the explosive shell of the 75. Few of them appear to have been wounded. You find them in the position in which they were struck, with their eyes staring from their heads, and a trickle of blood on their lips.'[7] But it was the shrapnel round that proved to be the real killer as reports from Paris in October 1914 made clear:

An appalling incident occurred on Monday. Five hundred Germans were caught on some flat fields. On the slopes on every side the French artillery quietly occupied positions, and when the moment came to open fire the officer commanding the battery said: 'Make me a cemetery down there'. The order was obeyed. The guns accounted for most of the 500, and rifle fire did the rest. Not a man escaped.[8]

Since the French 75 was intended to be used in a highly mobile role, it was purposly designed to be a relatively light unit, weighing 1,140kg (2,513kg) or just under one ton. Its detachment of six men would not have had too much trouble moving it short distances on firm ground: on soft ground though and over longer distances six horses were used to pull the gun and ammunition limber with another six pulling each additional limber and supply caisson. In total, a battery of four guns would be assigned 160 horses with most of them expected to pull extra limbers and repair and supply caissons even under fire and in rapid advances. Mechanized units were also available in the shape of the Fiat 70-horsepower artillery tractor. Other time-saving innovations included a tilting limber that presented the fixed rounds at a comfortable angle for swift collection. The detachment would also deploy wheel brakes under each wheel which operated during firing *en abattage*, literally, in slaughter, and, together with the trail spade, which dug itself into the ground under the force of the first round, provided a firm base. Clearly, setting the fuze at the head of the shell by hand with a fuze key could be a fiddly and slow process so an automatic fuze-setter had been included.

Figures vary as to how many 75s were ready at the outbreak of war: perhaps the most accurate came from General Frederick Georges Herr, Inspector General of French Artillery who wrote in 1917 that 3,840 were immediately available.[9] The guns were soon put to the test and the stakes could not have been higher with Paris threatened by the German advance in early September 1914. At the First Battle of the Marne around 2,000 75s, together with the infantry, succeeded in saving the capital and halting the enemy. But it came at a price, costing around 85,000 French fatalities due to poor co-ordination between the two arms resulting in unsupported infantry attacks. Writing after the war revealingly in 1920, the German *Generalleutnant* Rohne had no doubts about this stage of the war that 'French field artillery was superior to ours not only from the point of view of equipment, but also in its employment and the weight of bombardment'.[10]

The German Army's standard light field gun in 1914 and by far the most numerous in its arsenal was the 7.7cm *Feldkanone* 96 (*FK 96*) n.A, standing for *neuer Art* or new model. Germany entered the war with a staggering 5,086 guns and it remained an artillery workhorse for the entire conflict being used on all fronts and in all battles. This was an excellent field gun but not as spectacular in terms of its firing rate or as impressive in terms of its all-round capability as the French 75. Nonetheless, the Germans had performed a minor miracle transforming its antiquated predecessor into a commendable weapon, galvanized no doubt by the high standard set by the French gun. The breech mechanism was the Krupp-favoured single-motion sliding wedge type which was not as slick or as easy to operate as Nordenfelt's. The recoil system used a hydraulic buffer of simple but sturdy design containing glycerine and four recuperator springs within the cradle. Such an arrangement permitted a maximum firing rate of only ten rounds a minute and made more ponderous in the use of separate loading – that is, the two-stage process of loading the shell first followed by the cartridge.

The design of the 7.7cm *FK 96* n.A. had been dictated by German tactical doctrine prior to 1914. The German Army, like their French counterparts, was convinced that war would be one of manoeuvre, mobility and, as far as field artillery was concerned, speed of emplacement, so system lightness was given first priority in this gun's redesign. Considerable weight was saved by using a shorter barrel but this meant a lower muzzle velocity and range loss when compared with other field guns of the same calibre. Since the role of the gun was intended for close infantry support, the resulting range loss was not thought undesirable. Indeed, firing at ranges over 5,000m (3.1 miles) was considered both unnecessary and pointless. In many corps prior to 1914, firing at long ranges was expressly forbidden and considered a waste of ammunition! Five men formed the detachment and moving the gun required a team of six horses. Because of its lightness, the gun came into its own during the long, fast marches and brief encounters in the early autumn of 1914 but the tactical change from this type of open warfare to the static trench warfare revealed its short-comings which were lightness of shot and short range.

Uniquely, standard ammunition was a combined high explosive shell with shrapnel weighing 6.85kg (15lb) containing 294 lead bullets each of 10 grams in weight. Also available were separate rounds of high explosive and of shrapnel initiated by either a time fuze or a contact fuze, a smoke round, an illumination shell for night time use, from 1915, gas rounds and from 1917, an anti-tank projectile. Because of the distinctive sound of its round through the air, this gun was nicknamed 'whizz-bang' by British troops. The 'whizz' was the sound of the round travelling through the air faster than the speed of sound: the 'bang' was the sound of the round being fired and not of it exploding.

Like the French 75, when the tactics of the battlefield changed to trench warfare, the operational options of this gun were reduced. So, the Germans introduced an improved model in 1916 with a longer barrel and a howitzer-type carriage to increase its elevation and therefore range but this added 350kg (772lb) to the unit. It was designed to use the same ammunition as the *FK 96* n.A. Many of these guns contributed to the thousand or so that commenced firing along the six-mile French front on the first day of the Battle of Verdun on 21 February 1916. For the next nine months German artillery expended 21 million rounds. The experience of one French soldier was horrific. 'Men were squashed. Cut in two or divided from top to bottom. Blown into showers; bellies turned inside out; skulls forced into the chest as if by a blow from a club.'[11] Proof, surely, of the high esteem in which this weapon was regarded – and its usefulness to the German war effort – may be found during the successful and highly mobile German Spring offensive in 1918 when many batteries took the older but lighter and more mobile *FK 96* n.A. in favour of the newer and heavier *Feldkanone* 16.[12]

The British 18-pounder Mark I, introduced into service in 1904, was the Royal Field Artillery's standard light field gun.[13] This weapon benefitted in its design from the deficiencies experienced by British artillery during the Boer War and although a decade old by the start of the First World War, it remained a very good weapon. It was robust but the price to be paid for that was a heavy unit requiring a large detachment of ten men and a team of either six or eight horses to move the gun and limber – which held twenty-four rounds – with additional horses for the extra ammunition limber – which held thirty-eight rounds. In very heavy ground mechanized units like the 75-horsepower Holt tractor could be called upon. The carriage was a single pole trail which restricted the downward movement of the breech mechanism and therefore barrel elevation. As such, the maximum range for this gun, without improvisation, was 5,966m (6,525 yd) or 3.7 miles: digging the trail in improved this to 7,100m (7,800 yd) or just under 4.5 miles. As the war progressed the demand for greater range grew more forceful and later Marks were able to attain 8,500m (9,300 yd) or well over 5 miles and with an improved streamlined high explosive shell, 10,100m (11,100 yd) or under 6.5 miles. Only shrapnel and star shell were available for this gun in 1914. Unlike the other two field guns, high explosive rounds were under development and unavailable until 1915. Thereafter, incendiary, smoke, armour-piercing (for use against tanks) and chemical rounds were all used by the 18-pounder.

The table set out below summarises the important characteristics of the three light field guns. As well as its high rate of fire and other innovations, the French 75 was the most powerful of the three guns. This was due in part to its longer barrel (and therefore higher calibre) which imparted greater projectile speed or muzzle velocity at the point where it left the barrel.[14] This gave the gun an excellent range, indeed, the most far-reaching of the three at almost seven miles.

Gun	French 75mm	German 77mm	British 18pr
Bore diameter	75mm (2.95in)	77mm (3.1in)	83.8mm (3.3in)
Calibre	36.3	27	28
Barrel length	2,721mm (107in)	2,080mm (82in)	2,340mm (92in)
Introduced	1898	1896	1904
Min/Max elev.	-11° to +18°	-12° to +15°	-5° to +16°
Traverse	3°	4°	4.5°
Weight emplaced	1,140kg (2,513lb)	1,020kg (2,249lb)	1,284kg (2,813lb)
Shell wt. Shrapnel	7.2kg (16lb)	6.85kg (15lb)	8.4kg (18.5lb)
Shell wt. HE	5.3kg (12kg)	6.85kg (15lb)	
Muzzle Velocity	1,183mph	1,040mph	1,100mph
Max range theor.	11,104m (6.9 miles)	8,369m (5.2 miles)	7,100m (4.4 miles)
Max range prac.	8,851m (5.5 miles)	5,471m (3.4 miles)	5,955m (3.7 miles)
RPM	15 to 30	8 to 10	10 to 20
No. available 1914	3,840	5,086	1,226

Although heavier than the German gun it was considered mobile enough and expected to keep pace with the advancing infantry. Whilst its intentional shallow projectile trajectory dealt a deadlier spread of shrapnel, its limited elevation could not deliver plunging fire and its light shell, which although not designed to destroy enemy entrenchments or damage deeper bunkers, inevitably proved inadequate in trench warfare. Fortunately the French were in a fair position with nearly 4,000 in the field but still at a numerical disadvantage compared to the German number of over 5,000 light field guns. At the outbreak of war there were more German 77mm guns deployed than the combined number of British 18-pounders and French 75s! There was no doubting the effectiveness of the French 75 as a killing machine against troops in the open but the advent of trench warfare in 1915 removed that advantage and shrapnel rounds fell out of use in favour of aerodynamically improved high explosive rounds some of which could attain a range of 11,000 metres (6.1 miles). Additionally, chemical shells containing mustard gas and phosgene were coming into mass production. One of the French 75s' early problems and one that struck terror into any detachment was the premature explosion of a round in the barrel due to faulty fuzes.

The German gun had the shortest effective range of only 5,486m (6,000 yd) or 3.4 miles. This could be increased, however, to 8,410m (9,200 yd) or 5.2 miles by digging the trail in. The 18-pounder was the heaviest of the three light field guns at 1,284kg (2,831lb) or 1.6 tons, but it delivered a much weightier round. The biggest disadvantage for both the British and German gun was the use of springs in the recuperator which under the relaxed conditions of peacetime manufacture and then prolonged periods of fire either cracked or failed completely.

Heavy Field Howitzers

In 1914, the heavy field howitzers were the British 6in Howitzer of 30 cwt, the French 155mm *Rimailho Model 1904* and the German 15cm *schwere Feldhaubitze* (*sFH*) 02, arguably the best of the three. It had been developed by Krupp during 1899 and 1900 and subjected to extensive comparative field trials with its predecessor the *sFH 1893* and whilst performing well in most areas it was rejected on the grounds of its cumbersome and unmanageable nature in firing despite being the first artillery piece in the German army to use a modern recoil system incorporating springs and buffers.[15] Demands for a lighter howitzer involving a carriage redesign with a longer trail – enabling lifting by a strong man – were successful and it was introduced into service in June 1903 with a weight of 2,035kg (4,486lb) and a maximum range of 7,452 metres (4.6 miles). Additionally, and of particular effectiveness, was the introduction of an improved 40.5kg (89lb) high explosive shell introduced in 1904 with a delayed-action fuze for the penetration of covered entrenchments. Careful note of the rounds' effectiveness was taken during regular tactical manoeuvres and live-firing exercises such as the annual Kaiser Shooting Competitions. The Germans, unlike the French, had great faith in the tactical advantages that howitzers could bring and had built up their stocks of both the 10.5cm light field howitzer, the heavy field howitzer 02 and even its 1893 predecessor.

Improvements were made to the *sFH 02* in 1913 including the provision of a gun-shield for the better protection of the nine-man detachment, a longer barrel giving a more powerful weapon and the ability to send a slightly heavier shell of 42kg further to an effective range of 8,600m (9,405 yd). Although not available in the field until October 1914, the Germans were in the very strong position of being able thereafter to call on this weapon as well as its predecessor, the *sFH* 93. Later in the conflict, its relative mobility and capacity to deliver a lethal explosion to even the most entrenched troops more than made up for its lack of range. Each army corps had a battalion of them in four, four-gun batteries and detachments boasted that they could take the gun anywhere their comrades of the light artillery could go and demolish anything that held up the infantry.[16] Some idea of the regard in which this weapon and the heavy field howitzer had, can be gleaned from a letter sent to the Minister of War by the Army Supreme Commander in 1917 to the effect that they would continue to be the mainstay of battle in this war.[17] It was in reference to rounds from this gun exploding with black smoke that a British artillery officer referred to them as 'Jack Johnsons' after the first African-American world heavyweight boxing champion of the time. One of Paul Lintier's detachment of French 75s when they came under fire from this gun reported:

> Mon capitaine, I was in a trench . . . there was a lot of shelling, great black shells they were . . . First they burst behind us, a hundred yards away . . . As long as that went on we weren't worrying . . . But they started dropping right in amongst us . . . And then we cleared out!

They were also known as 5.9s after the barrel bore of 5.9 inches. On 3 August 1914, the day the Germans declared war on France, 416 howitzers of the 1902 model were in the field: 360 howitzers of the 1913 model had been ordered with 48 delivered by October 1914. In total, 3,409 were constructed, 2,676 by Krupp and 733 by Rheinmetall.

The British 6in howitzer of 30 cwt had been in service for eighteen years in 1914, having been introduced in 1896 as a replacement for the 5in breech-loading howitzer. Its service in France would be short and it was phased out during 1915 for the vastly improved 6in howitzer of 26cwt. The design was simple with recoil control dependent on a hydro-spring system as evidenced by the tell-tale double tube of springs appearing very prominently below the barrel. In terms of the historical development of artillery, this howitzer is of interest in that it represented an early attempt to combine the performance of a field gun and a howitzer in one system. That is, constructing a gun and carriage that permitted an interchange between field use and siege use. In other words, a capacity to send a heavy shell to the required distance with a high trajectory in siege, yet light enough and therefore mobile enough to be fired with a flatter trajectory more in the fashion of a field gun. This was achieved in a novel but cumbersome fashion by using two separate carriages and meant that it required more than the usual equipment: a wheeled travelling carriage and a siege mounting. For most of the time the gun sat on the wheeled travelling carriage allowing a maximum elevation of 35 degrees. At this angle, it could send a 45kg (100lb) shell 4,748m (5,192 yd). However, if tactics required high-angle plunging fire, then a siege mounting would be constructed, but it took time to set-up. This elevated the barrel to 70°, achieving a maximum range of 6,401m (7000 yd) or four miles despatching a 55kg (122kg) high explosive shell. Traverse could in theory be 360° all around the pivot. Twelve of these guns were present during the Second Boer War as part of the British siege train and it was here that its short range was felt. Greater range was achievable by using a lighter 45kg (100lb) shell and both high explosive and shrapnel rounds were produced which, on the travelling carriage at 35° elevation, improved its range to well over four miles from just under three. Around eighty of these guns were available at the start of the war and it served in all theatres until replaced by a new and very successful 6in 26cwt howitzer in late 1915.[18]

The French, never at ease with the concept of the howitzer, were still able in 1914 to bring the *Rimailho Model 1904 TR* (*tir rapide*, rapid fire), into the field. They could thank Captain Emile Rimailho who had made his name with the French 75 and in this case he seems to have had far more individual responsibility over its design than he had with the French 75. He must have been one of the few artillery officers who realised that excellent though the French 75 was for the artillery tactics for which it was designed, it did not have the flexibility to operate satisfactorily outside those parameters. His objective therefore was a demanding one. Namely, to produce a heavy howitzer modelled on the French 75, enjoying its high firing rate and incorporating some of its desirable features too – a tall order for a gun of this size at just over 6in bore. It was to have the same hydro-pneumatic recoil as the French 75 with semi-automatic loading but not the fast-action Nordenfelt breech mechanism. In service, a well-trained gun crew could achieve the remarkable rate of fifteen rounds a minute, but this placed great stress on the mechanically complex breech mechanism and carriage. Eventually five artillery regiments were equipped with it, each battery consisting of two guns accompanied by three ammunition wagons for each gun. By the outbreak of war, the French army had 104 pieces in service in twenty-six batteries. From 1915, it was supplemented by the *modèle 1915 St. Chamond* and replaced after 1917 by the *modèle 1917 Schneider*. None were in service at the end of the war. The table on page 223 provides statistical comparison of the French, German and British weapons just described.

These statistics provide strong evidence that the Germans were in possession of the best weapon; a very light howitzer with excellent range and over 400 available in 1914. It was easily the lightest of the three howitzers at 2,035kg (4,486lb), over a ton lighter than the French howitzer of 3,200kg (7,100lb) and nearly 1½ tons lighter than the British howitzer of 3,507kg (7,732lb). It also possessed the longest

Gun	German 15cm sFH 02	British 6in 30cwt	French 155mm
Bore diameter	149mm (5.9in)	6in (152.4mm)	155mm (6.1in)
Calibre	12	14	15
Barrel length	1,800mm (72in)	2,134mm (84in)	2,400mm (94in)
Introduced	1902	1896	1904
Min/Max elev.	0 to +42°	-10° to +35° (TC)	0 to +41°
		+35° to +70° (SC)	
Traverse	4°	360°	6°
Weight emplaced	2,035kg (4,486lb)	3,507kg (7,732lb)	3,200kg (7,100lb)
Shell wt.	40.5kg (89lb)	45.4kg (100lb)	42.9kg (94.6lb)
Muzzle Velocity	852mph	530mph	716mph
Max range theor.	7,452m (4.6 miles)	TC 4,748m (2.95 miles)	
Max range prac.		SC 6,401m (4 miles)	5,967m (3.7 miles)
RPM	3	2	15
No. available 1914	416	c.80	104

(TC is Travelling carriage. SC is Siege Carriage)

maximum range of 7,452m (8,150 yd), well over a thousand metres further than the British howitzer which was the next best. Fortunately the British had other howitzers in their arsenal including the excellent 4.5in field howitzer and the forthcoming 6in howitzer of 26cwt. The French never produced anything of a comparable nature to the German howitzer. Although the 155mm *Rimailho* had a much higher rate of fire than both of the other howitzers it was out-ranged by them. One temporary solution was to use larger amounts of propellant but this placed even more strain on the key components, the barrel, recuperator and carriage, to detrimental effect. The 6in 26cwt howitzer was the only true heavy artillery possessed by the British Army at the outbreak of the war. For this reason alone it was most welcome to the British Expeditionary Force but, having already spent eighteen years in service, many artillerists felt it to be obsolete in 1914. Its breech mechanism was ponderous and the exposed springs of the recoil system were vulnerable to shrapnel damage. Its advantages included shell weight, just over 10kg heavier than either of the other howitzers and a reasonable range on the siege carriage at further than four and a half miles which, although more than the French howitzer, was still slightly less than the German howitzer on its standard field carriage. Nonetheless, it was fortunate that eighty were ready at the start of the war.

The Barrage
All of the aforementioned artillery pieces would have played a part in the barrage, the epitome of mass artillery bombardment, so it is relevant to outline the purpose

of a barrage. It was a method of delivering heavy and co-ordinated artillery fire in either a defensive role to deny an advancing enemy easy progress or in an offensive role to neutralise enemy defences as far as possible, in order to give friendly forces the best chance of breaking into defensive positions. The British developed it during the Boer War and first used it, without great success, at the Battle of Neuve-Chapelle in 1915. Any successful infantry attack would depend on the barrage in the frequently vain hope that it had cleared enemy barbed wire, silenced artillery behind the lines and closer machine-gun emplacements.

As the war progressed, the barrage developed into several different types of a more complex and refined nature to try to maintain the element of surprise and to meet changing tactical situations.[19] All sides developed their own versions and variations on a theme through their experts, for example, Colonel Georg Bruchmüller for the Germans and Major-General Herbert Uniacke for the British. What sets Bruchmüller apart from Uniacke and others was his readiness to try the unconventional – and he had the authority to do so – in order to achieve his objectives. For example, light field guns usually supported the infantry whilst heavier guns engaged enemy artillery. Bruchmüller changed this around if he felt the tactical situation merited it.[20] It was universally realised that the key to delivering the infantry to the enemy's defensive positions with minimal loss was the ability to lay down sufficiently disruptive and destructive firepower but it required supreme coordination and a degree of luck. Once British artillery had overcome the high rate of rounds failing to explode, the actual shortage of ammunition and had developed the No.106 fuze which was sensitive enough to explode on contact with barbed wire, the barrage was fit for purpose and it would be the 18-pounders that took the lead.

A good illustration of this can be appreciated by comparing the essentials of the bombardment plan at Neuve-Chapelle in March 1915 with the fire-plan for the opening stage of the Battle of Amiens in August 1918. An attack at the former was intended to break through the German lines with the possibility of a further attack on Aubers Ridge behind. The First Army under General Haig, who carried responsibility for the attack, gave the artillery four tasks: first, to destroy the German wire and front-line trenches; second, flank protection; third, the delivery of concentrated fire behind the front-line trenches to prevent reinforcement, and fourth, the destruction of the German artillery and machine-guns.

Before the bombardment commenced, all the artillery had to be assembled, supplied and the guns registered without indicating that a major offensive was imminent. Ninety 18-pounders were placed in a semi-circle around Neuve-Chapelle and their task at a range of between 1,200 yards (1,097m) and 2,000 yards (1,829m) was the destruction of the German barbed wire. When ready, the artillery, each with a particular part to play at precise times, lined-up thus: 12 x 2.75in guns with 500 rounds per gun, 60 x 13-pounders with 600 rounds per gun, 324 x 18-pounders with 410 rounds per gun, 54 x 4.5in howitzers with 212 rounds per gun, 32 x 4.7in guns with 32 rounds per gun, 28 x 6in howitzers with 285 rounds per gun, 4 x 6in guns with 400 rounds per gun, 12 x 60-pounders with 450 rounds per gun, 3 x 9.2in howitzers with 333 rounds per gun and 1 x 15in howitzer with 40 rounds.

Phase 1, which included a 35-minute preliminary bombardment using a mix of 339 guns followed by an infantry assault on a front of 2,000 yards (1,829m) and a 200-yard (183m) charge to the enemy front trenches whilst the guns lifted to phase 2 targets, was successful apart from a 400-yard (366m) front where enemy defences remained intact resulting in heavy losses. The task of neutralising the German defences here had fallen to a battery of 6in guns that had not arrived at their positions until the day before the attack. This showed clearly how dependent the infantry was on accurate artillery support and that artillery could not be rushed into action. Another important feature of this phase of the attack was how quickly adjoining 18-pounder guns and 6in howitzers were able to re-direct their fire onto this section of German trench, destroying the defences and enabling the remaining infantry to occupy it without further loss.

Phase 2 required the infantry to clear the enemy front-line trenches and the supporting trenches 200 yards (183m) beyond, before attacking Neuve-Chapelle and the final objective thereafter. Half an hour was set aside with artillery support from the 13- and 18-pounders, 4.5in howitzers and the 6in and 9.2in howitzers. This was also deemed a success but then, for an unexplained reason, Phase 3 was delayed for five hours, giving the Germans valuable time to reorganise their defences. When the bombardment re-started it had been reassigned to a different division whose technique regarding artillery command and control was lacking and meant that the German deep defences were able to repel advancing British infantry. Forty thousand Allied troops took part during the battle. The British suffered 11,652 killed, missing and wounded with German casualties numbering about the same and with 1,687 prisoners taken: ten Victoria Crosses were awarded.[21]

The Battle of Amiens, which commenced on 8 August 1918, was the opening act of an Allied offensive that would later become known as the Hundred Days Offensive and ultimately lead to the end of the war. In total 1,386 field guns and howitzers and 684 heavy guns were assigned and a detailed fire plan compiled which depended on secrecy, intelligence and incorporating all the lessons that had been previously learnt. Great efforts were made to reduce any obvious build-up of guns and ammunition. The infantry had a good idea not only of the numbers of Germans before them but also of their physical condition and morale and the artillery had identified and mapped almost all of the positions occupied by German artillery through sound-ranging and photographic reconnaissance. These were to be destroyed at 'zero hour'. No preliminary bombardment or ranging shots were made to check accuracy of fire which had frequently given indication of an impending offensive. Just as the Australian, Canadian and British infantry advanced, the massed artillery commenced firing with a creeping barrage. For the 18-pounders, fall of shot was to be 200 yards ahead of the start line and would lift to 100 yards further on at zero hour +3 minutes, then lifting again a further 100 yards at zero hour +5 minutes and thereafter at three-minute intervals for eight lifts. At the eleventh lift the interval was raised to four minutes. Superimposed upon this was a barrage from the 4.5in howitzers and counter-battery fire from two-thirds of the heavy guns at zero hour and then a depth barrage for four hours.

The infantry soon achieved its first objective thanks to what was later described as an excellent barrage. At the same time, on infantry orders, designated field and howitzer batteries together with tanks moved forward. Some of the infantry were detained by a surviving enemy machine-gun battery that had survived the onslaught, but nonetheless, impressive lines of guns moved forward as quickly as possible in support of the second phase objective including 60-pounder field guns and 6in howitzers. Two German counter-attacks were attempted but were destroyed before they made any ground. Between them, the Canadian and Australian infantry captured 297 German officers, over 12,000 men and 334 guns. General Sir Martin Farndale, in the official history of the Royal Artillery wrote that on this day, possibly:

> The British Artillery reached the peak of perfection. Every aspect of the artillery plan was a success. The guns lifted the assault onto its objectives, they protected the flanks, they broke up counter-attacks, they prevented the enemy from using his guns effectively, they moved forward with the assault and repeated the process for the phase two objectives. It was a great triumph of method, skill and command, and the fruit of so much bitter trial and error for over three years.

The 18-pounders fired 40,000 rounds including 10,000 rounds of gas shell. The 4.5in howitzers fired 24,000 smoke rounds and the 6in howitzers 50,000 rounds of gas shell.[22] The logistics are staggering but all the planning and copious attention to detail was entirely dependent on supply by the horses, mules and donkeys. Without them it could not have been achieved.

Artillery Draught Horses

The dramatic film *War Horse* directed by Steven Spielberg, recounting the experiences of a horse engaged in military service on the Western Front, has graphically reminded its viewers of the terrible suffering of and sacrifice made by animals in the Great War. Mechanized transport was of course available but it was a relatively new invention, prone to breakdown and not very good in the mud. Without horses, the war would have ground to a halt; the numbers required are astonishing to the modern mind. The cavalry, reliant on over 75,000 horses, would have been redundant; officers would have had no means of easy transport without the horse, a number in excess of 111,000 employed in this role; supplies would have taken far longer to reach their destination requiring over half a million horses and mules; and moving the guns needing almost 88,000 more. Keeping such huge amounts of livestock healthy was a huge challenge. The average daily ration of a supply horse was 9kg (20lb) of fodder, one-fifth less than that recommended. This meant that a battalion required a weekly minimum of 3,556kg (7,840lb) of oats and hay to feed its fifty-six horses. The larger and stronger Clydesdales, favoured by the Royal Artillery to pull heavier loads, required 14kg (30lb) of fodder daily and could spend up to five hours a day eating. According to Doctor David Payne of the Western Front Association, the amount of fodder sent to the Western Front, over 5.5 million tons,[23] exceeded that of the ammunition at 5.2 million tons.[24] The British Army lost about 15 per cent of its horses annually with only a quarter, surprisingly, as a result of enemy action. Fortunately, over a thousand horses a week were being shipped to France from North America. The biggest killer and the greatest cause of pain to the horse was 'debility', a condition caused by exposure to the elements, hunger and illness. Death by enemy action was usually much quicker. Lieutenant-Colonel Neil Fraser-Tytler, serving with 30th Division Royal Field Artillery, recounted an horrific event on 2 August 1916, as he returned to his trench:

. . . the Hun started airing his famous 12-inch, 8in and 5.9in barrage, a very noisy and somewhat theatrical performance, but nevertheless it made the mile walk rather exciting. Just as I reached the road behind my position three passing teams were done in by a single big shell. I finished off as many of the horses as I could with a revolver . . .

Fraser-Tytler was an extraordinarily thick-skinned man liking nothing better than 'Hun-hunting' which he pursued by readily volunteering for the extremely dangerous pursuit of forward observation where he could personally direct the fire of his 18-pounder battery behind him. Later the same evening, an orderly with two horses brought him a message. He was contemplating sending them away when his trained ear heard another large shell heading in their general direction. He dived for safety into a shell crater just as the shell burst and later wrote that:

The shell must have burst on the back of one of the horses, as there was no crater on the ground. As soon as the shelling stopped, we began to clean up the place, finding one head, three legs and one hindquarters at distances of up to a hundred yards, while the remainder of the two horses was in small fragments over the whole position.[25]

For others more sentimentally minded, horses, mules and any animals – rats apart probably – were often adopted by the troops who became greatly attached to them no doubt providing a psychological release. It was different though when a favourite died. One horse called Sailor:

. . . would work for 24 hours a day without winking. He was as quiet as a lamb and as clever as a thoroughbred but he looked like nothing on earth so we lost him. The whole artillery battery kissed him goodbye and the drivers and gunners who fed him nearly cried.[26]

Eight million horses and countless more mules and donkeys perished in the Great War. One million were sent from this country and only 62,000 returned.[27]

It has been my intention in this chapter to give a comparative idea of the characteristics and performance of some of the field guns and howitzers used in action on the Western Front. The Germans possessed the largest artillery equipment in Belgium and France and should perhaps have gained the upper hand. The approximate ammunition expenditure on this Front by the British Army between 1914 and 1918 was 170 million rounds of which 100 million were fired by the British 18-pounder.[28] Germany expended 275 million rounds and France 200 million.[29] It is of course difficult to grasp such statistics and ghastly to comprehend their significance, but the Great War was truly an artillery war and as Colonel Georg Bruchmuller stated: 'The thanks of the infantry, in my opinion, must be treasured more by artillerymen than all decorations and citations.'[30]

Notes

1. Maj. Gen. J. B. A. Bailey, *Field Artillery and Firepower* (Annapolis: Naval Institute Press 2004), pp. 240–1 and J. Bailey, 'The First World War and the Birth of the Modern Style of Warfare' in The Strategic and Combat Studies Institute Occasional paper no. 22 (1996), p. 3.
2. Namely, 60pdr; 6in Howitzer of 30cwt; 4.5in Howitzer, 18pdr and 13pdr. *Life History of Ordnance used by the British Armies in France compiled from data collected in the Office of the Director of Ordnance Services by Order of the Quarter-Master-General G.H.Q. France* (c.1919), p. 4. A howitzer has a shorter barrel than a field gun, it uses smaller charges of propellant and the carriage on which it is mounted allows elevation to higher angles providing high trajectories of fire with a steep angle of descent. This is invaluable for firing over obstacles and is more effective against earthworks. The field gun has a longer barrel, uses larger propellant charges and its carriage permits limited angles of elevation imparting a much flatter projectile trajectory. This is useful against troops in the open, for clearing barbed wire using shrapnel and against individual targets like machine-gun posts using high explosive.
3. General Sir Martin Farndale, *History of the Royal Regiment of Artillery. Western Front 1914-18* (London: The Royal Artillery Institution, 1986), p. 342.
4. http://en.wikipedia.org/wiki/Canon_de_75 modèle_1897
5. J. Kinard, *Artillery. An Illustrated History of Its Impact* (USA: Abc-Clio, 2007), p. 245.
6. B. I. Gudmundsson, *On Artillery* (USA: Praeger, 1993), p. 21.
7. General Percin, 'The '75' – Marvel of Modern Quick-Firers'. http://archive.is/3kFrz
8. http://trove.nla.gov.au/ndp/del/title/16 No.17698 *The Brisbane Courier*, Monday 5 October 1914, p. 7.
9. F.G. Herr, 'Field Artillery: Past, Present and Future', *The Field Artillery Journal*, 17 (3) (1927), pp. 221–46. Available at: http://sill-www.army.mil/firesbulletin/archives
10. I. Sumner, *The First Battle of the Marne 1914* (Oxford: Osprey, 2010), p. 90.
11. http//www.historylearningsite.co.uk/battle_of_verdun.htm
12. http://www.landships.info/landships/artillery_articles.html?load=/landships/artillery_articles/Feldkanone_C96nA_1.html
13. The Royal Horse Artillery were issued with the lighter 13-pounder which was used to such

heroic effect during the action at Néry during the Battle of the Marne in September 1914. Three VCs were awarded.

14. Calibre in this case represents the ratio between barrel length and bore and can be considered a useful yardstick as to the relative power of guns of the same bore, since the longer the barrel the more powerful it is likely to be. So, in the case of the French 75, dividing a barrel length of 2,721mm by 75mm equals 36.3 or 36 calibres. The other clue to a gun's power comes from its muzzle velocity, that is, the speed at which the shell exits the barrel at the muzzle: generally speaking, the faster the speed, the longer the range and the more powerful the gun. But this is not the whole story since shell weight needs to be taken into account.

15. R. Haycock and K. Neilson, *Men, Machines and War* (Canada: Wilson Laurier Press 1998), p. 148.

16. Ibid.

17. http://www.lovettartillery.com/15cm_schwere_Feldhaubitze_1913./html

18. http://www.landships.info/landships/artillery_articles.html?load=/landships/artillery_articles/6in_30cwt_howitzer.html. Its designation introduced a peculiarity of British ordnance nomenclature, adding the weight of the barrel and breech mechanism into the title. This was done in order to differentiate between guns of similar calibre but of different performance and using different ammunition. The British Army in India, for example, were using a 6in howitzer of 25 cwt.

19. For example, creeping, rolling, moving, standing, block, box, quick and Chinese barrage.

20. Gudmundsson, *On Artillery*, pp. 88–90.

21. Farndale, *History of the Royal Regiment of Artillery. Western Front 1914-18*, pp. 82–92 and http://www.1914-1918.net 'The Battle of Neuve Chapelle March 1915 – The Long, Long Trail.

22. Farndale, *History of the Royal Regiment of Artillery. Western Front 1914-18*, pp. 287–90.

23. http://www.westernfrontassociation.com/great-war-on-land/73-weapons-equipment-uniforms /639-role-of-the-horse.htm

24. D. Kenyon, 'British Cavalry on the Western Front 1916-1918', Ph.D thesis submitted to Cranfield University, Defence College of Management and Technology (2007), p. 8.

25. Lt. Col. N. Fraser-Tytler, *Field Guns in France* (London: Hutchinson. 1922), p. 103.

26. http://www.historylearningsite.co.uk/horses_in_world_war_one.htm

27. http://www.animalsinwar.org.uk/index.cfm?asset_id=1375

28. Farndale, *History of the Royal Regiment of Artillery. Western Front 1914-18*, p. 342.

29. http://www.westernfrontassociation.com/great-war-on-land/weapons-equipment-uniform/68-ammo-supplies- western.html

30. http://www.military-quotes.com/artillery per cent20quotes.htm

Suggested Further Reading

Bailey, Maj. Gen. J. B. A., *Field Artillery and Firepower* (Annapolis, USA: Naval Institute Press, 2004).

Bidwell, S., and Graham, D., *Fire-Power. The British Army, Weapons & Theories of War 1904-1914* (Barnsley: Pen & Sword, 2004).

Gudmundsson, B. I., *On Artillery* (USA: Praeger, 1993).

Hogg, I., and Thurston, L. J., *British Artillery Weapons & Ammunition 1914-1918* (London: Ian Allan, 1972).

Lintier, P., *My Seventy-Five: The Journal of A French Gunner August-September 1914* (Solihull: Helion & Company Ltd, 2012).

Chapter 15

Silent Soldiers:
Animals in the Great War

* * *

Paul Skelton Stroud

Mankind has used a wide variety of animals in warfare since ancient times. The best known range from the long lines of horse-drawn chariots of the Egyptians as they fought the Nubians, the huge, ferocious war dogs of the Britons as they resisted the Romans, the war elephants used in India, Persia, Siam, China and even in Europe around the Mediterranean, the vast, powerful and efficient light cavalry of the Mongol hordes ranging huge distances and the heavily armoured horses of medieval knights that dominated their particular battlefields – all of these examples well documented. Other animals pressed into use in war would have to include asses and donkeys, oxen, camels and canaries, pigs and pigeons, reindeer and rats, geese and glow worms, and mules and mice.

Warfare presents us with a contradictory situation in that certainly in the Western World the inhabitants of most countries are expected to show either overt kindness to, or at least some form of respect for, animals in general. It is a hard and unfeeling person who cannot respond in some positive way to the companionship or affection shown by a horse, dog, cat or other animal which, although quite unable to respond in speech, nevertheless seems to be able to communicate its feelings directly or to reflect the person's feelings be they ones of happiness or sorrow. The relationship that can exist between man and animal serves to develop an air of trust intermingled with degrees of affection and outright devotion that should and does make a strong appeal to the best in us, and evoke the warmest and most enduring of all human emotions, that of friendship. That emotional link was sorely tested as animals were then deliberately used and exposed to the dreadful circumstances of the battlefields in the Great War.

Horses and Mules

The 1914–18 War was no different from earlier and ancient wars with regard to the use of animals and it is no surprise that at the commencement of hostilities the armies of all the belligerent nations had large numbers of horses in military service.

The outbreak of war in 1914 found the British Army with a total establishment of 25,000 horses and mules, with 1,200 remounts. Within twelve days, the establishment had been increased to 165,000 animals, entirely by impress, and a year later, in August 1915, to 534,971. At its peak in 1917, the Army establishment reached almost 870,000 horses and mules, with accommodation for a further 60,000 remounts.The Russian military forces in 1914 began the war with some thirty-six divisions of cavalry, standing in excess of one million horses available for service, a similar total recorded by the British and Commonwealth forces by the end of hostilities in 1918. The French started with 156,000 horses and after five months requisitioned a further 730,000 animals, eventually registering a total of 1,880,000 horses and mules from 1914 to 1918. Germany had 2,500,000 animals all told.

Horses were used in the transport and supply services and in the form of cavalry, although there had been for some years signs that the future of cavalry might be limited following advances in weapons' technology. Nevertheless, cavalry was a significantly large component in all armies in 1914, with the high command, on all sides, anticipating a very different war from what would, after a few months, develop, and having every expectation of deploying cavalry in action, in a reconnaissance role and, as exemplified by the Boers, as mounted infantry.

The Army Remount Service whose function was to purchase and supply horses and mules, was geared to that objective and as the war developed, particularly on the Western Front, the need for more horses and mules rose over and above the numbers listed as Army animals initially.

French cavalry went to war wearing gleaming breastplates and plumed helmets more appropriate to the days of Napoleon and wholly unsuited to the savage realities of the changes in warfare that lay before them. The cavalry of the Imperial German Army, by contrast, were in field-grey uniforms in 1914.

Such was the burgeoning demand for horses in the early stages of the war that most armies found that they had markedly insufficient numbers of horses and mules with which to prosecute the war. In Great Britain, some 165,000 animals were taken from farms, coal mines, factories and businesses, and in fact from any sphere of activity where horses were used, including riding schools. Even then, numbers were still inadequate. More animals were purchased from Canada and the USA, and from as far afield as Australia and Argentina. Such was the insatiable requirement to swell numbers and to cope with replacements that by the middle of 1917 Britain had procured 591,000 horses and 213,000 mules, as well as almost 60,000 camels and oxen.

Over the course of the entire war, a total of 468,323 horses was purchased in Great Britain itself; 428,608 horses and 275,097 mules were purchased from North America, to which were added some 6,000 horses and 1,500 mules from South America, and 3,700 more were obtained from Spain and Portugal. Shipping horses between the USA and Europe was costly and dangerous and over 6,500 horses and mules were drowned or killed on Allied ships lost to German surface ships and submarines. In addition, New Zealand lost around 3 per cent of the nearly 10,000 horses shipped from there during the war.

Between 1914 and 1920, the British Army Remount Department spent £67.5 million on purchasing, training and delivering horses and mules to the battle fronts, such that the British and Commonwealth total was somewhere in excess of one million horses and mules for military service, and that included 475,000 draught horses.

In the first weeks of the war, the German army mobilized 715,000 horses and the Austrians 600,000. More than 375,000 horses were taken from German-occupied French territory for use by the German military, and captured Ukrainian territory provided another 140,000, giving a total of over half a million animals to be added to their initial listed strength.

It has been reported that a total of eight million military horses and mules died during the entire conflict with around 256,000 of them being horses and mules in British service. How were these appalling losses allowed to develop and what were the reasons for it? A war zone is of course, far removed from an area of order and efficiency. The sheer number of horses and mules sent from Britain and elsewhere provided a huge logistics problem – where to house them and feed them and then where to care for them when they became sick or injured? Even before they got to the war zones there were major problems. Collecting great numbers of horses together, as in Canada and the United States, resulted in high mortality as infectious diseases took hold and overwhelmed local veterinary services. Such were the losses and concerns that British officers from the Army Veterinary Corps (AVC) had to be sent to both countries to organise and manage the situation, fortunately with considerable success. Further unnatural stress with consequent losses also occurred during shipping to Europe. It is surprising that in 1917 the American Expeditionary Forces had no veterinary organisation and their dreadful losses so alarmed British authorities that they insisted that one was formed and operated along European lines. The French were also concerned that incoming diseases from such imported animals might bring diseases which could easily spread into both their military and civilian animal populations, exacerbating an already fragile animal health situation.

On and near the battlefield, conditions could never be good and hastily erected temporary stables could not keep out the wind, rain and cold. Basic issues like the supply of water and fodder were not consistently upheld to a reasonable standard and the German army lost many animals through starvation. Both antagonists realised the conflict of interest between the needs for transport of military supplies and space requirements for their placement – ammunition being the most obvious example – and the far bulkier needs for animal fodder. The sheer number of animals gathered together caused major hygiene problems and posed a health risk to both the military horse population and in some instances to the troops as communicable diseases could spread very quickly.

Julian Grenfell movingly expressed his sympathetic admiration for the endurance of horses in his 1915 poem, written from Ypres, *Into Battle*:

In dreary, doubtful, waiting hours, before the brazen frenzy starts,
Horses show him nobler powers;
O patient eyes, courageous hearts!

Large numbers of horses and mules became ill through malnourishment, poor care, the demands of heavy physical work in appalling conditions and infectious diseases. Many died of sheer exhaustion or a combination of these factors and the overall harsh conditions, whilst some drowned after collapsing in the deep mud-filled shell holes created by the heavy artillery barrages.

The causes of animal death varied with the terrain of the battlefield, from the Western Front to the Balkans, the arid Middle East to the grasslands and forested areas of East Africa and the varied landscapes of the widely-separated areas of conflict in Russia. Climate was obviously a very important factor in each of these distinctive areas. Different types of warfare also influenced overall health and welfare – the static war on the Western Front contrasted starkly with the movement of animals through the harshness of the desert in the Middle East. Casualties from direct enemy action were considerable and superimposed upon them were thousands of cases of infectious diseases, malnourishment, debility and outright exhaustion.

On the Western Front, the devastating damage to the landscape by increasingly heavy artillery barrages pockmarked the battlefield with multiple huge craters. This destruction of the terrain was further compounded by damaged land drainage systems and small streams, and together with what seemed to be continual bad weather, the shell holes became water-filled and often with deep, viscous mud, severely impeding any but really determined movement by soldiers on foot. Cavalry horses could no longer move rapidly close behind the lines in training exercise or readiness for the long-awaited breakthrough but they still had to be available together with the huge numbers of horses and mules needed for draught purposes, hauling artillery pieces, ammunition, supply, field kitchens, communication cable wagons and ambulances.

As with the soldiers, horses and mules were exposed to shellfire, air attack, gas, barbed wire and such high levels of noise so that many were simply terrified. Horses and horse lines were specifically targeted by German artillery with devastating results. During the Battle of Verdun from late February 1916, one of attrition between French and German forces, a single shot fired from a French naval gun killed ninety-seven horses, amid a total of 7,000 horses killed by long-range shelling in a single day in March of that year. British Army horse losses between the Somme in 1916 and the end of the war comprised 58,090 horses killed in action, 77,410 wounded in action, 211 actually killed in gas attacks, 2,200 severely injured in gas attacks, and several hundred killed by bombs.

The AVC was initially under-recruited when war broke out, yet soon came into its own with significantly increased numbers of men. It started the war with six veterinary hospitals together with the astutely-formed mobile units to render immediate first aid for minor ailments, evacuation units to take serious cases out of the front line and the veterinary hospitals along the lines of communication or further in the rear to cure major disease/injuries so that animals later judged as fit could eventually be returned to service.

A total of 2.5 million animals was treated with an 80 per cent chance of being cured and thus two million were passed fit for further service – reflecting very highly upon the AVC and its professional standards, aided in France and at home by the significant contributions made by the Blue Cross and the RSPCA. The Blue Cross staffed their own horse and dog hospitals in France whilst many RSPCA staff joined the AVC and some served abroad. They also provided veterinary equipment and supplies, and numerous horse ambulances. Special units were formed to facilitate the disposal of carcases to reduce the risk of diseases in the front line as well as behind the lines.

For its part, the German Army is listed with over 250 veterinary hospitals throughout the entire country that participated in the war, with a recorded death in service rate of 27 per cent. This contrasted with the French who were forced to acknowledge that their military veterinary services were inadequate through poor organisation and a lack of resources, and with reported death rates of 80 per cent. Such was the poor state of the French military veterinary service overall, that it was only able to show some signs of coping following the intervention of the Blue Cross which established nine veterinary hospitals in France, properly supplied and staffed, and financed by donations from the concerned general public in Britain.

In East Africa, the Germans, their defensive campaign assisted of course by the need simply to evade and ambush when opportunity allowed, used the vast area of operations to retire behind the line of tsetse fly distribution, infections from which caused severe trypanosomiasis (sleeping sickness) in Allied mounted units resulting in the loss of 1,639 horses and mules on one march alone, and some 12,000 horse and mules overall, between August and October 1916.

Horses also served in the Near East in the Sinai and Palestine Campaign where the Desert Mounted Corps had three mounted divisions of British, Australian, New Zealand, Indian and French troops with a mixture of regular cavalry, Yeomanry, mounted infantry and horse artillery. The desert terrain was more suited to horses in general although day-long cavalry patrols without water for the horses (though grain stores were carried), did impose a serious and unwanted strain until they returned to base. Two mobile veterinary sections joined in April and July 1917. In the Middle East, General Allenby had 18,000 horses by the end of 1918 and although some laud the successful use of cavalry in several battles, traditional cavalry usage was being reduced and most troops fought as mounted infantry. Hardy 'walers' from Australia were highly regarded horses for these desert operations but even so, deaths from exhaustion, inadequate water supplies and wounds, continued to be recorded.

After hostilities ceased, we might wonder what happened to those animals that had survived being shelled, shot, wounded, gassed, malnourished, worked to the point of total exhaustion and exposed to the harsh conditions of the weather and the battlefield?. There are of course some notable survivors from horses which went to war and returned home – Warrior, the charger belonging to General Jack Seely, perhaps the most famous, actually surviving leading a cavalry charge at Moreau Wood in 1918, an exceptional circumstance. Warrior died in 1941. General 'Black Jack' Pershing, who commanded the American Expeditionary Force, also had a charger, Kidron, which was successfully repatriated in good health to the USA and lived until 1942. But what happened to the huge but anonymous number of horses and mules which had survived?

The British AVC had classified surviving horses in France into several categories, including a group returned to England for sale. However, good horses in other theatres of war, such as the Middle East, could not be repatriated to England and some could not be sold locally. 'The unfortunate consequence was that, after every available channel of useful [horse] disposal had been explored, there remained in some theatres of war a surplus of serviceable animals which could only be destroyed.'[1]

British losses were 484,000 horses and mules, and 62,000 British horses and mules were returned to Britain from the Western Front and such was the high level of care given to them by the AVC that no contagious diseases were brought into the country. Many others were sold either to French or Belgian farmers whose animals had been taken from them for the war effort, or for other kinds of civil work. The total sold in this direction was 7,775. Some 45,000 went into the meat trade to French horse butchers for meat and hides, and those 39,945 war horses and mules rated as unfit through injury, illness or age for either of these disposal routes were butchered and turned into by-products by the Horse Carcase Economiser Depots during the four months between the Armistice and the end of March 1919. 'A good market for horse flesh fit for human food was found' in France and Belgium, reported the official war history of the British Veterinary Service, noting the high demand for military contracts 'with approved firms of butchers in Paris'.[2]

Army Waste Products Ltd., a military trading company appointed by Britain's Army Council, took over the disposal of horse carcasses. When a severe meat shortage struck in England, officials set up a system to sell horsemeat in the cities of London and Liverpool. 'The plan worked well, and it became possible to dispose of large numbers of otherwise worthless animals at prices which varied between 9 Pounds and 12 Pounds,' is the relevant detail in a post-war report.[3]

The American Expeditionary Force recorded 63,000 as killed of the 182,000 animals brought into the war on the Western Front, of which a mere 200 went home. A total of 13,000 Australian horses survived until the end of the war with 11,000 going to the Indian Army as remounts – the remaining 2,000 were shot, as strict quarantine procedures together with significant transport costs prevented any being sent back to Australia. Similarly, New Zealand horses were distributed to the Egyptian or British Armies in Egypt, but the others were also shot to remove the risk of potential ill-treatment by other buyers.

In Egypt the situation for these ex-warhorses was far from ideal and even as late as 1930 there were so many ex-military horses from the former American, Australian and British Armies being ill-treated by their owners that Dorothy Brooke, wife of Major General Brooke, founded the Old Warhorse Memorial Hospital in Cairo in 1934 (now the Brooke Hospital for Animals) and, financed by donations from Britain, bought 5,000 of these creatures to stop further suffering. The exhausted and aged animals were humanely put down, leaving the remainder to be cared for, a practice which continues to this day.

The significant loss of draught horses in Britain led to some rather bizarre sights in some towns with circus elephants and even camels being used as draught animals to haul not only delivery carts but also to work on farms hauling ploughs. The Germans too were forced to use their circus animals on the Home Front as substitutes for their own horses which had been, like the British and French, drafted to the front, and on many occasions the better trained and more intelligent elephants were quite easy to manage, being far better suited and more useful than a horse. Such were the knock-on effects of removing horses by large-scale impressment to the military forces from their usual civilian uses.

Camels at War

The dromedary or Arabian camel is of course eminently suitable for military purposes in arid areas with its ability to go without food or water for long periods carrying either riders or supplies and so it was inevitable that they would be used in the Middle East during the war. Founded in December 1916, the Imperial Camel Corps Brigade (ICCB) was part of the Egyptian Expeditionary Force and fought extensively throughout the area in the Senussi, Sinai and Palestine Campaigns, and later in the Arab revolt until the disbandment of the Brigade in 1919.

It was found that camels, unlike horses, are not easily spooked by gunfire or shell detonations which, together with their hardiness, made them ideal for desert warfare to carry soldiers and also as draught animals. The soldiers fought as mounted infantry supported in the field by camel-borne mountain artillery guns. The ICCB was supported by a remount depot and a veterinary hospital near Cairo with an AVC sergeant in each company headquarters. By 1917, the lessons from the harsh realities on the Western Front had clearly been learned and a 42-man mobile veterinary section was present at brigade level. At one point there were 50,000 camels in the Egyptian Expeditionary Force, in addition to horses, mules and donkeys. Besides carrying the infantry, ammunition and other supplies, some thirty-five camels were also used to carry the wounded in side-mounted stretchers, called *cacolets*, strapped on either side of the camel, transport in which was described as acutely uncomfortable and often worse than being wounded.

Surprisingly, camels are sensitive to cold in particular, to rain and even more strangely, to excessive heat. The main cause of disease was mange which infected every single Egyptian camel and could have wiped out the entire force within a few months had drastic treatment not been initiated. Camel casualties and injuries recorded from the 2,000 camels in the Egyptian Camel Transport Corps are as follows: 1,000 animals killed in action, ninety-two shot due to battle injuries. As many animals were also reported to be overloaded it was inevitable that saddle/harness sores were a recurrent problem requiring constant veterinary vigilance and attention.

Pigeons

With birds encountering the extreme violence of the battlefield and particularly the horrendous noise, it never ceased to amaze soldiers that where trees and bushes still survived the devastation of the artillery bombardments, birds were sometimes seen trying to behave in an apparently normal way – flocking, perching to sing and building nests.

Everyone knows of the amazing and unerringly accurate ability for pigeons to return to their loft or roost after sometimes flying long distances so to do. Thus it was with military pigeons in the war, still seemingly capable of flying with reliable accuracy through the shattering noise of bursting shells and skies full of shrapnel. We should remember too that the lofts might well be mobile and temporary. Some in the British Army had considered pigeons obsolete as messages could be transmitted quicker by telephone and telegraph. Initially the Belgians and Germans both had more efficient Army Pigeon Services, but certainly on the Western Front, the ceaseless damage to the terrain caused by the artillery barrages broke wires as fast as they could be repaired, (often at extreme risk for the men involved in this work) and thus a British Army rethink of the value of pigeons was undertaken. Some 95 per cent of army messages sent by British pigeons was safely delivered in spite of this method being a neglected asset at the outset. By intriguing contrast, the British Admiralty had effectively used pigeons on minesweeping trawlers, submarines and seaplanes for some years. The French Army used considerable numbers of pigeons and was reported to have had some seventy-two military pigeon lofts at the time of the First Battle of the Marne early in September 1914. The Americans brought 600 birds with them, all donated by pigeon fanciers in the USA.

Reports state that in excess of 10,000 birds were used overall throughout the war. Individual birds, or, in pairs, were taken into the front line in baskets by the French and British troops whilst requisitioned London buses were converted into mobile temporary lofts immediately behind the lines. Individual birds were also carried in British tanks and were released through a small hatch in the hull, and pigeons were also released from Royal Flying Corps aircraft and from warships. The Germans had soldiers carrying backpacks containing several birds and some multiple bird containers were mounted on motorcycles.

The advantage of pigeons, in addition to their proven reliability, was the height at which they flew and their speed, with one bird, backed by a following wind, flying 38 miles in 20 minutes. Furthermore, they presented a small target for aimed rifle fire and they could fly in foggy conditions. There are many stories of wounded pigeons successfully reaching their battlefield destinations.

Such was the importance attributed to the military use of pigeons that six months imprisonment or a £100 fine were the penalties incurred in the United Kingdom by anyone caught infringing the Defence of the Realm Act relating to shooting or otherwise interfering with them on the Home Front, and there was a £5 reward for information leading to successful prosecution.

The Dogs of War

Dogs are man's oldest domesticated animal species and there can exist between man and dog a strong, tangible relationship based upon mutual trust. It is not really surprising that following on from antiquity dogs were used in the First World War. Their importance and usefulness was recognised early on in that the German Army commandeered all suitable dogs as they advanced through Belgium and France, sending them back for training backed by good veterinary oversight. Military dog numbers comprised: Germans, 30,000, Italians, 3,000 handled for their allies, British and French, 20,000.

Dogs were used for a range of tasks: guards and sentries, scouts, messengers, casualty dogs, explosives/mine detection, telephone line layers, draught animals, and rodent control. As sentries, in tandem with a soldier, dogs were highly efficient at scenting or hearing suspect movements, and responding with a warning growl or bark to alert both defender and aggressor. In this way they were effective in guarding military supply depots and were used in Salonika, Egypt, Mesopotamia, and in the early phases on the Western Front – but not by the British till around 1916 – and of course on the Home Front.

Scout dogs also patrolled with soldiers ahead of other troops detecting enemy soldiers moving or in ambush and they would quietly show such presence and direction by pointing and raising their hackles, whilst German scout dogs were trained to bark if an enemy trench were occupied. However, it was in the extensive Western Front trench network that dogs were valued as messengers. Telephone wires were frequently cut by artillery barrages and although mounted soldiers re-laid wires from spools on their horse and sometimes using similar but smaller reels on dogs, messenger dogs proved their value time and time again. Dogs could certainly run faster than soldiers used as 'runners', especially over any kind of broken ground, and were a much smaller target for snipers. A British Army messenger dog is credited with running over 4,000 metres in less than 60 minutes to a Brigade Headquarters.

Casualty dogs were introduced by the Germans to locate wounded soldiers. Some carried basic medical items for those soldiers who could treat themselves; other dogs guided stretcher bearers to the wounded, and some even tried to drag the wounded back whilst others lay beside the gravely wounded, identifying his position, providing some physical warmth and moral comfort. Casualty dogs could also work at night and in fog making good use of their training.

In the French army, and especially the Belgian army, dogs were used extensively as draught animals pulling small carts with general supplies, ammunition and machine-guns. Italy also used draught dogs, St. Bernards, to pull carts and sledges. On occasions, pack saddles were used on steep ground in snow, whilst imported Alaskan huskies were similarly used by French troops. This ability to carry a small load also enabled them to be used to carry spools of telephone wire to re-lay lines damaged by shellfire. Mines and other buried explosives were also detected by the superior scenting ability of military dogs.

The few dogs attached to French regiments were better organised from December 1914 with operational dog units attached to each Army Corps. Similarly, the Germans started with 6,000 trained dogs plus reserves and the Italians and Russians had military dogs too. Britain, however, had no official dog cover early in the war apart from two dogs with two different infantry regiments, the Durham Light Infantry and the Norfolk Regiment. It was only in 1915, through the persistence of Colonel Edwin Richardson, that this situation changed. He was a retired officer brought back into active service, and he had practical experience of war dogs, in training them and also of their proven success in action with other armies. His persuasive argument finally prevailed against those critics in the War Office who reluctantly agreed to the foundation of a British Army Dog Training School.

At the end of the war, it was estimated that 7,000 dogs were thought to have lost their lives. That number is disputed, however, and the United States Veterinary Corps put the total deaths at 16,000. As the French destroyed 15,000 war dogs and the United States, Great Britain, Germany, Italy and Russia also destroyed many, the actual total of dogs destroyed after the war is unknown.

Two factors impeded the successful return of British war dogs – rabies quarantine requirements together with the costs of transport and kennelling for that period of six months. The RSPCA defrayed these costs for 542 dogs for individual soldiers and sailors approved by the Army Council, whilst Battersea Dogs Home built new kennels to accommodate 452 dogs from France, twenty-five from Salonika, fifteen from Egypt and ten from Italy. Even so, several dogs were illegally and improperly smuggled in and rabies broke out in Plymouth, in South Wales, in London and in the Home Counties in 1918.

The appalling conditions in the trenches along the Western Front were paralleled elsewhere – in Gallipoli and on the Italian Front for example – resulting in the presence of huge rats in their thousands, feeding upon the discarded ration tins and upon unburied decomposing bodies in No Man's Land. They carried disease and were known even to scrabble over wounded and sleeping soldiers. It was forbidden to waste ammunition in shooting them, as that would never have seriously reduced their numbers, and so terriers became the best method of control.

Men, Mascots and Morale

Regimental or unit mascots have been known for a long time, taking part in ceremonial parades and they were much loved by the soldiers, many of the mascots were serving before the outbreak of the Great War. The Army had a variety, ranging from a black buck antelope, a goat, a ram, dogs, a pony and horses whilst the Royal Navy naturally had ship's cats, but also a lemur, monkeys, some dogs and even a pig. Such mascots were commonly gifts but some were obtained from foreign postings by adoption. All were regarded with a degree of affection and were sometimes permitted to appear on formal parades.

It is not surprising, given the circumstances on the fighting fronts, that men clung to anything that offered some degree of psychological comfort and detachment from the violence around them. Men became attached to their animals be they horse, mule, goat, donkey or dog as the companionship of a trusting animal was intensely personal and was often regarded as an extension of the soldier's own being. Mascots abounded throughout the Army and stray dogs as well as military dogs, horses, mules, donkeys and even pigeons were treated with genuine affection as they offered moments of escapism reminding the soldiers of their home life before the war when things were normal.

Some mascots were out of the ordinary and a baboon (the South African Scottish Regiment), a kangaroo, an eagle (in the Balkans), goats, donkeys, bears and rabbits, chickens and geese have all been documented as mascots as well as a pig. Some soldiers even tamed trench rats to come to them and accept bits of food, such was the deep-seated need for escapism from current circumstances. Mascots were often exposed to the hardships of the battlefield just as the men and other military animals. The wounding or even loss of an animal was keenly felt. Anecdotes are numerous but it was the emotional attachment which encouraged the repatriation of many mascots after the war to be pets or just to live out a peaceful life.

'Rags' was a Cairn terrier mix who served as the mascot of the US 1st Infantry Division. He 'joined up' in 1917 in France and held his title until his death in 1931. His greatest moment of heroism came during the Meuse-Argonne Campaign in 1918, when he ran a vital message through falling shells. Although the terrier was gassed and partially blinded, he survived. 'Sergeant Jimmy', a donkey, was born in 1916 during the Battle of the Somme and was wounded three times during the war. He learned to raise his hoof to those soldiers who cared for him and raised thousands of pounds for the RSPCA after the end of the war. 'Sammy', a terrier, served with the 1st/4th Northumberland Fusiliers, accompanying them to France in 1915 where he was, on occasion, buried, gassed and wounded. He 'served' in the Ypres Salient, and on the Somme.

A large white pig was kept was on board SMS *Dresden*, a German light cruiser that barely escaped the Battle of the Falkland Islands in December 1914, only to be cornered and scuttled in March 1915. The pig was spotted in the sea by the crew of HMS *Glasgow*, was rescued and taken aboard. Adopted by the crew as the ship's mascot, he was then, with typical British humour, named 'Tirpitz', after *Grossadmiral* Alfred von Tirpitz, Secretary of State of the German Imperial Naval Office. The pig was by all accounts very popular with all ranks and stayed aboard for a year before eventual transfer, after quarantine, to a shore station in Portsmouth. Auctioned off for a charity in 1919 he raised £1,785 for the Red Cross.

His stuffed and mounted head, seeming to show the suggestion of a grin, now resides in the Imperial War Museum.

Memorials

The inscription on the Animal War Memorial at Morley near Leeds, reads that 'worse than dying is to be forgotten' and there are of course innumerable memorials to the huge number of soldiers killed during the Great War in all the countries which fought and so it is entirely appropriate that memorials to military animals also exist. A particularly poignant and comprehensive one exists in Edinburgh on the south front of the Scottish National War Memorial, completed in 1927. It depicts canaries and mice, described as the 'Tunnelers' Friends', as they were used as indicators of foul air in tunnels dug on the Western Front. It also shows a mule, horse, camel, reindeer, dog, ox, elephant and carrier pigeons and is truly indicative of the many species which served.

In addition to the many personal memorials to individual animals placed by their owners or the regiments who cared for them, there were other institutional ones in Great Britain. In 1932, the RSPCA opened a memorial dispensary in London and the Royal Veterinary College started a fund to re-equip the college as their form of memorial. There is a bronze group by H. Heseltine, *Les revenants*, in the Imperial War Museum, showing worn-out and gassed horses returning from the Front, and in Dartmouth Park in Leeds, an animal memorial was erected in 2011. However, nothing was done on a national level until 2004, a strange omission, until the impressive and moving 'Animals in War' memorial in Park Lane, London, was dedicated. It shows heavily-laden and exhausted mules struggling towards a gap in the surrounding wall suggesting relief from the horrors of war, whilst the carvings on the wall depict the many species that served in the Great War.

Similar national memorials exist in Canada in the form of three distinctive and revealing bronze plaques showing horses in the deep mud of the Western Front and in Australia where the memorial is in the shape of a horse's head upon a granite column, the last remaining fragment of Charles Web Gilbert's original Desert Mounted Corps memorial (to the Australian Light Horse and the New Zealand Mounted Rifles), which stood at Port Said, Egypt, until it was destroyed during the Suez Crisis of 1956.

The Great War of 1914–18 had unexpected effects far outside the different theatres of war and the significant social and economic changes that lasted a considerable time. The persistence of poignant ceremonies of remembrance that are a constant reminder today of the huge losses suffered by all the belligerents will, it is to be hoped, cause some to pause and think of their animal comrades who also served, were injured and died – the 'Silent Soldiers'.

This chapter is written in constant memory of all those animals who served in the Great War, giving of their trust, unswerving loyalty and companionship – faithful even unto death.

Notes

1. An article in the *St Louis Beacon*, 6 July 2012, by Robert Koenig. See suggested further reading.
2. Blenkinsop, *The History of the Great War based on Official Documents: Veterinary Services*, pp. 682–8.
3. Ibid, p. 683 (Disposal of Animals).

Suggested Further Reading

Blenkinsop, Major General Sir L. J., and Rainey, Lieut. Colonel J. W. (eds), *The Official History of the Great War based on Official Documents:Veterinary Services* (HMSO, 1925).

Brereton, J. M., *The Horse in War 1914* (Newton Abbot: David & Charles, 1976).

Butler, Simon, *The War Horses:The Tragic Fate Of A Million Horses Sacrificed In The First World War* (Halsgrove, 2011).

Clabby, Brigadier John, *The History of the RAVC 1919-1961* (J. Allen, 1963).

Cooper, Jilly, *Animals in War* (Corgi, 1984).

Emden, Richard van, *Tommy's Ark, Soldiers and Their Animals in the Great War* (Bloomsbury, 2010).

Gray, Ernest, *Dogs of War* (Robert Hale Ltd, 1989).

Koenig, Robert, '"War Horse" and The Great War's Equine Holocaust', *St Louis Beacon*, 6 July 2012.

Leckie, Lieut. Colonel, *A Centaur Looks Back* (Hodder & Stoughton, 1946).

Moore, Major General Sir John, 'In The Beginning', *Journal of the Royal Army Vet. Corps*, Vol. 8, No. 1 (1938), pp. 10–123.

Seely, General Jack, Scott, Brough and Munnings, Alfred, *Warrior, The Amazing Story of a Real War Horse* (Racing Post Books, 2011).

Shaw Baker, Peter, *Animal War Heroes* (A&C Black Ltd, 1933).

Smith, Sir Frederick, *A History of the Royal Army Veterinary Corps 1796-1919* (Shrewsbury: Livesey Ltd, 1983).

Chapter 16

New Horizons –
A War in the Air, 1914

* * *

Nick Forder

Although the first sustained powered flight in Europe had only taken place in 1906, by August 1914 aviation was an accepted part of everyday life in Britain and much of Europe. Since Wilbur Wright visited France in 1908, the first aeroplane had flown in Britain in 1909; Blériot had flown across the Channel in the same year; and in that year the first all-British aeroplane had been built and flown; the following year, London and Manchester had been linked by air and the public had been thrilled by air races and exhibition pilots, courtesy of the *Daily Mail*. Preparations were under way to fly across the Atlantic.

From 1908, in France and Germany aviation grew in popularity too, with national organizations promoting the need for investment in military aviation. In 1912, Britain formed the Royal Flying Corps (RFC), with Military and Naval Wings and a shared Central Flying School. The Central Flying School was to train new pilots and provide advanced training for those who had gained their Royal Aero Club 'Tickets' through a civilian school. A retrospective grant was available to pay for civilian training. In addition, the Navy continued to train pilots at Eastchurch, using their own facilities. Army officers were seconded to the RFC from their regiments and corps, and an RFC Special Reserve was formed in parallel with the rest of the Army. Naval officers could be posted to the Naval Wing, but it was only for a period of time as aviation was not a distinct career path and 'sea time' was still needed for progression.

In 1914, Britain was, primarily, a naval power. Britain was a trading nation with the largest merchant fleet in the world. A primary role of the Royal Navy was protection of that trade, vital not just for prosperity but also because Britain did not produce enough food to feed itself without imports. Britain, of course, also depended on the Royal Navy for defence. Although the threat posed by the development of aviation had been identified by the newspaper owner, Lord Northcliffe, in November 1906, when he berated the editor of the *Daily Mail* for misreporting the first, sustained powered flight in Europe as 'Santos-Dumont flies

722 feet' when he believed the headline should have been 'England is no longer an island . . . It means the aerial chariots of a foe descending on British soil if war comes',[1] and entered the public consciousness when Blériot flew across the Channel less than three years later, it remained unclear how the Royal Navy could use aviation to support its primary aims.

The Naval Wing was to seek ways of co-operating with warships. Initially this was restricted to flying from coastal airfields, leading to an air-defence responsibility. The limited range of land-based aircraft made them unsuitable. Although airships, with their superior range, endurance and load-carrying capability, could act as aerial scouts for naval forces, development of this capability was less of a priority for a nation with a large navy and an existing force of surface cruisers. The situation was different in Germany where the rigid airship, the Zeppelin, was promoted as a national icon.

The key to the effective use of air power at sea was the aircraft carrier, the first design of which was presented to the Admiralty by William Beardmore in December 1912. The Admiralty correctly turned down the design as the concept was not practical until the problems of landing aeroplanes on ships had been solved and incorporated into the design. The seaplane carrier was an expedient compromise, as there was no need to land back on the ship and take off could be from the water too. Therefore the Admiralty was instructed to embrace the seaplane carrier as the platform for naval air operations, while continuing to experiment in the wider use of air power.

On 26 October, 1913, Winston Churchill, First Lord of the Admiralty, issued a minute recommending the development of three basic types of aircraft to fulfil a naval role:

1. A Fighting seaplane capable of operating from a ship and working over the sea.
2. A Scouting seaplane capable of working with the Fleet at sea.
3. A Service patrol aeroplane for coastal patrol duties and to repel enemy aircraft attacking vulnerable points in Britain.

By the outbreak of war, the Naval Wing had become the Royal Naval Air Service (RNAS). Its pilots had successfully taken off from a ship underway, developed seaborne seaplane operations, and experimented with the detection of submarines, bomb dropping and the use of aircraft for combat against other aircraft. A series of Naval Air Stations had been established around the coast with the intention of aerial defence and co-operation with the Fleet in coastal waters. The effective use of air power beyond the range of land-based aircraft remained elusive. Indeed, on 3 April 1915, Churchill chaired a conference at the Admiralty to review progress. He referred back to his minute of 1913 and expressed the opinion that 'the employment of aircraft in co-operation with the Fleets at sea had not been developed as much as had been anticipated would be the case'.[2]

Despite Britain being a sea power, the emergence of Germany as a major European power and discussions with the French established the notion of sending an Expeditionary Force to fight on the continent. This would include an air element, as Sefton Brancker, an RFC (Military Wing) Captain in 1914, explained:

It had been laid down in 1912 that this Expeditionary Force would require eight strong squadrons on mobilization, which meant a force comprising 200 pilots and 100 serviceable aeroplanes, and another 100 trained pilots and 100 serviceable aeroplanes in England for training purposes. Even in 1912 we had counted on annual wastage of at least 100 per cent pilots and machines.[3]

The Military Wing consisted of units known as Squadrons, with an establishment strength of three Flights, each of four aeroplanes, commanded by a Major. Both the French and the Germans preferred six-aircraft units.

On formation, the RFC was to inherit a number of aircraft types from the Royal Engineers' Air Battalion. These had been obtained, through purchase or gift, for evaluation purposes. Following similar trials in France in 1911, an aeroplane competition was announced and a design specification circulated. The primary role was seen as reconnaissance, though the need to arm aeroplanes for offensive and defensive purposes was anticipated. Such was the marginal performance of existing designs, with limited load carrying capabilities, that it was expected that airships would be developed to carry wireless sets and bombs.

The 'Military Trials' were open to foreign design also, though the governments of Germany and Austro-Hungary prevented their manufacturers from entering. Numbers of French designs were entered, some by British subsidiary companies. The pre-eminence of the French in aero-engine design was clear, with a number of British entrants having French engines. Unfortunately, the Military Trials failed to identify a standard design suitable for the RFC. The most successful design was deemed to be the Cody V biplane, although it was obsolescent and had strictly limited military potential. The RFC ordered two examples, the minimum it was obliged to purchase, and quickly retired the type after one fatal crash. The second aircraft can be seen today, preserved by the Science Museum in London.

However, one other design had made an impression at the Trials and this was the BE2. This 'Blériot Experimental' (i.e. it was a 'tractor' with a propeller facing forward) had been designed by Geoffrey de Havilland at the Royal Aircraft Factory, Farnborough. Technically ineligible for the Trials, it was, nevertheless, tested on an unofficial basis and seemed to offer all that the RFC required. Accordingly, it was put into production by contracted companies using plans provided by Farnborough. This, in itself, was significant as aeroplanes were generally built individually, using artisan skills, with reference to basic general arrangement drawings and sketches only. It was not usual for components to be chalked out, full size, on the workshop floor.

The performance of the BE2 was just adequate to meet the demands of the expanding role of the aeroplane. Its top speed was 65–70mph; it had a 'ceiling' of 10,000 feet and an endurance of three hours. Efforts were made to develop the BE2, focusing on making it easier to fly. This would make training pilots easier, and a stable aeroplane, capable of flying straight and level and allowing its pilot to undertake other tasks, in a non-hostile environment, was seen as a worthwhile goal. The inherently stable BE2c was just entering service on the outbreak of war and was adopted as the standardized design although it was not quite ready for contract production.

The BE2, in line with most military designs of the time, was configured for the benefit of the pilot and not the observer, in that it was flown from the rear seat. *Cabane* struts and wires surrounded the front seat, limiting the ability of the passenger to observe, operate equipment efficiently or defend the aeroplane from attack. So it was no great loss when the observer was left behind to increase speed, to maximize the useful load and carry more fuel, a machine-gun, a camera or a bomb instead. The early wireless sets weighed 75kgs. A Lewis Gun, mounting and two drums of ammunition weighed about 40kgs.

There was no intention to arm the BE2 beyond trials carried out in 1912, which led to the conclusion that, lacking a suitable means to fire forward through the propeller, and the constraints of the observer's position, a 'pusher' configuration, with the propeller behind the pilot, would be a more practical proposition. The Royal Aircraft Factory, FE2 (Farman Experimental 2: i.e. it was a 'pusher') was tested with a machine-gun fitted, but trials were discontinued to allow staff to concentrate on the BE2.

In the spring of 1913, the Royal Aircraft Factory resumed armament trials with the FE2 and the Henri Farman F20 pusher. The Farman was slower, but it was a proven design and was available for purchase from the Aircraft Manufacturing Company at Hendon. Limited resources, particularly finance, led to concentration on developing the BE2 and purchasing Farmans, as necessary. By the winter of 1913/14, Lieutenant-Colonel Frederick Sykes, commanding the Military Wing of the RFC, was pushing for standardization on the BE2. This was resisted by many of the RFC's pilots who championed the virtues of the Farman.

On the outbreak of war, aircraft type standardization barely extended beyond individual flights. Although no further competitions were held for aircraft, an attempt was made to stimulate British aero-engine design in a similar way. The RFC continued to purchase, or encourage the Royal Aircraft Factory to emulate the best designs produced by British or foreign manufacturers. Lieutenant Philip Joubert de la Ferté, 3 Squadron RFC, recalled: 'There were at least eight different types amongst the "hundred" serviceable aircraft, and of those only three were British. The engines were largely of French origin.'[4] By this time, the RFC Military Wing had worked on systems of co-operation with the infantry, cavalry and artillery. Experiments with machine-gun armament, wireless telegraphy and aerial photography had also been undertaken. Aircraft had participated in military manoeuvres, a long-distance deployment and flown successfully at night.

Backing British aviation was an industry employing about 1,000 workers, in a range of companies that were part of larger conglomerates, such as Vickers and Armstrong-Whitworth, independents such as Avro and Sopwith, British subsidiaries of foreign companies or builders of foreign designs such as Blériot and the Aircraft Manufacturing Company, and contract builders such as Hewlett & Blondeau.

The industry was in the process of establishing itself. A Sopwith had won the Schneider Trophy in 1914, British designs had been sold overseas, including to the German navy, and British and Colonial had set up a factory in Germany, at Halberstadt. However, production was small scale, supported by scarce military orders and a still developing domestic market dominated by French designs. Brancker summarized the situation:

> About eight firms were constructing aeroplanes for the War Office . . . but orders had been so small (none over six machines) that the whole of their output had been made by hand, and their experience in real bulk production of aircraft was practically nil. No satisfactory aeroplane engine had yet to be made in England, although a certain number had just been tried on the bench in the engine competition at Farnborough.[5]

Expansion of the RFC had been limited by lack of funds, aircraft being a very low priority compared with social welfare and capital ships needed to stay ahead in the naval race with Germany. The threat of European War made large funds available suddenly and it fell to Brancker to decide how to spend the money most effectively. Capacity orders were placed with an industry struggling to expand. Any increase in manufacturing needed skilled workers, plant and raw materials. Other industries, and then recruiting, competed for workers, while spruce had to be purchased and imported from the USA and Canada, engines from France and magnetos from Germany.

In theory, the Royal Aircraft Factory's BE2, the standardized design developed to meet the needs of the RFC and be capable of being produced by contracted companies, could be made by firms hitherto outside the aeroplane industry. The motor car industry was an obvious candidate for such expansion, employing all the necessary skills in engine and body manufacture and possessing a widening experience of volume production. However, Brancker concluded,

> We had practically no tried out and proved standard type of aeroplane which could be ordered at once in numbers. The first 80 h.p. Gnome Avros had just been delivered and we were still awaiting reports on their efficiency; the 80 h.p. Gnome Sopwith two-seater had been badly reported on [and replaced in 5 Squadron by Avros]; the Sopwith Bullet [Tabloid] had not yet flown in the Service; the latest Bristol two-seater was unsatisfactory; the Vickers Fighter [FB5 Gunbus] was being tried but its engine, the 100 h.p. Mono-Gnome, had so far proved very unreliable; the

BE2a and BE2b had just been replaced, in the small orders we had been able to give, by the BE2c, which was an untried type; and the Royal Aircraft Factory were making the RE5, also untried. This left us the Maurice and Henri Farmans, which were considered excellent for training, but which we knew were obsolescent, and the 80 h.p. Gnome Blériot, which had not been manufactured in England.[6]

Civilian aircraft, irrespective of their suitability for military tasks, were impressed into RFC and RNAS service. Brancker sought to source aircraft, engines and spares from overseas: 'We sent men to France to buy every Farman aeroplane and every Renault and Gnome engine they could lay hands on.'[7] The danger of relying on foreign production became clear when, in July 1914: 'This enterprise went splendidly until rumour in Paris established the idea that Great Britain was not going into the war, when our sources of supply suddenly dried up for a time.'[8]

Although France had the world's largest aircraft industry in 1914, employing some 3,000 workers, it was ill-prepared for war. Arguably, this was by design; in 1914 the expectation was that the next European War would be one of mobility, encounter and of short duration. It would be fought with available forces and materiel, and there would be little time to manufacture new aircraft. France depended on a conscripted army and, on the outbreak of war, reservists were to mobilize with their units while skeleton staffs completed partially-built aircraft. A similar situation existed for the companies and 2,500 workers of the German aircraft industry.

The air forces of all the major nations stripped training schools of aircraft and instructors, recruited civilian pilots and their aircraft, and struggled to meet the immediate demands of the war. 'The privately owned aircraft we gathered up were not of much value, but we got some good pilots; practically all the professionals at Hendon enlisted in the Military Wing and were made sergeant pilots soon afterwards.'[9] Brancker recalled:

> On Saturday, July 25, I was eating a hasty sandwich lunch at my office table when Henry Wilson walked suddenly into my room and said simply 'Are you ready for war?'. I think my reply was 'Good God, no, sir !' . . . I told him briefly what thought we could produce on mobilization – roughly, four weak squadrons and an Aircraft Park; he went out, and I sat with my head in a whirl.[10]

This was half the aircraft envisioned in 1912 to be available to support an Expeditionary Force (the BEF), and left little in reserve. In June 1914, the RFC had concentrated at Netheravon, and managed to put up no more than thirty aircraft on any one day. The Germans were in a no better state, having planned to equip their proposed air force by 1916. Although the Germans had about 240 operational aircraft at the beginning of the war, these were deployed on the Eastern as well as the Western Front, and forty were allocated to the aerial defence of cities such as Köln and Metz.

Although understrength, each RFC squadron was prepared to mobilize within four days and fly to Dover. A detachment of 6 Squadron was to prepare the aerodrome at Dover within two days of the mobilization order. Once concentrated at Dover, the squadrons would be deployed within two days. Additional mechanical transport was to be acquired through the Army Motor Reserve scheme or donation. The transport was to be driven to the embarkation port, while all else travelled by rail. 'The mechanics and transport went by sea to Boulogne.'[11] Brancker recorded. 'We had no transport of our own worth mentioning,'[12] recalled Lieutenant Philip Joubert de la Ferté, 3 Squadron RFC, the same source reporting that the vehicles made available were generally those the Army did not want, and that many went to war still wearing their civilian liveries. Brancker's description paints an unmilitary picture: 'The line of march of the RFC looked like a circus. Except for a fair sprinkling of 30-cwt. Leylands and the Daimlers every vehicle was different and still wore trade markings.'[13] The Aeroplane Park was to supply replacement aeroplanes and undertake repair and maintenance work beyond the capabilities of the squadrons. Its establishment strength was twelve officers, 162 other ranks and twenty-four aircraft. 'Spares were lamentably deficient',[14] as were workshop facilities to repair aircraft.

The RFC staff was to go with the BEF to command the squadrons. The BEF had priority for aeroplanes and pilots, and there was little provision for training replacements. According to Joubert, 'the reserve of pilots was derisory';[15] almost everyone left to join the BEF, albeit as a supernumary. 'It was generally expected that we should all be home by Christmas,'[16] noted Corporal James McCudden, 3 Squadron, RFC, and nobody wanted to miss out.

With the RFC deploying to France, concern was expressed at the vulnerability of Britain to air attack. Though not specific to aerial bombardment, international law enshrined in the Geneva and 1907 Hague Conventions was quite clear that the bombardment of undefended civilian targets was illegal. However, the bombardment of military targets was seen as legitimate. Pre-war science fiction writers, unfettered by interpretations of partially-ratified international conventions, adopted aerial bombing as a popular theme for their stories. Often, the superior load-carrying capability of the airship made it the more likely bomber. Supposed sightings of German airships off the English Coast before the war, and the secrecy surrounding the German airship programme, conjured up the Zeppelin as a potential threat.

The Admiralty had assumed responsibility for developing British airships but the failure of His Majesty's Airship No 1, and the reluctance to divert funding from warship building, meant that there was no relevant experience of airship operation to inform a view as to the capability of Zeppelins. Attempts to purchase a German airship failed, and naval attachés were forced to glean intelligence from published German sources and riding as passengers on DELAG civilian airships.

Over-estimating the capabilities of the Zeppelin, the British priority was to defend military targets against precision bombing. The Admiralty identified dockyards, ports, fuel and ammunition depots as vulnerable targets, and they were what the RNAS sought to defend. Anti-aircraft guns were sited, and patrols were flown from coastal air stations. No formal warning system existed, only makeshift weapons were carried, and it was unclear what offensive action would follow interception.

The RFC deployed aircraft too, in this defensive role, before war broke out. 'There were wild rumours of approaching Zeppelin raids and on July 31, No. 4 Squadron was sent hurriedly to Eastchurch to protect Woolwich Arsenal and London.'[17] noted Brancker, and even after the RFC went to France, 'one Flight of No. 4 Squadron on Maurice Farmans, under the command of Captain Chinnery, was left behind at Dover to protect the coast of Kent'.[18] While 4 Squadron was at Eastchurch, the RNAS Eastchurch Squadron was sent to Yorkshire to fly patrols between Naval Air Stations. RFC aircraft were sent too, mainly unarmed Blériots, impressed on the outbreak of war but of limited military use. One pilot was sent to investigate reports of Zeppelins operating from secret bases in Britain! Soon, however, these RFC units were incorporated into 6 Squadron and sent to join the BEF. The RNAS then assumed responsibility for air defence.

The first RFC aircraft landed in France on 13 August. The squadrons concentrated at Amiens where they were inspected by Sir John French, commander of the BEF, on 15 August. He was much impressed with the general efficiency of the aircraft force and made a point of telling the squadron commanders. What French did not tell the RFC officers was how he planned to use their aircraft. Despite demonstrating their potential during manoeuvres, the RFC was not integrated into army operational procedures. It was quite centralized, and its commanders sought to retain independence by not attaching units directly to army formations. In consequence, the RFC was an unknown, and thus untrusted, unit, and its commanders were too junior to exert their authority. Sir Douglas Haig, one of French's two Corps commanders, was of the opinion that: 'There is only one way for a commander to get information by reconnaissance and that is by the use of cavalry.'[19] Hence, although the RFC was soon to fulfil its role of providing intelligence reports, these reports were passed by the RFC Headquarters Staff to the Intelligence Officers at BEF GHQ for consideration along with information gleaned from cavalry patrols and from allied sources. Information from the RFC might be regarded as confirmation of other reports; it was not a primary source. In defence of GHQ, it must be said that the RFC lacked observers trained in interpreting what they saw and much of the information gathered was fragmentary.

It was expected that reconnaissance would be needed to locate enemy forces and during initial encounters, after which the descent of 'the fog of war' was anticipated and GHQ would be able to make little use of further reports. This was part of a wider issue, there being limited experience of commanding large bodies of troops in battle. The last major European war had ended in 1871, with colonial expansion and security actions providing different experiences with little relevance to the new circumstance. Commanders could no longer see across the entire battlefield. Except for the French, soldiers no longer wore brightly-coloured uniforms aiding identification, and battlefield communications were limited. Telephone systems were not flexible enough to support mobile warfare and wireless was under-developed. Sir John French was to be unaware of the beginning of the Battle of Mons, and, on 26 August, contact was lost with I Corps. Beyond that, liaison between the Allies was poor, as there were no clear lines of command or communication. General Joffre, commanding the French Army, could not issue orders direct to the BEF, and Sir John French was not obliged to consult his allies. Language was a barrier too, Sir John's stumbling attempts to speak French merely alienating his allies.

Meanwhile, the RFC deployed forward in support of the advancing BEF.

On 16 August we moved to Mauberge, leaving a small detachment to form the first overseas Aircraft Park. We also discarded a number of very undesirable machines, amongst which was the Entente Cordiale Blériot, a crock that must have been brought over for propaganda purposes, as it was certainly useless for anything else. [It had been bought from *Daily Mail* pilot Henri Salmet's wife for £800] . . . Its arrival at Amiens had created a furore amongst the populace, but it had not the same popularity amongst those who had to fly it.[20]

The RFC began operations three days later, the first task being to locate Belgian forces with which the BEF had no contact. Joubert was one of the two pilots chosen for this work:

On 19 August Lieutenant Gilbert Mapplebeck and I did the first reconnaissance . . . after getting lost over the coal-mining areas of Mons I finally decided to land at a large town where the houses still seemed to be flying the Belgian flag. This was Tournai . . . From there I took off again, lost myself once more and, running out of fuel, landed near Courtrai. Here my reception was not at all friendly. It had not occurred to the War Office to provide us with identification papers and a good many of us were to experience difficulty owing to this lack of forethought . . . Both reconnaissances were negative.[21]

Meanwhile, the German troops crossing the border into Belgium were supported by *Feldflieger-Abteilung* (*FFA*) *9*. The unit's *Taube* monoplanes carried out reconnaissance as far as Liege, dropping leaflets on the city demanding its surrender on 8 August and reinforcing the threat with bombs. Soon the word *Taube* (Dove) became the standard term for all German aircraft, though the Fokker A type monoplane and B type biplanes were in service also. Reconnaissance flights searching for Belgian troop concentrations followed, extending to Namur. On 11 August, four more *FFA*s were deployed, taking the first aerial photographs of the war and confirming the destruction of most of the bridges across the Meuse by the retreating Belgians. From 19 August, locating the BEF, which had landed in France on 8 August, became a priority for the German airmen. By 22 August, Belgian troops were reported retreating towards Antwerp, but the BEF remained unsighted. Confirmation that the BEF was in the field was to come from the air, but only after a 5 Squadron Avro was brought down by ground fire. German aerial reconnaissance should have located BEF units as, according to McCudden, 'About the 22nd August, a strange aeroplane flew over us at about 4,000 feet and the aerodrome look-out reported it to be a German machine, the first we had seen in the war.'[22] If the aircraft were German, its crew failed either to observe the aerodrome or identify it as being British.

All the major air forces went to war expected to undertake reconnaissance, and none was equipped to fulfil any other role efficiently. Neither equipped nor trained to fight other aircraft, the main threats facing the RFC continued to be ground fire and poor recognition. French and British infantry, as well as the Germans and Belgians, fired at every aeroplane that flew overhead.

> We had been told authoritatively in England that if we flew at 3,000 feet we were unlikely to be hit by small arms fire and gunfire was likely to be equally ineffective. We had hardly crossed the battle line at 4,000 feet before my machine was hit five times.[23] . . . Captain Charlton, DSO, of A Flight, did three reconnaissances during the morning in three separate Blériots, each one being badly shot about by rifle fire from the ground.[24]

RFC aircraft were marked with Union flags, and then roundels, to aid recognition. The loss of the Avro led to RFC pilots being ordered to fly above 5,000 feet, where they were expected to be safe from rifle fire.

The German Army's Zeppelins proved particularly vulnerable to ground fire, operating at low altitude and moving quite slowly. They left reconnaissance to the aeroplanes and concentrated on bombing, attacking both Antwerp and Ostend in 1914. Even this proved hazardous, and soon bombing was restricted to night raids on railway junctions and military bases behind Allied lines. Operation at night caused navigation problems and effective bombs and bomb sights had yet to be developed.

Reports continued to be made of German troop movements and concentrations in front of the advancing BEF, but, as stated above, GHQ tended to give priority to intelligence from the French or the BEF's cavalry screen. GHQ was inexperienced in interpreting intelligence from multiple sources, and unclear about co-operating with the French. Equally, relations between GHQ and the adjacent French Fifth Army were so poor that intelligence was withheld from the BEF. The result was the Battle of Mons, an action which would have been catastrophic for the BEF had not the British liaison officer serving with the French Fifth Army confirmed the implications of RFC reconnaissance. This indicated large German troop concentrations in front of the BEF, and caused Sir John French to order a pause in the advance. Thus the BEF was not so isolated when the advancing Germans were met, and an orderly withdrawal to conform with the French was possible.

The retreat from Mons made the processing and interpretation of intelligence from all sources even more difficult. RFC squadrons, RFC HQ and GHQ frequently moved bases, each time dislocating communications. Sometimes the dislocation of the RFC's established system had positive outcomes as it led to necessary decentralization. At Le Cateau, on 25 August, 4 Squadron was attached directly to II Corps for tactical reconnaissance. There is evidence, also, that Sir John French began to use the RFC to monitor the movements of his allies, events having led him to mistrust information received through liaison officers.

Although German aircraft were seen during the retreat from Mons, leading McCudden to record 'As soon as we got to a new aerodrome a German machine invariably found us',[25] there remained issues as to the interpretation of reports at German Army HQ also. It was thought that the BEF was withdrawing towards Mauberge and not Le Cateau. After the battle there, the fragmented BEF could not be located, leading the Germans to assume that it had been effectively destroyed and could be ignored. In consequence, the German First Army changed direction and moved against the flank of the retreating French Fifth Army.

The ingenuity of the RFC in adapting their aircraft grew during the retreat.

> At this time the RFC's principal work was reconnaissance and bomb-dropping, our bombs still being hand and rifle grenades, and also petrol bombs, which consisted of a gallon of petrol in a streamlined canister which was ignited on impact with the ground. These last proved very useful for dropping on German hangars.[26]

Attacking German aerodromes was aspirational at this time, though the German air units were in a similar position to the RFC and used temporary landing grounds as they moved forward in support of ground troops. This was necessary as the range of the *Tauben* and Fokkers was limited, and the first two *FFA* ground parties arrived at Mons on 24 August.

At first, bombs and grenades were dropped by hand, but soon:

> We started to fit little wooden racks to carry small hand grenades, which were to be used as bombs, because at the commencement of hostilities we had nothing in the way of aerial bombs of any sort whatever . . . we also received some flechettes, or steel darts, for dropping, but it was very obvious that these would not do much harm with head cover. We dropped a lot of these.[27]

Thought was given to attacking German aircraft in the air and 'all the machines which went up were loaded with hand-grenades, as the intention was to bring down a hostile aeroplane down by dropping bombs on it'.[28] The effectiveness of this tactic assumed superior performance of RFC aircraft, which did not exist, and indicates that it was easier to make grenades than to procure suitable guns.

Resupply and maintenance became an increasing problem as the BEF retreated, and contact was lost with ground parties.

> On these occasions we were away from our transport and mechanics for days, and the mechanics who flew with the flight therefore had their hands very full in order to keep the machine serviceable under difficulties, for we only carried a small tool kit on the machines.[29]

Although the Germans went to war with unarmed aircraft they, too, began to improvise. Hermann Koehl, flying in Fokker A1 monoplanes with *FFA* 41 from the end of October, noted:

> These light aircraft struggle to carry the 50 to 100 steel arrows, and throwing these missiles was also very difficult. . . By the end of 1914 we carried *Fliegermaueschen* on board: these were a type of grenade with a large fin to make it fall on its head.[30]

The closeness of the Germans to Paris was made obvious when a *Taube* flew around the Eiffel Tower and dropped the first bombs on the capital on 29 August. The RFC, concerned with monitoring the progress of the advancing Germans and the direction of the retreating French, began to bring back reports which suggested that the German First Army had changed its line of march. This was deduced as much from negative information as the identification of German formations.

Lieutenant Louis Strange, 5 Squadron RFC, recalled:

> On September 4th we received orders to move to Melun . . . Our first day at Melun proved most exciting, as from the first reconnaissance we were able to see Von Kluck's army streaming east instead of south, while the British troops were moving in a southerly direction instead of the northerly one in which we expected to find them. It took many confirmatory reports to convince the Higher Command that this was so, because the sudden break off of the German advance seemed almost a miracle, while I fear that there were still a number of old-fashioned officers who did not yet quite trust the efficiency of aeroplanes, and so credited us with no powers of observation.[31]

General Joffre, commanding the French Army, saw an opportunity for a counter-attack on the river Marne, supported by the BEF and a new French Army deployed on the left flank.

As the Allies now sought to capitalise on a successful stemming of the German advance at the resultant Battle of the Marne, they moved to cross the Aisne and strike for the heights above the far bank. The Battle of the Aisne began on 14 September, with the RFC squadrons now attached to the BEF's two Corps for tactical reconnaissance. Photographs were taken of German positions, involving trips to Paris in search of suitable cameras and thoughts of new designs.

> We were experimenting with two new developments, photographic reconnaissance . . . and artillery observation. The difficulty about photographic reconnaissance was that we had no mechanics trained to take photographs, and pilots, being very few in number, were not allowed to go up as observers in case two of them were lost together. And so it meant that we had laboriously to train others in the art while actually flying over the enemy lines. It was particularly irritating after one had spent an hour over the target and had been heavily shelled in the process to find, on developing the plates either that there was nothing on them at all or that some elementary mistake had been made which rendered the pictures useless.[32]

Aerial direction of artillery fire was now practical as static lines and the beginning of trench warfare allowed the practical deployment of the RFC's wireless capability for the first time on 22 September.

> At this time liaison with the Artillery was coming into practice. Captain Lewis RE, who was attached to HQ Flight, had a BE2a fitted up specially with wireless apparatus, and he was doing at this time very good work in his directing artillery from the air.[33]

A wireless flight, consisting of three officers, was attached to 4 Squadron on mobilization. The weight of the wireless sets meant that observers could not be carried and the system was dependent on horse-drawn ground stations, something of an anachronism for a corps with an establishment of mechanized transport only. 'Our portable wireless plant, which was erected at our landing place every time we stayed at home for more than a day. This wireless plant was being transported by road was housed on two high carts drawn by horses.'[34] The two ground stations were part of the RFC HQ and no practical system had been agreed to deploy them in support of the artillery.

As it was, there were not enough wireless aircraft and ground stations, so flares and message bags had to be used. 'At this time the principal method of signalling a correction to the gunners was by means of Very lights. A very simple code of signals was arranged.'[35] In the opinion of Joubert, 'This primitive method was very unsatisfactory and led to many misunderstandings.'[36]

German aircraft were not fitted with wireless. Initially, artillery spotting and reconnaissance were done by map, using the proximity to printed names and telephoning the battery on landing. Wireless sets were not to be fitted to German aircraft until mid-1915, though from 10 November, 1914, an air-to-ground communication system based on coloured flares was introduced for the attack on Ypres. Any system for directing fire remained cumbersome until simple codes were introduced and standardized. In the meantime, the Germans discovered that circling over the intended target was as effective a method as anything else.

Following the stalemate after the British and French crossed the Aisne but failed to advance further, monitoring Allied troop movements by rail became a priority for the *Fliegertruppe*, as well as supporting the cavalry leading the troops seeking to outflank the Allies and capture the French and Belgian ports vital to the British. The German Fourth Army was formed to break through to the Belgian Coast, with two *FFA* attached for air support. Similarly, a new formation was tasked with attacking Ypres on 30 October, complete with two *FFA*, though the support of other local air units could be called upon. On 23 October, orders were issued to be more pro-active, seeking targets for the artillery and bombing, rather than just reporting observations.

The Eastchurch Squadron of the RNAS and 6 Squadron RFC went overseas in September and October to help the Belgians defend their coastal ports. Along with a Naval Brigade and 7 Division, they arrived too late, though an opportunity to bomb the airship bases at Düsseldorf and Köln was grasped by the RNAS. The second raid, on 8 October, resulted in the destruction of a Zeppelin in its shed. German airship operations over Ostend and Antwerp had been largely ineffectual and, despite British propaganda to the contrary, the Kaiser was very reluctant to sanction air attacks on Britain, especially if this were to involve the bombing of civilian targets. Thus, in 1914, the Zeppelin raid remained an unfulfilled threat.

However, the opportunist raids by the RNAS on airship bases were promoted by Churchill as part of a developed strategy to defeat the Zeppelin. This and attempting to intercept returning raids was likely to be far more effective than flying endless standing patrols with low-performance aircraft. More elaborate raids followed, with the Zeppelin factory at Friedrichshafen being bombed on 21 November, and a combined operation against Cuxhaven by seaplane carriers on Christmas Day 1914. The latter raid highlighted a major problem with seaplanes. They had lower performance, due to the weight and drag of their floats and, until float design improved, could only take off in ideal conditions. French and German seaplanes were no better and, in many respects, less developed than British designs.

The viability of using seaplane carriers for fleet operations was compromised by the need for the carrier to stop in order to launch and recover aircraft. This made them and their accompanying ships vulnerable to torpedo attack. Ships converted as seaplane carriers tended to be slower than contemporary warships and this was a further disadvantage, making them more of a liability than an asset.

In fact, the operational limitations of the aircraft in use were becoming clear to all the air forces. The German *Tauben*, being monoplanes, had a restricted downward view that limited their usefulness. The Fokker A1, with celluloid side panels in the fuselage, was little better. The French impressed Morane-Saulnier Parasols, on order for Turkey, and soon realized the advantages of this type for observation, and adopted it as one of a small number of standard designs. The Germans began to see the advantages of biplanes. The LVG BI, which had entered production just before the outbreak of war, was a preferred type but, as with the BE2c, deliveries were slow. The RFC found that its French Blériots were too fragile to be left outside overnight, and the performance of their biplanes seriously compromised when fitted with bombs, wireless or machine-guns. Reserves from the Aircraft Park were soon exhausted, replacement aircraft were slow to arrive and increasing reliance was placed on the French. Joubert was sent to Paris to collect a replacement French aeroplane in August and, again, at the end of September. Strange missed the Marne battle as he was sent to Etampes to have the engine of his Farman overhauled by French mechanics, and then went to Buc to deliver Blériots to the RFC.

Much had been hoped for from the new designs then entering RFC service, some of which had gone to France with the Aircraft Park.

Soon after landing, we saw two very fast machines come in, and on inspection they proved to be Sopwith Tabloids . . . These machines were very speedy for those days, doing nearly 90mph as well as having a good climb. They did not avail us much as fighting machines, but they could and did perform excellently from the scouting point of view.[37]

The increasing aggressiveness of the German airmen, and the desire to disrupt enemy reconnaissance, led to requests for fighting aircraft from mid-September:

Towards the end of September two Bristol Scouts fitted with 80 h.p. Gnomes, arrived from England.[38] No one had accurately foreseen developments as regards fitting machine guns so they could be used with any effect from single-seater machines. The Bristol in No 3 Squadron was fitted with two rifles, one on each side of the fuselage, shooting at an angle of about 45 degrees in order to miss the air-screw.[39]

Innovation remained the order of the day. Strange recorded:

October 2nd – Fixed a safety strap to leading edge of top plane so as to enable passenger to stand up and fire rifle over top of plane and behind. Obtained permission from Major Higgins to try this out . . . Increases range of fire greatly, and I hear that these belts are to be fitted to all machines.[40]

McCudden also recorded of that month:

We were now receiving fairly large bombs for disposal. One type, which was painted red, weighed ten pounds, and had a small parachute attached to give it directional stability; it was called a shrapnel bomb. Another new type, which was called the Melinite bomb, weighed twenty-six pounds, and had a striker in the nose to detonate it. This bomb was really a converted French shell, and was afterwards condemned as being highly unsafe.[41]

The first of the new reconnaissance aircraft ordered by Brancker began to arrive, and Strange recorded that: 'October 15th was a red-letter day for me, for I was given a brand new 80 h.p. Gnome Avro that could put up a much better performance than the Henri Farman.'[42] McCudden agreed: 'These Avros, considering their low power, had a very good performance.'[43]

After the Battle of the Aisne, the so-called 'race to the sea' ensued and, once more, the RFC proved its worth in the reconnaissance role, and then increasingly so, following upon the First Battle of Ypres and the onset of trench warfare which so limited other means of intelligence-gathering. From November the RFC was offered an enormous opportunity to expand into a new role as the only force able to operate beyond the German trench line. The RFC was now the primary intelligence gatherer, offered the best vantage point for directing artillery fire and provided the only means of attacking targets behind the German trench lines.

During the winter, the RFC planned re-organization and re-equipment. New squadrons were forming with experienced pilots posted home to help. Joubert left France in October to command the new 15 Squadron. New aircraft, capable of carrying bombs and machine-gun, while retaining good performance, were demanded. The first of the machine-gun armed Vickers 'Fighting Biplanes' arrived in December. The inferiority of British spherical observation balloons, deployed in France from October, was addressed by ordering copies of the better French *Cacquot* kite balloon. The value of reconnaissance was increased by greater use of photography, allowing trained intelligence officers to interpret information gathered by themselves and not relying on the notes and sketches of the observers. Most importantly, static warfare allowed time for planning and integration, the establishment of a supporting infrastructure which did not need to be mobile, and the decentralization of the RFC by attaching squadrons directly to Army Corps.

The RFC had entered the war under-equipped and under-staffed, failing to achieve a vision set out in 1912. It was an unproven, and thus untrusted, part of the BEF. Four months later, the RFC could claim a significant role in preventing the early defeat of the BEF, was at least as effective as any other air force, either allied or enemy, and was regarded as an essential asset for the planning and execution of any future offensive.

However, by the end of 1914, the RNAS had still failed to address the central issue of the effective operation of aircraft in support of the fleet at sea, and thus the development of systems and procedures to achieve this was also neglected. The RNAS deployed to the Dardanelles in 1915 had no designated observers, and no experience of directing naval gunfire. Instead, the RNAS channelled resources into a range of innovations, including the development of the armoured car.

The Germans concentrated on expansion and re-equipment with better aircraft, more suited to the roles demanded of them. Although there were no plans to bomb Britain with Zeppelins on the outbreak of war, there were thoughts about using aeroplanes, hopefully from an aerodrome at Calais, should it fall to the Germans. In November, an aerodrome was built at Ghiselles near Ostend, for the unit codenamed the *Abteilung Brieftauben Ostend* (Ostend Carrier Pigeon Squadron). From December, Dunkirk was bombed, but the limited range of available aeroplanes precluded attacks on Britain. Zeppelins were capable of carrying a useful bomb load to Britain, but the Army airships fared badly on the Western Front and the Navy had a single operational airship, *L3*, on the outbreak of war. Five more Zeppelins were ordered in 1914, together with five more for the Army, but these were of limited performance and the priority of the High Seas Fleet was to use them as aerial scouts to make up for the shortage of cruisers and undertake defensive reconnaissance in the North Sea looking for British submarines and warships. This situation was to change in the New Year. Like the Eastchurch Squadron, RNAS, the German Navy deployed its own unit in Belgium. This was the *Marine Korps Flandern*, formed in August 1914 but not sent to Belgium until November. The *Wasserflugzeug Abteilung* (seaplane unit) arrived at Zeebrugge on 4 December, and began to patrol the Channel and southern part of the North Sea. Friedrichshafen FF29 seaplanes from Zeebrugge dropped the first bombs on Britain at the end of 1914.

Significantly, the first of the 'Vickers Fighting Biplanes', the FB5 or 'Gunbus', arrived in December. This was of 'pusher' configuration, with a top speed of 70mph, limited to 55mph at its maximum altitude of 9,000 feet. It was fitted with a forward-firing machine-gun but had an unreliable engine. Although the RFC had fought aerial combats already, and with some success, the Vickers was its first fighter aeroplane. 1915 would emphasise that the growing importance of air power required the attack of enemy aircraft and defence of one's own.

Notes

1. *Daily Mail*, 13 November 1906. See also Alfred Gollin, *No Longer an Island: Britain and the Wright Brothers 1902-1909* (Heinemann, 1984), and Alfred Gollin, *The Impact of Air Power on the British People and their Government, 1909-1914* (Stanford University Press, 1989).
2. See Stephen Roskill (ed.), *Documents Relating to the Royal Naval Air Service*, Navy Records Society (1969).
3. Norman MacMillan (ed.), *Sir Sefton Brancker* (Heinemann, 1935), p. 54.
4. Sir Philip Joubert de la Ferté, *The Fated Sky* (White Lion Publishers, 1977), p. 40.
5. MacMillan (ed.), *Sir Sefton Brancker*, pp. 54–5.
6. Ibid, p. 55.
7. Ibid, p. 56.
8. Ibid, pp. 56, 57.
9. Ibid, p. 60.
10. Ibid, p. 53.
11. Ibid, p. 63
12. Joubert de la Ferté, *The Fated Sky*, p. 40.

13. MacMillan (ed.), *Sir Sefton Brancker*, p. 61.
14. Joubert de la Ferté, *The Fated Sky*, p. 40
15. Ibid, p. 40.
16. Major J. T. McCudden, *Flying Fury: Five Years in the Royal Flying Corps* (Wrens Park reprint edition, 2000), p. 23.
17. MacMillan (ed.), *Sir Sefton Brancker*, p. 61
18. Ibid, p. 62
19. Haig's address to the Army Staff College, July 1914, quoted by Philip Hammond, Secretary of State for Defence, in his introduction to the Air Power Conference, 9 July 2014.
20. Joubert de la Ferté, *The Fated Sky*, pp. 42–3.
21. Ibid, pp. 43–4.
22. McCudden, *Flying Fury*, p. 26.
23. Joubert de la Ferté, *The Fated Sky*, p. 45.
24. McCudden, *Flying Fury*, p. 29.
25. Ibid, p. 36.
26. Ibid, p. 36.
27. Ibid, pp. 25–6.
28. Ibid, p. 28.
29. Ibid, p. 32.
30. Bernard Deneckere, *Above Ypres: The German Air Force in Flanders 1914–18* (FireStep Press, 2013), p. 21.
31. Louis A. Strange, *Recollections of an Airman* (The Aviation Book Club reprint edition, 1940), p. 50.
32. Joubert de la Ferté, *The Fated Sky*, pp. 53–4.
33. McCudden, *Flying Fury*, p. 44.
34. Ibid, pp. 46–7.
35. Ibid, p. 45.
36. Joubert de la Ferté, *The Fated Sky*, p. 54.
37. McCudden, *Flying Fury*, p. 34.
38. Ibid, p. 47.
39. Ibid.
40. Strange, *Recollections of an Airman*, p. 64.
41. McCudden, *Flying Fury*, p. 44.
42. Strange, *Recollections of an Airman*, p. 69.
43. McCudden, *Flying Fury*, p. 51.

Suggested Further Reading

Barker, Ralph, *A Brief History of the Royal Flying Corps in World War One* (Robinson, 2002).
Saunders, Hillary S., *Per Ardua: The Rise of British Air Power 1911-1939* (Oxford University Press, 1944).
Brett, R. Dallas, *History of British Aviation, 1908-14* (Air Research Publications, 1987).
Bruce, J. M., *Aeroplanes of the Royal Flying Corps (Military Wing)* (Putnam Publishing Group, 1982).
Castle, Ian, *The Zeppelin Base Raids* (Osprey Publishing Limited, 2011).
Cross and Cockade International: The First World War Aviation Society www.crossand cockade.com
Davies, Richard Bell, *Sailor in the Air: The Memoirs of Vice-Admiral Richard Bell Davies* (Peter Davies, 1967).
Robinson, Douglas H., *The Zeppelin in Combat* (GT Foulis and Company Limited, 1971).
Robinson, Douglas H., *Giants in the Sky: History of the Rigid Airship* (GT Foulis and Company Limited, 1973).
Samson, Charles Rumney, *Fights and Flights* (The Battery Press, 1990).

Chapter 17

The Mobilization and Experience of Nurses in the First World War

* * *

Alison S. Fell

The First World War is usually perceived and remembered through the experiences and perspectives of the men who fought it. However, female nurses enjoyed an unique perspective as chroniclers of the war and its consequences. Vera Brittain, perhaps the most well-known British Voluntary Aid Detachment (VAD) nurse, wrote the following in relation to her decision to write her well-known war memoir *Testament of Youth* in the early 1930s: 'With scientific precision, I studied the memoirs of Blunden, Sassoon, and Graves. Surely, I thought, my story is as interesting as theirs. Besides, I see things other than they have seen, and some of the things they perceived, I see differently.'[1] 'Seeing things differently' can be used more broadly in relation to nurses' roles in and experiences of the First World War. They witnessed the war in a way that no other group could. Their perspective was that of closely-involved participants in a destructive conflict, who were themselves neither combatants nor wounded.

Santanu Das has written compellingly of the 'impotence of sympathy' experienced by nurses, the extent to which their role obliged them to observe a suffering which they were powerless to prevent.[2] His observation allows us to view nurses as trapped in the machinery of war over which they had no power or influence. Yet, in another sense, nurses were not simply passive observers. They had a well-defined role: they healed the wounds of war, they 'patched up' the damaged bodies of their patients, and they offered support, both physical and emotional, to the men they nursed. In this way their perspectives differ, for example, from those of other non-combatants such as the chaplains or civilian relatives who more helplessly watched over the final hours of dying men. Nurses are therefore an important inclusion in any study of the First World War that aims to offer a rounded analysis of the diverse ways in which men and women responded and bore witness to the outbreak of war.

In this chapter I shall outline the mobilization of nurses in the Allied nations in 1914, discuss the different kinds of women who worked in First World War hospitals, and then explore from letters, diaries and memoirs the range of individual nurse responses to their mobilization.[3]

The Mobilization of Nurses in the Allied Nations

In Britain the military medical authorities had a small but well-established military nursing service on which to draw in 1914. There were three branches of the military nursing service: the Queen Alexandra's Imperial Military Nursing Service (QAIMNS), the Queen Alexandra's Imperial Military Nursing Service Reserve (QAIMNSR), and the Territorial Force Nursing Service (TFNS). Members of the military nursing service tended to be elite women, as the Army was keen to produce not only the highest standards of nursing practice, but equally women who came from a relatively high social class and whose appearances and behaviour were deemed appropriate. As nursing historian Sue Light comments: 'Shaking off any past reputation of nurses as being drunken, immoral and untrustworthy, [the British army] insisted that members of the Army Nursing Service and its successors were highly trained and educated women of impeccable social standing.'[4] Their numbers were relatively small in 1914 – around 2,300, but other trained nurses were quickly seconded from civilian hospitals and private homes to join their ranks.

In total, around 20,000 trained British nurses worked in different capacities in war hospitals at home and overseas during the war. These trained nurses were aided by volunteer VADs. The difficulties experienced by the British Army during the Boer War had led to various initiatives to improve the nation's readiness for war. This led to Haldane's 1907 Territorial scheme, and equally led in 1909 to the formation of the VADs, which recruited both male and female members. The idea of these detachments was to have a pool of men and women who could assist the work of the QAIMNS and the TFNS in time of war. By early 1914, 1,757 female and 519 male detachments had been registered with the War Office, whose members were given classes in First Aid and Home Nursing. Some VADs also did a few weeks of 'work experience' in local hospitals. During the war, the VADs were administered by the Joint War Committee of the British Red Cross Society and the Order of St John, and in total between 70,000 and 100,000 women worked as VADs at some point during the war. They worked either in the many large houses converted into convalescent hospitals during the war, in larger military hospitals, or overseas, as was the case with Vera Brittain. Their experiences therefore varied enormously, as did their length of service, which could be anything from a few weeks to five years.

The numbers of British nurses were swelled from the summer of 1915 onwards by the arrival of trained military nurses from Canada, Australia, New Zealand and South Africa, and these women worked in most of the areas of military operations.

In addition, there were British professional and volunteer nurses attached to organizations such as the Belgian and French Red Cross, the First Aid Nursing Yeomanry (FANY), the French Flag Nursing Corps, the Scottish Women's Hospital, and the Women's Sick and Wounded Convoy Corps, or to one of the privately-funded initiatives such as the hospitals set up in France by the Duchess of Sutherland and Duchess of Westminster. These organizations also recruited American volunteers, many of them wealthy women who could afford to travel and support their hospital work from their private incomes.[5] Other American women, such as the wealthy American heiress Mary Borden, set up their own hospitals under the auspices of the French medical authorities.[6]

The mobilization of nurses in other Allied nations depended to a large extent on the development (or lack of development) of the training and professionalization of nursing in the decades leading up to the outbreak of war. On the Western Front, France supplied large numbers of nurses, but only about 6,000 of them were trained nurses, either employed by the French state authorities (the *Assistance publique*), or attached to military hospitals. The majority of French women who nursed during the war were unpaid volunteers. By the end of 1918, more than 100,000 French women were working as nurses for one of the three organisations that made up the French Red Cross, of whom only 30,000 were paid. In addition, there were approximately 10,000 nuns and 10,000 other women who helped in various ways in hospitals.

In Belgium, there were relatively few trained nurses at the outbreak of war – Edith Cavell, who was to become known for the tragic circumstances of her death, was running a training college in Brussels before the war to increase the numbers of nurses. During the war, Belgium welcomed nurses from a range of Allied organizations. For example, Dr Antoine Depage, a Belgian doctor and president of its Red Cross society, recruited both British and French nurses for his well-known *Hôtel de l'Océan* hospital at La Panne.

In Russia, the numbers of Red Cross nurses, who were recruited from 'Sisters of Mercy' communities that were founded by aristocratic women in the nineteenth century, were relatively low at the outbreak of war – about 4,000. Training courses were shortened in a bid to recruit more women, and by 1916 their numbers had risen to 25,000, although there remained a serious shortage of qualified Russian medical personnel throughout the war. Other Allied nations, in which both military nursing and nursing as a profession were still in their infancy in comparison to Britain and the US, equally struggled to provide significant numbers of trained nurses at the outbreak of the war. As in Russia, Italian nurses were drawn from the voluntary sector, and only around 8,000 nurses worked for the Italian Red Cross during the war. Romania and Serbia also recruited volunteer nurses for their respective Red Cross Societies, which had been training volunteers and raising funds since the First Balkan War. These volunteers were often from the upper echelons of society, and as in other nations included members of royal families such as Queen Marie of Romania, who carried out fundraising activities and helped to raise the profile of the Red Cross rather than engaging in any actual nursing work.

The attempts to provide medical expertise to deal with high wartime casualty rates via the Red Cross proved inadequate in certain theatres. For example, the situation in Serbia and Romania was particularly acute in 1915 and 1916, with cholera and typhus epidemics adding to the obstacles already caused by the disadvantages of operating in a country under occupation. It is estimated that 65 per cent of Serbia's military deaths was due to disease rather than enemy action, and a severe shortage of trained personnel, both doctors and nurses, led to calls for help from the Allied nations via the International Red Cross Society. This was quickly forthcoming; organizations from Russia and Britain had already sent teams of doctors and nurses during the Balkan Wars. In some cases, the International Red Cross thereby facilitated the movement of medical personnel from one Allied nation to another. Small teams of Red Cross nurses were sent, for example, to Russia, France and Britain from Japan and Norway. The arrival of the Japanese nurses in particular was widely covered by the press. In other cases, the call for help was heeded by trained personnel from other nations, either individuals or smaller national organizations carrying out fundraising and making their own arrangements. It is for this reason that many of the surviving sources describing conditions and experiences in hospitals at the Serbian front, for example, are from the perspective of British women who volunteered to go there with organizations like the Serbian Relief Fund. Thus, although some trained women, such as British female doctors, were frustrated by the unwillingness of their national authorities to use their skills, so urgent was the need for medical care in certain theatres that 'a woman could find work on her own initiative'.[7]

Women in First World War Hospitals

As the above account makes clear, the kind of women who worked in hospitals, both at home and nearer to the front, varied considerably in terms of their skill, motivation, age, and social and professional background. It is important to distinguish between the women who performed nursing work, as their perspectives and experiences differed from those offering non-medical support. In France, for example, a nation in which political battles between Catholics and Republicans over control of the hospitals had dominated discussions over nursing as a profession in previous decades, Catholic nuns, trained nurses and volunteer Red Cross nurses worked side by side, and French accounts often highlight rivalries between nursing staff from these different sectors of French society. In the British case, the main dividing line was between professional nurses – either those belonging to one of the military nursing organizations or trained nurses who had worked in civilian hospitals before the war but who were mobilized for war-work – and volunteer VAD nurses. The latter underwent some first-aid training and many became highly skilled by the end of the war, but, at least in the first two years of the war, their role was to perform the 'domestic' work of the wards – preparing and serving meals, scrubbing, cleaning, dressing and undressing patients, letter-writing and so on – under the supervision of the trained nurses who performed more of the actual nursing work. The perspective of a trained professional who had already experienced medical trauma was bound to differ from that of an inexperienced volunteer, and this is reflected in the memoirs, letters and journals that both categories of nurses left behind.

In the eyes of the general public, however, volunteer nurses were more prominent than their professional colleagues, and this sometimes caused resentment and tension. Popular postcards and magazine articles often offered a highly romanticised image of nursing, with nurses being portrayed on the one hand as saintly paragons of virtue, or, on the other, as romantic heroines, their feminine charms coming as welcome relief to their soldier-patients. In many cases, little distinction is implied in such popular images between trained and volunteer nurses, whereas in other examples it is more likely to be volunteer nurses who are depicted, as the volunteer nurse functioned as the more respectable, and widely idealised, role-model for middle and upper-class women in all the Allied nations. These two romanticised images of nursing are evident, for example, in the popular magazine illustrations reproduced in the plate section of this book. One is taken from *The Illustrated War News* from October 1914, and illustrates an article discussing the mobilization of women for the French Red Cross. The image directly equates becoming a wartime nurse with 'taking the veil', or joining a religious order, thereby emphasising the role as a kind of sacred vocation. The other is taken from *Newnes Illustrated* from the following year and plays more on the nurse as romantic heroine with the caption 'A French Tommy enjoys an unlooked for pleasure. He little guessed a pretty nurse would manicure his nails in the trenches'. *Newnes Illustrated* was a weekly British magazine dedicated to war news. As with many such cheaply-printed magazines, it was more of a patriotically-inspired morale booster than a strictly informative publication, featuring a preponderance of illustrative material, both photographs and drawings, the latter being very comic-bookish in style, almost juvenile in their depiction of fighting and warfare. Its trivialization and romantic depiction of wartime nursing is therefore at the more extreme end of the spectrum, but it sits alongside a host of other images of nurses as pretty, romantic, heroines.

It is therefore unsurprising that many trained nurses were frustrated at what they saw as the lack of understanding and respect for nurses' work, as well as the public's inability to distinguish between trained and volunteer nurses. In both France and Britain the war represented an opportunity for women to prove their worth in a fight for greater professionalisation (particularly for the state registration of nurses), and they therefore sought public recognition of their service and its value. A French professional nurse, Geneviève Duhamel, for example, is keen in her war memoirs to contrast what she sees as the rose-tinted public image of the nurse with the more gritty reality:

Please don't believe the nice stories that you find in the newspapers several times a week: the model hospital set up in an old château, the wounded decorated officer, with a serious (although aesthetically pleasing) injury, the young nurse, blond beneath her white veil, who gave up dancing the tango for the Red Cross . . . invariably, they fall in love, or were in love, or will fall in love. I've seen more than 700 soldiers in my hospital, several had medals, but the highest ranked officer was the biggest pain in the neck![8]

Sometimes, trained nurses felt that their work was less recognised than that of the volunteer women that they trained and supervised on hospital wards. A 1919 letter published in *The Times*, for example, demanded to know why 'a regular Matron of the official Army Nursing Service, who has served throughout the war, may lay no claim to the war medal which is awarded to any VAD [. . .] not technically in the army at all, with possibly only a few weeks of service to her credit, during which she may have done little or no actual nursing.'[9]

Occasionally, the relationship between VAD volunteers and trained nurses was exacerbated by differences of social class. The former, and especially the ones who served abroad, tended to come from wealthier families, whereas, as the numbers of the military nursing services rapidly grew, the social classes from which they were drawn was more varied. However, this difference of social class should not be exaggerated as the background of both VADs and trained nurses varied. The differences and tensions that sometimes existed between the two groups of women stemmed more from their different motivations and experiences. We can see this if we examine the ways in which volunteer VADs, female doctors and trained nurses wrote about their experiences both during and after the war.

Christine Hallett notes that while VADs often saw themselves as women who 'brought a spark of humanity to the harsh discipline of the military hospital wall', professional nurses were often suspicious of their motives and classed them as 'romantic adventuresses'. Trained nurses had been taught the importance of setting strict emotional boundaries, whereas volunteer VADs were more likely to treat the soldiers as potential friends or comrades.[10] The differences between volunteer and professional nurses' ways of understanding and writing about their wartime work is also related to a broader distinction between 'work' and 'service' that often structured women's wartime roles. As historian Janet Watson argues:

Some members of the population, both male and female, while generally articulating a clear patriotism, saw their efforts on behalf of the war as work, Professional soldiers and trained nurses, for example, both identified an opportunity for career advancement. [. . .] Workers in munitions factories or women leaving domestic service, saw a chance for better wages and working conditions. [. . .] Other people in active war work, including some volunteer soldiers and volunteer nurses, identified more strongly with different conceptions of service – for King, Country or Empire.[11]

Whereas individual motivations for, and experiences of, war work obviously varied enormously, a broad distinction between 'work' and 'service' can be helpful in a discussion of the variation in nurses' attitudes towards, and written accounts of, their wartime lives. Professional nurses were more likely to understand their nursing practice as 'work' – albeit in a profession that was still often understood as a 'vocation' – and work that demanded appropriate pay and conditions from the state that would recognise their skills and experience. In contrast, the opening paragraph of a recruitment letter from Katharine Furse, head of the VAD, states:

> We hear a great deal about V.A.D. work. Praise and criticism but chiefly praise which is well deserved because both men and women have worked patiently and indefatigably without advertisement and with no thought of self except in a few who dress up in our uniform and are photographed for some picture paper. V.A.D. members serve. They fill the many unavoidable gaps in the care of the Sick and Wounded and they fill them so well that their nick-name, 'V.A.D.', which really stands for the Detachment and not for the individual is known throughout the whole country.[12]

We can see here that the idea of 'service', of selfless devotion to one's country in a time of crisis, is central to the recruitment rhetoric deployed by the VAD during the war.

The majority of women in hospital wards were employed as nurses, but it is important to note that there were also some female doctors who worked in First World War hospitals. For British female doctors, there were few opportunities on the Western Front, as they were not employed by the British army. In response to this, a few pioneering women decided to go it alone. Dr Elsie Inglis was a Scottish doctor and suffragist. In 1914, aged 49 and with 16 years of hospital experience behind her, she offered her services to the Royal Army Medical Corps (RAMC), but was turned down. However, Inglis used this opportunity to set up the Scottish Women's Hospitals for Foreign Service, which ran field hospitals and dressing stations in France, Serbia, Turkey and Russia. They performed valuable and skilled work in some of the most difficult circumstances. Interned in Serbia, Inglis returned home where she discovered she had cancer, but carried on her work, taking another unit to Russia. She died the day after she returned to Britain in November 1917.

Inglis was fighting battles on more than one front during the war: she was fighting to save the lives of men threatened by wounds and disease, and to prove women doctors could do wartime medical work as well as men. The female doctors, nurses and medical students who went with Inglis and the Scottish

Women's Hospital Units to nations who were desperate for trained medical staff, such as Serbia, Romania and Russia, often found working conditions that were particularly taxing. A lack of suitable premises, combined with constant movement due to invasion and retreat, a shortage of supplies, and epidemics of diseases like typhoid and cholera, could make the provision of effective medical care almost impossible.

Ellie Rendel was a final-year medical student when she signed up with a Scottish Women's Hospital Unit in August 1916, and worked in Romania and Russia. Her diary describes the terrible conditions with which her Units were sometimes faced, such as the following description of a hospital in Russia: 'Started to clean the hospital in afternoon. The dirt indescribable. Rubbish of every kind on the floor. Stores filled with old dressings, black beetles hopping about. Yard full of old bones, dressings and scrap iron. Dust & refuse inches deep.' Despite this, Ellie clearly relished the challenge, and her letters are resolutely cheerful, making light of the circumstances with sentences like 'We are as civilised as we can be but even doing our best we can't help being rather piggy' and 'Our outfit was not designed for city life and after camping and trekking and living in hovels for 3 months we feel most terribly shabby and ragged.'[13]

Women's Experiences of Mobilization as Nurses: Something so New

One of the most striking aspects of letters, diaries and memoirs produced by both trained and volunteer nurses, especially in the early months of their nursing service in a particular theatre of war, is their focus on the newness of their experience. For nurses who were posted abroad, their diaries can sometimes read like travel memoirs rather than accounts of life working in a military hospital. For example, two entries in the diary of VAD Sara Wilsdon, reveal her excitement at being in such an exotic location. They are accompanied by a photograph of her with two other VAD's riding camels. 'We need not have bothered to bring so many supplies with us as Cairo is strangely European – in parts – the native quarters are fascinating – such filthy bundles of rags on two legs & the women in black with nothing but their eyes showing. The Sphynx makes one feel such an uneducated, ignorant woman. She looks as if she knew, and kept all the hidden secrets of the world.' – and – 'I feel as if I were on a holiday – the best I've ever had. Took Hall to the 70th General, next door to see Pepper, who is there. Waugh took us through the Native Bazaars in Cairo. It was like something out of the Arabian Nights.' A young middle-class woman from Durham, she had never travelled. As was the case with many nurses who worked overseas, initially it is the novel experience of travel that the war brought her rather than that of nursing sick and wounded men that is most in evidence in her account.[14]

Sometimes what was new for nurses was the diversity of the patients they nursed. They often write about encounters with men of different races and nationalities. Many of them kept albums as mementoes of an experience they would never forget. The albums have photographs, sketches and short messages by both nurses and patients. One such album was kept by Ada Bramley, a trained British nurse who worked for the French Red Cross in a hospital in a converted college near Lyon.[15] Ada's album is full of warm notes of gratitude and thanks from French soldiers, many of whom also gave her copies of their photographs. An interesting aspect of this album is the reference the soldiers often make to the Franco-British alliance in their entries, seeing in Ada the embodiment of the willingness of British men and women to support French soldiers. One French soldier, for example, states: 'It is from the bottom of my heart that I thank Miss Ada Bramley for all the care she has given me as a night nurse on my ward. I will have good memories of my stay in hospital. Vive les Alliés!' Another comments that before meeting Ada he was prejudiced against the British, but his experience as her patient had changed his mind for good and convinced him of the 'brotherhood' of the French and British.

Of course, in the First World War the new encounters experienced by nurses were not only with soldiers from Allied nations but also from their respective Empires. Many nurses' diaries, letters and memoirs mention treating men from India and West Africa.[16] Some of these accounts of nursing non-white men are deeply marked by dominant imperialist discourses: the colonised soldier appears as infantilised and as a loyal 'simpleton soldier', as an exotic ethnographic 'type', or as a bloodthirsty 'savage native'. At other times, however, encounters with Indian and African soldiers provoke strong and unexpected responses, especially from nurse-narrators who were often interacting for the first time with non-white men from the colonies. It is possible to detect a fascination for the colonial soldiers' bodies and cultural habits, for example. Furthermore, in the case of nurses who spent extended periods of time interacting with their non-white patients, it is possible to chart an evolution in their attitudes, as well as evidence of the difficulties they experienced in trying to nurse men with whom communication was limited to a few words and gestures.

An interesting example can be found in a British memoir published anonymously in 1915 by the professional nurse Kate Evelyn Luard, *Diary of a Nursing Sister on the Western Front 1914-15*. Luard trained in London in the 1890s, and served in the QAIMNSR in the Boer War. She then held senior positions in several hospitals before going to France in 1914. She received the Royal Red Cross Medal in 1916, a bar in 1919, and was twice mentioned in despatches.[17] She was quite evidently an experienced professional when she nursed Indian troops on hospital trains in 1914–15, and her writing manifests a shift towards greater individualisation and understanding, despite the continued dominance of a confident colonial voice. Early in her diary she expresses her frustration at the inability of her Indian patients to articulate their needs and symptoms: 'The badly wounded Indians are such pathetic babies, just as inarticulate to us and crying as if it was a crèche' and in another entry attempts brief characterisations according to ethnic 'type': 'The Sikhs are rather whiney patients and very hard to please, but the little Gurkhas are absolute stoics and the Bengal Lancers, who are

Mohammedans, are splendid'.[18] Later on, however, she remarks: 'Three of my sitting-up Indians have temperatures of 104, so you can imagine what the lying-downs are like. They are very anxious cases to look after, partly because they are another race and partly because they can't explain their wants, and they seem to want to be let die quietly in a corner rather than fall in with your notions of their comfort.' Here, Luard reveals her frustration at her inability to perform her work in a satisfactory way and shows an increasing awareness of the problems created for nurses by language and cultural barriers with their Indian patients.

Another interesting example of nursing colonial soldiers can be found in the semi-fictionalised memoirs of Madeleine Clemenceau Jacquemaire, the daughter of the French Prime Minister. She had joined the French Red Cross in Bordeaux in 1914, where she was living with her father. She went on to publish her memoir *Les Hommes de bonne volonté* [*Men of Good Will*] in 1919, which often focuses on the hard conditions and psychological burdens of nursing work in the war, commenting for example on the heart-wrenching dilemmas faced by nurses who are asked to help heal soldiers only to send them back to the Front. One chapter offers a tragic account of the death of Kissis-a-Daouddah, a named French West African soldier. She describes in admiring tones his beauty and dignity when facing death:

> His skin was chestnut brown, very dark and shiny, like the wood of old furniture polished by generations of good housewives, and the damp purple cloth that crowned his head was arranged in such an original way that it was clear that the black soldier had redone the normal bandaging provided by the dressing station in his own fashion. [. . .] A human being could not have more dignity than did this bare naked soldier.

This description is ethnographic in tone, albeit positive in its dignified admiration of the soldier's body. However, what is more unusual is her final comment on his fate: 'Kissis will die and man loses his beauty before his life. He will die, in this climate so fatal for his race, for those who defeated his parents and annexed their territory.' Here, Madeleine Jacquemaire voices the irony of the fate of French African soldiers, who risked their lives for their colonisers. Treating patients from far-flung parts of the British and French empires therefore led some nurses to offer a more nuanced and more individualised account of colonial soldiers than that usually found in propagandistic postcards or newspaper articles.

Another, crucial, aspect of what was 'new' for First World War nurses concerns the kinds of wounds and illnesses they were dealing with, and the conditions under which they were working. Some of the nurses, and especially volunteer nurses who had not established psychological mechanisms necessary in dealing with witnessing medical trauma and extreme suffering, clearly wrote diaries and memoirs as a means of coming to terms with the disturbing nature of some of the cases they encountered. This can be seen in graphic descriptions of bodily mutilation that are often an important element in nurse narratives, and betray at least some sense of the psychological impact of the repeated sight of hitherto unimaginable bodily mutilation and suffering wrought by new weapons and worsened by the inadequate circumstances in which frequently the nurses had to work, especially in the first two years of the war. Gas warfare, burns, facial wounds, blinding, massive wounds from shell fragments, gangrene, death, could be, to say the least, a challenge to all but the most experienced nurse.

In the early years of the war, a key problem for the medical services was the infection that set in as wounded men were transported from battlefield to hospital. The length of time it took to do this (and of course the absence of antibiotics), meant that many soldiers died from infection rather than from the wound itself. Nurses often wrote of the difficulties of witnessing the damage caused to men's bodies by the new industrialised weapons of war.

Despite the patriotic tenor of many French and British nurse diaries and memoirs, it is clear that the daily spectacle of death and physical misery was at times difficult to bear, and in some cases led to psychological crises. It was, moreover, far from easy for women to record what they were seeing. In terms of memoirs published during the conflict, too much realism risked censorship. Further, even if the text were not intended originally for publication, women had not traditionally written in physical detail about bodies and did not have this as an accepted convention on which to draw. The technique most often used by the nurse-narrators when describing the mutilated bodies of their patients is simply to list the injuries without any commentary, deploying numbed, medicalised and apparently detached language. What is striking about the accounts written by many nurses is that the kind of injuries that they feel moved to write about tend to be the most disfiguring and dehumanising. Noëlle Roger, a Swiss writer who claimed to be publishing the memoirs of a nurse who had recently died, for example includes in her *Carnets d'une infirmière* [*Notebooks of a Nurse*] the following description:

> Oh! All the dreadful injuries that merge into each other in my memory: broken and shattered legs and arms. An ear hanging off, pierced by a bullet; a man with a swollen face, his mouth moved to one side. Another with a large portion of cheek missing. Another with a hole in his shoulder so big that one could put one's hand in it.[19]

Similar graphic descriptions appear in the recently published diary of a French nun from a nursing order who worked as a nurse in the occupied region of France: 'At about six o'clock, arrival in theatre of several seriously injured men from yesterday's battle – one no longer has a jawbone, and in addition he's wounded in his elbow, left leg and little finger. He's a real wreck of a man.'[20]

The American Mary Borden is equally graphic in her description of the ways in which men's injuries blurred the lines between human and non-human, and even between men and women: 'There are no men here, so why should I be a woman?

There are heads and knees and mangled testicles. There are chests with holes as big as your fist, and pulpy thighs, shapeless, and stumps where legs once were fastened. . . how could I be a woman and not die of it?'[21]

We should remember that unlike the text written by Sister Saint-Eleuthère, the French nun, Borden's text was written for publication, and she has crafted it in order to evoke pathos and sympathy from the reader, as well as to express her anti-war views. Nevertheless, it is similar to many descriptions of wounds in nurse memoirs, and all of these passages share a number of features. They focus relentlessly on the dehumanising aspect of the injuries suffered by First World War soldiers, the extent to which war has transformed young men into an unrecognisable jumble of misshapen body parts. Literary critics Jane Marcus and Margaret Higonnet have argued that these kinds of descriptions in nurse memoirs bear the hallmarks of a form of what was at the time referred to as shell-shock. They argue that the graphic nature of the images and the concentration on obscene details are suggestive of a type of 'hypersensitivity'. They also contend that the extent to which such images are evoked again and again can be compared with Freud's observation when treating shell-shocked soldiers that his patients were marked by a 'compulsion to repeat' their nightmarish experiences in the trenches, and were thus stuck in a psychological impasse.[22] There is plenty of evidence that, like their soldier patients, nurses suffered from both exhaustion and mental breakdowns as a result of their war experiences. The pension files kept at the British National Archives, for example, include those of several nurses diagnosed with 'neurasthenia', a catch-all term used during the period to refer to a range of mental health problems.[23] To try and deal with the potential breakdowns of nurses, the Army provided rest homes for them, and their service records sometimes note periods of time spent recuperating away from the hospitals.

To conclude, reading their letters, diaries and memoirs reveals that both trained and volunteer nurses perceived their work in the First World War to be valuable, showing pride in their essential contribution to the care of the sick and wounded. They also frequently express the extent to which they found the work, or the conditions of the hospitals, ships, trains and dressing stations where they nursed, to be challenging. For volunteers, the exposure to the realities of medical trauma, to the physical destruction caused by shrapnel, gas and other weaponry, was often shocking and sometimes traumatic. For professional nurses, the sheer numbers of men they were treating, and the prevalence of wounds and illnesses that they were not accustomed to dealing with, stretched the limits of their previous skills and experience.

Alice Slythe, an experienced trained nurse and a member of the TFNS, for example, kept a diary from 1914–16, when she worked in hospitals at bases behind the Western Front. In it, she records both her pride at her work and her despair at her inability to heal more of the servicemen whom she treats. Alongside many interjections at her pride in the excellence of her work and that of her fellow 'Terriers' (or TFNS nurses) there are occasional signs of strain in relation to the helplessness she sometimes experienced in relation to the care of the sick and wounded: 'The other Sisters all say they are glad & thankful to see the men die when they are really desperate, but I can not get used to it & I can't bear them all dying like flies, it seems as if we could prevent it & yet I know we can't.'[24] More generally though, even if nurses' memoirs provide evidence of the physical and psychological strain they were under, they rarely reveal overtly anti-war sentiments, especially in the early years of the war. They are largely accepting of the task in hand, and record the ways in which wartime nursing took them out of their usual environments in ways that were in turn exciting, challenging and, sometimes, traumatic.

Notes

1. Vera Brittain, 'War Service in Perspective', in George A. Panichas (ed.), *Promise of Greatness: The War of 1914-1918* (New York: Day, 1968), pp. 363–76.
2. Santanu Das, *Touch and Intimacy in First World War Literature* (Cambridge: Cambridge University Press, 2005).
3. An earlier version of my account of Allied nursing can be found in Christine E. Hallett and Alison S. Fell, 'Introduction', in Christine E. Hallett and Alison S. Fell (eds), *First World War Nursing: New Perspectives* (New York: Routledge, 2013), pp. 1–14.
4. Sue Light, www.scarletfinders.co.uk [Accessed 7 September 2014]. This website is to be highly recommended for offering an excellent introduction to researching British First World War nurses as well as reproducing valuable primary sources.
5. Subsequently, when the US entered the war in 1917, further trained military nurses were mobilized. Over 21,000 women served in the US Army Nurse Corps, 10,660 of them with the American Expeditionary Force.
6. Borden went on to publish her nursing memoir *The Forbidden Zone*, a hard-hitting account of a French military hospital that has recently been re-published and which has the hallmarks of a modernist literary text. Mary Borden, *The Forbidden Zone: A Nurse's Impression of the First World War* (London: Hesperus Press, 2008).
7. Leah Leneman, 'Medical Women and War 1914-1918', *Medical History* 38 (1994), pp. 160–77.
8. Geneviève Duhamel, *Ces dames de l'hôpital 336 [These ladies of Hospital 336]* (Paris: Albin Michel, 1917). This and all further translations from the original French are my own.
9. Anonymous letter, *The Times*, 18 August 1919.
10. Christine E. Hallett, 'Emotional Nursing': Involvement, Engagement and Detachment in the Writings of First World War Nurses and VADs' in Fell and Hallett, *First World War Nursing*, pp. 87–102 (p. 99).
11. Janet S. K. Watson, *Fighting Different Wars: Experience, Memory and the First World War in Britain* (Cambridge: Cambridge University Press, 2004), pp. 5–6.
12. Katharine Furse, Recruitment letter to VADs, 1917. Reproduced at www.scarletfinders.co.uk
13. Frances Elinor Rendel, Private Papers, Documents 20400, Imperial War Museum, London.
14. A radio drama based on the diaries of Sara Wilsdon entitled *The Camel Hospital* was broadcast in 2011 on Radio 4 *Woman's Hour*. The diaries are in the Liddle Collection, the University of Leeds.
15. I would like to express my gratitude to Sue Johnson, who generously shared her album and the photograph of her great aunt Ada Bramley with me.
16. For an extended discussion of this aspect of nurses' experiences see Alison S. Fell, 'Nursing the Other: the representation of colonial troops in French and British nursing memoirs', in Santanu Das, *Race, Empire and First World War Writing* (Cambridge: Cambridge University Press, 2011), pp. 158–75.

17. Unlike many professional First World War nurses, Luard praised the work of VADs in a 1922 letter to the *British Journal of Nursing*. In addition to the anonymous *Diary of a Nursing Sister on the Western Front 1914-15,* she published *Unknown Warriors*, a collection of further diary extracts, in 1930, which has been republished this year.
18. Anonymous [Kate Evelyn Luard], *Diary of a Nursing Sister on the Western Front 1914-15* (Edinburgh: William Blackwood and Sons, 1915), p. 57.
19. Noëlle Roger, *Les Carnets d'une Infirmière* [*Notebooks of a Nurse*] (Paris: Attinger Frères, 1915), p. 39.
20. Soeur Saint-Eleuthère, *Les carnets de guerre d'une soeur infirmière* [*Notebooks of a nursing sister*] (Noyon: Ysec éditions, 2003), p. 56.
21. Borden, *The Forbidden Zone*, p. 44.
22. See Margaret R. Higonnet, 'Introduction', in Margaret R. Higonnet (ed.), *Nurses at the Front: Writing the Wounds of War* (Boston: Northeastern University Press, 2001) and Jane Marcus, 'Corpus/Corps/Corpse: Writing the Body in/at War', in Helen M. Cooper et al. (eds), *Arms and the Woman* (Chapel Hill: University of North Carolina Press, 1989), pp. 124–67.
23. See TNA PIN 26.
24. Sister Alice Slythe, Diary, 25 June 1916, Liddle Collection, WO 107, University of Leeds.

Suggested Further Reading

Fell, Alison S. and Christine E. Hallett (eds), *First World War Nursing: New Perspectives* (New York: Routledge, 2013).
Hallett, Christine E., *Containing Trauma: Nursing Work in the First World War* (Manchester: Manchester University Press, 2009).
Hallett, Christine E., *Veiled Warriors: Allied Nurses of the First World War* (Oxford: Oxford University Press, 2014).
Harris, Kirsty, *More Bombs than Bandages: Australian Army Nurses at Work in World War I* (Newport: Big Sky Publishing, 2010).
Higonnet, Margaret R., *Nurses at the Front: Writing the Wounds of the Great War* (Boston: Northeastern University Press, 2001).
Macdonald, Lynn, *The Roses of No Man's Land* (London: Michael Joseph, 1980).
Powell, Anne, *Women in the War Zone: Hospital Service in the First World War* (Stroud: The History Press, 2009).

PART THREE

Chapter 18

Tracing Your Family's History in the Great War

* * *

Chris Baker

It is all my grandfather's fault. He died two years before I was born, so I had no chance to talk to him about his experience in the Great War. A single photograph in which he appears in army uniform and one of his medals were all that remained in our family, but they were enough to inspire me to want to find out more. After all I am a boy from that 1960s era of the *Victor* comic, Airfix kits and English v. German war games at playtime. It was a thrill to think that my own grandfather had been a soldier. Judging from stories handed down, he was also the most interesting and intriguing character in my immediate family.

Grandfather had apparently run away to sea at a young age and been in the Navy for many years before 1914, although we had no trace of evidence that this was the case. My own faltering entry into researching him began back to the days when all army service records were still held by the Ministry of Defence. You had to write to the people there for information – and all they would do was to send a typed summary. To my immense disappointment they said they had nothing on my grandfather's military or naval service. How could that possibly be? Years later, once the army service records had been released to the public and were on microfilm at the National Archives, we found him. There he was – Gunner 2245 Frank Hubert Wilson, Royal Field Artillery – with details of his enlistment, training, move to France, disciplinary record and the occasion on which he was severely wounded. I am still thinking of asking for my money back from the MOD. They had simply not done their job. The records have now been digitised, and the data entry clerks creating the index have spelled his name incorrectly and given the wrong regiment. Perhaps he is destined to remain difficult to find.

It was digitisation of records (with accurate indexing this time) and a very lucky break that allowed me to discover my grandfather's service at sea. It came from a wholly unexpected direction. The National Archives collection of militia service records was digitised and when they became available on the internet I entered his

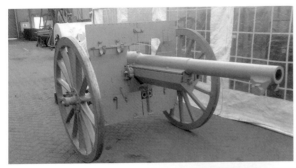

The famous French 75 field gun, *Canon de Mle 75, 1897.* (Courtesy of the Trustees of the Royal Armouries)

Canon de Mle 75, 1897, showing the breech mechanism (Courtesy of the Trustees of the Royal Armouries).

The German field gun, 77mm *FK 96 n.A.* (Courtesy of the Trustees of the Royal Armouries).

The British field gun, the 18-pounder Quick-Firing Gun. (Courtesy of the Trustees of the Royal Armouries).

French cuirassiers,
Paris, August 1914.
(Wikimedia Commons)

Mules floundering
in the mud of the
Western Front.
(Canada in the
Great War Series)

German motorcycle
pigeon carrier.
(http://justacarguy.bl
ogspot.com/)

British pilot with 'flying fox' mascot. (Mary Evans Picture Library)

Airedale messenger and first aid dogs, the latter wearing a gasmask. ('Animals in War Dedication Project, Canada')

Canadian War Memorial to Animals. ('Animals in War Dedication Project, Canada')

The Henri Farman F20, designed by a Englishman living in France. The F20 was built under licence at Hendon, its 'pusher' configuration giving both crew a better forward and downward view than the BE2. By moving the flying controls to the rear seat, the F20 could be fitted with a machine-gun easily but the added weight quite considerably affected the aircraft's performance. (Nick Forder)

Zeppelin *L3,* the sole operational rigid airship available to the German Navy on the outbreak of war. Its intended role was maritime reconnaissance. (Nick Forder)

Royal Aircraft Factory BE2. The pilot sat in the rear seat and the observer in the front. The view of the pilot was relatively good, but the wing struts and propeller hampered the work of the observer. In contemporary German aircraft, the observer was the aircraft commander and sat in the rear seat. The machine's top speed was 65–70 mph, maximum height, 10,000 feet, and it carried fuel for three hours. The developed BE2c, designed to fly 'straight and level' to allow inexperienced crew to concentrate on their work, was being prepared for production as war broke out. (Nick Forder)

Mobile Wireless Ground Station. Sefton Brancker wrote of such a vehicle: 'An old fashioned Royal Engineers' wireless wagon drawn by horses accompanied the transport, and perturbed the disembarkation officer at Boulogne considerably. He pointed out that no horses were allowed for in the mobilization tables of the RFC, and wanted to prevent their disembarkation in consequence.' (Nick Forder)

William Sefton Brancker was born in 1877, joining the Royal Artillery in 1896. He served in the Boer War and in India, where he made his first flight in 1910. He obtained his Royal Aero Club certificate in 1913. Brancker was appointed Assistant Director of Military Aeronautics in October, 1913. He was killed in the crash of the *R101* airship in 1930. (Royal Aero Club)

Philip Bennet Joubert de la Ferté was born in India in 1887. He served with the Royal Field Artillery from 1907 to 1913, when he was seconded to the RFC. Joining the BEF as part of the initial deployment of 3 Squadron, he flew one of the first two reconnaissances by the RFC. Joubert ended the war commanding the RAF in Italy, and continued serving as a regular officer until 1945. (Royal Aero Club)

Louis Arbon Strange. Strange was born in 1891, learned to fly in 1913, and applied for a commission in the RFC soon afterwards. He graduated from the Central Flying School in May, 1914. He joined 5 Squadron and flew a Farman F20 to France on 15 August. Strange won a bar to his Great War Distinguished Flying Cross for rescuing a Hurricane fighter plane from advancing Germans in 1940! (Royal Aero Club)

James Byford McCudden was born in 1895 and enlisted in the Royal Engineers in 1910 as a boy soldier. He joined the RFC in 1913 to become an engine fitter, with aspirations to be a pilot, and went to France with 3 Squadron. Promoted Corporal in November 1914, McCudden began to fly regularly, as an observer. He learned to fly in 1916, and after service with 20 Squadron, was to fly DH2 fighters with Number 29 Squadron. He scored his first confirmed victory in September1916, and was to achieve phenomenal success thereafter. Following upon his posting to 29 Squadron, he was to serve with 66 and 56 Squadrons. In March 1918 he was awarded the Victoria Cross. McCudden died from injuries sustained in a flying accident on 9 July 1918, *en route* to assume command of 60 Squadron. (Royal Aero Club)

Nurse Ada Bramley. (Family permission)

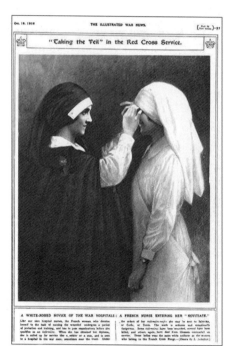

A Novitiate French nurse, *Illustrated War News,* 1916.

Adolphus, the mascot of Maurice le Blanc Smith, the Commanding Officer of 73 Squadron, RFC/RAF. 1918. (Liddle Collection, University of Leeds)

The popular image of the nurse, *Newnes Illustrated,* June 1915.

An annotated photograph from the album of T. L. W. Stallibrass, an Observer in 3 Squadron RFC, makes clear the loss of life in the air during the Battle of the Somme, in 1916. (Liddle Collection, University of Leeds)

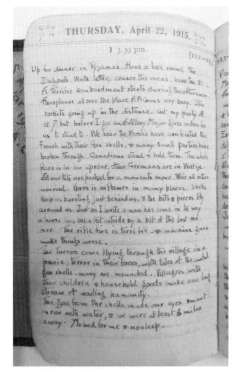

The envelope from a letter to the Field Punishment Barracks, Boulogne, where the recipient, Howard Marten, is being held, in June 1916, under arrest for Court-Martial proceedings for his refusal to drill. Marten was a Conscientious Objector, drafted into the Non Combatant Corps and sent to France. He was the first Conscientious Objector to be sentenced to death. The sentence was commuted. (Liddle Collection, University of Leeds)

A graphic diary account by a Sapper officer, of the panic spread initially by the German use of gas at the Second Battle of Ypres in April 1915. (N. C. Harbutt, Liddle Collection, University of Leeds)

A dramatic moment, 18 March 1915, at the Dardanelles, with the close-range bombardment of the Turkish forts. The battlecruiser, HMS *Inflexible,* has struck a mine; she may sink. Ratings strain at the capstan to haul a collision mat over the rent in the warship's beam. Two Royal Marine bandsmen play their fiddles to give rhythm to their efforts. (B. Sebastian, Liddle Collection, University of Leeds)

Lawnswood Cemetery, Leeds. The Ives
Memorial. (Andrea Hetherington)

Lawnswood Cemetery, Leeds. The War
Memorial. (Andrea Hetherington)

Lawnswood Cemetery, Leeds.
One of the brass plaques
adorning the War Memorial.
(Andrea Hetherington)

name, just from idle curiosity, but to my great surprise up he came. He had enlisted into the militia of the Royal Warwickshire Regiment and very soon afterwards was discharged as he had gone to sea – with the Royal Marines. Not only that, he had done so using a false name. No wonder the MOD could not find his naval story! By this time, the Royal Marine records had also been digitised and a quick search using the false name soon revealed his full story. I am indebted to the anonymous army clerk who had the presence of mind to note on his Royal Warwickshire papers the false name that my grandfather used when going to the Marines. How he came to know of it is still not clear to me, or why he troubled to write the details at all, but it proved to be my breakthrough. In a sense, the fact that we now know so much of my grandfather's story has come about because of three great developments in researching servicemen of the era: the release of records into the public domain; the cataloguing, indexing and digitisation of the records; and the evolution of a community of interested people who freely offer their help and expertise.

Finding out about my grandfather Frank might be said to be my first step into my eventual move into a full-time job as an independent military researcher, historian and occasional battlefield guide. By 1995 I was a veteran of many years of study of the Great War. Coupling my military history interest with another hobby of messing about with computers, I began a website about the British Army in the period. Called 'The Long, Long Trail', the site has long since been one of the most visited on the subject, with thousands of people using it every day. It spawned the discussion community, the 'Great War Forum', which has tens of thousands of members. It also led to people contacting me for help, and ultimately to my giving up my former career to concentrate on providing that help. I am grateful to every one of the 7,000 or so clients who have asked so far, for I have enjoyed researching every man and have learned something from each one.

Many people will just look things up, but I have always set out to do much more than that and really to determine who the man was, what happened to him and what effect it had on his life. No two men's stories are completely alike and I have found that to get under the skin and understand what took place and why, it is necessary to build up a body of knowledge of military law, regulations, methods of enlistment, army structures, regimental numbering schemes, battle histories, the social environment of the Great War period and of genealogy. Things have changed, research-wise, to the point where one might almost say that finding stuff is easy – anyone can do that – interpreting and understanding it all is the hard part and it requires broad and deep knowledge.

The Documented History of a Soldier

The following comments relate to soldiers of the British Army but the position with regard to men of the naval and air services is not dissimilar. We are fortunate in that the military life of a soldier was documented in great detail, mainly using forms that had been specifically designed for the purpose. Beginning with the form used to record the man's personal details at his enlistment, the documentation covered his postings to units, his medical history, disciplinary record, wounding, captivity, death or discharge from service. The longer and more complex the man's story, the more forms and more details recorded upon them. This collection of army forms is usually known as his 'service record'. In addition to this, there are documents to do with the issue of campaign medals, any pension that related to his service, gallantry medals and other special awards, and, in the case of officers, his promotions and appointments recorded in the 'Army List'. National newspapers carried casualty lists and reports and obituaries of officers; the local press often included portrait photographs, letters from the men, reports of their progress and well-being and often more. Taken together, the documentary evidence of a given soldier's military service can run to dozens of pieces of information. Sadly, in about 65 per cent of cases much or all of the 'army service record' was destroyed in an air raid fire that gutted the Army Record Centre at Walworth in South London in 1940. Destruction of a record in this way inevitably means that some of the finer details are lost forever, but most men's stories can be reconstructed to some extent by reference to the other types of information. This is Great War history at the most granular level. The records provide us with the rich minutiae of exactly how the military forces worked and how it affected the individual. How many campaign and battle histories have been written without any real comprehension of who the men were, how they were trained, whether they were good or bad soldiers, what physical condition they were in – that is other than for a few notable men – and when the author's focus is on the men, it is at the most meaningless aggregated level? Admittedly it has until recent years been difficult to determine these things but this has now changed. I expect many more histories now to take a much closer look at the men in the ranks and their regimental officers.

Finding the information that exists on an individual has become very much easier and quicker over the past two decades, mainly through digitisation and availability through the internet. With the imminent launch by Naval & Military Press of the campaign medal rolls, digitisation of most of the major documentary sources for non-commissioned soldiers who had left the army before 1921 will be complete. There are important exceptions: officers' service records and those of men of the Royal Marine Labour Corps are intact (although reduced by 'weeding') but still only available to see as originals at the National Archives, and records of many home and women's organisations are elusive. The records of most men at brigadier-general and above, are not generally available and it is not even clear if they were still to exist.

Records of disablement pensions are now in the hands of the Western Front Association, but may also be covered by the holdings of the War Pensions Agency in Blackpool. The army service records of men who were in the army in 1922 or later are still held by the Ministry of Defence, as yet with no announced date or method for release into the public domain.

Family Research

It seems that most of my clients are interested in the military story of their soldier, especially if he lost his life in the Great War, but are at least equally motivated by understanding his part in the family story. In some cases our clients express explicit hopes that the military records will provide information about the soldier's date of birth, the names of his parents, where he lived, whom he married and so on. This appears especially true if he has a relatively common name and that a genealogical approach (searching births, censuses, marriages, etc) has not helped.

Military records can be most helpful in this regard, depending on which documents have survived. In general, the man's next of kin and private addresses will only appear in his service and pension records, or in the registers of the Commonwealth War Graves Commission if he lost his life and his next of kin confirmed the information. His age might appear in the roll of the Silver War Badge denoting a man's honourable discharge, unfit for further service. Even without these things it is sometimes possible through an examination using his number to derive when and where he enlisted. In many cases we have found this led us to identify that he had been a pre-war regular soldier and we then went on to find him with his regiment in the 1911 census: that also gives us his age. In other words, it is far from guaranteed that military searches can provide family information but it is certainly possible.

State of Play

In comparative terms, Australia led the way in digitisation of its Great War service records. Australian army service records and the war diaries of its units and formations were among the first to be digitised, are available from a single source and are free to the user. Canada is not far behind, but for some years only had limited digitisation of each man's service record. This is now being addressed and it is likely that Canada will match Australia for the excellence of its search, the quality of its digitisation and the fact that the service is free of charge. New Zealand is now well into its digitisation. I am afraid that Britain makes for a sad comparison.

Each type of record has been licenced by the National Archives to different providers, each of which is a commercial venture and hungry for your money. Both Ancestry and Findmypast now have the digitised versions of the surviving army service records, which they allow you to search free of charge but one must pay for access. Quality of indexing has in some areas to date been little short of scandalous and searching has been rendered far too difficult as a result, although this appears to have been the subject of remedial attention in recent times. They are of course just one of many types of record that these service providers hold, and in general their services are focused on the genealogist rather than the military historian. The National Archives and Ancestry have campaign medal index cards, while Findmypast has a transcript of the card. Ancestry has the Silver War Badge rolls, whereas Findmypast has a transcript. None yet has a digitised version of the much more important campaign medal rolls, but this is the subject of Naval & Military Press's forthcoming development.

For the would-be researcher, it is now a little bewildering to be faced with a number of service providers claiming through their advertising to have army records, when in fact one of the heavier advertisers does not have them at all, and to sweep through all of the various types of digitised records would require working with at least two, and in most soldier's cases more like three to five, different providers of information. So the message is most definitely 'buyer beware' and my advice to researchers is to take time thoroughly to understand exactly what is on offer before you pay.

Researching soldiers has become a potentially expensive business, although Ancestry and Findmypast occasionally offer short periods of free or heavily-discounted access. Thank goodness that the records of the Commonwealth War Graves Commission, International Committee of the Red Cross and the *London Gazette* are excellent and without charge. The superb digitised archive of the *Times* newspaper can sometimes be found as a free of charge resource but generally only through a local library log-in. Access to the archives of local newspapers through the British Newspaper Archive (BNA), *The Scotsman* and the *Irish Times* is also increasingly digital but behind paywalls. BNA and 'The Scotsman' are commercial stablemates of Findmypast.

Armed with enough money and prepared to face the array of service providers who may or may not have records of the soldier concerned, today's researcher ought to be able to find the information that exists in digital form. They may need a little mental agility in navigating through search engines that often seem designed to darken rather than illuminate, and they may need to be tolerant of indexing that has rendered Hubert as Herbert and Royal Field Artillery as Royal Army Medical Corps, as in the case of my grandfather. There are thousands of very much worse mis-transcriptions, rendering an existing record impossible or very difficult to locate.

Fragmented, costly and often frustrating as the digitised British records are, thank your lucky stars that you are not researching a French, German, Italian, Belgian, American or soldier from any other country, for they are barely in the starting blocks as far as digitisation of personnel records is concerned.

Blind Alleys and Booby Traps

I always advise anyone who wishes to know more about a family member who took part in the Great War first to carry out an exhaustive search for information that is already held by the family. The man's medals will have his regiment, rank and number inscribed upon them. His discharge certificate will carry the same information. These are basics without which a search can be problematic, although not impossible. Photographs; letters and postcards sent home; pension details and membership of veteran's associations can all offer terrific clues. If a soldier married during his service or if his wife gave birth, the registration certificates will usually carry some military details. The man may also appear in the absent voters lists compiled in 1918 and 1919. It is worth spending time on all of these things before commencing a search for military service records, for every little snippet of knowledge can help in finding details and in interpreting the story they tell.

Researchers also need to be aware of potential blind alleys and booby traps that can waste much time and be very frustrating. I had no idea that at one point in his life my grandfather used a false name; I have no idea why or where the name came from. I have found when researching soldiers that this is by no means uncommon. I have had cases where a man enlisted using his brother's name, and another where he used his mother's maiden name. No evidence was called for when a man enlisted and all of the official documentation carried the name that the man gave. In both cases I found them only after an initially fruitless search for the real name, and then by some mental agility and luck. I have absolutely no doubt that there have been a few cases where our search found nothing, simply as the man used a name we could not even guess. Ages were often falsified, as were addresses and names of next of kin.

I have on many occasions had the pleasure of informing a client that their soldier achieved something of which they were unaware: men who were decorated, mentioned in despatches or even just present at a particular event. It is difficult to know why his descendants were unaware of such things but it appears that in many cases the man simply did not discuss it. In the opposite corner I have also dealt with a few where a photograph shows a man with medals or ribbons to which we found he was not entitled. This is obviously disappointing for his family but is also something that can exhaust a great deal of time, especially for people who are not experienced in research methods and sources.

Some Examples

It is too easy to describe cases where lots of information is found. The stories of these men are rich with detail, and either very interesting or rather run-of-the-mill depending on the nature of their service. As examples of the latter we have dealt with many cases of men of the Army Service Corps who worked at the vast dumps and warehouses at the Channel Ports; who worked as lorry drivers carrying such goods from ports to other locations, or from railheads to more forward areas. We got to know a lot about them and what valuable work they did, but it is not exactly 'Boy's Own' stuff. The same is true of the horse-handlers of the Remounts Service, the locomotive drivers, signalmen and permanent way labourers of the railways, the engineers in the workshops of the Army Ordnance Corps and many others in such unsung, fairly repetitive, work. We've had cases of such men killed in air raids and even one who drowned in the docks at Calais, but in general, by definition, men of the rear areas tend to have stories that were fairly uneventful.

At the other extreme we were invited to study a man who, on the face of it, looked as though he may have been one of the same type of soldier in that he was known to be a motor driver of the Army Service Corps. His name was James

Douglas. A search failed to locate his army service record and his campaign medal record was ordinary enough, giving us sufficient detail to work out when he enlisted and when he went overseas but not much else. His family however believed he has some sort of award, and from his number we found him in the *London Gazette*. He had won the Distinguished Conduct Medal, a gallantry award for men of non-commissioned rank. The citation was most intriguing, suggesting that he had been serving in the area of southern Russia and that he had been involved in a mission to rescue some 'allied consuls'. Not our everyday story of the Western Front, then! The next stage proved painstaking and lengthy, but with a wonderful result. We eventually made the linkage that proved he had been assigned as the private driver to a British officer, one George Goldsmith, who was part of a British 'Military Mission'. He was a spy, in effect.

The officer wrote a detailed narrative of his story, in which his driver is mentioned on a number of occasions. It is held in Foreign Office records, which is not a place we have to visit too often. The rescue mission was in Armenia. At 5am on 25 May 1918, Douglas drove a Ford car carrying Goldsmith and a guide of the Ingush Muslim tribe from Vladikavkaz where the Mission was now based, toward Kazbek. They were attempting to reach a group of British, French, Italian and other consuls and in some cases their wives, with a view to extracting them from what was an increasingly hostile area. A few hundred yards after crossing Dariel Bridge, the car came under fire from a Bolshevik force, which killed the guide. Goldsmith recommended James for his great gallantry, which eventually lead to the award of his DCM.

Not long afterwards, Douglas was sent with two Ingush to Nasran to persuade the local people to cease supporting Bolshevik attacks on local Cossacks. Douglas was dressed in local civilian clothing for this enterprise. The car was captured, the Ingush arrested and Douglas was subsequently recovered but only with great difficulty. Goldsmith and Douglas were later captured by the Bolsheviks and eventually returned home after diplomatic negotiations via Sweden. James Douglas stands out as a case in a number of ways: first, for the most unusual and rather thrilling story that emerged from an unpromising start, and second as an illustration that sometimes the most interesting military details turn up in non-military records.

Leading-Edge Techniques

Digitisation in another sense is also helping us pinpoint the location where a man died or was wounded. This is somewhat dependent on the records not of the man himself but of his unit. For example, if we find that a man was wounded on a certain date we can examine the war diary of his unit. This will give us a location and descriptive context: in some cases, the man is named. Some unit diaries are rather terse, and I often find that the diary of the formation to which it belonged (a brigade in the case of an infantry battalion) has more maps, orders, battle narratives and the like. This is all most helpful in determining what was going on at the time; whether he died in 'normal' trench warfare or was involved in a major action. The diaries usually give good information concerning location, quoting grid map references, names of trenches, villages and other features. It is possible of course to trace the location using paper records, but with digitised campaign and trench maps such as those available from Great War Digital it is possible to pinpoint locations to within a matter of yards if the right information is known. We have in many cases located the death or wounding of a soldier to such short distances. With GPS devices and free-to-use systems such as Google Earth, illustration of and visits to the locations are made very straightforward. A very recent development in this regard is the release by the Commonwealth War Graves Commission of information generated during the post-war period, when men's remains were being found and moved into those cemeteries that would remain. Through this we are now often able to determine where the man was originally buried and not just where he now lies. This adds considerable interest to what exactly happened to him when he died. There seems no doubt that such location-based technologies and emerging information like this will provide a considerable seam that can be mined by researchers in future.

Community, Connections and Crowdsourcing

I recall, back in the dim and distant pre-internet days, having conversations that suggested how terrific it would be if someone could compile a 'register of interests'. It was very evident that there were people out there who had interests and information that might be useful to you – but how would you ever know and find them? Digital means of communicating broke that barrier, and a key development from my own website has provided a large scale and serious platform for people to ask for help and to be provided with that help. Entirely voluntary and free of charge to use, the 'Great War Forum' has for some fifteen years enabled people to make great strides with their own research work. From 'I need to help in finding my grandfather' to the most unusual, complex and obscure technical questions about the Army, the forum has brought novices and experts together in tremendous, positive collaboration. The forum also led to the establishment of an annual conference and to occasional battlefield tours for members. It is a wonderful example of how a subject-focused internet discussion forum can work. With getting on for two million messages posted, many of which include photographs, maps and excellent advice, the forum is also now a splendid data repository. Search for any WW1-related term and the chances are that the forum and the 'Long, Long Trail' come out high on the list.

Of course, other formats for collaboration have now come along in the shape of Facebook, Twitter and other 'social media'. They all have their uses and value particularly for latest news, but what they are not is a good repository. Try finding something posted to Facebook more than a week or two ago, for instance, and you are probably going to have to give up. It is a pity as many people are now posting photographs and other useful material there.

The latest buzzword in use in the WW1 internet world is 'crowdsourcing', particularly for two major public projects. It means calling for public help and collaboration in improving or enriching existing websites and data. The Imperial War Museum has built its 'Lives of the Great War' site, a portal that in theory overcomes the fragmented nature of the various records by bringing them all together, and is currently advertising itself heavily in the social media, calling for people to add information to a soldier's record. The site calls itself a 'permanent digital memorial' and is showing large numbers of added facts that have come from the public. To see the records held by Ancestry, Findmypast etc, you still have to click a link to them and pay. 'Lives' essentially provides another search engine to these records. The National Archives' 'Operation War Diary' is asking for people to pick out place names, locations and other similar information that appears in the digitised unit war diaries and 'tag' them; the theory being that at some future point people will be able to search for wherever the tagged word appears. This approach obtains leverage from the power of accessing very large numbers of interested people. I do wonder, though, whether interest will be maintained and whether quality will be of an acceptably high standard. These are major developments, and it will be interesting to see how they evolve and whether they were to become an important part of the researcher's armoury. At the time of writing, this is not yet the case but, theoretically at least, things should change.

Interpretation needs Expertise

I mentioned above that my approach has always been to try to recreate the man's whole story, and to do so needs a broad range of knowledge. With the internet and digitisation making basic fact-searching easier, the emphasis on my time as a professional researcher is now definitely much more on the interpretation element than it is on searching. This trend will continue. Digital means of interpretation of records is currently either absent or crude, which is why so many people are turning to places like the 'Great War Forum' for help: what does this say? What exactly does this code mean? What does this date tell me? And so on. This is where there is scope for much academic, technical and other development. Tools to help family historians turn complex military documents into something meaningful would be of great value to the researcher, but they would be complex and expensive to develop. It remains to be seen whether the trend of the last decade or two, the incredible increase in interest in family history and the Great War will be sustained much beyond 2018, if that. At present there may be a 'business case' for investing in developing new forms of digital data from military records, websites that help search that data and tools to help interpret what the data means, but a reduction in public interest might quickly return the Great War to a quieter, more specialist backwater. There is as yet no date for release of servicemen's records for the Second World War, but the day cannot be far off, and I suspect that the interest and the money will switch very rapidly. Meanwhile, I intend to keep reading those codes and squiggles, and to keep doing my best to determine what happened to a man. I have my grandfather to thank for that.

Websites Mentioned in the Text

The Long, Long Trail http://www.1914-1918.net
The Great War Forum http://1914-1918.invisionzone.com/forums
The Naval & Military Press http://www.naval-military-press.com/
Ancestry http://www.ancestry.co.uk
Findmypast http://www.findmypast.co.uk
The Commonwealth War Graves Commission http://www.cwgc.org
The International Committee of the Red Cross http://grandeguerre.icrc.org/
The London Gazette https://www.thegazette.co.uk/
Great War Digital http://www.greatwardigital.com/
IWM Lives of the Great War https://livesofthefirstworldwar.org/
TNA Operation War Diary http://www.operationwardiary.org/

Chapter 19

The Liddle Collection of First World War Archival Materials in the University of Leeds

* * *

Peter Liddle

As a Comprehensive School teacher, a very inexperienced but keen Head of Department, I organised a First World War Commemoration exhibition in 1964 – fifty years after the outbreak of the war. The exhibition, with the presence of veterans answering questions and relating with the boys and girls, grew from my endeavour to nurture in the children a sense that history was all around them in their everyday life, not just in the past. Buildings, landscape, newspapers, radio, television, opinions, attitudes, music, politics, sport, holiday destinations, families, were full of history, and there was a life-enhancing magic about this if one were to choose to take advantage of it.

I used a variety of approaches to bring this home, from dramatic reconstruction to model-making or embroidery, from laying siege to a small medieval castle, to exploring un-modernised coalmines, from the use of documents in facsimile to the memories of people who had experienced events I was trying to bring to life.

In teaching myself how to tap into memory, how to interview elderly men and women about their youthful years, keeping them within the range of what they had seen, done, experienced and how they had reacted to that experience at the time, I became keenly, worryingly, aware that I was standing in the midst of vanishing history – memories were going to the grave and memorabilia associated with them was going in the dustbin. After teaching in Sunderland and Liverpool, and then at a college in Liverpool, a post training teachers in Sunderland enabled me to assist my students in recording memories and engage more and more seriously in this work. I was interviewing men and women about their lives pre-1914. Many had been miners, a few soldiers serving in the Second Boer War, and a similar number in sailing ships, one with initiation as an apprentice at the age of fourteen on a two-year voyage away from the United Kingdom, another, in the First World War, his vessel sunk by a German armed raider, the crew put onto an isolated island to await rescue. In the main, the women had given me their recall of their days at school, life in straitened circumstances, helping in the home, shopping for food in the town market late in the evening when bargains were on offer, the street vendors, church or chapel Christmas parties, and sources of entertainment like the silent films or Music Hall.

Of all I was recording I felt drawn in particular to memories of the First World War and was struck by hearing reactions to experiencing the war different from common perception among younger people. This was an additional spur to my awareness that I simply had to do something about this loss of our heritage. I had found what I wanted to do with my life – a rescue act before it was too late.

My appointment in a college where this could be done alongside preparing students for teaching history, was very fortunate. My first recordings were made in Sunderland in 1967. From 1968 my students were engaged in recording as part of their course work experience: one inspirationally, in relation to her dissertation, found a lady who had nursed with Edith Cavell.

In November 1970, I had a letter appeal published in the *Daily Telegraph* for contact with people who had Great War experience. It brought several hundred replies. I travelled to as many of the addresses given as I could, interviewed the respondents, was offered original letters, diaries and photographs, and began respectfully soliciting such material with a view somehow of placing it with the recordings in the public domain. I was shown great trust and, never mind my passion and sincerity, there was from early days the burden of conscience that I had no clear idea how a form of 'institutionalization' might be achieved, still less how difficult it would be. To compound this anxiety I had no professional training in archive practice. It would take twenty years to solve the first issue, for the second it had to be a question of learning on the hoof and trying to make as few mistakes as possible.

My travelling around the country to record men and women was introducing me to life experience that hitherto I had not even envisioned like the man trained before the war in man-lifting kites for observation of enemy activity, or the civilian interned near Berlin for the years of war, though commonsense should have introduced that topic to me. Meeting and recording separately the famous cricketing brothers the Ashtons who played key parts in the defeat of the all-conquering Australian team after the war was just one of innumerable bonus discoveries in my pursuit of anyone who had served in or lived through the war years.

I was recruiting volunteers who helped in all sorts of ways, most basically, in going through books of reference, like *Who's Who* and *Crockfords*, the Church of England directory, and the *British Medical Association Directory*, for people of the right age to write to. *Who's Who* was to bring Harold Macmillan within my reach and Victor Silvester, Arnold Ridley, Gordon Jacob, Barnes Wallis and Henry Moore; *Crockfords*, shoals of Padres in the war – surprisingly clergymen who had been in the German army but, fleeing from Hitler's Germany, had been given Livings in the Anglican Church; from the BMA, many regimental medical officers and surgeons, some engaged in experimental work.

I remember writing to the magazine *The Lady* in a successful search for VADs, to a Socialist journal for pacifist testimony, to Old Comrades Associations for those interested in contributing to what we were doing. It was an Old Contemptible – a man from the ranks – who further educated me away from any 'received wisdom' I may have retained that all soldiers were soon shocked into disillusionment on contact with the reality of war. Of course he was a Regular soldier, but, as to his social background, he was almost certainly kindred to the vast majority in the ranks of the New Army battalions.

Listening to this man's response to my questions, swiping aside any inappropriate concentration on factors of personal sensitivity or fragility of morale, encouraged me to consider the background of the average man in the ranks, accustomed as he was to the rough, demanding, accident-prone conditions under which he laboured in heavy industry or on the land – and the harsh world of the unemployed too. I was also becoming aware of the social background of the pre- and 1914 officer class, with its inbred obligation to lead and feel responsibility for the men they led, further inculcated by their education and military training. I was in the process of shedding the liberal-inspired myth of simmering resentment felt in the ranks towards the hermetically-sealed world of privilege of the officers. Not all of our appeals were successful: a letter in every coastal local newspaper in Britain did not bring in a single fisherman, docker or lifeboatman and the help of the then British ambassador in Moscow searching for contact with Russian soldiers was no more fruitful.

Volunteers were helping in more sophisticated ways than the necessary but mundane task of going through books of reference. I was strongly motivated by a responsibility to ferret out from original letters and diaries descriptions and opinions which cast light upon individual reaction to a man or a woman's experience. Behind this lay an understanding that legitimate generalisation might be drawn from such cross-referencing about this, that or the other, if a numerically strong body of evidence were to point in a certain direction. We might then really have sound evidence for judging how soldiers in 1917, for example, felt about the French or Belgian peasants eking out a living within reach of the lines, or about the resilience of a soldier's morale during his service in the Ypres Salient. This was the origin of the cross-reference catalogues, now replaced by digitisation, in what was to become the Liddle Collection in the Brotherton Library of the University of Leeds.

It was to be the task I shared with volunteers not just to list the holding of newly-donated material but, on a set proforma, to number in datal sequence a set of letters, identify to whom they were sent, and from where, though this might often be merely 'In the line', and note the matters of historical interest in the text – opinions expressed, descriptions, etc. A different proforma was designed for diaries, but then from both proformas, from photographs, recollections, ephemera and sometimes three-dimensional souvenirs, cross-references would be entered as appropriate in the hundreds of indices which would include attitudes and opinions expressed towards allies, enemy, the Government, the Press, reaction to topics such as health, recreation, food, brothels, the impact of service experience on Faith, and descriptions of involvement in the Battle of Aubers Ridge, or the German use of gas at the Second Battle of Ypres. This was designed to be a help to those who came to research at Sunderland, and among those who came as a post-graduate student was the distinguished keynote speaker at the Weetwood Conference, Gary Sheffield, now Professor of Military History at the University of Wolverhampton.

I may add that this cross-referencing work was also an enormous help to me in writing books on the war designed not least to demonstrate the burgeoning riches of the developing archive but also enabling me to join the efforts of others in encouraging thinking about the war differently from the received wisdom which had for long needed challenge.

It so happened that though, with help, I organised campaigns to find and record RFC pilots, merchant seamen, men who were at Jutland, women from the Scottish Women's Hospitals, Conscientious Objectors – and I found eight or nine of the thirty-four who heard the sentence of death pronounced upon them after court-martial (a sentence commuted) – somehow it was the Dardanelles/Gallipoli campaign which in particular caught my imagination. I travelled to every corner of the UK to meet men who had served on the Gallipoli Peninsula and in the surrounding waters, to Turkey, to Australia and New Zealand and four times to France, finding in all 650 who had survived the campaign, but truly if the reader's interest were in the East African campaign, or the one in South West Africa, even in the joint Anglo-Japanese expedition to clear the Germans out of Tsingtao in China, you will find in the Collection personal documentation related to that endeavour. Anyone keen to explore the testimony of the experience of women – in uniformed military service, as nurses, working in mills or munitions factories, or as wives, mothers or sisters – will find fascinating original and recollected material in the Collection.

It was not all plain sailing. At Sunderland there was some hostility towards any study of warfare as a subject at all. In the wider world, some historians were summarily dismissive of oral history having any real value as source material, and later, at Leeds, a member of the School of History courted the applause of the cynical by describing the work of the Collection, as 'badge collecting'.

From Sunderland it proved extremely difficult to get the developing archive into the public domain. Senior staff at the Imperial War Museum insisted that the Collection must be split into sections to fit into the departments of the IWM. I felt this would destroy a central feature of the archive, its integrated nature, everything associated with an individual kept together. Furthermore I wanted to be able to continue building the archive along these lines for the IWM, if ownership were now to be in their hands, and of course these were difficult issues to resolve, as was the sheer volumetric size of the Collection.

Four times a year I would go on five-day research trips to addresses listed regionally in the back of my diary – four appointments each day – and return with my car laden with original material and of course recordings. The visits would have provided further addresses of family and friends for later appointments. It was not just these tours which accounted for the mushrooming of the archive but the positive response from combing the commercial obituary columns of the *Daily Telegraph*, the distinguished entries too, in order to make a sensitively-judged approach for 1914–18 material.

Funding, space and fitting-out that space were going to be problems for any university library and creating a curatorial post too, but the answers were found at Leeds in 1988 with the then Librarian, Reg Carr, Professor David Dilks of the School of History, Colonel Alan Roberts, the Pro Chancellor, and several Trust Fund agencies, playing decisive roles. From twenty double-door lockable archive cabinets arranged around the walls of three lecture rooms, documentation of approximately 4,000 individuals, and then a thousand or so books, all the catalogues of what was held, the donor correspondence files and an enormous chest holding wartime newspapers, British, Belgian, French, German and Commonwealth, posters and trench maps, were transported in three enormous pantechnicons south to Leeds.

For the next ten years I was the Keeper of the Liddle Collection with the joy of developing it further, mounting 1914–18 exhibitions in London, Glasgow, and elsewhere, lecturing about the collection abroad, with colleagues, in particular Dr Hugh Cecil, arranging international conferences on the First World War in Leeds, and writing books on personal experience in the war, drawing upon the source material in the collection.

A new team of volunteers was enlisted – essential and invaluable but a concept which did not fit comfortably in the then hierarchical and highly formalized administration of Brotherton Library when, after a few years, the Collection was moved there from the pleasantly relaxed atmosphere of the Edward Boyle Library. An association of Friends was created, with its journal, *The Poppy and the Owl*, published three times a year. Through the active support of the Pro Chancellor, distinguished guests of the University regularly came to be shown the Collection, and researching visitors were coming in increasing numbers – undergraduates, postgraduates, some from overseas, the United States in particular, authors and media people. Both from the Sunderland base and from Leeds, TV companies made films resourced in the main from the archive. Imaginatively the authorities created a temporary post for Matthew Richardson, recent Leeds School of History and then Leicester University post-graduate. The Collection's work was enhanced by his presence. Matthew would have made a superb future Keeper of the Collection but sadly that was not to be.

Today, happily, a researcher can examine what is in the Collection through its website and then, following the library's procedures, freely research by appointment. There is extraordinary material available, some people with diaries for every year of the war, some with great numbers of original letters, some with three or more photograph albums. Two men, I recall, wrote unpublished memoirs of over 300 pages. There is a kilt which saw service in the trenches, a munition worker's dress or overall, a shrapnel ball-holed tunic, a shell fragment-torn Bible, logbooks for fighter, bomber and airship pilots, the sketch-illustrated letters of Adrian Hill, an Official War Artist, an exceptional collection of both unit newspapers and of trench maps for virtually every Front, but if I were to choose some items which still today send a tingle of excitement through me, I would select the following: Sapper Sergeant Jim Davey's diary of Boxing Day, 1914, and the Christmas Truce – 'Queerest Christmas I ever knew' – is a gem and to go with it is a German newspaper exchanged for a British officer's *Daily Mail*.

For anyone seeking first-hand evidence of the initial shock and degree of panic following upon the German use of gas at the Second Battle of Ypres on 22 April 1915, there could not be better evidence than the beautifully written diary of 2nd Lieutenant N. C. Harbutt detailing civilian and French Colonial soldier flight and Canadian efforts to hold the line.

The logbook and photographs of an RFC Observer, T. L. W. Stallibrass, are special treasures too.. The log includes a report on the first day of the Battle of the Somme, 1 July 1916, and describes the huge pall of smoke above the location of the La Boiselle mine explosion, the artillery barrage lifting and the British infantry leaving the trenches. This Morane Saulnier Observer's photographs of pilots and observers in his squadron are grimly personalized with dates for when the smiling faces were killed, wounded or missing. The diary for the same day of Regimental Medical Officer, G. D. Fairley, moving forward before Montauban to tend to wounded of the 2nd Battalion Royal Scots Fusiliers is in small writing but with graphic detail including that of being slightly wounded himself.

Photographically as dramatic is the record of Midshipman Brian Sebastian's album of the near-disaster of HMS *Inflexible* striking a mine in the great attack on the inner forts of the Narrows of the Dardanelles on 18 March 1915. A huge rent has been torn in the beam of the battlecruiser. An attempt is being made, under fire from the shore, to lower a collision mat in place over the gaping damage. Under the eye of a Petty Officer, ratings strain at the capstan hauling the large cumbersome cover. What can be seen in the photograph is two Royal Marine Bandsmen playing their fiddles for what may be presumed to be a shanty giving rhythm to the ratings' efforts.

Howard Marten's papers would come high on any list of gems. Drafted to France in the Non-Combatant Corps, he was the first Conscientious Objector to face court-martial in his refusal to drill. By refusing to obey the 'lawful command of an officer in the field', he was liable to court-martial and if convicted, the death sentence. Such was his fate, the first one promulgated of the thirty-four men in this circumstance. Their sentences were commuted. Marten's papers include his

Quaker testimony at his court-martial (two courts-martial in his case), written on the only paper available to him, toilet tissue. There are letters of support from Bertrand Russell and Philip Snowden and an autograph album from his later experience at Dartmoor, breaking stones on the Home Office Work Scheme.

One of the most touching treasures in the Collection is the little fluffy toy dog, Adolphus, the mascot given to fighter pilot and officer in command of his squadron, Major Maurice le Blanc Smith. His photographs, flying logbook and Flying Certificate accompany Adolphus.

There is a most unusual array of medals for a German Jew, German for service in the First World War, a veteran's medal actually presented by Adolf Hitler, and then perhaps less surprisingly, British Second World War service medals, but my final selection has to be a simply extraordinary, almost unbelievable item, though it is one which for me is symbolically sad. For about five years in the late 1990s I tried to persuade the library authorities that the Collection should embrace the Second World War as well – naturally so, from an historical and academic viewpoint. I believed the opportunity and the obligation were there. It was not formally sanctioned. With the authorities turning a blind eye occasionally, and my turning a blind eye more regularly, I did undertake Second World War work – the Duke of Edinburgh was recorded by his invitation, by invitation too, this time from the Society of Battle of Britain pilots, many of their members were recorded, then, through the Lords Haig and Harewood, considerable numbers of men incarcerated in Colditz Castle were recorded. The Liddle Collection website I think lists that there is material for 500 1939–45 men and women here, but I lost the battle quite disastrously. Everything, however, was not lost because with exceptional support I became centrally involved in the setting-up of the Second World War Experience Centre, originally in Leeds where it was privileged to have a visit from HRH the Prince of Wales, and now at Walton near Wetherby in Yorkshire. It now holds material for nearly 10,000 individuals, but my final item illustrates perfectly the irony of there being two separate archives.

For the Liddle Collection I had been recording a former 1917 Royal Naval Air Service Fitter, C. B. Simkins. Before I left he told me that in 1940 he had been a Technician at RAF Halton. He had taken a surprising phone call from the Air Ministry. He was instructed to make a longbow, a prototype for more to be made. He was told that it was in the current shortage of firearms and the possibility of invasion. That 1940 longbow is in the Liddle Collection for us all to wonder at during this centenary commemoration of the First World War, only one year short of the 600th anniversary of Agincourt. It certainly does something to illustrate the nation's peril in 1940 and if somehow it could be symbolically inspirational in a future union of the collections that really would be splendid.

Chapter 20

Lawnswood Cemetery in Leeds and the First World War

* * *

Andrea Hetherington

Lawnswood Cemetery, opened in 1875, is situated in Adel, North Leeds, around four miles from the city centre. It is distinctive in many ways – its original overall 'romantic' planning with meandering paths rather than neatly geometric rows, the architecture of its chapels and monuments, and the number of well-known men and women laid to rest within its borders.

The cemetery contains many echoes of the First World War, from soldiers to munitions workers, captains of industry to bereaved parents. There are the familiar Commonwealth War Graves Commission (CWGC) graves in the distinctive Portland stone, but also hundreds of commemorations on family graves, often for soldiers whose bodies remain abroad. In the days before cheap foreign travel, the prospect of families visiting the graves of their loved ones in France and beyond were slim, despite the schemes which were instituted by different organizations to allow such visits. In those circumstances families wanted a local place to visit to grieve and to commemorate their relatives, so included inscriptions on existing family plots for their sons and husbands who died overseas.

In terms of the military graves at Lawnswood, they fall into three categories – casualties who are buried at the cemetery, casualties who are simply commemorated there, and survivors of the First World War, their military service often recorded on the gravestone. One grave at the cemetery satisfies all three of those criteria, and that is the Ives family memorial.

Originally from the South East of England, the head of the family, Alfred Ives, was the proprietor of the Grand Restaurant in Leeds city centre. The family lived in Roundhay at a house called Greystones, which still exists today. The grave commemorates three sons of the Ives family, all of whom served in the First World War. The unique element of the grave is that it commemorates combatants in all three services.

Second Lieutenant Kenneth Ives was a solicitor by profession, having just qualified at the time the War broke out. He joined the Leeds Rifles, 1/8 West Yorkshire Regiment (TF), and was taking part in training at Strensall, near York, in December 1914 when he fell ill. He died on 9 December 1914, having never left the country. The cause of death was given as typhoid and double pneumonia. Kenneth Ives is one of the many Lawnswood military casualties who died in the United Kingdom from illness or accident and were brought to the cemetery at the request of their families.

Remembered on the gravestone is the youngest Ives brother, Derrick, who was a submariner – the only member of that branch of the Navy commemorated at the cemetery. He was a career sailor, a Lieutenant aboard the submarine *H10* with a crew of twenty-six. She failed to return from a routine patrol in the North Sea in January 1918 and was declared lost. The fate of the boat remains a mystery as it was not patrolling in an area known for mines and was not claimed as a 'kill' by any German warship. Derrick was 21 years old and is also commemorated on the sailors' memorial at Chatham in Kent.

The third brother on the family memorial is Edward Ives. Edward was in the Royal Flying Corps/Royal Air Force for the entire duration of the War and was a survivor. He served his country again in the Second World War and survived it, serving in the Royal Air Force. He died in 1948 at the age of 51, his service in the two world wars recorded on the memorial. Lawnswood has similar cases of First World War men, long surviving the war, having their Great War service recorded on their graves.

The 15th Battalion West Yorkshire Regiment – the Leeds Pals – is heavily represented at Lawnswood, as one might expect. The concept of battalions of Pals was central in the need for massive recruitment for the Army in the Autumn of 1914 but rather than being a regiment made up of men who had come out of the pits, heavy industry and factories together to enlist, the Leeds Pals was specifically 'marketed' as a 'businessmen's regiment'. The recruitment call went out for non-manual workers, aged 19–35, with no dependents. This rather exclusive element was turned on its head disparagingly, by the observation that they were men who could be spared with no great disruption to the life of the city! The initial recruitment target was soon filled and the new battalion went off for basic training in Colsterdale, near Masham, in September 1914. They were not deployed overseas until December 1915, partly due to the fact that further recruitment was required to bring the battalion up to strength as so many of their number were lost to commissions offered by other regiments.

Initially going to Egypt, the Leeds Pals arrived on the Western Front in March 1916 in preparation for the 'Big Push' which proved to be the Somme offensive. Their losses on 1 July were so severe that, as such, the battalion ceased to exist, the remnants being merged with the Leeds Bantams, the 17th Battalion West Yorkshire Regiment. The terrible toll is individually and collectively commemorated in France, but Lawnswood holds resonances too.

One of the men, the wonderfully-named Sgt Herbert Gladstone Pickles, whose name clearly betrays his father's political sensibilities, as Herbert Gladstone, the youngest son of the Prime Minister, had served as MP in Leeds in the 1880s. Herbert Pickles' father, Gladstone's great admirer, was the 'John Menzies' of his day. He started a newspaper distribution company in the early days of such things and had a large warehouse building in what is now the Chinatown section of Leeds city centre. Innovative before his time, Chas Pickles & Co suffered during the War with a loss of personnel and he eventually sold the firm to John Menzies, who had taken the concept of newspaper distribution much further than Charles ever could. Herbert himself was part of the original recruitment draft of the Leeds Pals. He survived the Somme but was killed during the Arras offensive in May 1917.

Some of Leeds' most renowned families of the time lost sons in the First World War. Two such families were the Haddocks and the Reffitts. The Haddocks were famous musically and were the founders of the Leeds College of Music at its original site on Woodhouse Lane in 1894. They include amongst their relatives the popular violinist George Haddock, who was famous enough to publish an autobiography in 1906 which sold in large numbers. The family member lost was George Percival Haddock, another teenager, who was known to friends and family as 'Val'. He had joined the Territorial Force in 1915 and was 19 when he died. He was a motorcycle despatch rider and was attached to a Signalling Company of the Royal Engineers. He was with his unit in Northamptonshire when he was killed in an accident, trying to jump on a moving truck and falling under the wheels. He died in hospital of his injuries and was returned to Leeds and given a funeral at Lawnswood with full military honours.

The Reffitt family owned a large dye works on the River Aire. A trade which grew massively due to the location of the booming clothing industry in Leeds, dyeing was an important business in the city in the late nineteenth century. Charles Reffitt was the sole surviving son of the family and was managing director at the time war broke out. Having initially been rejected for military service for some reason, he joined the Special Constabulary of Leeds instead. He rose swiftly to the rank of Inspector and in the shortage of manpower later was accepted into the Army and enlisted in the Royal Garrison Artillery. Though records of his service are scant, it seems that he died in a military hospital in Edinburgh in January 1917. His gravestone is a good example of the responsibility taken by the Commonwealth War Graves Commission for the maintenance of graves. Even though this is a family gravestone rather than a CWGC stone, the Commission ensures that the name of 'their' casualty remains legible, no matter what the condition of the rest of the inscription. For the CWGC to take responsibility, the death must occur due to military service and within the qualifying period which ends on 31 August 1921. The remains of the individual must be actually present at the site, rather than the man simply being commemorated there.

The Wilson family of Ossett near Wakefield have numbers of impressive monuments at Lawnswood. The family made their fortune in the worsted industry, making cloth for uniforms amongst other things, and operated mills in Leeds and

Bradford. The most poignant of the Wilson memorials is that to Norman Wilson, Captain in the 7th Battalion West Yorkshire Regiment (TF), the Leeds Rifles. He died during the Somme offensive in July 1916 and is buried at Authuile Military Cemetery. Norman Wilson's memorial at Lawnswood originally contained the cross which initially marked his grave at Authuile. His mother had already suffered great tragedy in her life when Norman's father, Andrew Wilson, had committed suicide in November 1896. She had remarried and moved to live in Scarborough at the time Norman died. Whether she visited France herself, or applied to the Imperial War Graves Commission, as it then was, for the grave marker, is unknown, but her heartbreak is evident – the inscription she chose from her allotted sixty-six letters for her son's grave records: 'Fell at Thiepval. Reunion is my hope'. The cross has now rotted away but the grave stands as a comparatively rare example of such markers being retained by the family.

No doubt Birmingham, Manchester and Glasgow would dispute such a claim but Leeds bids fair to having been the busiest city in the country in terms of the production of war materiel during the Great War. Shells and uniforms top the list of a huge range of war-related manufacturing. Many of the industries are represented at Lawnswood, with one of the more unusual examples being the grave of the Procter family.

Charles Procter, buried at Lawnswood, was one of the founders, with his brother, John, of a firm of wireworkers in Leeds. Procter Brothers made fencing, machine-guarding frames, mousetraps and a wide range of other wire products. They were responsible for producing the wire which was inserted into frames and then installed on the roof of Buckingham Palace to protect the royal residence from the threat of bombs dropped from Zeppelins. Procters made barbed wire and also wire frames for holding gauze on gas masks.

The Procter family grave also commemorates a First World War casualty, Captain Harry Mettam Procter, of the 9th Battalion West Yorkshire Regiment. Harry was Charles Procter's youngest son and a promising illustrator and cartoonist. He had just finished art school in London when war was declared. He joined the Army in August 1914 and in the following year served at Gallipoli where he had contracted first jaundice and then frostbite from the terrible November storm. He recovered from these afflictions but at age 22, met his end in the Ypres Salient in August 1917. Wilfred Owen may have written of the 'stinking Leeds/Bradford war profiteers', but it is a fact that many of the families of Leeds who made a profit out of the war also paid a huge personal price in the loss of their sons, Procter Brothers being just one example to be found at Lawnswood.

It is a point all too often ignored, but the poetry popular during the war was often markedly different in tone from that which, not least by the values of later times, has come to exemplify the war. The newspapers often published poems sent in by readers, some of which, though little better than doggerel, became wildly popular. Lawnswood has the distinction of having a war poet buried within its grounds, though she is little known in the wider culture today. Her name was Lucy

Whitmell, and she was the daughter of Sir William Foster, Baronet. Lucy was born in 1869 in Norfolk, where she no doubt had the privileged upbringing befitting a baronet's daughter. She had an interest in astronomy which led her to take part in an expedition to Spain in 1900 to observe a total solar eclipse. There she met her future husband, Charles Whitmell who was a schools inspector and keen scientist. They married in 1903, fairly late in life for the time, and lived together in Leeds. Lucy spoke Italian, and endowed a prize at the University of Leeds in Italian Studies which is still extant. In 1915, Lucy submitted a poem to the Spectator called 'Christ in Flanders'. Written from the viewpoint of a soldier, the poem bemoans the disappearance of Christ in everyday life before the War but ends with reassurance that he is always present.

Christ in Flanders

We had forgotten You, or very nearly
You did not seem to touch us very nearly
Of course we thought about You now and then;
Especially in any time of trouble
We knew that You were good in time of trouble
But we are very ordinary men . . .

Now we remember; over here in Flanders
(It isn't strange to think of You in Flanders)
This hideous warfare seems to make things clear.
We never thought about You much in England
But now that we are far away from England,
We have no doubts, we know that You are here.

First appearing in September 1915, the poem was immensely popular and gained wide distribution being quoted in sermons and printed by the *Spectator* in leaflet form throughout the war years. The derision of the modern critic may be unsurprising but then, different times, different needs and values come to mind. Lucy Whitmell does not appear to have been prolific, and this is the only poem which has survived the century. She died in 1917 and at the time of her death the poem clearly still resonated with the public, as 'She wrote "Christ in Flanders"' is displayed on her headstone at Lawnswood. Her gravestone is also an eloquent illustration of the position of women in England at the time, as the most visible fact about Lucy recorded there is that she was the daughter of Sir William Foster. Her artistic achievement is relegated to the side of the stone!

Underage soldiers are represented at Lawnswood in significant number. One of them was Geoffrey Arnold Denny. A product of the local public school, Leeds Grammar School, Denny is an interesting example of how younger soldiers slipped through the net. His CWGC citation shows no age, and he is one of the names on the war memorial at the University of Leeds, suggesting that he was at least 18 years old in order to be a student there. His attestation forms, which saw him into the Royal Army Medical Corps, record his age to be 18 years and 10 months at the time of enlistment on 13 August 1914. The relevance of this precise age was that he would have two months of basic training before he was eligible to serve abroad, the age for that posting being 19. Denny was part of the No. 7 West Yorkshire Casualty Clearing Station and went to France at the end of October 1914. He was there less than two months, dying of dysentery on 22 December 1914 and is buried at Merville Cemetery in France. His commemoration at Lawnswood Cemetery reveals the truth about Geoffrey Denny, as his family record that at the time of his death he was just 17 years old. He was never a student at the University of Leeds, having simply passed the entrance exam. He had just left Leeds Grammar School and was enjoying a holiday before starting at the University when the War intervened. The Leeds Grammar school magazine, *The Old Leodiensian*, gave him a lavish obituary:

> His happy disposition, his assiduous attention to the duties allotted, and his unselfish regard for others won him the admiration and respect of both officers and men, and his brave death revealed in a marked degree the unfeigned sorrow of all who came into contact with him.'[1]

As we have already seen, Lawnswood's First World War stories are not always about soldiers. One significant grave is that of James Graham, Director of Education for the City of Leeds from 1905 to 1931. As director, Graham was no doubt immensely proud of the brand-new teacher training college which had opened at Beckett Park in Headingley in June 1913. Purpose-built, in large grounds, with tennis courts and leafy surroundings, the college must have been the pride of the city. Less than a year after its opening, on 4 August 1914, some War Office top brass marched up the driveway and requisitioned the whole site for use as a military hospital. The 2nd Northern General Military Hospital – or Beckett's Park, as it remained known locally – operated as a military hospital until 1927 despite a number of attempts by the Board of Education to take it back into their control.

From 17 September 1914, with casualties wounded in the early engagements in Belgium and France, over 57,000 patients came through the doors of the hospital during the following three years. *Leeds in the Great War* records that only around 200 of those patients died. The hospital was not the first port of call for the very seriously wounded but it is an impressive record nevertheless. Staff at the hospital started to specialise in surgery, both orthopaedic and facial, and the opportunity to work with such injuries attracted an influx of American doctors from 1917 onwards. The hospital also played a significant part in the rehabilitation of disabled soldiers, with workshops instructing them in trades they might follow despite their injuries. A number of the Lawnswood casualties came from Beckett's Park and from other war hospitals which were established in Leeds under the command of the 2nd Northern General.

James Graham himself, like many of the notable citizens of Leeds, served on committees assisting the war administration. In Graham's case he chaired the local committee dealing with pensions and allowances for dependents. He appears to have had something of a puritanical streak and at the beginning of what was essentially a military occupation of the campus, students – mostly women – were still attending there for sport and other activities. Graham was appalled by the thought of soldiers ogling his female students as they played tennis, though he seems to have blamed the women for their conduct rather than the soldiers for looking!

Situated near Graham's monument is a poignant reminder of the lasting effects of the War upon those who lost family members. Rhodes Calvert was a solicitor and a respected member of the Leeds business community. He was for many years secretary to the Leeds Board of Trade and took a full part in the civic life of the city. Calvert had four sons, all of whom joined up when war was declared. The Calvert family tragically lost three of the four sons. Cyril Calvert had been serving with the Canadian forces when he was reported missing near Ypres in 1915. It took four years for the details of his death to reach the family, when they finally discovered that Cyril had been a victim of poison gas. Reginald Calvert was with the Leeds Rifles on the Somme in July 1916, receiving wounds from which he died later that month. The youngest son, Geoffrey, died of pneumonia and typhoid at a casualty clearing station in France in January 1919.

Rhodes Calvert was a broken man. In 1930, twelve years after the last of his sons was killed, Calvert was found dead at his house in Hollin Lane in Headingley. His wife made the awful discovery, finding him lying on a pillow in front of the gas fire with a tube nearby which had been attached to the gas outlet of the fire. The inquest heard that he had been very low of late and had in fact never recovered from the grief of losing his three sons. The impact of the War on the families left behind many years after the death of their loved ones is sometimes overlooked, but the story of Rhodes Calvert is a clear example of grief which had proved overwhelming.

Whilst the toll of death in the Calvert family is shocking, it is not the worst First World War accumulation of tragedy commemorated at Lawnswood. That particular distinction belongs to the Stewart family from Burley. The Stewarts were known as a musical family and a large one. Some of the sons were involved in the war industries of Leeds and were exempt, therefore, from military service. Five Stewart sons joined the Army and all perished. From 1915 until 1919, the Stewart family lost one son a year. The first to die was Private William Stewart, killed at Gallipoli in October 1915 whilst serving with the 8th Battalion Duke of Wellington's (West Riding) Regiment. William is commemorated, along with 21,000 others, on the Helles memorial at the tip of the Gallipoli Peninsula in Turkey.

The second casualty, Charles, was the only one of the sons who held officer's rank. He had already served four years in the Army from 1904 to 1907 with the Worcestershire Regiment. He was placed back on the strength again on the outbreak of war. After swift promotions through the ranks he was offered a commission with the Manchester Regiment in June 1916. By this time Second Lieutenant Stewart had already survived one serious wound the previous year when his legs were badly damaged by shell fragments, necessitating his evacuation to England. In September 1916 he received a wound to the head which looked as though it would prove fatal. As he was an officer, his mother was invited to visit France to see her son. It is not known whether Mrs Stewart actually got to see her son in time. A doctor in Folkestone provided a note to the War Office stating that it would be impossible for Mrs Stewart to make her way to France alone as she was quite deaf. Whether she was then accompanied to France is unclear, but Charles died a few days after the initial telegram notifying the family of his wound and was buried at Abbeville Communal Cemetery.

Leonard is the only son actually buried at Lawnswood, as he died in a military hospital in Manchester and his body was brought back to Leeds. He was the youngest of the Stewart casualties, being 21 years old at the time of his death. His elder brother, Alfred, was 29 and married with a daughter when he died whilst serving with the Yorks and Lancs Regiment.

The most tragic death in this litany of suffering is that of the last Stewart to die, Walter. Although the gravestone denotes that he died in British East Africa, the truth is more heart-rending, as Walter actually died on the boat on the way home to be demobbed, having caught a fever whilst in Africa. He was buried at sea.

Lawnswood has an impressive war memorial which has its own separate grassy area at the northern edge of what is known as the 1910 extension, near the New Adel Lane entrance. The cemetery authorities put aside some ground to accommodate casualties which were coming from Beckett's Park and other war hospitals in the city. Over eighty such casualties were buried in the vicinity of the war memorial and remain under the manicured lawn today. The casualties were from all branches of the armed services and from a range of countries. There are Australians, Canadians and even a Belgian soldier – one of the first batch of wounded Belgians who were brought to Beckett's Park in September 1914 under the welcoming scrutiny of the inhabitants of Leeds, who met their train at the central station and threw cigarettes and chocolate at the soldiers.

Visiting the Cemetery in October 1918, a journalist from the *Yorkshire Evening News* described the site in glowing terms:

But for the rumble and crash of an occasional car Leeds might have been many leagues away. The west wind, softly sighing with a hint of tears, wafted sound and smoke far south and verdant 'God's Acre' at Lawnswood was fair to see.[2]

It appears as though at least some of the graves did have individual markers at one point, but a decision was made to commemorate them on the bronze plaques behind the Cross of Sacrifice rather than with the Portland stone memorials. The plaques also record the names of the fifty-four casualties who are buried elsewhere in the cemetery, often in family plots. The memorial was completed in 1922, the chief stonemason being an ex-serviceman, John Bradley, who had returned to his family from a prisoner of war camp in Germany.

On the right-hand side of the CWGC plot is another large bronze plaque which records the casualties of both Wars who were originally buried at the Leeds General Cemetery. This cemetery is now part of the University of Leeds and is known as St George's Field. Largely cleared of monuments when sold to the University in 1969, it was decided to commemorate the war casualties at Lawnswood instead. The bodies were never exhumed and remain at St George's Field.

Lawnswood has a number of casualties of the influenza epidemic, some acknowledged, though many more registered with another cause of death. There are various theories on the origin of the pandemic, but all agree that it was spread so extensively by Allied soldiers and their movement around the world from 1918 onwards. Tragically, of course, that included returning home to their loved ones after surviving four years of war.

The first reports of the influenza cases began to appear in Leeds newspapers in June 1918, with a local GP reporting that he had seen thirty patients in the previous week, all suffering from symptoms of this new ailment – 'a new and particularly severe form of influenza'. There was no great alarm at this point, the doctor saying that he had not seen any really serious cases. However, by July, the chief medical officer of the Local Government Board was issuing the following statement: 'The disease is most infectious and it is necessary that all possible precautions should be taken. . . One case today may mean a hundred tomorrow and thousands within a week.'[3]

By October 1918, Leeds schools were being closed in an attempt to halt the spread of the epidemic. On 31 October it was being reported that 100 people in Leeds had died from influenza in the preceding week alone. Less than a week later, this number had doubled. By January 1919, numbers of fatalities had dropped to around twenty per week, only drastically to increase again to eighty-two per week in late February when soldiers began to arrive home in greater numbers.

The whole process of returning soldiers to their civilian lives was fraught with difficulty and controversy. Men felt strongly that the first to enlist should also be the first to go home, but this proved hard to implement and caused a lot of ill-feeling amongst the troops, many of whom were now being kept in camps in Britain having been brought home from the Western Front. It was said that if the malcontents started a riot, it would be the first time in history that the rioters were better trained than the police who would have to stop them.

One of the unhappy consequences of the demobilisation catastrophe was that soldiers were keen to avoid anything which might result in a delay in their release.

They were asked to sign a statement as to disability before their discharge, including a declaration that they were not suffering from any illness or disability attributable to their military service. There was a concern amongst them that disclosing any illness would mean that they had to spend longer in uniform. Inevitably this resulted in influenza victims returning to the general population whilst suffering from the virus.

Sgt George Atack was a veteran soldier, having previously served with the 2nd Battalion West Yorkshire Regiment. He was working in a forge when war broke out and was 47 years old, a married man with four children. He enlisted again as a private, 12 years after his previous period of service, a month after the start of the War. Initially in the Territorial Force, in October 1915 he agreed to serve abroad and found himself in the 20th Battalion Rifle Brigade. In January 1916 he was posted to Egypt, the battalion being used for garrison duty there. He remained there it seems for the rest of the war. He had returned home in February 1919, but had not yet been officially demobilised, his official discharge date being 20 March 1919. George had signed his 'Statement as to Disability' form in Egypt in February 1919. He died of influenza on 4 March 1919, less than a month after returning to Leeds.

Private Hanson Stephenson is another known influenza casualty at Lawnswood. He was a fishmonger by trade and worked for a firm in Harrogate. He was married with three children and was called up for service in 1917. He never went overseas and spent his time with the Army Ordnance Corps at the Woolwich Arsenal in London as a storeman. The end of the War saw him stationed in Ireland. In July 1918, he spent 6 days in hospital in Ireland suffering from influenza. He appeared to have made a recovery and, like George Atack on leaving the Army, he did not claim to be suffering from any disability caused by his war service. He was discharged in February 1919 and died three months later, on 7 May, from influenza. Poignantly, the Stephenson grave carries two casualties – Hanson, and his son, Gunner Frederick Stephenson. Frederick was a casualty of the Second World War – a war his father's generation thought would never happen again. Suspiciously large numbers of military casualties at Lawnswood died of 'pneumonia' in 1918 and 1919. It is highly likely that at least some of these individuals were also victims of the influenza pandemic.

There are many other First World War stories at Lawnswood but certainly no claim is being made here that this cemetery is unique. Every major city or large town has its 'Lawnswood' but the stones and memorials in those cemeteries have so much to tell us about the war and about the community. It is perhaps an unusual way to study the War, but one which opens up a wide range of subjects and a deeper understanding of the scale of the loss and its impact on the city during those years.

The Friends of Lawnswood Cemetery is a voluntary organisation. We try to work with Leeds City Council to improve the condition of the cemetery and to promote it as an historical resource. We have regular action days at the cemetery where we carry out basic gardening and maintenance tasks and are one of the most active volunteer groups in Leeds. We rely entirely upon donations and membership fees and can be contacted at friendsoflawnswoodcemetery@yahoo.co.uk

Notes

1. *The Leodiensian*, Vol. XXXIV, No. 3 (June 1915), pp. 50–1.
2. *Yorkshire Evening News*, 21 October 1918.
3. *Yorkshire Evening Post*, 1 July 1918.

Suggested Further Reading

Scott, William Herbert, *Leeds in the Great War* (Leeds Libraries and Arts Committees, 1923).

Notes on Contributors

Professor Gary Sheffield FRHistS. FRSA, was appointed to the newly-created Chair of War Studies at the University of Wolverhampton in 2013. Previously he held Professorial Chairs at the University of Birmingham and King's College London, the latter post held concurrently with that of Land Warfare Historian on the Higher Command and Staff Course at the UK's Joint Services Command and Staff College.

A leading authority on the First World War, his publications include *Forgotten Victory: The First World War – Myths and Realities* (2001), *Douglas Haig: War Diaries and Letters 1914-1918* (co-editor with John Bourne, 2005) and *The Chief: Douglas Haig and the British Army* (2011). With John Bourne, he is currently editing the diaries and letters of General Sir Henry Rawlinson.

Sheffield is President of the International Guild of Battlefield Guides, and a Vice-President of the Western Front Association.

Professor John Bourne FRHistS, taught History at Birmingham University for thirty years before moving to Wolverhampton University. He founded the Centre for First World War Studies at Birmingham, of which he was Director from 2002 to 2009, as well as the MA in British First World War Studies. He has written widely on the British experience of the Great War, including *Britain and the Great War* (1989; 1991; 1994), *Who's Who in the First World War* (2001), and (with Gary Sheffield), *Douglas Haig: War Diaries and Letters 1914-1918* (2005).

He is currently completing a multi-biography of Britain's Western Front Generals and an edition of the letters and diaries of General Sir Henry Rawlinson, again with Gary Sheffield. He is a Vice President of the Western Front Association, and a Member of the British Commission for Military History

Dr Catriona Pennell FRHistS is a Senior Lecturer in History at the University of Exeter. She completed her doctorate in 2008 at Trinity College, Dublin, during the course of which she was awarded two major scholarships.

Her research focuses on the social and cultural history of war, particularly the First World War. Her first book, *A Kingdom United: Popular Responses to the Outbreak of the First World War in Britain and Ireland*, was published by Oxford University Press in March 2012. Her latest project, funded by the British Academy, continues investigating Irish participation in the war by examining the home and fighting front experiences of the 36th (Ulster) and 16th (Irish) Divisions during the Somme offensives of 1916 and March 1918. She is also PI on an AHRC-funded project 'The First World War in the Classroom: Teaching and the Construction of

Cultural Memory.' In 2011 she was the *An Foras Feasa* Visiting Fellow at the NUI Maynooth, Ireland.

Professor Edward M. Spiers has been the Professor of Strategic Studies at Leeds University since 1993. He has written many books and articles on military history and contemporary strategic studies, including *Haldane – An Army Reformer* (1980), *The Army and Society, 1815-1914* (1980), *Chemical Warfare* (1985), *Chemical Weaponry: A Continuing Challenge* (1989), *The Late Victorian Army, 1868-1902* (1992), *The Scottish Soldier and Empire, 1854-1902* (2006) and co-edited *A Military History of Scotland* (2012).

Professor Dominic Tweddle was appointed Director of the Royal Naval Museum in 2009 after a career in academia, the charity sector and in business. He has worked at the British Museum, was the Assistant Director at the York Archaeological Trust, and is a Visiting Professor at University College, London. He has lectured widely abroad for the British Council and the Department of Trade and Industry, and published a number of books.

Dominic is a Trustee of the Society of Antiquaries of London, a Fellow of the Society of Antiquaries of Scotland, and a member of both the Institute of Directors and the Institute of Field Archaeologists.

Dr. Spencer Jones is Senior Lecturer in Armed Forces and War Studies at the University of Wolverhampton and currently serves as the Regimental Historian for the Royal Regiment of Artillery.

His previous publications include *From Boer War to World War: Tactical Reform of the British Army 1902 – 1914* (2012) and *Stemming the Tide: Officers and Leadership in the British Expeditionary Force 1914* (2013).

Professor Peter Simkins MBE worked at the Imperial War Museum for over thirty-five years, retiring as its Senior Historian in 1999, when he was awarded the MBE. He was Honorary Professor in Modern History at the University of Birmingham from 1999 to 2010 and is now Visiting Lecturer in that university's Centre for First World War Studies, having helped to teach the MA programme in British First World War Studies since 2005.

He is President of the Western Front Association, a Fellow of the Royal Historical Society, and a member of the Army Records Society and the British Commission for Military History. He is the author of numerous books and articles on the Great War, including *Kitchener's Army: The Raising of the New Armies, 1914-16* (1988), which was awarded the Templer Medal by the Society for Army Historical Research.

Matthew Richardson is currently Curator of Social History at Manx National Heritage, Douglas, Isle of Man, a post which involves the care and interpretation of a diverse range of collections relating to the history of the Isle of Man. He has produced a number of highly regarded exhibitions in recent years, notably several reflecting the Island's strong association with motorcycle racing through the famous TT races. He is currently engaged in directing and shaping Manx National Heritage's response to the 100th anniversary of the outbreak of the First World War.

Prior to this he was for a number of years Curator at Saddleworth Museum and Art Gallery in the Pennines. Matthew's abiding interest – and topic for much of his research – is the First and Second World Wars as experienced by ordinary people, particularly in the British Isles. A formative post early in his career was as assistant to Peter Liddle at the Liddle Collection, in the Brotherton Library, University of Leeds. It was this post in particular which shaped his understanding of and reinforced his passion for the history of the First World War. He has published a number of works reflecting his interest in military history, on the Leicester Tigers in both World Wars, on the Distinguished Conduct Medal and most recently, *1914, Voices from the Battlefields* (2013).

Major Roger Chapman MBE was the Curator/Director of The Green Howards Museum in Richmond, North Yorkshire until this 312-year-old infantry regiment was amalgamated in 2006. He still acts as an advisor to the Museum.

From Pembroke College, Oxford, and National Service, he became a regular officer in The Green Howards from 1959–1976. He was an Instructor at R.M.A Sandhurst and later Director of Plans on Operation Drake and Raleigh. His main interest has been in the Victorian Army. He has written three books about The Green Howards: *Beyond their Duty – the story of Green Howard VC & GC holders* (2001), *Echoes from the Crimea* (2004), and *The History of the Green Howards in Photographs 1854-2006* (2006).

Dr Peter Liddle, FRHistS has for more than forty years been concerned with the study of the First World War. His work in rescuing personal experience evidence of the war led to the establishment of the Liddle Collection in the Brotherton Library, University of Leeds which documents the wartime experience of some 4,500 individuals by original letters, diaries, photographs, artwork and recollections.

He has written and edited numerous books on the Great War including volumes on Gallipoli, the Somme, the Third Battle of Ypres, the Armistice. and a book of his interviews with men and women who had striking war experience, *Captured Memories: Across the Threshold of War, 1900-18* (2010). His most recent book, published in 2015, is a re-evaluation of the Dardanelles/Gallipoli Campaign. His research, his publications and the three conferences on the war he had previously directed, have been fuelled by an undiminished enthusiasm for so fundamentally formative a period in our history

Clive Harris served in the Royal Signals BAOR, Cyprus, Germany and France before taking up a permanent staff post at the Royal Military Academy, Sandhurst. On leaving the army he joined his local Constabulary as a specialist communications officer and control-room manager. In his spare time he became a trustee of the Western Front Association and joined the Committee of the Gallipoli Association.

In 1998 he began working as a speaker, writer, researcher and battlefield guide and since then has guided groups the length of the Western Front & Gallipoli for the Great War, alongside Normandy, Arnhem, The Italian Campaign and the London Blitz for the 1939/45 war.

Clive is a member of the British Commission for Military History and is the co-owner of Battle Honours Ltd, the specialist battlefield tour operator. He has had had three books published, *Walking the London Blitz* (2013), *A Wander Through Wartime London* (2013) and *The Greater Game – Sportsman who Fell in the Great War* (2014).

Lieutenant Colonel John Whitchurch joined the Royal Engineers in 1975 as a Junior Leader and transferred to the Small Arms School Corps (SASC) in 1984. His most notable appointments prior to commissioning were at the RAC Gunnery School, the Australian Infantry School, the Royal Military Academy, Sandhurst and, as the Regimental Sergeant Major of the SASC. Since commissioning he has completed tours with various units including the AFV Gunnery School, Infantry Battle School, the British Military Advisory and Training Team (Czech Republic), the Defence Ordnance Safety Group and the Army Training Centre. He assumed command of the SASC on 26 September 2011.

Philip Magrath has a Masters Degree in Museum Studies and an Honours Degree in History. He has been Curator of Artillery for the Royal Armouries since 2001 at the Museum of Artillery, Fort Nelson near Portsmouth. This houses one of the finest and largest collection of historic cannon in the world including a fifteenth-century Turkish Bombard, Mallet's Mortar, built for the Crimean War and the last 14in Mark VII naval gun constructed in 1946. A First World War exhibition is planned for 2014 featuring a fully conserved 18-pounder Field Gun and Limber and a 25cm *Minenwerfer*.

Philip was also part of the team formed by Gosport Borough Council to create Explosion! The Museum of Naval Firepower at Priddy's Hard, for its 2001 opening. Although he likes to maintain a level of expertise about artillery from all periods he has a particular interest in Victorian artillery and artillery of the First World War.

Major Paul Skelton-Stroud's higher education was at the Royal Military Academy, Sandhurst, the University of Liverpool and the University of Surrey. His academic qualifications are in veterinary science, physiology, toxicological pathology and the pathology of tropical parasitic diseases.

A bioscience pathologist by training, he worked on the development of a wide range of new medical drugs for humans. Initially involved with the pathological investigations he later became the author for preclinical safety reports on new human drugs submitted to the various national and international health regulatory bodies around the world, and was scientifically and legally responsible for their content and integrity.

During the 2001 outbreak of foot-and-mouth disease he worked at Defra as a veterinary adviser and remained to assist in the early developmental stages of the Animal Welfare Bill, and authored papers on some aspects of small animal welfare.

He served in the Royal Army Veterinary Corps (Territorial Army Officers Pool) for eight years, and keenly maintains his interest in military history.

Nick Forder, following professional museum work as Curator of Transport at The Museum of Science & Industry (MOSI) in Manchester, set up a private consultancy in the history of flight before taking a post at the Imperial War Museum, Duxford. He has curated regimental collections earlier in his career. Work with the British Aviation Preservation Council has included management of initiatives to develop a National Aviation Heritage Strategy and promote education provision in aviation museums. The latter includes a project centered on the Great War.

An interest in the Great War and aerial defence led to a graduate dissertation on Zeppelins and Gothas, and membership of Cross & Cockade (Society of WW1 Air Historians) for more than 30 years; contributing both to that Society's journal and 'World War 1 Aeroplanes'. Current research projects include the impact of the Great War on freight railways and the role of French manufacturers in supplying aircraft to the RFC and RNAS, 1914–1916.

Professor Alison Fell holds the Chair of French Cultural History at the University of Leeds and has published extensively on French and British women's roles in the First World War. She is currently writing about the legacy of First World War service on women's careers and aspirations in the 1920s, and has recently published a book with Professor Christine Hallett entitled *First World War Nursing: New Perspectives* (2013).

Since 2010 she has been leading the 'Legacies of War' project at the University of Leeds, (http://arts.leeds.ac.uk/legaciesofwar) which involves collaborations with numerous cultural organisations and community groups in partnership with Leeds City Council. She is on an advisory committee for the Imperial War Museum, London and has recently acted as historical consultant for several BBC First World War-related broadcasts.

Chris Baker is a former Chairman of the Western Front Association and an Honorary Research Fellow of the Centre for First World War Studies at the University of Birmingham. A former manufacturing engineer who rose to become

Operations Director of one of the UK's largest automotive components businesses, he spent more than 20 years as a consultant to manufacturers before focusing on his lifelong interest in the Great War.

The author and founder of the renowned Long, Long Trail and Great War Forum websites, he now spends most of his time researching the lives of soldiers and has examined more than 5,000 men. His first book *The Battle for Flanders: German defeat on the Lys 1918*, was published in April 2011 and he is now also an in-house military expert for *Your Family History* magazine as well as an advisor to two TV companies making family history programmes.

Andrea Hetherington is a solicitor by profession, but now spends more time as a freelance researcher and writer. She delivers talks to local history societies on a range of subjects and is much in demand in this Centenary period. She has appeared by invitation at literary festivals and has assisted the Commonwealth War Graves Commission with research and the locating of graves for those missing from the CWGC register. She carries out family history and military history research for private clients and for academics and has worked closely with the University of Leeds' 'Legacies of War' project since its commencement.

A founder member of the Friends of Lawnswood Cemetery, Andrea conducts guided tours at Lawnswood Cemetery on various topics, although the First World War has become a speciality. She has recently been commissioned to write a book on the history of one of Leeds' oldest family firms.

Index

Ranks, titles, positions, offices held, principally given as for 1914